Whither Hong Kong:

China's Shadow or Visionary Gleam?

Albert H. Yee, Editor

香 港 何 去 何 從

與 中 國 如 影 隨 形 歟

抑 爲 其 閃 出 遠 見 之 曙 光

余 元 愷 編

University Press of America,® Inc.
Lanham • New York • Oxford

Copyright © 1999 by
University Press of America,® Inc.
4720 Boston Way
Lanham, Maryland 20706

12 Hid's Copse Rd.
Cumnor Hill, Oxford OX2 9JJ

Library of Congress Cataloging-in-Publication Data

Whither Hong Kong : China's shadow or visionary gleam? / Albert
H. Yee, editor = Hsiang-kang ho ch' ü ho ts'ung : yü Chung-kuo ju
ying sui hsing yü, i wei ch' i shan ch' u yüan chien chih shu kuang /
Yü Yüan-k 'ai pien.
p.   cm.
Includes index.
l. Hong Kong (China)—History. I. Yee, Albert H. II. Title:
Hsiang-kang ho ch' ü ho ts' ung.
DS796.H757W48 1999 951.25—dc21   99—24366 CIP

ISBN 0-7618-1393-4 (cloth: alk. ppr.)
ISBN 0-7618-1394-2- (pbk: alk. ppr.)

⊖™The paper used in this publication meets the minimum
requirements of American National Standard for Information
Sciences—Permanence of Paper for Printed Library Materials,
ANSI Z39.48—1984

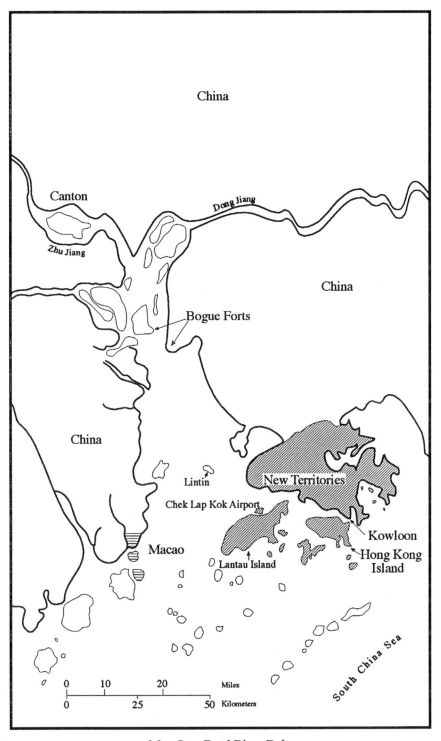

- Map One, Pearl River Delta -

Contents

Illustrations

Display

Figure

Maps

Tables

Preface

Hong Kong's return to China's sovereignty on July 1, 1997 was an unparalleled event in world history. As the British lowered their flag and Chinese rule resumed, emotions filled millions worldwide; the buglers sounded "Sunset" and rain flowed down their faces like tears of sadness and joy. Wordsworth's verse fits that moment, "Whither is fled, the visionary gleam? Where is it now, the glory and the dream?"

After 156 years, there was much to celebrate and regret. Great Britain's colonies have come and gone, but none have resembled the loss and transition of its "Pearl of the East." For Hong Kong is the first and only colony that Britain did not grant independent self-rule, and the people had no say in the negotiations and decisions that culminated into the Sino-British Joint Declaration of 1984 that sealed their fate. Taking Hong Kong's return as its natural parent, Mainland China is hardly the dying colossus that consented to its forced adoption by Britain, also vastly changed since its former imperious nature. With a population that approximates London and is larger than Los Angeles and Chicago combined and an economy that has ranked among the world's best, far ahead of both Britain and China in per capita terms, Hong Kong today is nothing like it was in 1841. Indeed, its history and prospects deserve a fair telling.

Since this book attempts to relate Hong Kong's past to today's realities and tomorrow's possibilities, nary one or two persons commands the expertise for the comprehensiveness desired. Thus, as editor, I recruited distinguished authors who know Hong Kong intimately and have lived and worked there professionally for many years. Providing relevant history and critical analysis, each chapter discusses Hong Kong from critical perspectives that its author has been involved with for long and knows firsthand. For example, Frank Ching's Chapter Seven on change and community in Hong Kong since 1984 and China's influence therein comes from his many years reporting from Beijing for the *New York Times* and *Wall Street Journal* and service as senior editor of and columnist for the *Far Eastern Economic Review* in Hong Kong where he continues.

xi

The Overview and our chapters, therefore, review Britain's rule, Sino-British relations, American involvements, the people and institutions of Hong Kong, and prospects for what is now named the Hong Kong Special Administrative Region (SAR) of the People's Republic of China (PRC). This book represents our knowledge, insights and sentiments grown out of lifetimes and many years in the territory and concerns for its future.

A number of books on Hong Kong, which the Overview surveys, that were published before the handover were quickly outdated after July 1, 1997. Focused mainly on the political ramifications of the change of sovereignty, they tended to be narrowly framed and quite negative about the SAR's prospects. Many attacked Britain for its "betrayal." There seemed to be great need for a book that was unconstrained by the moment and its unknowns. Thus, we began to produce a book that would have the benefit of time following the handover and would be comprehensive, reflective, and perhaps lasting.

Examining imperialism and colonialism in Hong Kong for over a century and a half, *Whither Hong Kong: China's Shadow or Visionary Gleam?* identifies who and what were beneficial, humane, constructive, racist, avaricious, and autocratic. In pursuit of those goals, the Editor worked very closely with each contributor on content, style, and research, typically through five drafts. Since the handover several years ago, the new SAR's administration has revealed itself, China's leadership has changed somewhat, Sino-American relations continue in fits and starts, and Hong Kong and East Asia have fallen into serious recession.

Yes, whither the course of Hong Kong. Those of us who know the place well and appreciate its past and potentials wonder, Will its finest days come in the new century or will the vision and dream fade into the shadows of its past?

Acknowledgments

Dr. George Shen, who authored Chapter Four, kindly provided the literal translation of the book's title in Chinese -- "Whither Hong Kong: As a Shadow of China or Gleam of Vision." The lower four characters are the Editor's Chinese name, Yu Yuankai (Yee Yuanhoy in Cantonese) and Editor.

Grateful acknowledgment is accorded the following: (1) Lonely Planet Publications Pty Ltd, for permission to work from its map in Steve Shipp's (1995). *Hong Kong, China,* page 3, which was used in drafting Map One, Pearl River Delta (p. iii) ; (2) Professor Winberg Chai, for permission to use his translation of Confucius Analects, 6:28 (p. 1); (3) Oxford University Press, for verifying that the Wordsworth verse used in the Preface is out of copyright (p. xi); (4) Random House UT Ltd, for permission to quote in Chapter One from *A Soldiers View of Empire, The Reminiscences of James Bodell 1831-1892* by Andrew Newton, edited by Keith Sinclair (The Bodley Head, 1982); (5) Bantam Doubleday Dell, for verifying that *Rudyard Kipling's Verse 1885-1932* (1934) is in the public domain (p. 106); (6) HarperCollins *Publishers*, London and the Irene Skolnick Literary Agency, New York for permission to quote from Frank Welsh's (1993) *History of Hong Kong*; and (7) *Far Eastern Economic Review* for permission to reprint part of Frank Ching's June 18, 1998 column on the HK's election results.

To research material and verify details for each contributor and his own works, the Editor spent many enjoyable days at the libraries of the following universities in 1995-99 and expresses gratitude for access to their stacks: University of Montana (Mansfield Library), University of Washington, University of Oregon, Oregon State University, University of California, Berkeley, Harvard University (Yenching Library), and The University of Texas, Austin. After searching in vain on both sides of the Atlantic for the full text of the above mentioned Kipling verse, the Reference Section of the Library of Congress came to the rescue.

James Diefenderfer, a geography student at the University of Montana, drew the three maps and Figure One of the Overview.

A Hong Kong philanthropist who wishes to be anonymous contributed a grant in support of the Editor's efforts; his generosity in early 1999 was most welcomed. Pages 14, 40, and 235 gratefully acknowledge three individuals for their assistance and encouragement. Mrs. Bev Van Canagan graciously typed the handwritten draft of one chapter for word-processing. To the many friends, relatives, and groups whose enthusiastic encouragement helped to spur this project along, we extend our warm appreciation and affection.

AHY
Missoula, MT

xiii

Names and Such

Whither Hong Kong? uses names for places and persons that are most commonly found in English-language works, such as Canton instead of Guangzhou. In most cases, alternative names as in *pinyin,* are given in parentheses following the first use. The Editor has also worked to maintain consistency in the use of American spellings and punctuation and to avoid repetitions when not vital to the discussion. Page references are often noted in the text (p. = page; pp. = pages) to aid readers who might want to cross-check related information elsewhere in the book and other sources. When an entire chapter is suggested, it means that much of that chapter deals with the topic at hand. Although the Editor was a taskmaster who worked closely with each contributor throughout the production, authors had the final say and are responsible for the substance of their chapters.

As the Overview attempts to explain, China has unique distinctions that differ from other nation-states, such as the people's identity to their culture versus their counter-allegiance to the state. Thus, we have differentiated between regimes, such as that of the Qing (Ch'ing, Manchu) Dynasty rulers (1644-1912), Chiang Kai-shek (1927-1949), Mao Zedong (1949-76), etc. When Chiang Kai-shek and his forces fled to Taiwan, the "two Chinas" issue added a special dimension to the meaning of China as a state. Although that issue is somewhat muted today, the use of "China" can be confusing if not argumentative. We avoid the journalistic use of "Chinese" to represent whatever referent is at hand.

Also, different names are used for the China of chief concern to Hong Kong today -- Mainland China, the Mainland, People's Republic of China (PRC), and of course, China. We often refer to the PRC Government by use of the capital city, Beijing, as we do with London or Whitehall (London thoroughfare where the British Government is centered) to specify the British Government. Other usages, such as HK for Hong Kong, SAR for the Hong Kong Special Administrative Region, and U.S. for the United States, should be obvious. To arbitrate between various spellings for Chinese names, such as Kai Chow, Kiaochow, or Jiaozhou, the Editor referred to *The Columbia Encyclopedia* (5th ed.), 1993.

The style guidelines of the American Psychological Association were utilized; chief exception was citing authors' first names in full instead of initials.

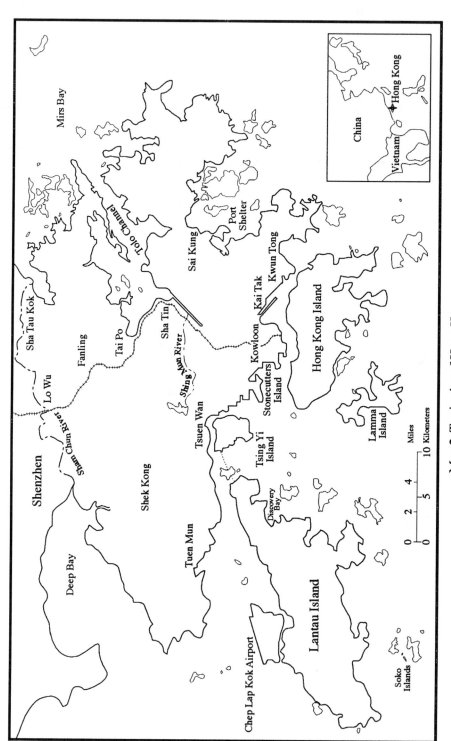

- Map 2, Territories of Hong Kong -

Overview

Albert H. Yee

A man of jen (humanity) is one who, in seeking to establish himself, finds a foothold
for others and who, desiring attainment for himself, helps others to attain.
                                    Confucius, *Analects*, 6:28 (Trans., Chai & Chai, 1965, pp. 26-27)

This overview discusses a number of themes as it provides historical background and reflection for the chapters that follow. One significant theme is the
ageold predominance of authoritarianism (autocracy) over humanitarianism (humanism, morality) in the history and institutions of China and Hong Kong. Another important theme is the self-sufficiency of the Chinese people and their
capacity to uphold their civilization against tremendous odds. Attempt is given to
portraying events in meaningful context and groups and individuals as people
with personalities and choices that influenced outcomes. The views expressed
are the author's alone.

Hong Kong Preliminaries: Lin versus Elliot

When Americans staged the Boston Tea Party on their march to the War of Independence, acrimony brewed in China over alien encroachments. With its
Crown monopoly on China trade (1600-1834), the British East India Company
enriched itself and Britain's tax revenues as Britons and Americans increased
their thirst for tea. By 1770, 4,500 tons of tea were exported from China, three
times greater than a decade earlier. Benjamin Franklin (Fleming, 1972, pp. 312-
313) groaned over the colonies' trade deficit brought on by tea imports. By 1830,
Britain's take on tea import duties alone amounted to 10% of its domestic revenues. The tea vogue also enhanced demand for China porcelain and other goods.
However, there was one very big problem; the Chinese sold much more than

they bought and Westerners were forced to cover their shortfall with lots of cash. Scurrying worldwide for goods to sell China, the East India Co. finally found something that it could grow cheaply at its doorstep in India, which was opium. By 1804, the narcotic reversed the trade deficit to stay as its import into China steadily increased -- nearly fivefold from 400 tons in 1800 to 1,900 tons in 1832; 3,200+ in 1838 . . . (Keay, 1991, pp. 349 & 453; Spence, 1990, pp. 128-132 & 149).

Lin Zexu. Sino-British tensions finally came to a head in 1839 when China decided to abolish opium imports at Canton (Guangzhou), the only place where China permitted foreign trade. As Map One shows, Canton is at the head of the Pearl River Delta, traversed by innumerable war and merchant sailing ships. After a year's study, Emperor Daoguang appointed Lin Zexu as High Commissioner to stamp out the nefarious import. Governor of Hubei and Hunan, Lin had already fought opium without compromise and was seen to fit the ideals for scholar-officials so well that his nickname was "Blue Sky." The 53-year-old's reputation included settling a peasant uprising in 1823 by crossing a torrid river to discuss the rebels' grievances.

According to Chinese values, morality not materialism is the true key to social status and civilized behavior. Drafting a letter to Queen Victoria but not sent, Lin Zexu explained China's viewpoint: "The Way of Heaven is fairness to all; it does not suffer us to harm others in order to benefit ourselves. Men are alike in this all the world over: that they cherish life and hate what endangers life." Lin continued, although "trade has flourished" in Canton for about 130 years, "there is a class of evil foreigners that makes opium and brings it for sale, tempting fools to destroy themselves, merely in order to reap profit. Formerly the number of opium smokers was small; but now the vice has spread far and wide and the poison penetrated deeper and deeper" (Waley, 1958, pp. 28-31).

Assuming command at Canton, Lin required teachers to help suppress addiction among students by forming student groups of five to swear off of the drug and support each others' withdrawal, blamed everyone from the educated elite to peasants for putting their province of Guangdong into disrepute by opium-smoking, and called one and all to throw off the "foreign mud" (Beeching, 1975, 74-75). After he toured the foreigners' compound and read translations of their books and journals, Lin concluded that the merchants were in fact "betraying the great favors bestowed upon them by the Emperor" by wheeling and dealing in opium and in huge quantities. On March 18, 1839, he ordered the traders to surrender their entire stock of opium and to guarantee that they would not import opium to China again (Collis, 1946, pp. 207-208).

Charles Elliot. In 1792-94, a British expedition led by Lord George Macartney and paid for by the British East India Co. took shiploads of British goods, including up-to-date artillery, to Beijing to effect a trade treaty with Emperor Qianlong. Grand as the mission was, it failed to get a treaty. China did not desire foreign goods. The British noted everything but neglected to study the language.

However, the 11-year-old page, Thomas Staunton, delighted Qianlong by speaking Chinese that he learned from interpreters. The British became convinced that the "Celestial Empire" had magnificent trade potentials, but they viewed China as backward and inferior to Europe's progress, science, enterprise, and military -- hardly worthy of the accolades of Marco Polo, the Jesuits, Voltaire, and others. Thus, "Macartney and his companions made a notable contribution to the exultation of Anglo-Saxon superiority that spread throughout the world for 200 years" (Peyrefitte, 1992, p. 545; also see Spence, 1998, pp. 56-61).

In 1816, a less ostentatious mission but deemed no less important, led by Lord Amherst and his No. two, Sir Thomas Staunton, now grown and on his second trip to the capital, failed to obtain an audience with Qianlong's son, Emperor Jiaqing. The court had learned 23 years earlier that the British would not observe the ceremonial protocol of kowtowing to the emperor and would jeopardize their entire mission by refusing to perform the homage. Refusing to kowtow despite a scuffle with court officials, Amherst and Staunton also departed China minus a trade agreement.

After Parliament abolished the East India Co.'s China monopoly in the name of free trade for all comers in 1834, the British Government appointed Lord Napier as the first Chief Superintendent of Trade of British Subjects in China. His primary mission was to establish a trade agreement with the viceroy at Canton where the East India Co. had posted traders since 1684. Napier brought an elaborate company with him, including his wife and two daughters, as he intended to fulfill a term of office and bring about results. Perhaps it was thought that circumventing the Imperial Court might overcome the problem of the kow-tow and get down to business, i.e., replace the tribute system with free trade at long last. Ignorant of the Chinese and unversed in diplomacy, Napier was ill-equipped for his mission.

Rebuffing Napier's credentials, Viceroy Lu K'un referred to the emissary in the third person -- foreigners were obliged to deal with Chinese brokers, who were responsible for their conduct and business. The Viceroy added that it was not his duty to instruct the "foreign devils," who should "Tremble hereat -- intensely, intensely tremble!" (Fay, 1975, p. 71). Yet, the Viceroy's comments regarding Napier's tour did include conciliatory remarks that the "Barbarian Eye" had come "myriad leagues" and could be excused for not knowing China's laws and ways (Collis, 1946, pp. 128-129).

In frustration, Napier slipped into Canton on a small boat with little concern that he lacked the required travel visa. The British traders welcoming him with enthusiasm, opium *taipans* William Jardine and Lancelot Dent buffooned the Viceroy and encouraged Lord Napier to assert himself. His anger at high pitch, the Superintendent let it be known that the Chinese should honor his status. Lu then answered by mounting a trade boycott, which halted tea sales and panicked the foreign traders.

Somehow deciding that hostilities would open doors, Napier ordered cannonades by two frigates along the Pearl River to Whampoa (Huangpu), Canton's port, and called for an army from India. In retaliation, Lu built blockades that trapped the frigates at Whampoa. Thoroughly stalemated and malaria-stricken, Napier finally agreed to accept a humiliating permit to depart Canton on a small boat after it was verified that the frigates had sailed to sea. Four months after landing in Macau, the first Superintendent of Trade died on October 11, 1834.

The poor results caused London to downsize the Superintendency to half of Napier's salary of 6,000 pounds per year and from four to one deputy when Captain Charles Elliot RN at age 36 became the fourth to assume the post in 1836. Elliot first experienced "the crash of cannon and the smell of powder" as a 15-year-old midshipman on the ship-of-the-line HMS *Minden*. Commanded by Lord Exmouth, the 74-gun *Minden* along with other Anglo-Dutch warships bombarded Algerian pirates in 1816 with nearly 50,000 rounds of which Elliot's ship fired an amazing 4,710. Elliot achieved notoriety by sitting nonchalantly at ship stern under an umbrella while Napier's frigates exchanged bombardments with the Bogue Forts (see Map One). He had served as protector of slaves in British Guiana before being recalled to assist plans to abolish colonial slavery, work that may have engendered or reinforced humaneness that would appear later.

When Elliot assumed the Superintendency, China was poised to crack down on opium. His predecessor, Sir George Robinson, had conducted his business aboard the tiny cutter, *Louisa*, anchored by Lintin island (see Map One), 23 miles NW of HK amidst the Pearl, where he recorded shipping, inspected manifests, etc. and turned a blind eye to opium smuggling. Since the action was in Canton, Elliot decided that was where he belonged. Avoiding Napier's intrusiveness, Elliot submitted a formal petition through the trade broker, Howqua, and obtained permission to move to the foreign compound in Canton [see Spence (1996, pp. 1-13) for a detailed description of the compound]. When the Chinese learned that he was a British official seeking trade talks, Elliot was forced to work out of Macau, the tiny Portuguese settlement extant since 1557 where the traders leisured off-season and kept their families and mistresses in grand mansions.

The Early Rounds

In receipt of Lin's order, Captain Elliot rushed to Canton in full naval uniform to protest and refused to sign a bond certifying the end of opium imports and sales. Reality soon struck the pampered foreigners when servants, clerks, and teachers failed to report for work and they were forced to care for themselves. Resident Americans "served up ham and eggs the consistency and color of shoe leather" and "produced hardboiled eggs that resembled grapeshot and rice indistinguishable from glue" (Fay, 1975, p. 150).

After a brief standoff, Elliot ordered the surrender of 20,283 chests of opium (about 1,217 tons of opium) on March 27, 1839 in order to secure the safe passage of the foreign community to Macau. Although all the British departed, the Americans stayed behind. Robert Bennet Forbes, resident head of the U.S. firm,

Russell & Co., foreswore opium sales and traded in cotton and other goods to the consternation of the British (see Kerr, 1996). Forbes told Elliot that "he would retreat step by step buying and selling as long as there was trade," to which the British traders complained, "While we hold the horns, they milk the cow" (Chang, 1964, pp. 207-208).

In June, Lin dumped the opium hoard into ditches along the Pearl River and mixed it with lime and salt. He ordered the immediate execution of at least one worker who stole some of the opium. Not knowing that their victory over the "foreign devils" would be short-lived, the Chinese took great pride and satisfaction in the destruction. Early on, Lin had noted with pleasure that William Jardine had returned to England -- the "ring-leader in the opium-smuggling trade," a "particularly unscrupulous foreign merchant. Being of a sly and crafty disposition he has known how to take a mean advantage of our dynasty's traditional policy: 'Deal gently with those from afar' " (Waley, 1958, p. 22).

However, Jardine's return home foretold retaliation, for the "prince of opium" sought the ear of the Foreign Secretary, Lord Palmerston. Thus, the ambitious scheme of Jardine and other opium dealers began to take form -- provoke armed hostilities between China and Britain and achieve trade concessions after China's defeat.

A year before Lin's appointment, Elliot began to forewarn the Foreign Office of problems caused by the opium traffic. Palmerston's response was noncommittal. Publishing the reply in the *Canton Register*, one of several newspapers printed at the Canton compound, Elliot took criticism from traders who said that he should not have drawn Whitehall's attention to their opium trading. Now with Lin's action they turned full circle and agitated for retribution. Without a warship, Elliot was forced into a passive waiting game. Infuriated by their predicament and Elliot's decision to surrender the opium, the traders sent volumes of letters by every ship en route home demanding action.

The traders had a long wait before they would learn what London would do, as one-way sailing time between Hong Kong and London was about 3-4 months. Completion of the Suez Canal 30 years later (1869) would cut the time by half. In the 1870s, installation of telegraph cable systems from Suez to Europe and throughout Asia brought further revolutionary changes (Coates, 1990). Relating the sailing hazards of the 19th century, Fay (1975, p. 188) wrote: "when Matheson wrote Jardine the full story of the opium crisis . . . , he committed seven copies of his letter to seven different ships!"

A Chinese man was stabbed to death in July 1839 during a drunken riot by British and American seamen seeking women and drink. The murder was in a village in Kowloon, located today about where the docks in Tsimshatsui (see Map 3)are for the Star Ferry and liners, such as the Queen Elizabeth II. Elliot tried to hush the incident by spreading $2,000 around the village and fined and imprisoned five sailors, but the specific culprit could not be identified. Chinese officials whipped up public outrage and noisy demands for the murderer. In similar straits in Canton, seamen handed over to officials had been promptly strangled with little pretence of trials. Thousands of Chinese troops took position and war junks threatened the British ships in Hong Kong harbor. The plight of the foreigners took a distressing turn in August when Macau's Governor, Adriao Accacio da Silva Pinto, under pressure as always from Chinese officials (China never ceded Macau to Portugal), said that he could not be responsible for the safety of the British. With nowhere else to go, the traders and their families took refuge on cramped merchant ships in Hong Kong. An attack on the schooner, ironically named the *Black Joke*, with loss of one man's ear added to everyone's distress. Americans stayed in Macau since Lin only targeted the British and at least one Briton, heavy with child, stayed behind with the Americans. Although the summer of 1839 was milder than normal, the situation grew increasingly uncomfortable when every effort by Elliot to obtain water and food failed because of the uproar over the Kowloon murder.

Hostilities Commence

Two British frigates, the 26-gun *Volage* and 18-gun *Hyacinth*, finally arrived in August 1839, but an army and more warships were needed. Pestered by the merchants to put the two frigates and the *Louisa* into action, Elliot abandoned his caution on November 3rd and ordered cannon fire on three war junks that were moving more aggressively that day. Deadly grape shot finally subdued the mismatched junks. As it is one thing to order gunfire and another to see its effect, Elliot reported to London "feelings of irritation which have betrayed me" (Collis, 1946, p. 246).

More British warships reached the Pearl River and arrogance replaced passivity. *The Canton Press* of December 12, 1840 (microfiche, University of Hong Kong) expressed gratitude for Captains Henry Smith of HMS *Druid* and William Warren of HMS *Hyacinth* for "valuable service" and "energy and zeal . . . during a period of difficulty and danger unexampled in the history of British intercourse with China." Smith was presented with "a service of plates of the value of six hundred guineas" and Warren the same valued at 400 guineas. Dent & Co. was the first of 60 signatories, followed by archrival Jardine Matheson & Co., painter George Chinnery, and R. J. Gilman, who would found Gilman & Co. (of Inchcape plc today) in Hong Kong.

Britain's armed forces did not seek war. While he doubted the value of trading with "an empire so little versed in western ways," First Lord of the Admiralty, Sir James Graham, who knew the grievances of traders and ship captains, advocated persuasion 'by the mildest means' and the 'plastic adoption of our manners to theirs.' However, the First Lord stationed a Vice-Admiral in a line-of-battle ship to India to convey "the full impression . . . (to) China . . . (of) the predominance of our power" (Bartlett, 1963, p. 99). Instead of crediting the military for the war with China, historians blame the traders for fomenting war hysteria and misrepresenting Lin, who tried to reason (Beeching, 1975, Chapter 4; Fay, 1975, Chapter 12; Spence, 1990, Chapter 7). In the end, for the British, "the imperative was money" (Fay, 1975, p. 189); for the Chinese, it was control of their territory. Ever since Marco Polo and Lord Macartney, while the West misjudged China for their own purposes, the Chinese misjudged their inviolability (Spence, 1998).

The warmongers. Although Charles Elliot did his best for his countrymen, he abhorred the opium trade and the dealers knew it. Elliot characterized the trade as 'plain buccaneering' in letters to Palmerston. Writing home on November 4, 1840, his wife, Clara, wrote that "Charlie" was brokenhearted over the conflict and "the discontent and ill feeling of his own countrymen . . . Never was I so brought in contact with the mercantile world as of late and truly they have lowered the English character in *my* eyes -- they sacrifice every thing, every feeling, for *dollar making*" (Hoe, 1991, p. 23).

As hostilities escalated, the traders could see that their strategy was working. Agitating and making the most of their grievances long before 1839, the Canton merchants received support from compatriots, such as the Calcutta and Glasgow chambers of commerce. Pooling thousands of pounds, the traders had sent representatives to London to lobby, such as Robert Inglis, Hugh Hamilton Lindsay and Alexander Matheson, all aggressive opium dealers. During lobbying tours, Matheson affirmed that opium smoking in China was equivalent to drinking brandy and champagne and that he had never seen a Chinese "in the least bestialized" (Fay, 1975, pp. 190-191).

Touring Britain as Chairman of the British Chamber of Commerce in Canton, James Matheson was adept in arousing support and published a popular pamphlet entitled, *The Present and Future Prospects of Trade in China* in 1836. Hardly mentioning opium, Matheson said that it was necessary "in the name of justice and national honour to end the abuses Englishmen had suffered too long at the hands of the Chinese" (Coates, 1988, p. 172).

Britain's decision to force open the China market to free trade with arms presented a confrontation of diametrically opposing viewpoints. To the Chinese, the strange manners and behavior of the "foreign devils" were abhorrent. Confucian traditions ranked the social standing of scholars, farmers, and craftsmen much higher than merchants since they were seen as socially contributive instead of mainly acquisitive and self-centered. By nature of their deadly work, warriors did not rate a respectful ranking.

Guangdong Viceroy Lu K'u, reported in 1834: ". . . the barbarians are by nature avaricious and the more forbearance and indulgence are shown to them the more do they become proud and overbearing." ". . . the common disposition of the English barbarians is ferocious, and what they trust in are the strength of their ships and the effectiveness of their guns" (Endacott, 1973, p. 7).

Indeed, the British and Americans were unlike foreigners of the past, such as the Polos in the 13th century and traders traversing the Silk Road to and from Rome and the Middle East. Making obeisant tribute to the emperor, the early traders departed loaded with valuable goods over lengthy land routes controlled by Chinese forces. The Anglo-Americans baffled the Chinese by their swift sea transport and hustling mercantilism. Instead of curbing the opium traders, Lin Zexu played right into their strategy of forcing a confrontation.

When Elliot's report of the crisis reached Lord Palmerston, the Foreign Secretary thundered that relations with China had to be settled once and for all. Never one to take half measures, Palmerston demanded a commercial treaty with secure trading rights and the ceding of a port where his countrymen could live and work under their own laws. He argued that the merchants had surrendered their property in Canton in order to save their lives, which in fact were never in real danger. An advocate of Adam Smith's free-trade philosophy (*Wealth of Nations*, 1776), Palmerston sided fully with the merchants and sought their counsel.

Advising strong action, William Jardine provided every assistance -- maps, papers, and the use (not taken) of his opium fleet. Politically intertwined, Jardine joined the Whig Parliament in 1841; and Palmerston, famed for shifting ground to gain advantage, moved to the Whigs and was reappointed Foreign Secretary. Thus, the meeting of minds as what to do about China, that "arrogant, ridiculous colossus," could not have been better.

The First Opium War, 1839-42

Lord Palmerston quickly despatched warships and an army of 4,000 to China. Unsure of China's fighting ability at first, the British soon learned that her defenses were archaic and feeble. Lining both banks of the Pearl River, cannon of the Bogue Forts (see Map One) turned out to be more bluff than real threats. A naval expedition of 40 ships led by Charles Elliot and his cousin, Rear Admiral George Elliot, sailed north to Taku at the mouth of the Beiho River leading to the capital and left after presenting Palmerston's demands. Hoping to settle matters through diplomacy, Elliot wanted to avoid unnecessary bloodshed on both sides. Having overwhelmed the Bogue Forts, Elliot's officers wanted to impress the Chinese further with their superior firepower.

Cannon versus cross-bows. Spence's (1996, pp. 52-53) description of the conflict near Canton shows how one-sided the battles really were: "By May of 1841 the shifting tides of war had sent Chinese crowds surging through the abandoned foreign factories, gutting all . . . , smashing or stealing . . . what remained. The British fleet . . . and their guns raze much of the waterfront . . . ." In the Sanyuanli area, British troops destroyed ripening rice fields and property, stole food, clothes, and animals, raped women, and violated gravesites. Assembled with hoes, spears, and a few guns, 5,700 villagers "joined in chaotic combat over the outrage," but "the British lines hold firm, although some of their men are literally hooked out of the rain-soaked ranks by Chinese wielding weapons like enormous shepherd's crooks attached to bamboo poles, and badly wounded." At Fort Chuenpi in the Bogue narrows, 600 elite Manchu soldiers and their brigadier fought to their deaths in "a frightful scene of slaughter," versus only 30 British wounded (Beeching, 1975, pp. 124-125).

Although China had cannon, they were mostly out-dated and poorly used. By tradition, the Chinese rewarded military skill with swords, cross-bows, and spears and viewed guns as beneath chivalrous combat, as did the Japanese until the 19th century (see pp. 78-79).

Ceasefire and Elliot's exit. Realizing that the Chinese were helpless in battle with his forces, Elliot negotiated with Qishan (Kishen), Lin Zexu's replacement. Fighting stopped when they agreed to the Chuenpi Convention on January 20, 1841, ceding Hong Kong to Britain and $6 million for the confiscated opium. The Emperor condemned the proposed treaty and imprisoned Qishan. Also rejecting the agreement in anger, Palmerston complained that Hong Kong had little or no value. Still fuming over their losses, the traders continued to foment war. Palmerston charged Elliot for being lenient and not using his military advantage to strike a harder bargain and holding on to the main island in the Chusan (Zhoushan) archipelago near the Yangzi River. Hardly a pliant act, Elliot had evacuated Chusan in order to obtain the release of maltreated British prisoners that Lin had captured through bounties.

Elliot's replacement was Sir Henry Pottinger (Pottinger, 1997), recently retired from the British East India Co., where he had a tough, no-nonsense reputation. Chapter One (pp. 72-74 & 76-81) covers the Opium Wars in detail. Concluded on August 29, 1842, Pottinger's Treaty of Nanking ceded Hong Kong to Britain in perpetuity and named five treaty ports for free trading, It also extracted $21 million for the lost opium in Canton, other debts, and war expenses. Frustrated by many restrictions in Canton, British traders had argued for a port governed by their own nation's laws and authority and now they had one.

Faulting Lin but not the emperor for Britain's actions, Palmerston provided a face-saving outlet. Since by definition China's rulers are infallible, the Qing court blamed Lin Zexu for Britain's aggression and banished him to remote Sinkiang. His successor, Qishan, was exiled to the border with Siberia. While Lin, Qishan, and Elliot suffered postings to faraway places, they fared better later on. Although disposed to the then rough-and-tumble Republic of Texas, Captain Elliot, more humanist than warrior, became an admiral in later years. Lionizing Lin's stand against the foreigners and using him as an example of Qing duplicity, the People's Republic of China (PRC) built a huge, heroic statue of the Commissioner on a prominent hill in Macau overlooking the Pearl R. in the mid-1980s.

Famed historians, Fairbank & Reischauer (1973, p. 277), wrote: "No episode in modern history has provided more occasion for the charge of 'imperialist aggression' than the First Anglo-Chinese War of 1839-42 -- a war that was precipitated by the Chinese government's effort to suppress a pernicious contraband trade in opium, concluded by the superior firepower of British warships, and followed by humiliating treaties that gave Westerners special privileges in China."
After the Second Opium War (see pp. 76-81), the British Ambassador to Peking reported to Parliament, "We forced the Chinese Government to enter into a Treaty to allow their subjects to take opium" (Booth, 1998, p. 145).

The Improbable Colony of British Hong Kong

John Bull personified. While Britain's parliamentary system is democratic, it continues to be criticized for concentrating too much power in the central executive (Weir & Beetham, 1998). With a political career extending from 1807-1865, Lord Palmerston (Henry John Temple, 3rd Viscount) was in his late fifties and had been in the highest echelons of government for over 30 years when he first heard of Hong Kong. Reporting to Queen Victoria on April 10, 1841, he said that "Viscount Palmerston has felt greatly mortified and disappointed . . . (with Elliot's) expedition to China, and he much fears that the sequel of the negotiation . . . will not (be worthy). Even the cession of Hong Kong has been coupled with a condition about the payment of duties . . . ." Writing to her uncle, King Leopold I of Belgium, the Queen faulted Elliot's "unaccountably strange conduct" and said that "you would find the East not only as 'absurd' as the West, but very barbarous, cruel, and dangerous into the bargain . . . . Albert is so much amused at my having got the Island of Hong Kong, and we think Victoria ought to be called Princess of Hong Kong in addition to Princess Royal." (Benson & Esher, 1908, pp. 260-262).

Although Victoria generally supported his efforts, such as the independence of Belgium in 1839, Crimean War of 1853-56, and the Indian Mutiny of 1857-58, Palmerston clashed with Victoria's beloved Prince Albert. All too often, acting "by instinct -- by a quick eye and a strong hand," manhandling crises, the Foreign Minister dismissed the meticulous, thoughtful Prince as an alien nobody and earned Victoria's and Albert's dislike. With boldness often bordering on rashness but supremely self-confident and proud of his country and himself, Lord Palmerston was John Bull personified (Strachey, 1949, pp. 154-156; Weintraub, 1997). His penchant in bullying weaker nations and his habit of usurping the Queen hardened her displeasure. She and Albert privately nicknamed Palmerston "Pilgerstein."

Although Palmerston opposed slavery, it was an open secret that he and many of the elite favored the South, perhaps in part because of the sorely needed cotton. Souring Anglo-American relations until Britain paid America a compensation of $15 million six years after the Civil War ended, British shipyards built cruisers for the Confederate Navy equipped with deady nine-inch rifled cannon and underwater rams. Harassing Union merchantmen and whalers in the Atlantic, Gulf of Mexico, and round the world, the rebel raiders caused shippers to register their ships in Britain and elsewhere. Except for times of wars, America's merchant shipping would never recover. The famous *Alabama* sailed from Liverpool in 1862 to take nearly 70 Northern ships before the USS *Kearsarge* sank her offshore of Cherbourg in 1864. Somehow, French artists happened to be on scene, and Edouard Manet painted a work of the spectacular battle (Churchill, 1958, pp. 231-232; Delaney, 1972) that resides at the Philadelphia Museum of Art today. Aide to his diplomat father in London, John Quincy Adams, Henry Adams

(1917, p. 212) wrote that the last two years in England, 1866-68, were "agreeable and amusing. Minister Adams became, in 1866, almost an historical monument in London; he held a position altogether his own. His old opponents disappeared. Lord Palmerston died in October, 1865; . . ."

Palmerston's England. As national leaders do not operate in a vacuum, valuable images of 19-century Britain have been preserved by novelists, such as Charles Dickens (1812-70) and William Makepeace Thackeray (1811-1863). Dickens' *Oliver Twist* and *Nicholas Nickleby* were printed in book form in 1838 and 1839, respectively; and *A Christmas Carol* was published with its unforgettable character of Scrooge in 1843, a year after the signing of the Treaty of Nanking. Portraying life in Britain with its social contrasts and wants -- harsh poverty of the poor, opulence of the elite and disparities in humanitarianism, Dicken's writings and tours were highly popular in Britain and America. His father an East India official and Calcutta born, Thackeray complemented Dickens' romanticization of the poor by satirizing the upper classes, as in *Vanity Fair* (1847-48).

The gap between social classes in Victorian Britain was near impossible to bridge for the disadvantaged. Risk-taking and luck for those with some education and means could spell the difference between a bountiful versus common life. If all went well, young opium dealers could amass a princely fortune after only four to five years work at Canton.

Wages and living costs in 19th-century England were low, as a London bobby earning one guinea (16 shillings) per week lived fairly well. Less well off, London stereodores were paid six pence per hour. Beyond Britain, $1.00 per day and keep for Texas cowhands attracted British seamen to jump ship and forfeit top wages of $25 per month. Gunners on opium clippers got $45 a month, and top pay for coolies was about $9 per month (Beeching, 1975, pp. 332-333). One dollar then was equivalent to 4-5 British shillings. American clipper captains made about $300 per month with rich extras that could run into thousands, such as bonuses and cargo space reserved for the captains. A new clipper ship cost about $25,000.

The value of a chest of opium weighing from 160-170 pounds of which 120 lbs. was narcotics fluctuated but the average price in the first half of 1842 was about $314 or £90-100 (for details on opium preparation and use, see Fairbank, 1969, pp. 64-65 , Fay, 1975, pp. 3-9, and Booth, 1998, pp. 5-10). Early British profits on opium exceeded the total U.S. federal revenues. (Freuchen, 1957, pp. 150-163).

In 1844, opium *taipan*, James Matheson, built Lews Castle on his own Scottish island for 514,000 pounds sterling. His nephew, Alexander Matheson, spent £773,020 pounds for much of Inverness County and £300,000 pounds on property in Ross-shire (Welsh, 1993, p. 144). Dying early, William Jardine (but not his partner, James) lent partial credence to the whispered prophecy that opium dealers did not enjoy their wealth for long. However, Jardine Matheson & Co. remains active in Hong Kong today, albeit with Bermuda company registration since 1984. It deregistered from HK before the Sino-British Agreement was signed.

In Commons and Lords debates, many questioned the morality of aggressing China for trade and profits; but Palmerston, who knew how to control his party and Parliament, persisted in his conviction that China needed persuasion through might. A speech full of contraditions by Sir George Staunton, whose father had been to Beijing twice as mentioned earlier, confused Commons about China and opium. While Napier fired the first shots, Palmerston was the first to articulate gunboat diplomacy in China waters. Thus, ministering through Elliot and Pottinger, Palmerston unintentionally hatched the colony of Hong Kong.

As Pemberton (1954, p. 78) wrote, trouble with China was sure to come after the Crown assumed responsibility in 1834 for British interests in China trade, for "the presence of Palmerston at the Foreign Office made it a certainty." Yet, parlimentary politics and sea communications being what they were, Palmerston had been out of office for months before Pottinger learned that the Tories had been returned to power. By then, Palmerston's instructions had been fulfilled in the signing of the Treaty of Nanking. Lord George Aberdeen became the new Foreign Secretary in Sir Robert Peel's Tory administration of 1841-46, which had little interest in China as the first Afghan-British War (1838-1842) and Ireland's Great Famine (1845-49) consumed their attention.

Albion in South China. Replete with coincidences and unlikely outcomes, history often surpasses fiction. Omitting the merchants, British Hong Kong came about through a series of unlikely events involving five individuals. First, on his initiative, Charles Elliot included the ceding of Hong Kong in the Convention of Chuenpi. Safely aboard 40 or so ships overloaded with 700 dependents in Hong Kong harbor for months no doubt attached Elliot to the place. As a missionary wrote about that time, "Hong Kong is indeed, a most romantic spot, and said to be the finest harbor in the world" (Hoe, 1991, p. 21). Between the island and the jetting peninsula of Kowloon (Nine Dragons), the harbor provides superb anchorage and shelter. Unlike Macao's shallow waters, HK's 90-foot depth by the Kowloon side can accommodate the largest ships. However, behemoth U.S. aircraft carriers anchor west of Central towards Lantau Island.

Soon after he completed the Chuenpi agreement in January 1841, Elliot sent his deputy, Alexander Johnston, to Hong Kong as resident administrator. Six months later, Elliot learned of his own fate from the *Canton Press*, which Jardine Matheson & Co. owned and supplied with news through their swift clipper fleet. Left to his own devices, Johnston took it upon himself to develop infrastructure, such as barracks, warehouses, and roads. Most significantly, no doubt pressed by the merchants, he also advertised and sold many plots of land -- £20 an acre in town and £2 an acre for outer lots. Johnston also "rented" choice bazaar locations to locals. Another example of the communications lag, all of this took place without a valid treaty (Welsh, 1993, pp. 132-141).

After Pottinger fulfilled Palmerston's instructions, he despatched the Treaty of Nanking to London for approval and turned his attention to Hong Kong, where he was aghast to find that his orders to cease land sales and nonmilitary construction had been disregarded. After two years of Johnston's administration, Hong Kong was a bustling community -- stone buildings, a waterfront road built by the Royal Engineers, a newspaper, ongoing commerce, and a growing population of 15,000. Johnstone's initiatives produced a tangled mess for the frustrated Pottinger, such as land titles and permanent works that Pottinger had to square with Aberdeen's instructions (see Mr. Topley's Chapter Two, pp. 111-114).

Aberdeen replaces Palmerston. Foreign Secretary from 1841-46, Lord Aberdeen (George Hamilton-Gordon, 4th Earl of) contrasted with his predecessor as night and day. Unpretentious and reflective, he tried to "establish Christian methods in the conduct of foreign affairs" in sharp difference to Palmerston's principle of every nation and man for themselves (Cecil, 1927, p. 91). Aberdeen's achievements are a testimony to the best of British diplomacy. While his predecessor's rough style rowed France and the United States, Aberdeen improved relations with both. Compared to the blusterer, Aberdeen was a humanist

For example, the 1842 Webster-Ashburton Treaty settled longstanding Anglo-American disputes in the border regions of the Great Lakes and Maine where the Aroostook War of 1839 had been fought. Setting the peaceful pattern for future Anglo-American relations, the Treaty also included cooperation in suppressing the African slave trade and the extradition of criminals. Aberdeen is reminiscent of the Englishmen who wrote the Declaration of Independence and the Constitution versus those who foolishly lost America.

Prime Minister (PM) from 1852-55, Aberdeen appointed Palmerston his Home Secretary. In 1855, the ever-brazen Palmerston forced Aberdeen to resign and replaced him over the issue of supporting the Ottoman Empire, thus launching Britain into the Crimean War against Russia. While Palmerston's popularity never soared higher, the most positive outcome of that deadly war was Florence Nightingale's crusade to modernize military medicine (Strachey, 1949, 1969).

Lord Aberdeen had wanted to use Hong Kong as a temporary military outpost and bargaining chip to obtain trading rights from China, not to hold permanently. PM Peel and Aberdeen left HK affairs mainly to the Governor-General of India, first Lord George Auckland, a cousin of Charles Elliot, and then Lord Edward Ellenborough. Aberdeen had ordered that no permanent buildings or works were to be completed; but those instructions had gone to Pottinger while he was absent with his war expedition in the north and not to Johnston. After his assessment of HK, Pottinger wrote to Ellenborough in May 1842: "I have done as much as I could to retard, without injuring this settlement, but the disposition to colonize under our protection is so strong that I behold a large and wealthy City springing up under my temporizing measures, and the chief difficulty I now have is the provision of locations for the respectable and opulent Chinese Traders who are flocking to this island." The last was a gross exaggeration as few gentry would be in HK for many years. Pottinger also informed Foreign Secretary Aberdeen that the settlement had "already advanced too far" to satisfy his orders and that the commanding general (see p. 74) urged improved defenses.

The British Government realized that a permanent possession was a *fait accompli* when the Treaty of Nanking reached London for ratification; its terms specifically ceded Hong Kong to Britain in perpetuity. On January 4, 1843, Aberdeen wrote to acknowledge receipt of the Treaty and instructed Pottinger to "assume the Government of the Island of Hong Kong, then become a Possession of the British Crown . . . ." Reaching HK six months later, the ratification led to a formal change of sovereignty on June 26, 1843 (Welsh, 1993, pp. 141, 124-125).

In short order, the Government drafted a charter that granted extraordinary discretionary powers to Governor Pottinger and his successors. Chapter Two (pp. 112-113) discusses the charter and other developments, and Chapters One (pp. 75-76) and Three (pp. 153-155) tell of the devastating death rate of the British in early HK.

Although no landmarks in Hong Kong commemorate Palmerston, who was so instrumental in HK's cession, Aberdeen's name was given to the cove area on HK island's southwest (see Map 2). One relishes the memory of quaint dining there aboard junks in the late 1940s with live fish to pick from bulging nets hanging from the swaying sides. That romantic scene has been replaced by industry and floating tourist restaurants. Aberdeen is also remembered with four HK streets. One street each has been named after Pottinger and Elliot in Central (courtesy of Grace Lee, HK Survey & Mapping Office, August 1997).

Geographical and Psychological Stepping-Stone

Prior to 1841, Hong Kong was sparsely populated, which made it easier for the British to develop without interference. The Chinese population increased as lower-class types rushed in to seek work and quick cash. Gentry and those with means shunned the colony for some time because of xenophobia and HK's crime rates of the worst types of foreigners and Chinese, but in time they started to come as China's turmoils grew and word circulated of the British colony and its opportunities.

Coolie exports. The Chinese soon realized that among HK's opportunities was transport abroad. Life became so harsh in China that from 1849 to 1875, about 1.5 million men (compared to 2 m. African slaves taken to the New World in the 19th c.) shipped to Southeast Asia and the Western Hemisphere as coolie laborers. The end of the African slave trade created worldwide demand for cheap labor. Using Havana as its terminus, South America offered the deadliest destinations, especially the hellish guano mines of Peru's Chincha Islands from which few survived. Spanish planters paid $400 to $1,000 for each coolie, whom they treated as slaves.

Supposedly respectable firms at home and in the colony were found to be closely involved in the lucrative business. Anglo-American statesmen, such as Foreign Secretary Lord Clarendon and Secretary of State William Henry Seward, denounced the "dreadful trade," and the public was appalled by the "horrors connected with numerous mutinies on Macau coolie ships" (Eitel, 1895, pp. 458-459; Lubbock, 1981). When the HK Government established some humane standards and restricted coolie sailings to British territories, Macau picked up the slack. Anglo-American pressure on Portugal finally curbed the trade in 1875.

In common then when foreigners could find rogues to do their dirty work, agents subdued the innocent by force or drug and turned them over to shippers. Desperate men and families in China could be found in abundance; there were plenty of takers who would indenture themselves and kin to "contracts" of work overseas with a pittance paid on the spot. Honest brokers and schemes existed; but the gullible made it easy for rogue agents. Once majestic and swift, worn clippers hauled the Chinese in inhuman conditions similar to that of the African slave trade. Therefore, opium importation the reason that Hong Kong became a British colony, the coolie trade thus became HK's first major export enterprise.

A great diaspora. Chinese emigration to SE Asia, the Americas, and Australia swelled from the 1850s and Hong Kong appointed its first emigration officer in 1854. The diaspora extended to and picked up after World War II (Lyman, 1975), especially to North America. All of this began with British Hong Kong.

The Taiping Rebellion lasting 14 years, other revolts, and the Opium Wars destroyed the people's confidence in China's Qing rulers. Also, the population languished in a drug stupor which Lord Elgin could readily observe, as translation of the Peking Convention of 1860 ratifying the Treaty of Tientsin progressed at snail's pace because the officials were addicted. Qing authorities lost control over the people, especially in South China around Hong Kong, a region which suffered over-population due to the introduction of the sweet potato to the food supply (Ho, 1959).

As China's laws punished emigration with beheading, HK provided the perfect solution; for as foreign territory with its own laws, the colony provided protection and escape from Qing edicts and control. Unlike Portuguese Macau on the eastern side of the broad Pearl River Delta, the British colony had the protection of the world's dominant power that had already humbled China in war. Seeing the escape hatch and finding the British unperturbed by their comings and go-ings, more and more Chinese used HK as a stepping-stone -- a haven and diaspora springboard from troubled China to opportunities abroad.

It is estimated that 2-3 million Chinese, mostly males, lived outside of China in 1876 with the number growing to 8-9 million by 1908 (Bastid-Bruguiere, 1980, p. 584). Today, "Overseas Chinese" are estimated to number 55 million who control $2 trillion in assets as "expatriate wizards," which is considerable when "Japan, with about twice as many people, had only $3 trillion in assets in 1990" (Seagrave, 1995, p. 3). Since the 55 million includes Chinese in HK, N. America, SE Asia, etc., they are diverse and often many generations removed from ancestral roots (Lever-Tracy, Ip, & Tracy, 1996). However, many in SE Asia and in HK maintain PRC ties, especially new immigrants and the super-wealthy who invest in the PRC. U.S. higher education has been a magnet for many Chinese for long.

Since the 1980s, Chinese students have been the first or second largest foreign student group in America (42,503 in 1996, 9.3% of the total; Desruisseaux, 1997). Mid-century gold rushes in California and Australia attracted thousands of Chinese who joined the diggings and sought work in the camps. For a decade, up to 10,000 Chinese worked on the transcontinental railroad across the hazardous Sierra Nevada mountains until completed in 1869.

Hong Kong as stepping-stone entrepot. As the number of Overseas Chinese expanded, they desired native provisions, such as rice, tea, medicines, spices, and many other native goods. First as transients and later as customers, the growing numbers of Chinese in SE Asia and North America promoted the stepping-stone's commerce, and more Chinese came to live and work in Hong Kong. In 1880 when colonialism remained steadfast, the Chinese already dominated HK's trade and were the biggest property tax payers, signs of the growing numbers of prosperous Chinese (Endacott, 1973, p. 196). By 1915, a world import-export network and local trading class, with about 1,700 commercial firms, handled indigenous goods. After World War II, Chinese participation in the economy advanced apace.

Tsai (1993, pp. 23-35) verifies that HK's importance as an entrepot developed early, as the colony in 1871-73 handled 32.5% in value of China's total import trade and 14.7% of her exports. As Shanghai developed into its own and siphoned off HK's trade business, a HK-Shanghai corridor developed which Shanghai dominated. The Cantonese took advantage of the corridor's import-export business as in-house compradors or brokers for foreign firms and as entrepreneurs. By 1907, almost 510,000 vessels handled over 36 million tons of shipping in and out of Hong Kong (Tsai, 1993, p. 34).

Besides the old opium firms that entered other markets, new foreign companies became giants in China, such as British-run Butterfield and Swire Co., Gibb, Livingston & Co., and Dodwell & Co., the American-run Standard Oil Co. of New York, the Singer Sewing Machine Co., the British-American Tobacco Corp., Japan's Mitsui in insurance and shipping, Germany's Carlowitz (rail and mining machinery and Krupp weapons) and Sienssen & Co., and many others. Sun Yat-sen and many Chinese spoke out against the "new imperialism of foreign companies" profiting on China's soil (Spence, 1990, p. 329; Feuerwerker, 1983).

Hong Kong became the world financial center it is today in part because Overseas Chinese made use of the currency exchange and bank system to trade and to send funds to relatives in China and the colony (Lattimore, 1940, p. 190). Local trading firms established the Hongkong and Shanghai Banking Corporation (HSBC) in 1864 to facilitate their local and East Asian trade and exchange activities (Collis, 1965). After World War II, the HSBC provided liberal loans to promote the colony's recovery. It also cleaned up the currency mess that the Japanese left by honoring the $119 million (about £7½ million) the Japanese overprinted in HSBC's belief that repudiating banknotes unlawfully issued would have harmed the Bank.

Today, HSBC is one of the world's largest financial corporation with many holdings beyond the SAR (see p. 295). After the 1911 Revolution, the Bank of Canton opened in Hong Kong with $2 million put up by Chinese American shareholders and many other banks opened in time. The stepping-stone became a regional clearinghouse and banker for resources and funds, setting roots for today's sophisticated financial infrastructure. The communists have made good use of HK's financial system and diverse commercial opportunities. The PRC's Bank of China is HK's second largest bank, and more than 15,000 mainland-owned firms employ four percent of the population. Using HK as an opportunity stepping-stone themselves, mainlanders participate fully as capitalists as p. 278 mentions.

Geographically, HK could not have been better located. Deep in South China, the territory has benefited from its great distance from Beijing. In the main, provincial and Canton officials have accommodated trade and travel with Hong Kong, in part because they found ways to line their pockets and also they understood regional ways. Preferred by the opium barons over HK, Chusan mentioned earlier was well within Beijing's easy reach. Also, Chusan's waters are dangerous to traverse during the monsoon and importantly, its established population versus HK's sparseness would have made it much harder to develop and administer, especially with Beijing and neighboring Hangzhou ready to create trouble.

The venturesome Cantonese were primed to take advantage of HK's opportunities and they remain predominant today. Northern Chinese often refer to the Cantonese as "revolutionaries" because Taiping chief, Hong Xiuquan, and China's revolutionary father, Sun Yat-sen, were born and raised near Canton and launched their anti-Qing activities in the same area. The Cantonese are known for their outspokenness and self-confidence, characteristics that often irritate Westerners and the more demure Northerners. Also, their eight-toned dialect and chattering manner are grating to Northerners' ears.

However, the Southerners preserve the dialect of the great Tang Dynasty (618-907) and oldtimers in Guangdong's hinterland still identify themselves of "people of the Tang." From the days when almost all Chinese in the U.S. were Cantonese, the Chinese name for Sacramento Street in San Francisco's Chinatown is *Tang yun gai,* as can be seen on bilingual street signs.

Not only did Hong Kong become an English colony by happenstance, indeed, the British unwittingly established the unique stepping-stone to and from China for the Chinese, primarily the Cantonese, who developed radical, new ways of perceiving themselves and the world.

The goose that lays golden eggs. Compared to its meager beginnings, Hong Kong today is a bustling, capitalistic center of far-reaching world importance. In 1997, its 6.3+ million people had a per capita income that was about US$29,000, which was comparable to America, about $7,000 more than Britain, and more than 20 times that of China. HK's GDP of about US$190 billion surpassed Switzerland's $125 b. with only 40% of its population. As HK's Chief Secretary, Anson

Chan, once proudly asserted at trade fairs: "Given our track record as the eighth largest trading entity, our tight control of public expenditure, our substantial reserves and the sheer competence and competitiveness of our economy, you would have to be a very courageous speculator indeed to bet against us." Chapter Six discusses the HK golden goose and how it began to fall on its face in late 1997.

In contrast to its July 6, 1998 issue, *Forbes'* (July 29, 1997) list of the world's 100 richest persons, 11 were Chinese: Hong Kong (5), Indonesia (1), Philippines (1), Singapore (2), and Taiwan (2). HK realtor, Lee Shau Kee, with US$14.7 billion was the richest before HK's property collapse of 1997-98. According to the World Bank, the gap between HK's rich and poor is among the highest in the world (Palpal-latoc, 1997). While many humanitarians have risen above greed to found hospitals (Chapter Three), universities and schools (Chapter Five), and many foundations, HK originated from and remains dedicated to free enterprise .

During several weeks' stay in May 1998, I could see that HK was poised between its preceding 13 years of prosperity and recession. Soon afterwards, the HK Government announced a 2% GDP drop in the first quarter. As property collapsed as much as 50%, many struggled to bolster their loans since lenders require fair-market financing. Since my last stay in 1992, prices were higher, new high-rises decked the skyline; the harbor, streets, and walkways were cleaner (no black blots from chewing gum and grime; perhaps a carry-over from the scrubbing for the 1997 handover); and shops and hotels seemed more luxurious. However, as unfinished high-rises stood void of workers and layoffs grew, one could see that HK was facing bad times. In March 1999, unemployment rose to 6% and underemployment increased to 3%.

HK's Causeway Bay lost its rank as the world's most expensive shopping property (annual rent from US$8,280 to $5,835 sq. metre) to New York's Madison Avenue ($5,920/sq. metre) (*HK Standard*, Nov. 15, 1998, Internet Edition). Late in 1998, the once sacrosanct government policy of providing relatively free health and medical services was under critical review, as Health and Welfare Secretary Katherine Fok Lo Chiu-ching forewarned adoption of a "user-pays" plan to meet increasing costs, estimated to increase 50% by 2010 (Wan, 1998). With the announcement on January 6, 1999 by PRC finance minister, Xiang Huaicheng, that the Mainland's economy was turning bad with "no room for optimism" plus his prediction that the Asian financial crisis was worsening (O'Neill, 1999), Hong Kong may experience tough times for years (see pp. 286-288).

At a Tokyo forum on Asia's future, Lee Kuan Yew, famed for his draconian pronouncements, said that Beijing would have to devalue the yuan within 18 months, a move that would be a huge negative for the SAR. While Anson Chan disputed that by saying that Premier Zhu Rongji was set against devaluation, Lee and others said that Zhu's promise was destined to be broken (Fulford, 1998).

If HK's recession deepens, how will it affect democratic expectations? HK's Constitutional Affairs Secretary gave an answer to a US Congressional Delegation -- democracy is no longer the public's priority; the economy is (McNamara, 1999). In the 1992 presidential race, Bill Clinton's cry was, "It's the economy, stupid!"

The Chinese Stepping-Stone Syndrome (CSS)

Let's broaden the discussion with concepts and a theoretical framework that can promote specificity and generalization. In 1990, I wrote that "China has been a civilization of more than 3,000 years but not a nation." Pye (1990, p. 58) said it better: "China is a civilization pretending to be a state. The story of modern China could be described as the effort by both Chinese and foreigners to squeeze civilization into the arbitrary, constraining framework of the modern state, ... In Western terms the China of today is as if the Europe of the Roman Empire and of Charlemagne had lasted until this day and were trying to function as a single nationhood."

Peyrefitte's (1992) excellent work on Britain's first mission to obtain free-trade rights in China in 1792-94 includes many insights into East-West differences and his concerns for future developments. One observation is apt here; he wrote that going from Hong Kong to China in 1960: "I was immediately struck by this society's resemblance to the one described by Macartney's companions. . . . China had a very Chinese way of rebelling against itself. Even while seeking to break with its past, it plumbed that past for precedents to grasp in asserting its own invariance" (p. xix). *How can all of this be explained?* If the nation-state of China is something archaic and separate from civilization, how does it function and relate with the people? How have the Chinese survived for thousands of years and maintained their great civilization?

Some social-science theory and concepts will help us to focus on and examine some of the complexities in the behavior and psychology of the Chinese people and how they have coped with indigenous misrule and foreign colonialism as well as the manner and role of authorities governing them.

Let's consider two forces that have shaped the nature of China -- the autocracy of the rulers and the self-reliance of the people as they organized and preserved themselves. To answer the question that journalist Bill McGurn put to me in 1988, "What makes the Chinese tick?," the Chinese Stepping-Stone Syndrome (Yee, 1992b; Yee & Cheng, 1999) was devised to explain the Chinese and HK.

With the CSS, I view Hong Kong as a geographical and psychological stepping-stone. That is, in location vis-a-vis China, from 1841-1997, HK was a British colony operating with British law and laissez-faire, free trade principles. As such, therefore, HK has provided an extraordinary, otherworldly refuge (escape hatch, egress) from China's misrule and constraints. The fact of the foreign colony at China's doorstep elicited the CSS psyche (driving spirit) of the Chinese people for self-determination, security, and prosperity. The term, stepping-stone, is defined here as a means of progress and path to advancement that can be unsure but emboldening and expedient of circumstances.

Since people adapt to change by adjusting more or less what they know, fear and value, the CSS is not a radically new phenomenon brought about only by the coming of British HK; but rather, it is a longstanding characteristic of the Chinese that stemmed from ageold conditions in China.

The CSS is a social-psychological complex that is characterized by opposing inclinations, such as opportunism versus prudence, fortitude versus submission, and approach versus avoidance and materialistic versus ideological behavior. As a stepping-stone or "foothold" (from the Confucius quotation, p. 1), the establishment of British HK opened the way for millions of Chinese to find greater life options and unleash the bolder aspects of their CSS nature. As HK's colonialism declined after WW II, that CSS nature or spirit seemed boundless in developing an energetic and prosperous world economy.

The Chinese in Taiwan, of course, are also imbrued with the CSS complex. As the *Economist* (In praise of paranoia, 1998) survey said, "It may be a cliche that the Chinese are possibly the world's best entrepreneurs, and would shine even more if their governments did not so often get in the way . . . ." Close to the question that McGurn raised, the *Economist* asked, "What is it about the Chinese? . . . . They work hard. They are financially conservative, which is to say they dislike debt and watch their pennies. At the same time they are natural gamblers (entrepreneurs) with a keen eye for opportunity and an appreciation of managed risk. They are motivated by pragmatic self-interest and self-preservation . . . ." "Taiwan's greatest strengths are a healthy paranoia in combination with the best of Chinese business acumen. These qualities show up in lots of ways, from conservative government policies to prudent corporate financial management."

Presented as a social-psychological construct with various factors, the CSS has two intersecting elements as shown in Figure One.

China's Autocratic Rule

Representing China's variable conditions of state rule, the vertical continuum, termed *authoritarian paternalism*, ranges between the poles of extreme oppression ($A+$) and uncontrol ($A-$). $A+$ characterized the brutal reign of the Qin king (221-207 B.C.), who created his title of First Emperor, *Shi huangdi*. Centralizing state government, he built much of the Great Wall 2,200 years ago with slave labor and buried alive hundreds of scholars to ensure his rule. Fairbank (1992, p. 55) said that the Qin used policy such as: " 'If you glorify the good, errors will be hidden; if you put scoundrels in charge, crime will be punished.' The ruler's aim was to preserve his power, never mind benefiting the people. There was no harmony of interests assumed between ruler and people." Illustrating their depravity, as a youth, Puyi, the last Qing emperor, regularly ordered servants flogged before him for his entertainment (Brackman, 1975, p. 79).

China's rulers grasped and held power by controlling and applying the means of violence. One dynasty typically changed to another through conquest and usurpation. China's authoritarianism matches Muller's (1985) "regime repressiveness hypothesis" in which no dissident individuals and groups and their resources are permitted and are absolutely repressed through violence if any should appear. $A+$ is well-illustrated by those who directed the tanks that not only murdered Tiananmen demonstrators in 1989 but had them ground the tracks over the

- Figure One -

MODEL OF THE CHINESE STEPPING-STONE SYNDROME

Authoritarian Paternalism

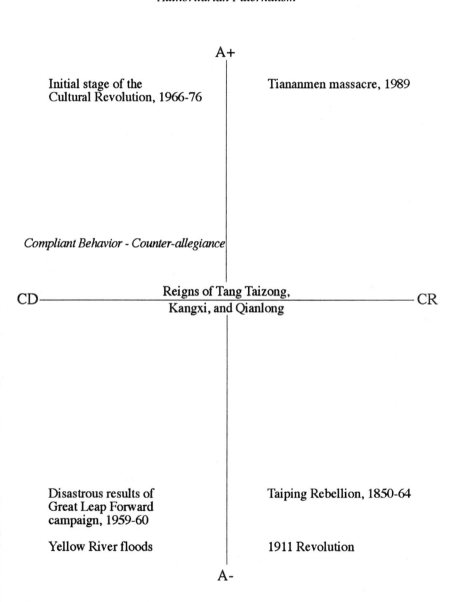

A+

Initial stage of the
Cultural Revolution, 1966-76

Tiananmen massacre, 1989

Compliant Behavior - Counter-allegiance

CD —————————— Reigns of Tang Taizong,
Kangxi, and Qianlong —————————— CR

Disastrous results of
Great Leap Forward
campaign, 1959-60

Taiping Rebellion, 1850-64

Yellow River floods

1911 Revolution

A-

bodies to obliterate any hope of identity. Unrestrained brutality marks totalitarianism, as shown in the Holocaust and the mass execution of entire Southern
Song armies defeated by the Mongols in 1268-79, the 1927 purge of leftists in
Shanghai and Canton, the slaughter of 10,000 Taiwanese on February 28, 1947,
and untold mayhem suffered by smaller groups and individuals. Suffering state
persecution for millennia, the Chinese have yearned not for democracy, but for
more reasonable rulers and political stability, i.e., no warfare or big changes, so
they could get on with their lives.

The other polar extreme (*A*-) represents anarchy, the rulers' inability to control
events and the people -- weak, ineffective rule or impasse, such as during natural
calamities bringing floods and famine as well as dynastic decline. In 1852, the
Yellow River (*Huanghe*) overwhelmed the dikes east of Kaifeng and misery persisted for long. The river racked horrendous devastation on a vast region as it
gouged a new channel to the Yellow Sea north of Shandong (Shantung). When
Governor Chang Ju-mei, neglected the all-important dikes, at places 60-70 feet
above the plains because of the incessant silting, "China's sorrow" inundated
thousands of square miles in 1898. As if that wasn't enough, locust plagues and
two years of drought extended bitter famine and homelessness. Enshrined by the
Chinese as their origin, the Yellow River symbolizes their persistent struggle and
longing for a better life.

While Emperor Qianlong's (1736-95) and some rulers provided limited relief,
the people never became dependent on state welfare. Whenever it came, aid was
arbitrary and meager, and even the best emperors ruled as tyrants. Also, by the
17th century, rich landowners who had moved to the cities took no responsibility
for the populace during catastrophes as in the past and humanitarian relief efforts
by local gentry, such as soup kitchens, were inadequate (Elvin, 1973, pp. 260-
267). Will (1990, p. 13) found that available reports of famine relief give "the impression of an administration conspicuously absent from the field." Therefore,
the *A* continuum is like a thermometer, the state ruling with brute force and arro-
grance at one polar extreme (*A*+) and gradations downward to uncontrol (anarchy) at the opposite end (*A*-). Since the people have had little choice in who their
rulers were and how they were ruled, a crucial question arises, how did they cope
with the state? The CSS helps to explain Hong Kong and the Chinese and how
and why they differ so from Westerners and others in many ways.

Leadership-followership. Gernet's (1982, pp. 492-493) classic synthesis of Chinese civilization characterized the golden age of "great emperors K'ang-hsi"
(Kangxi, 1662-1722), and his grandson (Qianlong), whose reigns he said accomplished so much, as "enlightened despots." Gernet also termed the entire Qing
Dynasty era as "authoritarian paternalism," and said that "China suffered from an
unhealthy degree of centralization. Peking expected to settle all questions, even
in the smallest details, all over this immense empire . . . ." Sun Yat-sen called it
"absolutism." Describing himself as "*heshang dasan wufa wutian*," meaning one
who is unbridled by law or God, Mao Zedong was a megalomaniac who insisted

on knowing and deciding everything, no matter how minor (Li, 1994, pp. 120-127). Close to Mao Zedong for 22 years, Li Zhisui (1994) told how thoroughly compliant and gullible the masses were in following the dictator's ridiculous orders to cast steel in backyard furnaces and substitute communes for families. It is pathetic to learn from one who was right on scene how sycophantic other PRC leaders, including Premier Zhou Enlai, acted towards Mao when they knew full well that his schemes were disasterous. Credit must be given to the few who spoke up, notably Deng Xiaoping, who suffered more than one purge for disputing Mao and the Gang of Four. Ironically, of all of China's rulers Mao came the closest to reaching the hearts of the Chinese people. Clutching his "little red book," they blindly identified with Mao as their great father-figure, whom they called the "Great Helmsman." Dictating destructive campaigns, Mao and his inner clique put China to waste with no opposing restraint, all of which distressed the HK people who witnessed all that was happening across the border.

Mao and the Chinese Communist Party (CCP) came to power by gaining the support of the peasantry in their struggle against Chiang Kai-shek and the Kuomintang Party (KMT), which the CCP branded as tyrants of the old order. After their mainland victory in 1949 and Chiang's retreat to Taiwan, the CCP presented the peasants new alternatives to traditional compliance and hardship, such as redistributing the land with the demise of the former owners (take from the rich to give to the poor), laws raising the rights of women and other oppressed groups, and cadre and soldiers who helped in harvests and construction .

Even so, in time it became clear that the PRC dominated family and village affairs and relationships to a far greater degree than even the KMT and former landlords ever dared. While life conditions improved, especially after Deng abolished Mao's communes and resurrected family farming, state rule became increasingly omnipresent and omnipotent throughout the land (Moore, 1966). In other words, the CCP enhanced authoritarianism at the same time that the people felt that the CCP was their salvation and thus obeyed.

Aboard Mao's train streaming through the night during the Great Leap Forward campaign of the late 1950s to catch up with the West, Mao's physician, Li (1994) saw disaster in the flaring flames of backyard foundries throughout the countryside. "As the drive to produce steel continued at an ever more frenetic pace, people were forced to contribute their pots and pans, their doorknobs, the steel from their wrought-iron gates, shovels, and spades. There was not enough coal . . . , so the fires were fed with the peasants' wooden furniture -- their tables, chairs, and beds" (p. 283). What came out of the foundries was useless and the fields were unattended. The CCP Standing Committee and cadre throughout the PRC were so fearful of the tyrant's commitment to the Great Leap Forward that their reports of harvest and production output were outrageously falsified.

During the 1930s Great Depression, millions worldwide denounced democracy and capitalism as fraudulent and embraced authoritarianism. As fascism, racism, and propaganda replaced reason and democracy, World War II ensued. On this, Drucker (1939) said that Germans and others became so hopelessly disenchanted with political instability and poverty that the rational character of society disintegrated and "economic man" was replaced by "heroic man." In CSS terms, as *A* is relative to perceptions as well as actions, tyranny is in the eyes of the people. Recall the thunderous acclaim to Hitler and Mao. Following the Cultural Revolution (1966-76), Mao's disasters finally reversed the people's trust in their heroic "Helmsman" and their *state-people* bond with him. In 1972 Beijing, Canton and Shanghai, I witnessed the madness of Maoism and the fearful submission of the people. Since no ruler had mesmerized the people as Mao had and thrown them asunder, the old antipathy towards the state returned reinforced.

In capitalistic HK, where "economic man" reigned, the people witnessed the CR and shuddered. Many assisted the droves of refugees that fled China into the colony, even after the HK Government said that refugees had to reach Central HK to qualify to stay in the stepping-stone, a marathon hurdle that had never been required before. While powerless to do anything whenever the CCP mounted one of its rank campaigns, the HK people have empathized with relatives and compatriots in China. For example, during the 1960s famine, the HK community sent food and money; £2.4 million in one drive alone (Becker, 1996, p. 297) and more over the years, such as during the devastating floods of 1998.

To maintain power and control, the PRC has the largest, best organized, and most technologically advanced military and security forces in East Asia. While outsiders try to assess China's war potentials abroad, which are almost nil, they do not realize the extent to which the numerous security forces and the People's Liberation Army (PLA) scrutinize and control the people. Viewing the issue as a domestic affair, China's militancy towards Taiwan is meant to bring the "renegade province" back into the fold as was done with Hong Kong.

Therefore, for thousands of years China's nation-state has been one dictatorship after another, functioning with little or no opposition. Even the most capable rulers have been tyrants, more concerned with their absolute power than the welfare of the people. The harsh reality of China's state authoritarianism (*A*) stems from antiquity and the corruption of Confucian principles.

Compliance and Counter-allegiance

The horizontal CSS continuum concerns the people, whose behavior in interaction with the rulers is submissive compliance under duress. I enfold compliance into *counter-allegiance* to stress the negative *state-people* relationship. Fending for themselves, the Chinese people organized their basic human activities into family and kinship relationships to survive and cope. While they did their best to avoid soldiers and state agents, they had to endure the inescapable *state-people* relationship and comply as well as they could. Taking many forms, counter-allegiance involves compliance behavior loaded with degrees of animosity and resistance, perhaps akin to immates of a prison facing arbitrariness and corrupt guards. Matching avoidance behavior with passivity, the Chinese follow a live-and-let-live attitude, which Lin Yutang (1977, pp. 45-49) identified as "indifference" -- "not a high moral virtue but a social attitude made necessary by the absence of legal protection" (p. 47).

Foreigners since Marco Polo have observed that the Chinese appear to be cheerful and conforming to authority. However, what they saw was the facade, not the people's true feelings and conditions. Facing an overbearing state, the Chinese are non-confrontational to officials and shirk attention. Using anonymity as in faceless groups, however, the docile Chinese reveal a subtle, taunting style of counter-allegiance. With no respect for personal privacy in China, the state has always mandated that people report any wrongdoing by others, even family members, a policy which the PRC has intensified to the extreme. After a Tiananmen demonstrator took shelter in his sister's home, she reported her brother to the police who arrested the young student. State and social constraints in China, therefore, have not only stymied the CSS psyche of the Chinese, they probably originated it across millennia of stultifying conditions. HK was such a contrast!

Direct confrontation in the PRC can be frightful and tricky. For example, Wudunn (Kristoff & Wudunn, 1994, p. 395), a Chinese American journalist in Beijing, wrote about her narrow escape from police arrest: "When it came to the Chinese authorities, I discovered that if you pushed a little, you usually got a lot. But you had to push at the right time and with the right amount of force. If you didn't push enough, you got nothing. If you pushed too hard, you got into a fistfight. That is also a metaphor for relations between China and the West."

CCP leaders constantly receive signals, Chinese-styled, that never let them forget the counter-allegiance underlying the people's compliance. Distinctive of Chinese societies, counter-allegiance is an ongoing expression of the people's attitude towards the ruling state. Strong action is taken when the rulers perceive people going too far. To maintain control, Deng Xiaoping often said with unmistakable scorn: "Slaughter a chicken in front of the monkeys." Contrast that and Mao's mentality with the words of Confucius at the start of this Overview.

The line dividing counter-allegiance from discretion and danger is clear, but many brave Chinese still act on their inner values and put themselves into jeopardy. Famous from world television, a young man, named Wang Weilin, courageously challenged a tank column near Tiananmen on June 5, 1989. Wang was arrested and hasn't been heard from since, also many others taken during the purge. Those viewed as going too far and used as examples are relegated to subhuman status as *feirenmin* (non-people) as millions were during the Cultural Revolution. [see Nien Cheng's (1986) haunting tale of her imprisonment during the CR. As I wrote (1992b, p. 175), After Tiananmen, the Chinese people suffered "remorseful shame -- the kind a mother and child feel when they must seek help from outside the family to save them from the tyrannic father's cruelties and dissipation."]

It has been said that history repeats itself because people forget the lessons of the past. What should never be forgotten is the CCP's record of volatile intrusions in HK during the 12 years after the Declaration was signed (see Chapter 7). Consider Xu Jiatun, Beijing's headman in HK during the 1980s and Deng's confi-

fidant. Always seeking the limelight, Xu often rocked the territory with his voci-
ferous and humorous rhetoric in fluent Cantonese. After a fallout with the CCP
Standing Committee in 1990, perhaps over Tiananmen repercussions, Xu fled to
the U.S. where he remains in subdued exile with his family. Few Westerners
have heard of him, but Hong Kongers saw Xu's bombast and downfall both as
exemplary of Beijing's arrogance and the constant power struggle within the
CCP elite. Commending Xu for discarding his offical mask, HK delighted in his
sensational flight to safety that not only countered the regime but also symbolized HK's precious stepping-stone feature -- an escape hatch from China.

Since its founding in 1949, the PRC has had numerous wild and violent up-
heavals; some campaigns not mentioned earlier are: the Anti-Rightist campaign,
1957; anti-Lin Biao and anti-Confucius campaigns, 1973-75; the second "Hundred Flowers" rise and fall and suppression of the "Democracy (Wall) Movement, both 1979; "Campaign Against Spiritual Polluticn," 1983; "Anti-Bour-
geois Liberalism campaign, 1987-88, etc. Amnesty International and the U.S.
State Department denounce the PRC's human rights record as the world's worst.

Indeed, China is a colossus in culture and population (i.e., *culture-people*), yet its
state governance remains autocratic and archaic. The way Chinese are treated
versus non-Chinese is telling; as PRC agents prounce on Chinese, even those
with foreign passports, and order them not to betray state secrets or doing anything to damage the PRC, as was done in the weeks before President Clinton's
visit to China (Shenon, 1998). In that stance, they assume that one is guilty until
proven innocent and that whether one is China or foreign born or a national of
another nation, a Chinese is a Chinese. In preparations for Clinton's visit, a
Beijing book on the U.S. President's sex problems, etc., *The Temperment of Bill
Clinton*, was banned from sales. Will that ever happen in Hong Kong?

The Chinese Family and the CSS

Sinologists have uniformly praised the cohesiveness and durability of the Chinese family without delving much into behavioral explanations that the CSS tries
to initiate. The respected China scholar, Lucian Pye (1992, p. 88) has written:
"The Chinese familial system has been one of the great and distinctive institutions in all human history." According to another famed sinologist, John Fairbank (1992, p. 18), the Chinese family is "a microcosm, the state in miniature":

> . . . the amazing thing about the Chinese farming people has been their ability to
> maintain a highly civilized life under these poor conditions. The answer lies in
> their social institutions, which have carried the individuals of each family through
> the phases and vicissitudes of human existence according to deeply ingrained pat-
> terns of behavior. These institutions and behavior patterns are among the oldest and
> most persistent phenomena in the world. China has been the stronghold of the
> family system and has derived both strength and inertia from it.

Since survival in China demanded a hardy breed, the social behavior of the Chinese can be best understood through their family institution, as in Hong Kong (see Lau & Kuan, 1988). Organized first and foremost as such, the Chinese have related to life situations and authorities through the bipolar extremes of despair **(CD)** and rancor **(CR)** of Figure One. The middle was the best that could be hoped for and will be discussed soon.

Fatalistic capitulation **(CD)** is shown by the pathetic close to Lao She's (Lai She) *Ricksha Boy*, when the once hardworking laborer who tried to provide for his family ends up as a destitute prop in funeral processions. When Mao's Great Leap Forward (1957-60) failed, the people, who did their utmost to obey their "helmsman," fell in exhausted despair and capitulation and over 30 million died from starvation (Becker, 1996). Stemming from family loyalties and a history of calamity and misery, the famed Chinese work ethic is as much for gain as it is paranoia of misfortune.

It has taken tremendous provocation for Chinese to revolt, since rebellion would put their families in severe jeopardy. During the PRC's liberal climate in 1996-98, people felt freer to speak their mind; but the limit remained absolutely no opposition to CCP rule. As p. 135 relates, the HK Chinese never revolted or used arms against the British even when there were crises, such as Shanghai and Canton massacres in 1925; instead, they abandoned the colony on strike. When student rancor and smoldering resentment **(CR)** approached breakpoint revolt at Tiananmen in 1989, CCP leaders saw the threat and crushed it with classic ruthlessness. So that the populace remembers the limit, the CCP has been relentless in its persecution of dissidents, such as the 1999 crackdown and pro-democrats, Wei Jingsheng , Wang Dan , and others.

Rancor flared after Qing defeats to foreign imperialists, such as the loss of Vietnam to the French in 1885. That was the last straw for revolutionists such as Sun Yat-sen and others in Hong Kong; but as Sun complained the people offered little collective unity because their concerns were for their families, not China as a nation-state (Scalapino & Yu, 1985, pp. 148-230). Famed 1920s activist writer, Lu Xun, said China was a deadly "windowless, iron house" and berated the people's passivity and condemned the family for its lack of commitment beyond itself.

As 1998 ended, the CCP issued a crackdown on dissent that ended its toleration of criticism for several years. Typically young voices, critics attacked a host of problems. He Qing-lian published a well-argued, footnoted "critique of the economic and social consequences of China's 20-year-old economic reform programme" in which she lambasted the "power-holders" and "hangers-on" of failed state enterprises (Lawrence, 1998, p. 12; Binyan & Link, 1998). According to He, *Behind the Pitfalls of Modernization* became a bestseller with 3 million copies sold in legitimate and pirated copies.

During the Cultural Revolution, Ms. He's father, a Chinese medicine doctor, died after being savagely persecuted by Red Guards and the family barely survived as He pushed carts and hauled bricks for pittances. After the CR, she studied and graduated with an economics master's degree from the prestigious Fudan University. It seems clear that her family and personal experiences with the state incurred her strong criticism.

Writings by Yu Jie have been circulating in the PRC since 1993 (Nightingale's Song, 1998). Also speaking in indignation from family experiences, Yu has criticized much in China, including the daring issue of political tyranny. Echoing Lu Xun, Yu wrote: "From time immemorial, China has had people who obey, and people who are thugs, but China has never had citizens. Its people are like turtles who shrink into their shells, . . ." Turtles, however, know how to survive and live long lives. Since critics such as He and Yu skirt the edge of political tolerance, what happens to such voices during the "anti-group dissent" crackdown in 1999 will reveal how the PRC enters the 21st century.

China's strongest social institution, the Chinese family has been the most self-sufficient family institution in the world and explains how the people have survived millennia of authoritarianism and calamities. Because they have had to fend for themselves, the Chinese have used family cohesiveness, loyalty, and sacrifice to the utmost in order to survive and progress. Their fulfillment of basic human activities through the family is shown in the still-prevalent practice of family businesses, even in large corporations where key executives are related, and obtaining loans and investments through relatives and family friends. Enduring through the ages, the family has preserved Chinese civilization and identity through love for China's culture, arts, etc. The *culture-people* bond has been their bulwark against tyranny in China and colonialism in Hong Kong.

Years ago, I saw a Taiwan-made movie of Shanghai's resolute defense in 1932 against invading Japanese forces. During the fighting, KMT soldiers fortified a block of buildings and heroically fought off waves of Japanese for weeks. In the film of that famous battle, not once but several times wives and children came on scene to plead and cry for their husbands to abandon the fighting before they were killed, leaving them destitute. At the film's close, the officer in charge was shown escaping alive across a burning bridge -- yes, calling for his family!

It is impossible to imagine the same scenes in Western war movies, which in contrast would stress patriotism for the nation-state. Perfectly understandable to the Chinese, the film instead made the most of family devotion. No words and theory can put it better.

State-People Dyad: Authoritarianism vs. Humanitarianism

Over the ages, the autocratic rule of men has persisted in China as opposed to the rule of law in the West (Li, 1991; Yahuda, 1996, pp. 140-141). Confucian humanitarianism and benevolence became lip service as the sage's teachings on hierarchical authority and loyalty took precedence. Second only to Confucius, Mencius believed that the people's well-being is the ruler's chief reason for being and that any ruler that subjects the people to penury and selfishness should be deposed. Little known until the 11th century, Mencius (about 371-288 BC) is revered along with Confucius (551-479 B.C.).

Forsaking the ancients altogether, the CCP has gone further than past rulers and escalated totalitarianism through modern technological and military means. Van Kemenade (1997, p. 393) said it well, "Until the (end of the Qing), China had a tra- dition of state omnipotence (*quan-neng zhu-yi*), . . . After . . . 1949, the remnants of feudal state omnipotence expanded into rigorous, modern authoritarianism . . . The dividing line between society and the state disappeared entirely." The CCP has promoted communism "with Chinese characteristics," i.e., whatever the CCP intends. Criticism was tolerated in 1996-98, because critics said what CCP leaders wanted to say themselves. Yet, both Mao and Deng welcomed debate before clamping down again. Speaking on nationalism, Sun Yat-sen (1943, pp. 4-9) touched on China's nation versus state disparities as compared to other nations; but he did not pursue the point very far. He would be bitterly disappointed to see how regimented China as a state is today.

Authoritarianism versus pragmatism. Elected to a second five-year term in September 1997, PRC President Jiang Zemin could prove to be less authoritarian than "emperors" Mao and Deng. Jiang and Zhu Rongji, the pragmatic economist who became Premier in March 1998, could foretell a future that is less dogmatic. Zhu's nickname is "one chop," which comes from his efforts to curb red tape. Both have advocated economic reforms and pledged to ensure HK's autonomy. While "Deng Xiaoping theory," i.e., material progress is the chief measure of political success, became state creed at the 15th CCP Congress in 1997, everyone senses two needs -- political reform and relate Jiang's rule to Mao and Deng.

It would surely be revolutionary if Jiang Zemin and the Standing Committee revised dogma which views the CCP as synonymous with the state and opposes above all else any diminution of CCP power, i.e., no threat to *A*. In contrast to Beijing authorities, such as former premier Li Peng, infamous for the Tiananmen crackdown, Jiang and Zhu settled protests in late 1980s Shanghai without bloodshed (Goldman, 1994). Since hierarchical authority runs through all Chinese institutions, there is much inertia to overcome. Autocratic rule has continued for millennia because change proponents lacked united power, such as Sun Yat-sen, or were false reformers, such as Yuan Shikai (Scalapino & Yu, 1985, pp. 38-147).

In early 1999, Jiang attacked "destabilizing factors" that challenge one-party rule. Zigzagging between tolerant and tough lines as in the past, the CCP struck broadly against those who rock the boat -- dissidents, media, corrupt officials, inefficient state industries, unemployment, and stagnating rural incomes. The abrupt reversal signalled that the CCP was asserting itself before harder times hit home as well as boost plans to establish Jiang as the "new-style philosopher king" and revise the constitution during the 50th year of the PRC (Lam, 1999).

Because revolution is improbable, the only hope has been that the CCP would introduce incremental change towards a freer state. When Chinese speak of China as a state, they typically refer to the leaders and what they are saying and doing. Deng Xiaoping's nickname was *yi yan tang* (one-word boss), which means as absolute dictator what he said was *it*, right or wrong. Westerners who referred to him as "paramount leader" had it almost right. Deng's famous assertion, that it didn't matter whether a cat was white or black as long it caught rats was electrifying throughout the PRC, because it was Deng's way to abolish Mao's syllogism about being a true Communist (Red) first and then a capable worker, etc. Deng's analogy meant that results should take priority. Seemingly trivial outside, Deng's words opened a new era. Pressure mounts on Jiang and Zhu to modernize with political reforms. They must find a workable and lasting CSS center for the 21st century. However, China's traditions of tyranny offer few guidelines.

HK's society and media as well as increasing consumer demands and awareness of the world in the PRC increase pressures for progressive reforms. An estimated three million in the PRC with Internet access obtain limited information with tens of thousands of new *wangchong* (net bugs) getting online each month, despite CCP controls. In contrast to HK's freedoms, filters in the PRC block what is judged unfit, such as the BBC and *New York Times*. The hardline that began the last week of 1998 increased restrictions on the net bugs. However, with such ubiquitous devices and communication demands today, Jiang and the CCP elite will be sorely tested. One bad scenario is that they take extreme measures $(A+)$ to show who's boss, fail to exert control, and tougher types take over.

Walking about Beijing, Shanghai, and Canton in 1972, I had the streets almost to myself. It was eerie touring the empty Palace Museum (Forbidden City), Temple of Heaven, etc. The people secluded themselves indoors during the Cultural Revolution; the few outside looked forlorn and wore an unisex, baggy uniform. In sharp contrast, people in the PRC today as in HK are everywhere wearing a colorful variety of clothes, speaking animatedly, and have means. China's autocratic line has remained in place through good times or bad, but the people are clearly less pliant today. Assessing the lack of political reforms in China by 1997, Pye wrote that PRC "progress" has only been "old-fashioned varieties of money politics." That was not to say, however, that China would face the dilemma of reform and control with more certainty and debate in 1999.

Deng Xiaoping made it clear throughout his reign as paramount leader that China should never have another dominating personality leader such as Mao Zedong again. Head of the CCP and the military, President Jiang holds the power reins, but he lacks the charisma as well as the desire to be a supreme dictator. Time will only tell if Jiang, Zhu, and their "reform" clique can stay in power and how different they really are.

Soon after he became Premier, Zhu Rongji wowed foreign reporters with his humor, enthusiasm, and self-confidence. He has charmed leaders and journalists in Europe, Hong Kong, Japan and in the U.S. However, anecdotes circulating in Beijing in 1998 may be prophetic, such as: (1) One guy with middling intelligence has left the State Council . . . to be succeeded by a smart madman. (2) Li Peng's wife teased her husband soon after the new premier's now-famous press conference: "You were premier for 10 years and Zhu for one day. But you never had this kind of adulation from the media." Mr. Li replied: "But I'm sure Old Zhu won't last 10 years" (Lam, 1998).

Harmony is at the center. Midpoint intersection of the CSS continuums (to form four equal quadrants) represents the best of times -- stable, functioning society and rational dictatorship (not too fierce nor ineffective) and conforming, achieving people, such as the Golden Age of Tang Taizong's reign (627-650).

How to gain and hold the CSS center involves many factors. In the past, the people conformed in their desire for stability. Exerting selfish authority, rulers did not pursue the center much. Deeply ingrained then, Chinese compliance has been malleable as a family to a stern patriarch or the Germans to Nazism. Saying that China's stance to the world is defensive, Nathan & Ross (1997) suggest that the PRC faces two big tasks, first as in the past, control and harmony within, and second, security internationally. While Nathan, Shi, & Ho (1998) argue that democracy is possible in the PRC, they are astonished to find that the people are unaware of how intrusive the state is in their lives and see no option to CCP rule. Dickson's (1997) provocative study of democratic developments in Taiwan, however, gives concrete basis to believe that the CSS center can evolve into an expanding "even playing field," when authorities can be forced to interact and interchange with the people. Perhaps free societies can be portrayed as an ongoing CSS center, a circle minus the authoritarian aspects of the CSS model.

A basic Chinese ethic is following the middle course as most prudent and wise. The oft-used concept of middle relates to harmony and compatibility. While Westerners are intrigued with the Chinese character for crisis, a combination of the characters for danger and opportunity, few realize how their coupling reflects the Chinese sense of balanced wholeness. Also, few are aware of the *Book of Changes* (Wilhelm, 1970) and *feng shui* (Thompson, 1996), ancient beliefs based on mystical harmony, which many Chinese apply to their daily lives as in HK.

Westerners view the world chiefly through the self (the "I" and "me"), reductionist causality, and oppositional premises, such as heaven versus hell, etc. Instead of the individual, the Chinese perceive the world and life through significant others (the "we"), nature's wholistic being, and vigilant work to avoid and temper the bad. Helping to explain CSS psyche, Potter (1988, p. 206) captures this East-West difference: Instead of using "emotion in order to symbolize and affirm human relationships" as in the West, "the social world of the Chinese villager is remarkable for its insistent emphasis on drudgery and production. The Chinese devote endless attention to work and the rewards for work." The Confucian/ Daoist sense of equilibrium conceives the universe as integrated (inseparable) wholes, the seasons, man/woman, etc. Such values are deeply ingrained in Hong Kong.

Culture-people bond. Thousands of years of oppression and hardship have shaped the behavioral characteristics of the Chinese and Jews, two peoples with the oldest, continuous civilizations. Since their life conditions have been marked by autocracy and self-sufficiency across thousands of years, they share interesting, unique characteristics (Yee & Laytner, under review). One is a psychological dissociation that is not found among other peoples, which arises from the fact that their long histories lack compatibility and cohesion in *culture-state-people* or (civilization-nation/state-family/person) identity. While other peoples have enjoyed positive triadic relationships and take them for granted, such as Americans and British, the Chinese and Jews have suffered alienation in their negative *state-people* dyadic relationships (dyad = two interacting entities). Thus, they have made much of their *culture-people* bond (bond = the positive relationship between two entities) and organized themselves in strong family and kin relationships to provide for their basic human activities. This lack of a positive *state-people* bond across millennia has contributed to CSS social-psychological traits that are evident in many Jews and Chinese (especially HK), as manifested by opportunism and risk-taking urges versus prudence and apprehension of life's vicissitudes.

Emphasizing their vital *culture-people* bonds, the Chinese and Jews have related their cultural heritage and significance as distinct, worthy peoples wherever they may be in the world, a trait much noted by others. Their traditional sense of family and culture have promoted their work ethic, materialism, and drive for educational achievement. Thus, the *culture-people* bond placed greater demands on family socialization and kin ties than for others. For the Chinese, their sense of family is their hope for eternity; their identity by state symbols has been far less relevant. For while the Stars & Stripes and the Tricolor are emulated by their peoples, the Chinese have had no inspirational equivalent and have envied the citizens of strong nations. HK's Bauhinia flag elicits little or no "patriotism."

Just consider how many flags have flown over Tiananmen Square, the misnamed Gate of Heavenly Peace, in this century alone? Comparing the profusion of monuments in Washington, Paris, and London to the relative paucity in Beijing, one finds nothing heroic spanning China's dynasties. The Ming tombs, Xian diggings, and Great Wall are testimonies to ruthless autocracy, alas, unbeknownst to the common tourist. Rationality and humanitarianism emanated from the *people-culture* bond, not the *state-people* dyad. Modern Israel carries immense meaning for Jews, the likes of which the Chinese have been yearning for -- within the land of their ancestors but where they have been misruled. For it is not just the soil but everything that goes with nationhood, as clearly shown by the patriotism of peoples with true *culture-state-people* triadic relations.

Visiting the New York Metropolitan Museum of Art in 1998, I came across a beautiful scroll of calligraphy identified as follows: "This poem is a plea for humanitarian rule. It ends with the admonition: 'Despotic officials and shyster underofficials may feel ashamed.' Yelu Chucai's (1190-1244) Poem of farewell to Liu Man." The poem reflects the ageold disparity between reality and Confucian humanism in China, which has persisted because men have ruled, not law.

Martyrdom and identity. The Chinese harbor counter-allegiance as a shield against their rulers, the epitome of which is to memorialize heroes martyred through state injustice and misrule, such as Song General Yue Fei, Ch'u Yuan of the Dragon Boat Festival, etc. Demonstrating at first to honor Hu Yaobang as a martyr during his funeral, weeks later the Tiananmen students became martyrs themselves when they were slaughtered. Hu spoke of reform and humanism before his ouster from power as Party chief by Deng and CCP archconservatives.

Great grief also followed Premier Zhou Enlai's death in 1976. Against the orders of the Gang of Four led by Mao's wife, Jiang Qing, the people massed at the Heroes' Monument in Tiananmen to honor Zhou whom the Gang of Four had treated as an enemy. When the effusive placards and flowers, many homemade of paper, were quickly deposed and edicts against further demonstrations were issued, the people came forth again with great heaps of the same, thus provoking a crisis when many were arrested and punished. While Zhou and Hu shared responsibility for CCP excesses, they nevertheless showed openness, flexibility, and humanitarian concern for the people. Honoring them as martyrs, the people achieved what they wanted by signaling counter-allegiance to the CCP Standing Committee that was resounding enough to provoke its ire.

The Chinese view their identity and homeland in kinship and abstract, cultural terms, i.e., "We are descendents of the Yellow Emperor," a HK 1980s pop song referring to the mythical first emperor, *Huang-di*, who invented medicine and always benefited the people. The song of course expressed counter-allegiance to the CCP. Another song, "Embracing the Blood-Soaked Flag," an emotional, patriotic lament that the CCP flourished during the 1979 Sino-Vietnamese War, was also used in satiric derision in Hong Kong after Tiananmen -- "our blood, your flag!" Since it's impossible to picture the Chinese without it, counter-allegiance will not dissipate; its wonderous shades of satire, sarcasm, irony, and scorn deserve much study. Chapter 4 has examples of media satire and sarcasm.

The unity of *culture-state-people* associations for the Japanese is illustrative, as seen in their traditional sense of nationalism, homogeneity and union or *Nihonjinron*. For while the Japanese family is close-knit, boys are socialized to achieve outside their families in corporations and the government, i.e., for Japan. General MacArthur and others were surely correct in believing that retaining the emperor's symbolic role would fit well into a democratic Japan, quite the opposite for the Chinese. Chinese youth are raised to be loyal to the family for life, which explains the propensity of Chinese family businesses in HK and elsewhere.

As the Qing Dynasty deteriorated (lower half of Figure One's vertical axis, *A*-) throughout the 19th century to its 1912 demise, the people shifted to the right of center and became uncharacteristically assertive. With China in anarchy and poverty, they moved boldly beyond *CR* rancor and cast off compliance to the Qing rulers, as evident by rebellions, warlordism, banditry, and unprecedented emigration through Hong Kong and Macau beginning in the 1850s. Men, who once prided their queues although mandated by the Qing, had them cut off with oaths aimed at the failed rulers. Is there an equivalent in the West?

Secret societies, rebel savants such as Lin Qing in 1813, and many disaffected, rootless men added to China's turmoil (Spence, 1990, pp. 165-193). Of the CSS's four extreme corners representing chaos *(luan)*, which the Chinese abhor and seek to avoid, China was in Quadrant IV chaos -- the rulers were in disarray and the people were in arms and recalcitrant. Such was China after Hong Kong was lost in the First Opium War. From one regime to the next, dictatorship ruled.

Social-psychological studies show that authoritarian groups are highly dependent on their leaders and become unstructured in the leaders' absence and lack of supervision. Democratic groups, however, identify as a unit and are generally self-controlling and seek leaders who can coordinate and guide versus dictate and dominate. While authoritarian climates are cold and formalized, democratic groups generally operate with openness and humaneness (Lewin, et al., 1939; Lippitt, 1940). Such contrasts relate to the *state-people* dyad of the Chinese. See Yee & Cheng (1999) for greater depiction and analysis of the CSS construct.

Hong Kong: The Good, Quaint, Bad, and Ugly

This section is a potpourri of issues regarding Hong Kong -- colonialism, the people, the sale of opium for revenue, Sino-American relations, governors, etc.

Unlike the missionaries and philanthropists discussed in Chapters Three and Five, foreign traders and others in China disparaged the Chinese and rested on their own values and interests. Except for Anglo-American missionaries and translators (Yee, 1992b, pp. 56-57) who painstakingly gained competence in Chinese, both sides relied on *pidgin* English, a shortcut means of communication which the Chinese concocted from English words and Chinese syntax, "a most wonderful gibberish" (Ball, 1892, p. 455). In time, Chinese became competent in English by completing studies in HK secondary schools and in Britain and America. *Pidgin* itself came from the word, business. Used to connote varied fees, *cumshaw* originated from "come shore," an expression coined by boat-people calling sailors to go ashore aboard their sampans. The sailors would reply, "How muchee cumshaw?" Overworked *pidgin* sayings, such as, "Can do" and "No can do," are still heard in Singapore and Malaysia today but only rarely in HK. Yet English fluency in HK has been a big problem (see pp. 263-264).

To the common people, the foreigners' language, dress, and diet were offensively weird; the reverse impression was the same. Xenophobia aside, British autocracy resembled that of China's rulers. Appointed Hong Kong's first Chief Magistrate in 1841, Captain William Caine, late of the Cameronians, strutted about the colony looking for provocation. As typical of British and U.S. military and shipping of those days, Caine firmly believed in "discipline reinforced by frequent floggings" (Welsh, 1993, p. 133). During their 1803-1806 expedition of the Louisiana Purchase, Captains Meriwether Lewis and William Clark maintained discipline in the Corps of Discovery with floggings; one man received 100 lashes (Ambrose, 1996).

Change, however, was evident in the 18th century; as General George Washington found it effective to cajol and reason with his civilian soldiers while frequent floggings maintained discipline among their opposing Redcoats. The British maintained law and order in Hong Kong with rough methods for long (see pp. 126 & 135-136).

Inured to tyranny in China, the Chinese were not altogether surprised by British colonialism in HK and knew how to handle it. 'When a citizen is maltreated by a mandarin, he has no choice but to resign himself' (Peyrefitte, 1992, p. 403). In short, the CSS model applied to British HK as well as China. However, the Chinese observed that some Westerners, unlike most, were humanistic and gentle as some people were in their own society.

Although most governors tended to be humane, they were far removed from the people and sympathy is keenest in the abstract. Up to recent times, the British ran HK to suit themselves, not the Chinese. Note (pp. 127-128) that one high point of Kennedy's term (1872-1877) was his being the first Governor to invite Chinese to Government House, for which he was highly criticized by the British community. Yet HK's colonial rule had its significant contrasts.

British Law and Colonialism

Nothing shows the difference between China and the West better than law and justice (e.g., Li, 1991), a contrast that continues today. In turn, nothing highlights the disparity between Western values and practices more than colonial bias. For example, the bread poisoning incident of 1857 (see p. 121) raised hysteria among the HK British community demanding that suspects be "strung up." Gov. John Bowring stopped lynchings, trials ensued, and a British jury acquitted suspects for lack of evidence. Before emotions cooled, however, an inquisition stormed with more than 600 Chinese jailed in inhuman conditions, which British doctors protested. Many Chinese were exiled to Hainan and Bowring was driven to overlook some vigilantism (Endacott, 1973, pp. 93-94; Welsh, 1993, pp. 214-215).

The poisoned bread panic revealed the following: (1) the biased behavior of the colonial community toward the Chinese as opposed to the HK Governor, even when he had personal cause to be rowed since his wife had been stricken and later died; (2) the rule of law and justice administered fairly by the courts; and (3) Parliament's oversight which demanded an enquiry.

In contrast to China's corruption, justice prevailed in Hong Kong on matters of law. The Chinese were simply amazed to see that the law ruled men in the colony and that they were treated as equally as Westerners, even in hangings and canings (see pp. 117 & 122 on the autonomy of HK attorney generals). They embraced Western law as it was reliable and conformed with seldom-achieved Chinese values of justice. However, no set of laws cover all societal concerns. As in the U.S., for example, it was possible to discriminate by race, age, gender, etc. before civil rights laws were passed only several decades ago. Inciting a 1905-06 boycott against American goods in HK, U.S. Chinese exclusion laws in the late 19th and early 20th centuries were highly discriminatory until they were declared unconstitutional decades later (Tsai, 1993, Chap. 7).

In HK, blatant colonialism, such as biased education and property and physical abuse in public, did not begin to really fade until the 1970s. Since colonialism in Hong Kong resembled what they knew in China, the Chinese took it in stride.

Early Chinese emigrants to the U.S. showed that they had learned the essentials of British law and justice in Hong Kong and applied them in America. Facing bias and violence in the American West, they took grievances to trial and were often successful, especially at the U.S. Supreme Court. One famous discrimination case involving the Chinese, *Yick Wo vs. Hopkins* in 1885, concerned fire-safety licenses for laundries in San Francisco, a law which was enforced upon the 150 Chinese laundries but not on the 170 White laundries. In the end, the U.S. Supreme Court ruled that even though the ordinance was proper, its discriminatory enforcement was unjust as the Constitution mandates "equal treatment under the law." Cases such as *Yick Wo* are a magnificent consequent of the mingling of East and West and unheralded outcome of British legal justice in Hong Kong.

However, jurispudence was one thing; colonial bigotry and discrimination were another. Shifting their compliance and counter-allegiance to British authority, the Chinese in HK did not expect equality and saw little reason to change their ways. Both sides perceived glaring peculiarities in the other, but relations boiled down to who had power; autocratic elitism and social distance grew accordingly. Sino-British rapprochement was glacial because both sides believed that they were distinct people and superior culturally.

Persistent in English-speaking societies (e.g., Australia's "One Nation" racist party led by Pauline Hanson, race murders in America, & London's police racism -- the 1999 Macpherson Report), the myth of racial superiority thrived long before Hitler.

The idea of biological race was institutionalized by Social Darwinists with a superior-inferior hierarchy to justify imperialism and the subjugation of colored peoples (Fredrickson, 1988; Lieberman, 1968). Americans used the dehumanizing myth to justify their enslavement of Blacks and genocide of Native Indians (Fredrickson, 1981; Yee et al., 1993). With the upper hand in HK, the British segregated by race until colonialism slowly faded. A cricket field in Central HK strictly off limits to Chinese across from the also restricted HK Club offended locals until it was replaced by a public park about 1980. However, it did not brandish a sign as at a Shanghai park for Westerners, "No dogs or Chinese allowed."

Hong Kong's Pernicious History of Opium

Expressing *A+* arrogance towards the people, the HK Government derived sizable revenue from its opium sales (see pp. 134-136) right up to Japan's 1941 attack. Its greatest profits came in the late 1930s as Japanese forces swept southward to capture Canton on October 21, 1938. The Chinese flew in hysteria and terror of Japanese atrocities, especially after the inhumane Rape of Nanjing (Chang, 1997). Responding to demand in China for narcotic escape and suicide, opium sales by the HK Government monopoly soared. In October 1939, sales reached 1,000 taels (one tael is 1½ oz.) per day, which was the monthly level in 1936. To bolster its supply, the HK Government imported Persian opium, the last being 750 chests (45 tons of opium) in November 1941, just before Japan's occupation (Yee, 1992b, p. 40). As Miners (1987, p. 273) wrote: "Demand remained strong throughout 1940, and the Hong Kong Government fretted that it could not supply a demand estimated at 25,000 taels a month."

Ironically, opium sales ended after HK surrendered. As U.S. submarines and bombers hampered the use of HK harbor, the Japanese did not sell opium and did all they could to reduce the population by forcing people into China.

In 1943, the U.S. Commissioner for Narcotics pressed for a postwar policy that eliminated opium in all Japanese-held territories taken by U.S. forces. The British Foreign Office asked the Colonial Office for a statement to help it handle this latest incident in their longstanding confrontations with the Americans over opium. After studying the issue "exhaustively," the Colonial Office announced in concert with France and Holland that opium monopolies would not be resurrected after the war. The decision came without the 'advice' of their colonial administrators, who had autonomous control of their revenues and budgets, since most were in Japanese prisons (Miners, 1987, pp. 274-275).

Obviously, British officials felt little guilt in being drug suppliers; consumers were at fault. Aggression to force opium onto China was bad enough, but the $A+$proned use of the drug to raise substantial revenue up to World War II is an indelible stain. In common with HK, including opium farm leases, colonial Singapore's history is as bad or worst. It is hard to understand why Singapore continues to honor Sir Stamford Raffles, who settled the island in 1819 as an East India Co. transit center for opium. In Singapore and the Straits, opium was shamelessly used as wages for laborers, who then became addicted if not already. As Trocki (1990, p. 223) said of the revenue source: "Opium paid for free trade . . . ."

Opium imperialism and profiteering from human misery represent the ugliest side of British rule in Asia. It set an egregious precedent of unforeseen consequences. Today, HK security forces cooperate closely with Interpol and U.S. agencies to stem the flow of opium and its derivatives from the Golden Triangle (see p. 159 on treatment). Including cocaine, the world drug trade today is estimated to be worth US$750 billion a year (Booth, 1998, p. 352).

Chinese Patriotism and Loyalty

Westerners have always found it hard to understand the Chinese, mainly because they were unaware of CSS psychology and its difference from their own sense of self and nationalism. Apprehensive about *state-people* relations, the Chinese approached state officials and agents when there was no other recourse and when they saw a possible state interest which they could use to advantage. Propagandists have alluded to the "patriotism" of HK Chinese who looked to Chiang Kai-shek's KMT or CCP China for leadership and help whenever the British went too far. Yet the terms, patriotism and patriot, are questionable.

When the people rallied, such as the "United Front" during the Sino-Japanese War (1937-45), in league with China's rulers, they really meant alliance and common cause rather than inspired commitment to the state as in the West and Japan. As said earlier, the Chinese have lacked an inspirational symbol such as the British Crown or Stars & Stripes. Translated as patriotism, *aiguo*, literally meaning "love country," implies the *culture-people* attachment. Responding if the circumstances could further their aims, the CCP and KMT have provided covert funds and agents to assist and nurture allies in Hong Kong and wherever large populations of Chinese reside. Located by Happy Valley, Xinhua (China News Agency) is well-known as the PRC headquarters in Hong Kong. (See Chapter Four for the sensational court case involving *Ta Kung Pao*, pp. 197-198, a newspaper funded by Beijing, and coverage of CCP and KMT "patriotic" activities).

The PRC's and Taiwan's long feud can be understood through the CSS. Since the *A* axis brooks no rival, both have claimed China and battled for power. Spectators in such struggles, the people are "patriotic" and "loyal" according to which side rules them. Thus, whether in *state-people* relations with the Qing, British, KMT, or CCP, the reality of counter-allegiance was always in play. Indeed, colonialism reinforced the people's counter-allegiance to authority. Increasingly used in HK, the CCP's use of the term, "motherland," cleverly encroaches emotionally into the *culture-people* bond.

After the HK Government began to provide respectable social services during Governor Maclehose's tenure (see pp. 145-147), the services, especially housing, were well-received but with public feeling that they were long overdue. Before the 1970s, the people had to fend for themselves in HK's "cruel society," especially the horrible shantytowns. One important feature of the social services that facilitated them was that the people dealt with Chinese civil servants, medics, educators, etc. The Government began to represent more than foreign faces.

The HK police and public cooperation gradually improved as more Chinese were recruited into the police force and held rank. As late as 1941, the few Chinese promoted to the rank of subinspector took orders from British officers junior to them (Welsh, 1993, p. 381). The bugaboo that the Cantonese, unlike Indians, could not be trusted to control their own and serve responsibly was proven fallacious as Chinese were promoted into the higher police ranks in the 1980s.

The British misread Cantonese manners and saucy counter-allegiance to mean that they were untrustworthy, an unfair charge that hardliners, such as Gov. Francis May, set in concrete. Although the Chinese never viewed foreigners as one and the same, the blanket racism towards the Chinese and the assumption of colonials that all Britons were proper was an either-or fallacy. Governors failed to act on the rampant corruption throughout the Royal HK Police until the sensational case of Chief Superintendent Peter Godber erupted in 1973. Chapter Two covers Gov. May, the Godber case, and formation of the Independent Commission Against Corruption (ICAC), which is recognized as one of the world's finest anti-graft agencies (Fraser, 1998).

HK's positive attitudes towards the provision of social services by the HK Government did not mean the demise of counter-allegiance and advent of Western-styled loyalty; it was more like, "OK, but what have you done for us today?"

According to Lindsay's (1978, pp. 32-33) definitive work on HK's defense during WW II: "Many Chinese had enlisted in the Garrison's . . . Volunteer infantry and artillery batteries, and as drivers, engineers, signallers, sailors, airmen and medical orderlies." Although the British were unsure of their fighting ability and some drivers and sailors deserted, "most Chinese were to fight with considerable ferocity and courage." Many brave Chinese provided Westerners imprisoned at Stanley Camp substantial aid as well as the British Army Aid Group led by Lindsay Ride in Free China. After the Japanese apprehended and executed the Chinese guerrillas assisting the BAAG, communications with Stanley Prison were terminated (see pp. 92 & 171-172).

The Chinese will struggle and die for a cause that they believe in, especially when led by a humane leader of integrity. The closest most Hong Kongers have come to give heartfelt "loyalty" to a Briton was to Governor Edward Youde, whose untimely death in office truly grieved the people. Anyone who understands that will not demean the Chinese for lack of trust and faithfulness.

Reviewing HK's history from 1842-1913, Tsai (1993) found considerable social unrest and Chinese agitation, especially after the 1911 Revolution, that is not covered as well elsewhere. His work could be viewed as revelations of counter-allegiance in the colony. HK was better than China but never "easy street." While commoners fended for themselves, as in China and often in poverty, those Chinese with wealth and position knew how to protect and enlarge their rice bowls and make the most of British law and colonialism.

According to Tsai (p. 268), Acting Governor Francis May (1903-04) wrote to London, " '. . . the real feelings of the mass of the population towards Englishmen in this Colony' could be described in one word -- '*animosity*,' " which approximates the CSS concept of rancor. Responsible for putting the choice real estate of the Peak off limits to the Chinese, May, who became Governor in his own right (1912-1919), was more racist and hostile to the Chinese than any other governor (see pp. 135-136), even calling Sir Kai Ho Kai "treacherous" (Welsh, 1993, p. 342). As Dr. Choa's Chapter Three makes clear, Ho Kai should be remembered as one of HK's most outstanding figures.

As Chapter Four relates, Hong Kong looks quite different when one reads the Chinese- versus the two English-language papers. Numerous and outspoken, the former provide much more information and views on issues, groups, and persons locally and and in China, especially government foibles. Beyond their personal affairs, the Chinese may be slow to act, but as great spectators and critics, they are eager to know the issues, what's what, and who's involved.

Anglo-American Differences

Through most of their history in East Asia, Americans have enjoyed warmer relations with the Chinese than the British and other Europeans. When Yankee ships first appeared in the Pearl River Delta soon after the War of Independence ended, the Chinese were confused by the new breed of English speakers. They called the Americans the "new people," maybe because the U.S. seamen tried to tell the Chinese that they sailed from New England. The Chinese commended their flag as *fa-khey*, meaning "colorful flag" in Cantonese. Americans would be called the "people of the colorful flag" and their nation nicknamed as *Fa-khey*.

The standing name for the United States has been *meiguo* or "beautiful Country," which has a phonetic quality. Red Guards and their banners sloganizing against the U.S. during the Vietnam War blared, "Down with the Beautiful Country and their running dogs!" and the like. Everyday, the Chinese everywhere speak and read about the "Beautiful Country." Yet a name is just a name, especially one based on phonics. For America, the Japanese use the similar sounding character of grain rice or "Rice Country." The Chinese name for England, *Yingguo* or "Brave Country," reflects the fact that "Britain" and "British" came into use after England's 1707 union with Scotland and Wales and that on early contacts with the Chinese, seamen used "England."

The Chinese quickly saw how different the British and Americans were. Compared to the formality of the British, the more personable manner of the Americans forged strong friendly relations between them and the Chinese. A U.S. ship captain and China trader, Forbes (1844, p. 19) wrote: ". . . in our experience we have never had the good fortune to deal with men to whom the above character more appropriately belongs." In friendly good humor, Americans built and named a clipper after the famed Canton broker, *Howqua*, and put a figurehead of him at the bow, a mark of respect that astounded the British. We can imagine the amazement of the broker and his countrymen! A fast ship, its maiden voyage in 1844 from New York to HK took only 95 days. Seamen liked the *Howqua*; under Captain Nathaniel Palmer it had the rare reputation of being a happy ship with lots of good food (Stackpole, 1954, pp. 28-29).

As British historian Ridley (1970, pp. 248-249) wrote, "The ordinary English trader in China despised the Chinese as much as the Chinese mandarin despised the English. It was a common occurrence if a Chinese annoyed an Englishman by making a noise in front of his house, or in some other way, for the Englishman to seize him and flog him without more ado."

The distinguished British author and HK official (who encouraged this book project and would have joined it but for the cancer that finally caused his death), Austin Coates (1988, pp. 144-146) wrote: "The American attitude that the British in general tended to exaggerate the difficulties was shared by many Chinese, in particular by Howqua, who preferred the Americans to the British, though he dealt with both . . . . As he and other critics saw it, the British were insufferable sticklers on matters of dignity and principle."

Sino-British animosity stemmed in part from their mutual taste for ceremonial form, which irritated both sides. Because the Qing were inflexible with their customs, such as the kowtow, the British stuck it to the Chinese whenever they had the upper hand. In a chapter on Britain's imperial style, Morris (1973, p. 274) described Lord Elgin's entrance into Peking after his victory in 1860 as follows:

Three miles up the highway to the House of Ceremonies the British majestically marched -- General Sir Robert Napier in the van, Lord Elgin in a sumptuous sedan chair with another horseback general at his side, then 400 marching soldiers, and 100 sailors, and two bands -- through the symbolic gates of the hall, through the ornamental gardens, up the cobbled way -- and when, near the Grand Entrance, Prince Kung, attended by 500 mandarins, closed his hands before his face in submissive greeting, 'Lord Elgin', we are told, 'returned him a proud contemptuous look, and merely bowed slightly, which must have made the blood run cold in the poor Prince's veins'.

Regarding the people versus the state, Coates also said that the positive nature of Sino-American relations continues today "for such things do not change," suggesting a cultural compatibility. Sun Yat-sen (1943) and other revolutionists were inspired by the American and French revolutions and saw humaneness in their sage heroes, e.g., Rousseau, Washington, and Lincoln (Sun, 1943, pp. 173-174, 216, 228, 232-235; Scalapino & Yu, 1985, pp. 155). There were no British equivalents.

Yet to be fair, the British operated under far greater scrutiny than the Yanks in the Pearl River delta, first as East India Co. men and then under the anxious gaze of their government's officers. The Americans were less class and status conscious than the British. Also, it was Britain that humiliated China in war. While U.S. warships accompanying British expeditions at times violated their presidents' orders to stay neutral, the Chinese never considered the Americans as aggressors. The Yankees were on their own in China and could be themselves.

History neglected. Even though they coveted Chinese goods in the 18th and 19th century, Americans knew little about China and HK. While museums boast the artisan silk, porcelain, paintings, furniture, silverware, etc., Americans today remain ignorant of the China trade of the past and today. Historians and educators, being Eurocentric, have been derelict in their neglect of Sino-American relations and full details of the Stamp Act, etc. that brought about the War of Independence. While the Boston Tea Party is well-known, why is it that Americans are unaware of the historical circumstances surrounding the tea and its source?

There is even failure to note that among the long list of complaints against King George III in the 1776 Declaration of Independence is one that infuriated 18th-century Americans -- "For cutting off our Trade with all Parts of the World." They resented Britain's prohibition against their participation in foreign trade and sailing to China and Asia and round the world on their own.

President Thomas Jefferson's objectives for the Lewis and Clark expedition (1803-06) exploring the Louisana Purchase included the search for the elusive water passage to the Pacific and warding off British trappers and traders encroaching from Canada (Ambrose, 1996). Anglo-American rivalry in China trade and seafaring continued for long (see Yee, 1992b, pp. 7-20 for details).

Unlike the U.S. with its vast resources and nation-building across the frontier, the island nation of Britain looked to China as it did to India as a great revenue producer. The British harbored few illusions in what they were doing. In 1830, the British Government's income on tea import duties alone amounted to over three million pounds a year, "almost one tenth of its total revenue receipts from the whole of England" (Keay, 1991, p. 452). It was revealed during 1840 Commons debate on hostilities in China that "one sixth of the whole united revenue of

Great Britain and India depended on the China trade, for British import duties on goods from that country amounted to £4,200,000 (and) the income derived by India from the trade was no less than £2,000,000" (Collis, 1946, p. 267).

For the U.S., such taxes and thus records did not exist, but American traders and ships participated in about 20% of the opium trade. Many prominent Atlantic Coast families derived their original fortunes through opium, a dark history that awaits the full light of day.

Because biographers and historians have dodged the issue, few Americans know that the maternal grandfather of the great President, Franklin Delano Roosevelt, derived two fortunes, first in Canton and the second in HK, and that FDR's mother, Sara, lived several years in Hong Kong as a youth. Besides Warren Delano, other American drug-dealers who enriched themselves and their posterity through opium include the names of Coolidge, Forbes, Heard, Low, Perkins, Russell, Sturgis, etc. (see Downs, 1997; Kerr, 1996). However, a few such as David W. C. Olyphant and his associates opposed the opium trade (see pp. 220-221).

In China, therefore, the Americans had the best position to take -- (1) follow the lead of British aggression and trade advances; (2) stand aside and remain neutral in conflicts with the Chinese; (3) give the British a run for their money; and (4) be everybody's friend. This then allowed them to preach against opium to the British and to preach evangelism to the Chinese. Thus, Thomson et al. (1981) could characterize the Americans as "sentimental imperialists" [also see Jespersen (1996), Madsen (1995), & Spence (1998)].

Active in the Pearl River Delta after they won independence, Americans were among the first to enter the new colony (see pp. 220-222). They opened HK's first school, church, and big hotel, the 1,000-room HK Hilton, and an American dentist owned HK's first auto. The U.S. Navy knows HK well, as the respective fleets of Perry and Dewey quartered there before they sailed to open Japan and take the Philippines from Spain; and its subs prevented use of the harbor during WW II. During the Vietnam War, thousands of U.S. servicemen enjoyed "Rest and Recreation" in the colony. Riders on the Star ferries frequently see warships flying the Stars and Stripes amidst one of the world's most memorable scenes.

Hong Kong is residence and workplace for about 40,000 Americans today, perhaps four times more than Britons, as 2,000 U.S. corporations have offices, plants, and regional centers in the SAR. Americans find the place to be bustling and relatively crime-free; the murder rate is less than 2% that of New York. The American Consulate in HK has a larger staff than most U.S. embassies, and the PRC has accused it of being a spy center. So echoing what was said in 1839, while the British held the horns up to the handover the Americans milked the cow.

If the U.S. had somehow possessed Hong Kong and muddled its way into the 1997 issue, it's doubtful that any president, the Congress and people would have handed the people of Hong Kong to the Communists as easily as PM Margaret Thatcher and Parliament did. If HK had been American territory, it might be like Puerto Rico today (see pp. 140-141; democracy in HK was first proposed and then stymied). Although the Vietnam War was a unmitigated disaster for America, one seldom mentioned point of pride is that amidst the throes of defeat the U.S. brought out millions of Indo-Chinese allies to its shores instead of leaving them to death and cruelty at the hands of the communists. After decades of strict denial, London finally granted British passports in 1997 to the few aged widows of HK men who had served in the colony's defense in World War II. Successful at last during Patten's tenure, Jack Edwards, a humanist and retired Briton war veteran in HK, campaigned relentlessly on behalf of the widows for many years.

However, America did not possess Hong Kong and President Ronald Reagan did not dispute what his good friend, PM Thatcher, did with the colony and its people in the 1984 Declaration. Without a doubt, he would have acted differently if the situation had been reversed. The two nations have related with a "special relationship" for long, and the expression, "An ally is an ally," has been evoked by presidents and prime ministers since. Today's relationship is still valuable to both but not equally (Renwick, 1996), as seen in China relations. Following President Jiang's state visit to the U.S. in 1997 (see pp. 323-324), President Clinton's visit to the PRC in 1998 firmed up a "constructive strategic partnership," which Premier Zhu's visit to the U.S. in April 1999 underlined. PM Blair and Britain cannot deal the same with China. The importance of US-PRC relations today reflects America's superpower role, China's ascension, and realpolitik.

Racism in Hong Kong

An American journalist who lived in and about China for long, Emily Hahn (1944) knew Hong Kong before and after World War II. She wrote: "One of the irritating things about the British point of view which you noticed in the Hong Kong residents was their stubborn refusal to consider the Far East situation. The war meant to them the war in Europe." About the Chinese, Hahn said that they "have stubbornly resisted change, and in Hong Kong you will find many old customs and traditions flourishing in a lively manner which you can't find anywhere else in China." It's noteworthy that Hahn said that both peoples held stubbornly to their ways and outlook -- two distinct peoples and cultures in the same place. She said that HK's provincialism made her appreciate Shanghai's cosmopolitanism, but she made her observations in the 1930s and 1940s.

Because they were both White and Chinese, HK Eurasians never seemed to escape the sting of racism, especially among the British. None more celebrated and wealthy, Sir Robert Ho Tung served as Jardine's comprador in HK from 1883 to 1900. Ho Tung became a multimillionaire and a China Coast leader in most business lines. Though his father was a Belgian and his wife an Eurasian, he lived as a Chinese and was the first Chinese to reside on the Peak. Knighted in 1915 by King George V, Ho Tung was a generous philanthropist, especially in education. He epitomized the model of a successful HK Chinese (Cheng, 1976) and remains a local legend even today. Even Sir Robert could not escape the stings of racism. A school that he donated for English instruction and to be open to all was used by the HK Government for an exclusive school for British youth. Consenting with regret, Ho Tung said that the change was "so much opposed to the spirit which prompted my offer of the school to the colony" (Endacott, 1973, p. 281). One of Sir Robert's ten children, Jean Gittins (1969) spent World War II at Stanley Camp and her Eurasian husband, Billy, died in Japan after he was sent to labor there with other prisoners. She wrote about her bitter disappointment and hurt when European internees blamed the inclusion of Eurasians in the camp for their collective poor rations.

While Anglo-American jurisprudence represents a solid good of democracy and freedom, the attitudes and discretionary behavior of the very same peoples who prize and enjoy such values for themselves often seemed contradictory. The negatives of colonialism are hard to excuse by reason of the times, since many Britons clearly contradicted their faith and hardly behaved the same at home, where they lived far less well than they did in Asia. Welsh (1993, pp. 380-386) wrote of the "stultifying snobbishness" and "nervous adhesion to pro-prieties" of HK's colonial society with its pecking order and rigid "no Chinese" ban. He also told how every few minutes colonials struck down and insulted Chinese in public for no real reason, cruelties that the people acquiesced to as they did in China before government agents and soldiers.

Experiencing the same in 1947-48 Hong Kong and Shanghai, I however did not take it lying down; my resistance did not bring further abuse probably because of my fluent English. When I was struck down from behind by an European for no other reason than being Chinese, a British colonel whom schoolmates and I befriended on the ship from the U.S. cared for me. Yes, Britons are as varied as others, and it has been my good fortune to have known more of the best -- in Hong Kong, China, and as a "G.I." in the Korean War.

On racism, Morris (1968, pp. 131-155) said that "Clearly the British responded most warmly to what they would think of as Nordic qualities" and that "The British recognized the strength of the Chinese" -- as excellent gardeners, farm workers, workmen, cooks, all with honesty and lawfulness. When not so supercilious, Morris (p. 150) said that colonialism was not all "arrogance or condescension" -- "the particular was often far more attractive" than the general.

Humanitarians in the missionary service, hospitals, universities, schools, private sector, and civil service contrasted sharply with the bias of the majority. Compared to the Japanese occupation, however, the British were paragons of virtue. Yet Dr. Choa tells of one humane Japanese soldier (p. 156).

Britain's defeats in East Asia made it difficult to reimpose colonial rule after World War II, surely as it had been. Singapore's falling with little resistance though built into a fortress was especially humiliating (see Chapter One on HK's valiant but futile defense). French and Dutch colonies were also in great jeopardy after the war. In CSS terms, Asians viewed European rule after the war as having no legitimacy and falling below center towards uncontrol (A-). Gone was the aura of autocratic might that bolstered colonialism. As with the Qing in China, Asians resented the fact that the Europeans, who had lorded over them with arms and airs, could not stop the Japanese and prevent their suffering. Unlike the people of Singapore, Burma, Malaysia, Indonesia, and Indo-China, however, the HK people remained unconfrontational because at China's very doorstep they saw little advantage if and when the British departed. The British would have to change and over the years they did.

Describing racism in HK before progressive changes began, such as replacing the horrible shantytowns with housing developments, Cameron (1978, p. 124) wrote: "Yet, in its xenophobic Western outlook, Hong Kong was unable to allow the Chinese anything more than the most subservient positions, the most miserable opportunities. Only rich Chinese could afford anything resembling an education, a decent place to live, or any degree of human recognition."

On the other hand, China's revolutionary father, Sun Yat-sen emphasized the colony's positives in contrast to Qing China. Speaking to a cheering crowd at the University of Hong Kong in 1923, Dr. Sun said that his revolutionary ideas originated in HK. He said that while studying at the College of Medicine (see pp. 167-169 & 228-229), the orderliness and attractiveness of the city impressed him deeply. On trips back to his native village just north of Macau, Heungshan, he could see the contrast between Hong Kong and China. While he had to seek protection for his family with firearms and felt surrounded by corruption and filth in China [see Park's (1997) study of China's corruption], "he thought of the beautiful streets, the artistic parks, and wondered why Englishmen could do such a thing on this barren rock within seventy or eighty years. Why could not China, in the last four thousand years, have a place like this?" (Jen & Ride, 1970, pp. 21-22). Thus, HK's advantages helped to inspire Sun's crusade to uplift China.

Although segregated housing in Hong Kong ended in 1946, the first Chinese was only appointed to a Secretariat post in 1992. Unlike the Indian Civil Service, Britons held all of HK's senior posts until close to 1997. British HK institutionalized bias with differentials in salary, perks, etc. for the same work based on nationality and race. That said, however, the Chinese hardly ever complained publicly, even those who had status and been knighted, because they were fairly satisfied in terms of family and economic concerns, i.e., the CSS middle. They would hold their fire until the 1984 Declaration marked the end of the British dynasty and the start of the 1997 transition and the pro-democracy movement.

A Resolution of Mind and Heart

Trying to have the last word but appearing rather pathetic, some Britons departing Hong Kong for home in 1997 on month-long luxury cruises, one of their last colonial perks, lambasted their job losses to the "localisation" policy. One would like to think that such views are in the minority, as Britons continue to be HK civil servants and those recently retired might have left feeling that they were fortunate to have had excellent years in the place and could turn over duties to competent Chinese whom they helped to train. Also, they could look forward to excellent pensions that followed outstanding salaries.

Attitudes in Britain have been marred by superciliousness towards the HK people and Asians in general. Responding to grave concerns raised in Parliament by Liberal leader, Paddy Ashdown, and others for HK's people the day after Tiananmen, PM Thatcher retorted: "Do you want to see more than three million Chinese come to Britain!?" Labour leaders of that day echoing her and several Conservatives gushing racism, every MP knew what she meant. Hearing the debate on BBC, Hong Kong fell into despair at first and then rose in *CR* rancor against such unfeeling arrogance. It wasn't so much that they wanted to emigrate to Britain, no jobs anyway; some empathy would have been timely.

Britons have exposed themselves in their amused toleration of anti-Asian slurs in the media. Bob Borzello, a London publisher, protested the national sport of referring to the Chinese with the derogatory term of "Chinks." When Britain's Press Council and other authorities refused to lift a hand, the media continued its childish sport of finding innovative ways to utter the slur for long (Hubbard, 1989). The longstanding hostility of Heathrow officers towards HK passport holders forced Lord Glenarthur, Minister for Special Responsibility for HK in the late 1980s, to fix the problem after Lady Lydia Dunn complained.

Erudition does not help to excuse the general bias, e.g., *The Cambridge Encyclopedia of China* (Hook & Twitchett, 1991, p. 218) actually faults the Chinese for the First Opium War: "The British government found cause for war with China in the unreasonable behaviour of Commissioner Lin Zexu at Canton. . . ."

In time, more Britons may come to grips with their history in HK and China. Contradictory attitudes, some arrogant and belittling versus the nostalgic and humane, may last for long if race continues to be an issue. It can be surmised that superciliousness persists because of ignorance and that many cannot face what's so regrettable about their nation's rule in HK and Asia, i.e., don't reflect; buffoon the other. It's hardly a desirable resolution of mind and heart.

Britons can be proud of much in HK (see Chapter Three) and still face up to the bad. They can also take pride in certain governors, especially Youde and Patten, whose humanism exemplified the best of their country (see pp. 147-149 & 308-328). Inasmuch as Britain committed itself to see that the PRC upholds the word and spirit of the Joint Declaration, Britons should see that their Government follows through on that pledge. We shall see if trade and such conflicts with that assurance. Let's end this section as follows (Yee, 1992b, p. 85):

> Hong Kong grew out of the crass commercialism and commitment of British traders and their Government to free commerce and their unshaking belief in the China market. No reasonable person would argue that Hong Kong is worse off today than it would have been if China had not lost it. Law and order as well as humanitarianism have helped to build Hong Kong. Its history also involves the participation of the Chinese and the development of the HK Chinese as an integral, major aspect of its growth and progress. A stepping-stone for opportunity and escape, a bridge between China and the West, a marketplace and entrepot, Hong Kong is what people would make of it. For all that can and should be said to point out shortcomings, in many ways Hong Kong is quite a place.

Administrative Purview

During the brief euphoria after the signing of the Joint Declaration, one oft-repeated accolade in HK was "Stability and Prosperity!" Since the British and Chinese in HK went separate ways in the main, one to administer and officiate and the other to make money, CSS configurations were seen to stay mostly in the ideal center and neither side wanted to rock the boat.

Fortunately, the British sent more capable governors than not; for while some underlings took gifts and cash until the Independent Commission Against Corruption was formed (see p. 146), the governors and top officials were corruption-free. Out of a scale of 10 on corruption, Hong Kong (7.28) is ranked higher than Japan (6.57) and just lower than the U.S. (7.61) by the *Far Eastern Economic Review* (December 11, 1997, p. 69). HK's generous civil-service salaries, perks, and pensions are defended by the claim that they prevent corruption; but since its formation, the ICAC has undoubtedly been the best deterrent.

HK's worst CSS disruptions arose from external crises, such as the Cultural Revolution-induced riots of 1967-67 and massacres in Shanghai and Canton by British troops leading to the 1925-26 General Strike and Boycott. Domestic dissent followed rash actions, such as by Governor May, who segregated the Peak and passed the Boycott Prevention Ordinance in 1912. However, local crises were mild compared to those caused by external forces.

Some British authorities in Hong Kong twisted facts and the truth beyond the norm of politicians in the West, even when they were obviously less than circumspect. They could do that with wide latitude and straight faces because the HK people could not vote, no matter the retorts of a free press. Scant accountability to farway London and much independent purview put autocratic power in the hands of those who might otherwise have functioned more fairly and reasonably. Britons, such as John Walden, a former high official in Hong Kong, helped to expose the foibles of British rule and colonialism in Asia. His out-spoken presence and humanist values needled the establishment and gave credibility and support to the pro-democracy movement (Wong, 1996).

Pages 136-137 relate Governor Stubbs' brash attempts to end the 1925-26 General Strike and Boycott through bribe proposals and more. Pages 300-303 review the 1987 survey on representative government, a classic example of political chicanery that textbooks on survey methods and opinion polls should use as a case study. Other examples of unaccountability to decency and the people was satisfying Beijing's demands to expel Sun Yat-sen from HK and to reject the petitions of pro-democracy exiles from the PRC to remain in the colony.

While the HK Government never fully admitted the problem, many saw the emigrant outflow as a serious danger; as the people voted on the 1984 Declaration by emigrating with their families. The American Consulate in Hong Kong reported in October 1989 "that overall emigration is increasing and that a considerable portion of it represents an outflow of scarce talents . . . . the economic consequences . . . are already being felt and will become increasingly evident . . .

." (McGurn, 1991, p. 135). Canada's Commissioner (Consul General) in Hong Kong, Anne M. Doyle, also disputed the Government's estimates of exit emigrants in 1989, saying that they were "presumably designed to support their own arguments." Taking most of the emigrants, North America surely knew the extent of the brain drain. In early 1998, however, the HK Government reported that the 1997 emigration rate dropped 25% from 1996 to 30,900, the lowest in a decade, and predicted that emigration would continue to drop and more emigrants returning. The economic downturn that gathered force in 1998 will probably reverse those trends.

The steady decline in English-language competence helped to verify the brain drain (Yee, 1992b, pp. 286-287, 304-307). In the 1990s, the HK Government raised civil-service and teaching salaries to high levels and increased university admissions from about 5% in 1985 to 18.6% (see pp. 261-262), which had the effect of slowing the emigration rate. As many emigrants returned to work in HK after fulfilling residency obligations abroad, the turnabout so pleased the Government that it began to subsidize international schools (Miners, 1995, p. 241).

A Hong Kong Identity: Something of Value

As the economy expanded and the idea of democratic self-rule emerged in the 1980s, the identity of the people became more solidly attached to Hong Kong. Many family ties in China having frayed into insignificance, especially after the Cultural Revolution, HK became home, not just as noted on ID cards and passports. Also, many families have lived in the territory for generations and education and prosperity gave them self-confidence and self-realization that the place belonged to them (see pp. 198-201 & 294-295), i.e., stepping-stone as home.

Much identity-building came in the late 1980s when many political leaders, such as Martin Chu-ming Lee, Emily Lau Wai-hing, Christine Loh Kung-wai, and Szeto Wah, rallied community support for democracy and outrage over Tiananmen. Giving voice to populist counter-allegiance, they won election to Legco and harassed London and Beijing.

Adjusting to SAR restrictions against candidates for office holding foreign passports, Emily Lau replied to a reporter's question whether she regarded herself as British or Chinese, "I always consider myself a Hong Konger. I have British citizenship, but I am an ethnic Chinese" (Choy, 1997). A survey that I conducted of 400 HK university students in 1989 (after Tiananmen) found that they identified themselves as "Hong Kong Chinese." While quite positive to America and Canada, their attitudes were very negative towards the PRC and Britain.

Before the Sino-British Joint Declaration was signed in 1984, the HK people were indifferent to politics, as the CSS can explain. However, dissent rose over ambiguities in the Joint Declaration and machinations during Governor Wilson's tenure (see Chapter Seven). Shattering what complacency remained, Tiananmen shook Hong Kong to its core. Unprecedented, the people stormed in extreme rancor as a million marched in the streets and hurled protests at Xinhua, the local PRC offices. Of all of the many demonstrations, marchers, taxis, minibuses, etc. those several weeks, the most memorable was the long chain of tugs and small boats that crisscrossed the harbor, shrilling horns as they passed Government House. One dynamic spokesman emerged at that time named Martin Lee, who declared to the masses, "Hong Kong has discovered her spirit."

Senior Exco member, (Baroness) Lydia Dunn said the day after Tiananmen, "The events in China have highlighted how very different the systems of the two places are. We in Hong Kong, no matter how angry we are, must put all our energies in preserving the freedom of expression and the press. Our future depends on the maintenance of our existing system and on our continued stability."

With the 1997 handover approaching, the HK people's gut feelings of themselves and their future coalesced into an integral identity in 1989. The stepping-stone psyche matured beyond the elusive transience as captured by the familiar expression, "borrowed place, borrowed time," into new dedication and commitment that went further than family and individual gain. Not just a here and now stopover between destinations, Hong Kong was something to preserve and cherish as unique and precious. More and more, the people identified themselves as Hong Kong Chinese, not just Chinese (see pp. 145, 198-201, 294-295)

Even before the handover, a pro-CCP type has emerged to wave the PRC flag. A provisional legislator chastised professors in 1997 for criticizing his plan for "patriotic education" and called for their dismissal. As discussed on pp. 213-214, a HK publisher declared that the SAR-funded RTHK should not air criticisms of the PRC and SAR Govenment (Choy, 1998). Both were lambasted by the public. The "patriots" also echo Beijing's warnings against further commemorations of Tiananmen. Yet estimates of up to 40,000 braved heavy rain on June 4, 1998 to memorialize the massacre nine years earlier and demanded that China reverse its Tiananmen verdict and promote democracy. How many will turn out in 2000?

As HK's recession deepened in 1999, democracy and Tiananmen were said to slip in the people's priorities. Since the SAR economy is vitally linked to the PRC, such issues might seem imprudent and untimely, a real test for identity.

Fuzzy leadership and identity? "The key to Hong Kong's future lies in the quality of the people chosen to lead it after 1997" (Starr, 1997, p. 265). Anointed SAR chief executive by Beijing, Tung Chee-hwa is one of HK's innumerable examples of the meeting of East and West, a *taipan* who understands HK, China and the West (see pp. 291-292, 316-320 & 326-327). Working part-time to support his education in Britain, Tung has also lived in the U.S. for years.

While his family shipping empire owes much to HK's free-enterprise system, it is also indebted to Beijing for bailing out the firm in the past. Tung exhibits energy and a positive personality; strengths that are needed; but he is viewed as overly sensitive to Beijing and fuzzy on HK's international status and strengths. The 1998 legislative election was controversial as soon as Tung narrowed the electorate and two million lost their votes. Nevertheless, the people turned out in the name of democracy on May 24th, as discussed on pp. 324-326

In his first Policy Address on October 8, 1997, Tung said, "We must work to build HK for ourselves and for future generations: a HK that is civilized, prosperous, stable and democratic, filled with a new vitality." He said that the earliest date for universal suffrage for his post and legco would be 2007. Property, the one business area in which the Government has intruded from 1841on, is where Tung aimed to dampen speculation and then dropped when prices collapsed.

Following his second Policy Address in October 1998 when Tung intimated that HK needed to emphasize its "Chineseness," liberals criticized Tung as "incompetent" and his pro-Beijing stance. Two years after the handover, his relations with Legco are cool and the public wonders about Tung's loyalties (see pp. 291-292 316-320 & 326-327). The HK Human Rights Monitor labelled Tung's Administration as "enemies of democracy" for favoring big business (Fraser & Yi, 1998). In February 1999, his weak response to Beijing's rebuke of the decision by HK's Court of Last Resort to permit Mainland children of HK residents to enter the SAR intensified the complaints. Yet, given what is known about the CCP and how it has intruded into HK affairs (see Chapter 7), Tung could very well deserve praise if we were privy to his deliberations with Beijing.

Unlike British governors who could call London when problems with China arose, Tung has no recourse but to deal with CCP authorities -- an one-sided ordeal. However, HKers are not alone; Mainland and Taiwan Chinese also want HK's autonomy to stand. Excitement in the PRC over HK's return was ebullient long before July 1, 1997, as a chronograph in Beijing counted the days remaining for the return of the lost territory to China beginning with 1,000. Identifying with HK's wealth, drive, and modernity, the people have made it clear that they want the PRC to approximate the SAR, signalling counter-allegiance. All comes down to the nature of China as a dictatorship -- of the past or one in transition?

Authoritarianism versus Democratic Paternalism

The identity of the HK people is maturing at the same time that the SAR is at the crossroads. The SAR's long-term nature and direction will be uncertain for years. This is understandable by CSS terms since the people's identity (culture-people bond; who we are) is distinct from those who rule them (*state-people* dyad). The SAR Government has the dual difficulties of managing a smooth transition to avoid perceptions that its administration is inferior to the British as well as to working out its relations with Beijing. In 1999, the people have doubts of the Tung Administration and some say that they miss the British.

Will PRC sovereignty bring increments of authoritarianism or will democracy progress? If the former, CSS shifts will surely move into the dangerous right-hand quadrant. If democracy progresses as promised, then paternalism might eventually replace authoritarianism as in Japan and the CSS configuration will be at the center. It is crucial to see how Beijing handles HK's autonomy when the going gets desperate as will inevitably happen someday, if not by 2000? Will regimentation be more insidious from within than without, i.e., media self-censorship and sycophantic moves to placate Beijing (see Dr. Shen's concerns in Chapter Four)? While the catastrophe devastated China, Western leftists resident in the PRC, such as Anna Louise Strong, and CCP leaders closed their eyes to the 1960s famine and continued to extol Mao (Becker, 1996, p. 293).

Amidst Asia's financial crisis as discussed in Chapter Six, many feared that the PRC and HK would eventually have to devalue their currency. The Indonesian rupiah lost 75% of its value at one point and fiscally-sound Singapore saw its dollar plunge about 40%. HK's U.S. dollar peg has ensured stability for long, but at such levels HK's services, labor, etc. cannot compete with SE Asia. Through 1998 and into early 1999, fears of HK being an overpriced business location and predictions that the PRC and SAR would devalue clashed in the tense atmosphere, e.g., the Royal Bank of Scotland moved its HK operations to Singapore. How long can HK and Beijing continue to be among the world's most expensive cities for foreigners to live and work, more costly than New York and London?

Hong Kong has strong reserves and a sophisticated fiscal system; yet unlike the past, it is not fully independent of China and its vagaries. The PRC yuan is artificially valued at 8.3 to one U.S. dollar because it's not fully convertible. If the HK and PRC units are tied together somehow, the former would depreciate greatly. Also worrisome is that a crisis in the PRC, such as a severe recession or power struggle, could destroy any hope for political reform and possibly bring irrational demands, such as transferring SAR funds to Beijing.

The PRC's history is full of disasters induced by CCP leaders, so many in fact that the question is, when will the next one come? When Taiwan's President, Lee Teng-hui, visited his alma mater, Cornell University, in 1996 with U.S. permission, Beijing erupted into frenzied resentment that lasted months and culminated in a dangerous and reckless rocket-firing exhibition in Taiwan waters (Fulghum, 1996). The Taiwan issue is so volatile that just raising it shifts the CSS meter to the right-hand corner. Every October 10th, Taiwan's KMT flag was flown in HK to commemorate the Chinese Revolution and of course to taunt the CCP (same flag used by Sun Yat-sen's republic). Although the British never pulled down flags, the SAR police did just that months after the handover but not in 1998. Whether Taiwan, bad times, etc., CCP autocracy has often reared its worst face.

Democratic paternalism. Asian societies will not become democracies as in the West. Their social-political and cultural backgrounds favor strong, authoritative (not authoritarian) administrations, which are lawful and effective. As Lee Kwan Yew, former Singapore PM, and others have often said, Asians do not want to substitute their cultural values for those of the West, which are seen as often decadent and unsuitable for Asians. For example, crimes in East Asia are punished with little indulgence, e.g., executions follow drug convictions. When South Korea's President, Kim Dae-jung, pardoned more than 5.5 million prisoners in his inauguration amnesty, the world was shocked to learn that the crimes of many were for petty traffic violations and related to the National Security Law, prohibiting all contacts with North Korea (Wiltrout, 1998).

Many in the West regard Singapore as highly regulated ("squeaky clean") but nothing as autocratic as China (e.g., State Department, 1995, pp. 679-688). In CSS terms, Singapore is lower on the $A+$ scale than the PRC. Yet Singaporeans have free elections in which they have voted the People's Action Party to power with almost 100% control of the legislature ever since the Republic's founding in 1965. They have done so because the PAP has maintained the CSS center or stayed close to it. One party rule has been mostly true in Japan as well. In Taiwan, KMT legislative and mayoral ballot victories in December 1998 reflect the same pattern. Lee Kwan Yew attributes the East-West difference as: "A Confucianist view of order between subject and ruler -- this helps in the rapid transformation of a society . . . in other words, you fit yourself into society -- the exact opposite of the American rights of the individual" (Gibney, 1992, p. 257).

Therefore, if HK expands democracy, its vertical CSS axis could evolve from authoritarianism to paternalism (as Confucian benevolence, paternalism isn't viewed as a negative; also called "parentalism"). Democratic paternalism (my term) upholds the importance to Confucian Asians of maintaining an interdependent, balanced relationship between an effective, clean government and an industrious people.

While the Government would be expected to continue social services, such as education, health, housing, etc., its traditional laissez-faire stance towards business, finances, etc. would persist. Seldom stated, it should be understood that the last point implies CSS initiative and making the most of opportunities. Sociocentric though they may be, especially as families, the Chinese are rugged individuals and abhor government interference in business and capitalism. Entering 1999, HK's business community complained that HK was becoming too socialistic and neglecting capitalism. That may be prescient of future politics, since HK tycoons had lobbied behind the scenes in the past (Hon, 1998).

If the CCP can restrain itself and maintain HK's autonomy, HK politics will focus more on community issues than political parties and dissent; and one party that's pro-HK and business-oriented will take control of Legco. However, if Beijing meddles and disrupts as in the past, all bets are off and the SAR Government will be seen as its lackey. The A axis would then be seen as the CCP and Beijing instead of the SAR Government. Reviewing the cultural orientation of the Chinese to "an all-embracing socio-political order centering on a particularly powerful conception of universal kingship" (i.e., the CSS), Schwartz (1996, pp. 114-124) said that post-Mao China might move away from absolutism to "spaces of autonomy," as in the economy and other domains, under one national roof.

What's crucial is the direction of the PRC itself (see p. 29). What adjustments will the CCP make in a world where autocracy become increasingly harder to maintain? Thoughtful analysis of Confucianism and modern Chinese thinkers by Metzger (1990) brought out the notion of "optimistic this-worldliness," i.e., Confucian stress on developing and perfecting the knowing, moral (humanistic) individual (self) as touched on earlier. Metzger sees this ethos functioning in the modern, international world as potentially interactive with and open to the widest range of views. What Schwartz and Metzger wrote seem related to what has been discussed as CSS psyche and democratic paternalism, a shift from absolute authority to paternalism that leads to a brand of democracy that modern Chinese will increasingly demand. However, ascribing Chinese behavior to "optimism" and Confucianism seems over-simplistic. As covered above, especially pp. 19-34 and more in Yee & Cheng (1999) and Yee (1992b), CSS psyche is most complex.

Chinese intellectuals have debated reform issues at great length (Furth, 1968). In the past, most have been reluctant to overhaul Chinese traditions significantly by adopting Western ideas to any extent. For example, Liang Shuming (1917), an activist scholar and humanist, saw little good in blending Western and Chinese values, but his studies of the West may have influenced him in part to attack China's over-emphasis on traditional authority and neglect of Confucius' chief aim, the worthy, individual humanist. However, as Nathan (1990) and Goldman (1994) have stressed, modern Chinese intellectuals study Western ideas and by dint of their aim to modernize China do think hard on sociopolitical issues without regard to cultural source. Addressing skeptics who say that Chinese thinkers cannot entertain cultural pluralism or that China can never develop democratic processes, Nathan (1990, p. 312) said that those who believe that Western values are irrelevant to China are blind "to the reality of a cross-cultural dialogue . . . ."

Those who openly favor democracy in China require courage and patience. In April 1998, the PRC paroled dissident student leader, Wang Dan, from prison and allowed him to fly to the U.S. on the eve of President Clinton's PRC visit. Although Wang suffered harsh imprisonment after founding the Beijing Autonomous Students' Federation during the Tiananmen demonstrations, he has remained true to his values. After his first release in 1995, he made statements such as: "A society still needs idealists, people who are willing to sacrifice themselves to uphold the basic ideals of freedom and democracy" (*South China Morning Post*, Internet edition, April 20, 1998). Wang was then detained for 17 months without charges and then handed an 11-year sentence in 1996.

Regaining his political rights on June 2, 1998, Bao Tong, the most senior CCP official jailed after Tiananmen, met with foreign reporters and said that China must mesh political and economic reforms and that free elections were needed to avoid tyrants and autocratic power (Becker, 1998). Bao's interviews were an example of overt counter-allegiance that he pursued to test PRC laws on free speech, i.e., dare you to suppress me for doing what you say is lawful.

Former aide to the deposed CCP Chief, Zhao Ziyang, who is still under guard, Bao said that if Zhao had stayed in power HK would have one-man, one-vote elections. Two days after his interviews, Beijing police silenced Bao by saying that interviews with foreign reporters were forbidden without permission, a rule that is enforced arbitrarily. It was Zhao who signed the Sino-British Declaration of 1984. After his arrest following Tiananmen, air- brushing was used to remove Zhao from photos of the event. We may not have heard the last of Zhao and those who favor political reform. Although "optimism" hardly begins to explain Chinese behavior, an optimist could say the potential for PRC reforms is real.

In late 1998, however, clamping down on dissent, PRC President Jiang declared that "the Western mode of political systems must never be copied" (Chu, 1998). Could it be that as the CCP elite observed President Bill Clinton's long and embarrassing trials in 1998-99, they mused: "So that's democracy?"

Wilson and Patten: A Study of Contrasts

As Chapter Seven shows, HK's last two British administrations differed greatly. Appointed by PM Thatcher and guided by Beijing-placating policy which he helped to draft, David Wilson (1987-92) hindered democratization. He argued that HK never had the ballot, since there had been a "consultative process" to gain public opinion, which meant that governors spoke with Exco. The Daya Bay nuclear plant controversy occurred during his tenure (Yee, 1992b, pp. 325-331). As sycophants became Wilson's pet appointees, cynicism about 1997 increased.

Replacing Wilson, Christopher Patten became the 28th and last British Governor of HK. Besides their contrasting backgrounds, the personalities of the last two governors were about as different as Palmerston and Aberdeen. Appointed by PM John Major, Thatcher's protégé turned opponent when the "Iron Lady" faltered, Patten came from a political versus a foreign-office background. He was a populist, pro-democracy Governor that Beijing could never accept. Insisting that Patten should be denied a speaking role during the handover ceremonies, Beijing gave in when London countered that they could choose their own speakers.

The people took to the experienced politician, who refused the customary knighthood that came with the job (see Dimbleby, 1997). Sensing that London had changed its "convergence" stance, many rallied around Patten. He gave vent to their counter-allegiance by articulating pro-democracy views (see pp. 308-312). However, Flowerdew (1998) points out low points in Patten's tenure, such as a visit to a housing settlement when the residents exhibited and threw dead rats at his Rolls-Royce to protest their miserable living conditions (p. 157). The chatty Cantonese enjoy using nicknames and verbal shorthand for almost everything, especially newsmakers (see pp. 216-217 for Wilson's and Patten's nicknames).

A realist, Percy Cradock, PM Thatcher's foreign affairs adviser, played a leading role in negotiating the 1984 Declaration. Roberti (1996) and others branded Cradock, Wilson and the Foreign Office as HK's chief betrayers. One of the most perceptive analyses was by Johnson (1997), which countered Cradock's self-defense and criticisms of Patten. He said that Sir Percy's reasoning was pitifully weak -- "A shameful silence would have been more dignified" (p. 14).

Seeing how CCP negotiators, led by the urbane, iron-fisted Zhou Nan, became more untractable after the 1984 Declaration was signed, Cradock and Wilson formulated the policy of obsequious "convergence" towards Beijing, which was inferred as protecting British interests in future China trade. Cradock served as a troubleshooter whenever Beijing flexed its muscles, such as its holding up the US $21+ billion Chek Lap Kok project hostile for concessions. Fulfilling policies that

that he and Cradock find hard to defend, Wilson did not implement democracy as promised. Because of the footdragging and maneuvers during Gov, Wilson's term, a full and free election of Legco members came about only in 1995, which Patten cleverly maneuvered (see pp. 312-313). Therefore, while Wilson stressed a get-along-with-China policy to the detriment of his HK subjects and was rewarded with appointment to the House of Lords, Patten stressed democratization, confronted Beijing, and then wrote a book.

Yet it should not be forgotten that Britain's interests were always the first priority of HK's administrations; it was the nature of the job. In that light, Tung Chee-hwa's work is much tougher and trickier. In the 1980s, Britain's first concern was getting out as gracefully as possible, which meant dealing with Beijing. In that triad, the HK people came third and last. Although Elliot, Pottinger, and Elgin of the Opium Wars hated the opium trade, they still did their duty. However, PM Major gave Patten extraordinary free rein (see pp. 326-327) so that Patten could put HK first and foil with Beijing , degrees of freedom that Tung lacks.

PM John Major's reelection wizard, Patten was rewarded with the governorship and its US$425,000 salary. Patten and Governor Sir Edward Youde (1982-86), who as a young diplomat performed courageously in the HMS *Amethyst* affair of 1949, probably came the closest of all the governors to giving the people forthright priority and a real sense of humaneness. Juggling HK, London, and Beijing concerns, Youde was the only governor to die in office (see pp. 147-149). PM Thatcher never should have overtaxed him with the burden of wrestling with Beijing on implementation of the 1997 handover; that job alone could have caused a stroke. Therefore, the best of British rule in Hong Kong comes down again to individual character and personality.

Contrasts between the Wilson and Patten administrations reflect the strengths and weaknesses of Britian's parliamentary democracy, which in a peculiar way might have been seen in Beijing as resembling their own ways. HK's history would be significantly different if the terriory had been given elective representation in Parliament, a notion that most Britons would scoff at but such a reaction if true just points out Anglo-American differences discussed earlier.

If free elections had only been started years earlier, even 1988, Hong Kong would have had some solid experience with an elected legislature, etc. and made it harder for China to replace the elected members with those it handpicked just before the handover. If Governor Young's (1941-47) plan for democracy had only been adopted, even the diluted version that was trashed during his successor's term (see pp. 140-141), the SAR would have started with a freely elected legislature that had a solid track record, democratic traditions, and community networks that the CCP would be loath to tamper with.

While Wilson's machinations succeeded because the people had little voice, his tenure is a matter of record. The likes of Morris' (1997, pp. 297-299) paean of Wilson's HK ("handsomely fulfilled") see only the superficial glitter and dynamism. Flittering in and out of HK to write about the place for decades, Jan Morris obfuscated and oversimplified Hong Kong's character and the far-reaching issues of Britain's last years in Hong Kong and the people's welfare, which Chapter 7 covers. On HK's character, Booth's (1994) expatriate view is superior.

Patten was so different that cynics suspicioned that London planted him as the last Governor to show the worst of Beijing in contrast to the best of Britain, but I disagree. His stated aim was to bring British rule to an honorable conclusion with lasting humane outcomes. True to his views of the CCP, Patten joined the June 5, 1998 Tiananmen vigil outside of the PRC Embassy in Washington, D.C. to show his "support and concern for the development of democracy in China."

In 1998, Patten sued HarperCollins for breach of contract when it cancelled his book on Hong Kong and won a six-figure out-of-court settlement. He alleged that the publisher disapproved of his criticism of Beijing. The *Independent* newspapers, which Patten later joined as non-executive director, the *Telegraph*, and others accused Rupert Murdoch of cancelling the book in order to protect his business ambitions in the PRC. The largest shareholder of HarperCollins, Murdoch also controls the *Times*, which rivals say has treated the PRC with kid gloves. See pp. 326-327on Patten's enthusiastic visit to HK in November 1998.

The book affair underlined the follies of media self-censorship when China is involved, as Chapter Four discusses at length. Evident from the early 1800s, China somehow brings out the worst and best of many Westerners. The CCP preys on the greed that the Qing failed to control.

The Substance of Hong Kong

Visiting Hong Kong, tourists often credit Asian modernity to Western rule, a notion that Barlow (1997) challenges at length. Tourists should have seen Hong Kong and Singapore during colonialism's heyday when the Chinese were held back. The profuse views of HK by Western dignitaries and travellers (White, 1996; Wise, 1996) have been highly superficial. Movies and novelists, such as James Clavell's *Taipan* and Richard Mason's *The World of Suzie Wong*, have portrayed HK as an exotic and mysterious otherworld and fed the fantasies and illusions of millions. Reality has always been something else.

Some Westerners have shown penetrating insights into the unique place and people. Learning to appreciate the East and its confrontation with the West, they (e.g., Bonavia, 1982; Cameron, 1989; Coates, 1968; Miners, 1987; Welsh, 1993) went beyond the veil of obviousness. Britons, such as Sir Philip Haddon-Cave, Sir Jack Cater, Lady Pamela Youde, Elsie Tu, Jimmy McGregor, and others mentioned elsewhere continue to maintain steady, humanist hands in HK affairs. Many Britons have spoken when their country mishandled HK and tried to do what was right. The Chinese have not been easy for Westerners to understand, but those who succeeded became enamored with them and their culture.

The humanitarians and their legacy. Chapters Three and Five relate inspiring stories of physicians, educators, and missionaries who devoted themselves to the people's social and health needs. In contrast to the indifferent and avaricious, they were true humanitarians as were numerous others in HK. Chapter Three tells of medical heroes at wartime and peace who should not be forgotten and whose histories are more exciting than fiction. Their education of practitioners and laying the foundation for modern medical training and comprehensive health care comprise their great contribution. Starting with medical-school graduates, such as Dr. Sun Yat-sen, and others who were educated in the West, such as Sir Kai Ho Kai, British physicians and untold others achieved an East-West unity that expanded in unforeseen directions, such as affecting China's Revolution through Dr. Sun's education. What they started became so successful that educational and low-cost health and medical services are now taken for granted.

The World Health Organization (Chan & Smith, 1998) reported that HK women are among the least likely in the world to die during childbirth. HK's rate of one death out of 9,200 pregnant women is better than in the U.S. where twice as many women die of birth-related complications. Also, since all pre- and post-natal care have been free into 1999, the cost of having a baby in the SAR is less than US$50 compared to thousands in the U.S. (see page 18).

A positive foundation. Although the British introduced democracy in a woefully tardy and reluctant manner, a foundation for democracy has been flourishing for long. While Chapters 2 & 4 report some ripples, there was never any doubt that home traditions of free speech and press as well as jurisprudence should be implemented and maintained in HK; any diminution would have affected the British and free trade. Promoting the CSS middle ground, those traditions of free societies are at the crux of Hong Kong's contrast with China.

Even when HK was known as a "cruel society," a persistent humanitarian theme can be traced as this book relates. Whether inspired by Confucianism, Christianity, or human nature, the place often exhibited charity and the best in people beyond their normal loyalties to family and self-interest.

While HK's legal system restraints the people as well as the Government and is laissez-faire towards business, no person or group, including the Government is above the law. This is opposed to the PRC where the state dictates and uses the law to dominate versus facilitate the populace. The CCP, which is synonymous with the state, is presumed above the law. Promulgated in 1990, the HK Basic Law, which is the SAR's mini-constitution, is controversial in key parts; as many legal minds believe that it allows the PRC too much room to work its will.

For example, replacing Britain's Privy Council, HK's Court of Final Appeal could be hampered by PRC intrusions, since the CFA "shall have no jurisdiction over acts of state such as defense and foreign affairs." With deep British roots and a century and a half in use, HK's legal system, unlike the PRC, is as sophisticated as any in the Free World. As such, any CCP efforts to disrupt it, as occurred in early 1999 on a PRC challenge to the CFA's decision on immigrant children, would bring tremendous protest and consternation in HK (see pp. 214-215).

In Chapter Four, modesty omits full mention of the high repute of and praise given to the *Hong Kong Economic Journal*, where the author, George Shen, worked

58 Whither Hong Kong?

ed as the respected Chief Editor for long. Dimbleby (1997, p. 220) wrote: "Of the mainstream Chinese-language papers, only the *Hong Kong Economic Journal* was stalwart in support of democratic reform; most of the rest sheltered behind the demand for 'consensus' and 'compromise' without specifying how these admirable objectives might be achieved in the circumstances." Supporting democracy as HKEJ has marks true humanism. Lau (1997, pp. 164-165) said the HKEJ:

> is a quality financial daily enjoying high esteem. Founder Lam Shan-muk has fearlessly maintained his independence while other papers have bent with the wind to tone down their criticism of China. His daily column has continued to criticize China where it is due. Lam's column is 'required reading' for the territory's elite, who also take seriously the views expressed by academics and professionals in the paper's extensive opinion pages.

Deng Xiaoping said that HK's reporters provoked him because they never stopped trying to get information from him, unlike PRC journalists. Free speech and press have gone hand in hand with what made the HK a world entrepot. As Dr. Shen (1994) has said, "The media do not serve any economic system. Rather, market economy provides the media with vitality and information for the media to disseminate. Hence it is market economy that serves the media."

Dependable, longitudinal data are crucial to free markets. The reason why the Canton traders profited from publishing newspapers was that the foreign community needed information -- market prices, inventories, ship arrivals and departures, home news, etc. As Chapter Six shows, the HK Government and other sources regularly report data to indicate how HK and other markets are doing.

President Jiang and Premier Zhu have said that the PRC's 2,000 or so bankrupt and unproductive state industries should be sold or closed. They should also fault state secrecy and controls, i.e., lack of accountability and Marxist ideology that stymie productivity. Production figures rose ridiculously during the Great Leap Forward, because nobody dared to incur Mao's wrath by reporting bad news. Although the GLF led to the starvation of 30+ million (Becker, 1996), the CCP holds to the absurd line that Mao was 80% right and good, 20% wrong! Yet Jiang and Zhu have shown signs of being more progressive than Mao and Deng.

A 1999 survey found that insular attitudes in HK, such as xenophobia and protectionism, were low compared to other Asian societies. S. Korea, India, Vietnam, China, Indonesia, Malaysia, Thailand, Taiwan, and Japan are more "nationalistic" than HK. Besides *state-people* animosity omitting patriotism, HK is imbrued with openness and welcomes investments and all comers (Chan, 1999).

Therefore, a solid foundation bolstering Hong Kong as China's beacon, its visionary gleam, stands ready to promote modernization and democracy -- humanitarian spirit, legal system, speech and press freedoms (see Chapter 4), fiscal and anti-corruption safeguards (see Chapter 2), social services (see Chapters 3 & 5), laissez-faire commerce and finances (see Chapter 6), and professional and business data and information networks fostering free trade.

Hong Kong's Prospects

"One country, two systems?" The sloganized formula for HK seems as specious to me as it does to Milton Friedman (Patten, 1998, p. 20). It's hard to understand why more do not question it, for it assumes the feasibility of two contrary economic and political systems existing under one roof. Since HK and the PRC have been closely related economically and ethnically long before the handover, those relations will continue and expand. The formula might make sense if HK could truly go its own way albeit under PRC sovereignty. Yet a moment's reflection brings one to see that the highly touted formula is more of a bromide blessing to a shot-gun wedding, i.e., given the CCP's record and nature, how conceivable is it that HK's autonomy will be preserved for long (see pp. 49-54)?

Putting aside the socioeconomic disparities, we can see how very different the "two systems" are in human rights and stability. The formula should become "one country with compatible economic and political systems." As the PRC, with its record of dictatorship, relates hand-in-hand with HK, the world's exemplar of capitalism, their disparate economic and political systems can only clash unless one or both adjust. Segal (1993, pp. 206-208) prophesied that Hong Kong would slow down to China's pace and ways, but on the other hand it could be argued that Hong Kong could become the tail that wags the dog. Which way will it go?

Predictions. Over the years leading up to the 1997 handover, much was written about HK's return to China; most predicted the worst. Let's take a sample.

David K. P. Li (1996), the Cambridge-educated, urbane Chairman and CEO of the Bank of East Asia, predicted that by 2046 China "will be one of the world's richest countries" and that "Hong Kong, the focal point of a metropolis covering the Pearl River Delta, will be the world's leading financial centre."

McGurn (1991, p. 134) wrote: "What the British achieved in Hong Kong could be said to reflect a Chinese ideal. The veteran Chinese journalist Tsang Ki-fan put it this way just before he died in 1988: 'This is the only Chinese society that, for a brief span of 100 years, lived through an ideal never realized at any time in the history of Chinese societies -- a time when no man had to live in fear of the midnight knock on the door.' How sad to see it all sacrificed at the precise moment when history has vindicated the experiment."

Probing the quote by Mr. Tsang, I contacted his son, Terence, with Mr. McGurn's assistance. The son explained that his father's reference to "100 years" of relative security in Hong Kong was dated from the reduced fears of British collusion with Qing Dynasty authorities, not as it would seem at first, i.e., that the British had always upheld human rights and tolerated dissension.

His answer helped to reinforce the point that the British supported Qing rule and resisted the dynasty's downfall -- until the irrational Boxer Uprising of 1898-1900 made it clear that the Qing were in hopeless disarray. Why did the British support the Qing regime? Because Britain had arrangements with the Qing rulers that profited both sides handsomely after 1860 and there was the New Territories deal (see pp. 83-84 & 132).

According to Welsh (1993, pp. 321 & 338), Gov. William Robinson's (1891-98) desire to extend the colony's borders was so keen that he actually recommended to London that Sun Yat-sen and other "scoundrelly leaders" be extradited to Qing China as a quid pro quo. Colonial Secretary Joseph Chamberlain denounced Robinson's idea as "monsterous," but he did approve of the 99-year New Territories lease, which sealed HK's 1997 fate. Yet, Robinson, who disliked the rebels as did other governors during the revolutionary era [Henry Blake (1898-1903), an exception], exiled Sun from HK in 1895 (see pp. 131-133).

Tsang (1997, pp. 220-221) likened HK's handover to a forced wedding: "Hong Kong's prospects of surviving the handover are fair, though it is unlikely to be able to continue exactly as before . . . . (with) no possibility of a divorce . . . . Although her husband is prone to bullying, he wants to make a success of the marriage and thus provides a glimpse of hope." China's shadow or visionary gleam?

A former HK senior policeman, Annieson (1989, pp. 212-213) condemned Britain's refusal to provide the over three million who were British dependent subjects the protective "right of abode" in Britain when Portugal granted 500,000 Macau citizens full Portuguese citizenship. Annieson concluded: ". . . what the British are doing to their own people, is racism concealed in white kid gloves!"

Mueller & Tan (1997, pp. 124-126) concluded by saying that "China is *in* the information age, but it is not yet *of* it." Also, "from the standpoint of Hong Kong and the West, the one country, two systems arrangement appears historically unique and fraught with drama and danger. From mainland China's perspective, however, ... (its) political administration already contains many special zones and autonomous or semiautonomous regions with slightly different systems."

De Mesquita, Newman, & Rabushka (1996, pp. 101-119) wrote depressingly about HK's future, saying that daily activities, such as reading newspapers, shopping, and conducting business, ". . . look very different in free societies from the way they look in controlled societies." "The political and economic landscape will be filled with uncertainty, cronyism, lost freedoms, and more corruption than has been known in the recent past. It is a bleak picture indeed."

Seeing a parallel with Shanghai, Patrikeeff (1989, pp. 214-215) said that HK may go the same way, "frozen in its heyday." He closed by saying: "Hong Kong too may find itself inheriting this twilight status: changed from a window on the world to just another Chinese city." In 1999, HK does seem to be regressing.

Menski (1995, p. 187) wrote: "The inescapable conclusion is that Hong Kong has already learnt to live with its future and shows all the signs of making an immense success of it."

Commending the indomitable strengths of the Chinese people in HK, Johnson (1997) wrote: ". . . the Trojan Horse of Hong Kong will prove an important perhaps determining factor. That is why I do not regard the surrender of Free HK . . . . as an unrelieved tragedy. It may, on the contrary, be the opening of a new chapter of hope for the Chinese people as a whole. Not least of the ironies which mark the history of British colonialism, and of its last and most exotic flower, HK may be the Phoenix-like rebirth of freedom within the Communist monolith, just at the moment when its lamp seems to be extinguished."

Abbas (1997, p. 6) said that "administering the HK 'special administrative region' after 1997 may be for the Chinese authorities a little like handling a gadget from the future." His main theme is since 1984 HK has been "a space of transit" captive to a "culture of disappearance" (e.g., architecture, films). However, he mistakes the surface for the real thing. The people's indomitable CSS psyche does not change so easily and should be seen as adjusting to new conditions.

Roberti (1996, p. 309) charged: "Without an adequately representative government, ironclad protection against human rights abuses, and the guarantee of an independent judiciary, the people of Hong Kong have been consigned to an uncertain future. They have every right to feel that Britain has betrayed them."

Wei Jingsheng, a famous dissident who was released from prison to the U.S. after President Jiang's 1997 visit to America, is pessimistic about HK's future: "He said that 'the one country, two systems' formula . . . is a Chinese sham.. . . . 'Just wait a year or two. They don't care about economics that much. If they see Hong Kong as an enemy place, they'll smash it'," (Mirsky, 1998). In December 1998, the PRC imprisoned three democracy dissidents to more than 10 years. They committed the ultimate crime (blatant counter-allegiance) of challenging the CCP's one-party rule by advocating a democracy party (Langfitt, 1998).

Analyzing the crisis over Beijing's (jurisdiction) and the HK people's (great costs) protests over the ruling by the HK Court of Final Appeal to allow hundreds of thousands of PRC children to join HK parents, Lau Siu-kai (1999) wrote that the balance of power between liberals and "pro-China" forces has been broken, "even though the liberals are still likely to maintain their lead."

On the handover, Buruma (1997) wrote: "Now, for the first time since the 1920s and 1930s, two kinds of Chinese patriotism will clash under one Chinese flag: The authoritarian kind and Martin Lee's kind, the May 4th kind. On the face of it, Lee and his fellow democrats don't stand a chance. The official patriots have the money and the guns. But in the long run, the love of liberty might yet turn out to be stronger. In that happy event, HK's homecoming will prove to have been the most dangerous tribute ever to fall into a Chinese tyrant's lap."

A crucible potent with contrasting possibilities, some highly explosive, HK will reflect the nature of China in the 21st century when some predict that China will become predominant in Asia. Picking up on Johnson's and Buruma's predictions, my greatest fear is that a militant CCP ($A+$) will resurface, as it has in bad times, and perceive the "Trojan horse" or "dangerous tribute" as a threat to its power and seek to subjugate the HKSAR into its shadow. It can do that with incremental moves that will lead the people to rancor (CR) but not to revolt.

My hope (against hope) is that China's leaders will address the challenge of Hong Kong with visionary gleam -- moderating authoritarianism and resurrecting the humanistic roots of China's culture.

References

Abbas, Ackbar (1997). *Hong Kong: Culture and the politics of disappearance.* Minneapolis, MN: University of Minnesota Press.

Adams, Henry (1918). *The education of Henry Adams.* NY: Random House.

Ambrose, Stephen E. (1996). *Undaunted courage: Meriwether Lewis, Thomas Jefferson and the opening of America's West.* New York: Simon & Schuster.

Annieson, Anthony (1989). *The one-eyed dragon: The inside story of a Hong Kong policeman.* Moffat, Scotland: Lochar.

Ball, J. D. (1892). *Things Chinese.* London: Sampson Low. (Reprinted Kelly and Walsh, Shanghai, 1925; Oxford University Press, Hong Kong, 1982).

Barlow, Tani E. (Ed.) (1997). *Formations of colonial modernity in East Asia.* Durham, NC: Duke University Press.

Bartlett, C. J. (1963). *Great Britain and sea power 1815-1853.* Oxford: Clarendon.

Bastid-Bruguierre, Marianne (1980). Currents of social change. In J. K. Fairbank & K. C. Liu (Eds.), *The Cambridge history of China.* (Vol. 2, Late Ch'ing, 1800-1911, Part 2) (pp. 535-602). Cambridge: Cambridge University Press.

Becker, Jasper (1996). *Hungry ghosts: Mao's secret famine.* New York: Holt.

Becker, Jasper (1998, June 4). Democratise or fail, Zhu told. *South China Morning Post,* Internet Edition.

Beeching, Jack (1975).*The Chinese opium wars.* NY: Harcourt Brace Jovanovich.

Benson, Arthur C. & Viscount Esher (1908). *The letters of Queen Victoria* (Vol. 1 -- 1837-1843). London: John Murray.

Bonavia, David (1982). *The Chinese.* New York: Penguin.

Booth, Martin (1994). *The dragon and the pearl: A Hong Kong notebook.* London: Simon & Schuster.

Booth, Martin (1998). *Opium: A history.* New York: St. Martin's.

Brackman, Arnold C. (1975). *The last emperor.* New York: Carroll & Graf.

Buruma, Ian (1997, August 14). Selling out Hong Kong. *The New York Review of Books,* pp. 26-27.

Cameron, Nigel (1978). *Hong Kong: The cultured pearl.* New York: Oxford University Press.

Cameron, Nigel (1989). *Barbarians and mandarins: Thirteen centuries of Western travellers in China.* Hong Kong: Oxford University Press.

Cecil, Algernon (1927). *British foreign secretaries 1807-1916: Studies in personality and policy.* New York: G. P. Putnam's.

Chu, Henry (1998, December 19). Chinese leader lauds economic reforms but he criticizes U.S.-style democracy. *San Francisco Chronicle,* Internet Edition.

Chai, Ch'u & Chai, Winberg (Ed. & Trans.) (1965). *The humanist way in ancient China: Essential works of Confucius.* New York: Bantam.

Chan, Quinton & Smith, Alison (1998, March 13). SAR safest place to give birth. *South China Morning Post,* Internet edition.

Chan, Zoe (1999, February 21). Low sense of nationalism 'a boon to economy. *Hong Kong Standard,* Internet Edition.

Chang, Hsin-pao (1964). *Commissioner Lin and the Opium War*. Cambridge, MA: Harvard University Press.

Chang, Iris (1997). *The rape of Nanking: The forgotten holocaust of World War II*. New York: Basic.

Cheng, Irene (1976). *Clara Ho Tung: A Hong Kong lady, her family and her times*. Hong Kong: The Chinese University of Hong Kong.

Cheng, Nien (1986). *Life and death in Shanghai*. London: Grafton.

Choy, Linda (1997, Dec. 16). Emily Lau to give up British passport. *South China Morning Post*, Internet edition.

Choy, Linda (1998, March 10). HK deputies warned not to meddle. *South China Morning Post*, Internet edition.

Churchill, Winston S. (1958). *The great democracies*. New York: Dodd, Mead.

Coates, Austin (1968). *Myself a mandarin*. New York: John Day.

Coates, Austin (1988). *Macau and the British 1637-1842: Prelude to Hong Kong*. Hong Kong: Oxford University Press.

Coates, Austin (1990). *Quick tidings of Hong Kong*. Hong Kong: Oxford University Press.

Collis, Maurice (1946). *Foreign mud: Anglo-Chinese opium war*. Singapore: Graham Brash.

Collis, Maurice (1965). *Wayfoong: The Hongkong and Shanghai Banking Corporation*. London: Faber & Faber.

De Mesquita, Bueno, Newman, Bruce, & Rabuska, Alvin (1996). *Red flag over Hong Kong*. Chatham, NJ: Chatham House.

Delaney, Norman C. (1972). The end of the *Alabama*. *American Heritage*, *23*(3), 58-69 & 102.

Dickson, Bruce J. (1997). *Democratization in China and Taiwan: The adaptablity of Leninist parties*. Oxford: Clarendon Press.

Dimbleby, Jonathan (1997). *The last governor*. London: Little, Brown.

Down, Jacques, M. (1997). *The golden ghetto: The American commercial community at Canton and the shaping of American China policy, 1784-1844*. Bethlehem, PA: Lehigh University Press,

Drucker, Peter (1939). *The end of economic man: A study of the new totalitarianism*. New York: John Day.

Ebrey, Patricia B. (1991). *Confucianism and family rituals in imperial China: A social history of writing about rites*. Princeton, NJ: Princeton University Press.

Eitel, E. J. (1895). *Europe in China*. Hong Kong: Kelly & Walsh (Reprinted: Oxford University Press, Hong Kong, 1983).

Elvin, Mark (1973). *The pattern of the Chinese past: A social and economic interpretation*. Stanford, CA: Stanford University Press.

Endacott, G. B. (1973). *A history of Hong Kong*. Hong Kong: Oxford University Press.

Fairbank, John K. (1969). *Trade and diplomacy on the China coast*. Stanford: Stanford University Press.

Fairbank, John K. (1992). *China: A new history*. Cambridge, MA: Belknap.

Fay, Peter W. (1975). *The opium war 1840-1842.* New York: Norton.

Feuerwerker, Albert (1983). The foreign presence in China. In J. K. Fairbank (Ed.), *The Cambridge history of China* (Vol. 12, Republican China 1912-1940, Part One) (pp. 128-208). Cambridge: Cambridge University Press.

Fleming, Thomas (Ed.) (1972). *Benjamin Franklin.* NY: Newsweek.

Flowerdew, John (1998). The final years of British Hong Kong: The discourse of colonial withdrawal. New York: St. Martin's.

Forbes, Robert B. (1844). *Remarks on China and the China trade.* Boston: Dickinson.

Fraser, Niall (1998, November 10). ICAC acclaimed as world leader in graft-busting. *South China Morning Post,* Internet Edition.

Fraser, Niall & Yi, Cheung (1998, December 26). Tung named 'an enemy of democracy.' *South China Morning Post.* Internet Edition.

Fredrickson, George M. (1981). *White supremacy: A comparative study in American and South African history.* New York: Oxford University Press.

Fredrickson, George M. (1988). *The arrogance of race: Perspectives on slavery, racism and social inequality.* Middletown, CT: Weleyan University Press.

Freuchen, Peter (1957).*Peter Freuchen's book of the Seven Seas.* NY: Messner.

Fulford, Benjamin (1998, June 6). Singapore notes yuan threat to peg. *South China Morning Post,* Internet Edition

Fulghum, David A. (1996, March 18). Chinese missile shots: Only a prelude? *Aviation Week & Space Technology,* pp. 22-24).

Furth, Charlotte (1983). Intellectual change: From the reform movement to the May Fourth movement, 1895-1920. In John K. Fairbank (Ed.), *The Cambridge History of China* (Vol. 12, Republican China 1912-1949, Part I, pp. 322-405). Cambridge: Cambridge University Press.

Gernet, Jacques (1982). *A history of Chinese civilization* (J. R. Foster, Trans.). Cambridge: Cambridge University Press.

Gibney, Frank (1992). *The Pacific century: America and Asia in a changing world.* New York: Scribner's.

Gittins, Jean (1969). *Eastern windows -- Western skies.* Hong Kong: South China Morning Post.

Goldman, Merle (1994). *Sowing the seeds of democracy in China: Political reform in the Deng Xiaoping era.* Cambridge, MA: Harvard University Press.

Hahn, Emily (1944). *China to me:A partial autobiography.*Philadephia: Blakiston.

Ho Ping-ti (1959). *Studies on the population of China, 1368-1953.* Cambridge, MA: Harvard University Press.

Hoe, Susanna (1991). *The private life of old Hong Kong.* Hong Kong: Oxford University Press.

Hon, May Sin-Mi (1998, December 24). SAR 'moving from capitalism to socialism.' *South China Morning Post,* Internet Edition.

Hook, Brian & Twitchett, Denis (1991). *The Cambridge Encyclopedia of China* (2nd. ed.). Cambridge: Cambridge University Press.

Hubbard, A. (1989, October 17). Briton wages lone fight against newspapers' racist slurs on Chinese. *Straits Times,* p. 25.

In praise of paranoia (1998, November 7). *The Economist*, pp. 4-18.

Jen, Y. W. & Ride, Lindsay (1970). *Sun Yat-sen: Two commemorative essays*. Hong Kong: Centre of Asian Studies, University of Hong Kong.

Jespersen, T. Christopher (1996). *American images of China 1931-1949*. Stanford, CA: Stanford University Press.

Johnson, Paul (1997). A contrarian view of colonialism. *In Far Eastern Economic Review's* special issue, *Hong Kong: A new beginning* (pp. 8-16).

Keay, John (1991). *The honourable company: A history of the English East India Company*. New York: Macmillan.

Kerr, Phyllis Forbes (Ed.) (1996). *Letters from China: The Canton-Boston correspondence of Robert Bennet Forbes, 1838-1840*. Mystic, CT: Mystic Seaport Museum.

Kristoff, Nicholas D. (1991, March 3). New China propaganda wrinkle: Enjoyment. *New York Times Magazine*, pp. 28-31, 49-51.

Kristroff, Nicholas D. & Wudunn, Sheryl (1994). *China wakes: The struggle for the soul of a rising power*. New York: Random House.

Lam, Willy Wo-Lap (1998, May 20). Rough ride for Zhu the reformer. *South China Morning Post*, p. 17.

Lam, Willy Wo-Lap (1999, February 19). Jiang quotes Deng on military line. *South China Morning Post*, Internet Edition.

Langfitt, Frank (1998, December 22). China sentences leading dissidents. *San Francisco Chronicle*, Internet Edition.

Lattimore, O. (1940). *China memoirs: Chiang Kai-shek and the war with Japan* . (Compiled by Fujiko Isono). Tokyo: University of Tokyo Press.

Lau Chi Kuen (1997). *Hong Kong's colonial legacy*. HK: Chinese University Press.

Lau Siu-Kai (1999, March 2). Verdict tips the political balance. *SCMP*, Internet Edition.

Lau, S. K. & Kuan, H. C. (1988). *The ethos of the Hong Kong Chinese*. HK: Chinese University Press.

Lawrence, Susan V. (1998, October 22). Celebrity critic. *Far Eastern Economic Review*, pp. 12-14.

Lever-Tracy, Constance, Ip, David, & Tracy, Noel (1996). *The Chinese diaspora and Mainland China: An emerging economic survey*. London: Macmillan.

Li, David K. P. (1996, October, 50th commemorative edition). China in 2046. *Far Eastern Economic Review*, pp. 188-189.

Li, Victor (1991). Two models of law. In Robert F. Dernberger, et al (Eds.), *The Chinese: Adapting the past, facing the future* (pp. 243-247). Ann Arbor, MI: Center for Chinese Studies.

Li, Zhisui (1994). *The private life of Chairman Mao* (Tai Hung-chao, Trans). New York: Random House.

Liang, Shuming (1917). *Eastern and Western civilizations and their philosophies*. Reprinted 1969: Taipei: Hung-ch'iao shu-tien.

Lin, Binyan & Link, Perry (1998, October 8). A great leap backward? *The New York Review of Books*, pp. 19-23.

Lin, Yutang (1977). *My country and my people*. Hong Kong: Heinemann.

Lindsay, Oliver (1978). *The lasting honour:The fall of Hong Kong 1941*. London: Sphere.

Lewin, Kurt (1939). Patterns of aggressive behavior in experimentally created social climates. *Journal of Social Psychology, 10*, 271-299.

Lieberman, L. (1968). The debate over race: A study in the sociology of knowledge. *Phylon, 29*, 127-141.

Lubbock, Basil (1976). *The opium clippers.* Glasgow: Brown, Son & Ferguson.

Lubbock, Basil (1981).*Coolie ships and oil sailers.* Glasgow: Brown, Son & Ferguson.

Lyman, Stanford M. (1975). The Chinese diaspora in America. In T. W. Chinn (Ed.), *The Life, influence and the role of the Chinese in the United States, 1776-1960* (pp. 128-146). San Francisco: Chinese Historical Society of America.

Madsen, Richard (1995). *China and the American dream: A moral inquiry.* Berkeley: University of California Press.

Malone, Dumas (1948-81). *Jefferson and his time* (Vol. 1-6). Boston: Little Brown.

McGurn, William (1991). *Perfidious Albion: The abandonment of Hong Kong 1997.* Washington, DC: Ethics and Public Policy Center.

McNamara, Sheila (1999, January 11). US group told SAR 'not interested in elections.' *South China Morning Post,* Internet Edition.

Menski, Werner (1995). *Coping with 1997: The reaction of the Hong Kong people to the transfer of power.* London: Trentham.

Metzger, Thomas A. (1990). Continuities between modern and premodern China: Some neglected methodological and substantive issues. In Paul A. Cohen & Merle Goldman (Eds.), *Ideas across cultures: Essays on Chinese thought in honor of Benjamin I. Schwartz* (pp. 204-292). Cambridge, MA: Council on East Asian Studies, Harvard University.

Miners, Norman (1987). *Hong Kong under imperial rule 1912-1941.* HK: Oxford University Press.

Miners, Norman (1995). *The government and politics of Hong Kong* (5th ed.). Hong Kong: Oxford University Press.

Mirsky, Jonathan (1998, March 5). Talking with Wei Jingsheng. *The New York Review of Books,* p. 39.

Moore, Barrington, Jr. (1966). The decay of imperial China and the origins of the communist variant. In his *Social origins of dictatorship and democracy: Lord and peasant in the making of the modern world* (Chapter 4, pp. 162-227). Boston: Beacon.

Morris, James (1968). *Pax Britannica: The climax of an empire.* San Diego, CA: Harcourt Brace.

Morris, James (1973). *Heaven's command: An imperial progress.* San Diego, CA: Harcourt Brace.

Morris, Jan (1997). *Hong Kong* (rev.). New York: Vintage.

Mueller, Milton & Tan Zixiang (1997). *China in the information age: Telecommunications and the dilemmas of reform.* Westport, CT: Praeger.

Muller, Edward N. (1985). Income inequality, regime repressiveness, and political violence. *American Sociological Review, 50*(2), 47-61.

Nathan, Andrew J. (1990). The place of values in cross-cultural studies: The example of democracy and China. In P. A. Cohen & M. Goldman (Eds.), *Ideas across cultures: Essays on Chinese thought in honor of Benjamin I. Schwartz* (pp. 293-314). Cambridge, MA: Council on East Asian Studies, Harvard University.

Nathan, Andrew J. & Ross, Robert S. (1997). *The great wall and the empty fortress: China's search for security.* New York: Norton.

Nathan, Andrew J., Shi, Tianjian, & Ho, Helena V. S. *(1998). China's transition.* New York: Columbia University Press.

Nightingale's Song (1998, May 14). *Far Eastern Economic Review,* p. 30.

O'Neill, Mark (1999, January 7). Dark days ahead for economy, says Beijing. *South China Morning Post,* Internet Edition.

Palpal-latoc, Lucia (1997, September 21). Rich-poor gap among highest in world. *Hong Kong Standard,* Internet edition.

Park, Nancy E. (1997). Corruption in eighteenth-century China. *Journal of Asian Studies, 56*(4), 967-1005.

Patrikeeff, Felix (1989). *Mouldering pearl: Hong Kong at the crossroads.* London: George Philip.

Patten, Christopher (1998). *East and West: China, power, and the future of Asia.* New York: Times/Random House.

Pemberton, W. Baring (1954). *Lord Palmerston.* London: Batchworth Press.

Peyrefitte, Alain (1992). *The immobile empire* (J. Rothschild, Trans.). NY: Knopf.

Pottinger, George (1997). *Sir Henry Pottinger: First governor of Hong Kong.* New York: St. Martin's.

Potter, Sulamith H. (1988). The cultural construction of emotion in rural Chinese social life. *Ethos, 16*(2) 181-208.

Pye, Lucian W. (1990). China: Erratic state, frustrated society. *Foreign Affairs, 69*(4), 56-74.

Pye, Lucian W. (1992). *The spirit of Chinese politics* (2nd ed., rev.). Cambridge, MA: Harvard University Press.

Pye, Lucian W. (1997). Money politics and transition to democracy in East Asia. *Asian Survey, 37*(3), 213-228.

Renwick, Robin (1996). *Fighting with allies: America and Britain in peace and war.* London: Macmillian.

Ridley, Jasper (1970). *Lord Palmerston.* London: Constable.

Roberti, Mark (1996). *The fall of Hong Kong: China's triumph & Britain's betrayal* (rev.). New York: Wiley.

Scalapino, Robert A. & Yu, George T. (1985). *Modern China and its revolutionary process. Recurrent challenges to the traditional order 1850-1920.* Berkeley, CA: University of California Press.

Schwartz, Benjamin I. (1996). *China and other matters.* Cambridge, MA: Harvard Univeristy. Press.

Seagrave, Sterling (1992). *Dragon lady: The life and legend of the last empress of China.* New York: Knopf.

Seagrave, Sterling (1995). *Lords of the rim: The invisible empire of the Overseas Chinese*. New York: Putnam.

Segal, Gerald (1993). *The fate of Hong Kong*. New York: St. Martin's.

Shenon, Philip (1998, June 9, 1998). U.S.-based Chinese harassed by police on visits home. *South China Morning Post*, Internet edition.

Shen, George (1994, September 16-22). How should the media serve the market economy? Two Sides of the Taiwan Strait and HK News Symposium, held in Hong Kong and sponsored by the HK News Executives' Association.

Spence, Jonathan D. (1990). *The search for modern China*. New York: Norton.

Spence, Jonathan D. (1996). *God's Chinese son: The Taiping heavenly kingdom of Hong Xiuquan*. New York: Norton.

Spence, Jonathan D. (1998). *The Chan's great continent: China in Western minds*. New York: Norton.

Stackpole, Edouard. A. (1954). *Captain Prescott and the opium smugglers*. Mystic, CT: Marine Historical Association.

Starr, John B. (1997). *Understanding China: A guide to China's economy, history, and political structure*. New York: Hill and Wang.

State Department (1995). *Country reports on human rights practices for 1994*. Washington, DC: U.S. Government Printing Office.

Strachey, Lytton (1949). *Queen Victoria*. San Diego, CA: Harcourt Brace Jovanovich.

Strachey, Lytton (1969) *Eminent Victorians*. San Diego, CA: Harcourt Brace Jovanovich.

Sun Yat-sen (1943). *The three principles of the people*. Chungking, China: Ministry of Information of the Republic of China.

Thomson, J. C. Jr., Stanley, P. W., & Peery, J. D. (1981). *Sentimental imperialist: The American experience in East Asia*. New York: Harper and Row.

Thompson, Angel (1996). *Feng shui*. New York: St. Martin's.

Trocki, Carl A. (1990). *Opium and empire: Chinese society in colonial Singapore, 1800-1910*. Ithaca, NY: Cornell University Press.

Tsai Jung-fang (1993). *Hong Kong in Chinese history: Community and social unrest in the British colony 1842-1913*. New York: Columbia University Press.

Unintended consequences (1998, May 30). *Economist*, p. 41.

Tsang, Steve (1997). Hong Kong: Appointment with China. London: Tauris.

Van Kemenade, Willem (1997). *China, Hong Kong, Taiwan, Inc.* (DianeWebb, Trans.). New York, Knopf.

Waley, Arthur (1958). *The Opium War through Chinese eyes*. Stanford: Stanford University Press.

Wan, Rhonda Lam (1998, December 8). Patients will have to pay in overhaul: health chief. *South China Morning Post*, Internet edition.

Weintraub, S. (1997). *Uncrowned king: The life of Prince Albert*. New York: Free Press.

Weir, Stuart & Beetham, David (1998). *Political power and democratic control in Britain*. London: Routledge.

Welsh, Frank (1993). *A history of Hong Kong*. London: HarperCollins

Wilhelm, Richard (1967). *I ching or book of changes*. London: Routledge & Kegan.

Will, Pierre-Etienne (1990). *Bureaucracy and famine in eighteenth-century China* (E. Forster, Trans.). Stanford, CA: Stanford University Press.

Wise, Michael & Wise, Mun Him (Eds.) (1996). *Travellers' tales of old Hong Kong and the South China coast*. Brighton, UK: In Print.

White, Barbara-Sue (Ed.) (1996). *Hong Kong: Somewhere between heaven and earth*. Hong Kong: Oxford University Press.

Wiltrout, Kate (1998, March 14). Shock as 5.5m offenders pardoned. *South China Morning Post*, Internet Edition.

Wong, Jesse (1996, August 28). British official-turned-critic fights on. *Asian Wall Street Journal*, p. 1.

Yahuda, Michael (1996). *Hong Kong: China's challenge*. London: Routledge.

Yee, Albert H. (1989, Feb. 9). China's big lie. *Far Eastern Economic Review*, pp. 18-19.

Yee, Albert H. (1992a). Asians as stereotypes and students: Misperceptions that persist. *Educational Psychology Review, 4*(1), 95-132.

Yee, Albert H. (1992b). *A people misruled: The Chinese stepping-stone syndrome* (2nd ed., rev.). Singapore: Heinemann Asia.

Yee, Albert H. & Cheng, Joseph Y. S. (1999). Enhancing China studies: Social psychology and the Chinese stepping-stone syndrome. *Asian Thought and Society. 24*(71), 113-133.

Yee, Albert H., Fairchild, Halford H., Weizmann, Frederic, and Wyatt, Gail E. (1993). Addressing psychology's problems with race. *American Psychologist, 48*(11), 1132-1140.

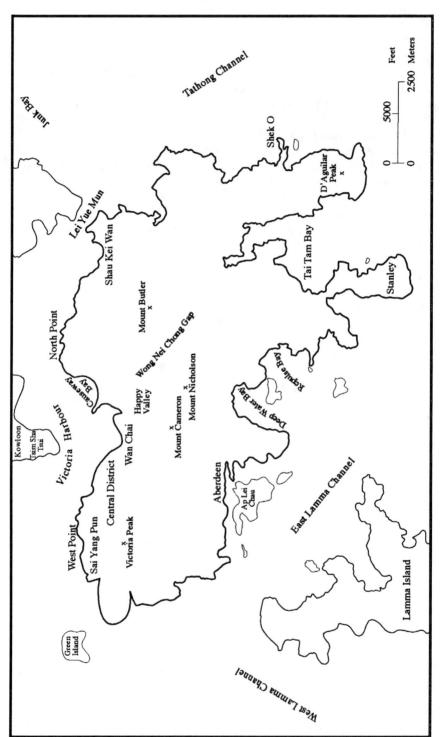

- Map 3, Hong Kong Island -

CHAPTER ONE

Hong Kong's Military History and the Wars of Aggression

Oliver Lindsay

Prologue

The Shingmun Redoubt, Hong Kong. It was nearly midnight on Saturday 6th December 1941. Beyond Kowloon, up in the mountains at the Redoubt, the men of the Royal Scots watched the rapidly changing shadows as the clouds raced across the moon. To their right were the Rajputs and Punjabis. The digging of trenches continued. Patrols groped forward to check that the perimeter wire was still in place. At Shamshuipo Sydney Skelton of the Royal Rifles of Canada tucked the diary which he was writing for his fiancee into his large pack. This battalion was to move to battle stations at first light. Covered by the massive guns of Stanley Fort, His Majesty's torpedo boats patrolled far out into the South China Sea.

Thirty miles to the north, the officers of Colonel Doi Teihichi's 228 Imperial Japanese Regiment studied markings in crimson ink upon their maps. Their objective was the Shingmun Redoubt, and then the British Crown Colony of Hong Kong itself -- a prosperous colony which boasted a magnificent natural harbor. Colonel Doi was a man of courage, intellect and initiative. Nevertheless it would never have occurred to him that, 56 years later, the British would hand Hong Kong over to the Chinese People's Liberation Army -- an amicable and peaceful handover, moreover, with bands, flags, a Royal yacht, The Prince of Wales, all amidst some optimism for Hong Kong's future.

Nor, when Colonel Doi saw the stately homes on Hong Kong's Peak, the magnificent colonial government buildings and elegant country clubs, would he have imagined that Hong Kong was once a desolate place, inhabited by a few Chinese fishermen.

The Opium Wars

British interests in China in the early 19th century rested upon trade, which unfortunately centered on opium, the narcotic that was grown and processed cheaply cheaply in India and shipped into China through the Pearl River delta for huge profits. Opium was capable of enslaving addicts even more completely than alcohol, creating intense agonies -- "fiction can paint nothing of horror half so horrible." But many in England and India were unaware that the traffic even existed. Since this book's Overview traces the people and events leading to Sino-British conflict, this chapter will highlight some military aspects of the Opium Wars before dealing more thoroughly with HK during and after World War II.

The first shots of the First China War were actually fired on September 4, 1839 in Hong Kong Harbor. Short of provisions and menaced seige-like by war-junks, about 40 British ships had laid at anchor for several months. Since August 25th they were overloaded with 700 or so merchants and family members who had fled Macao, including Captain Charles Elliot's wife and daughter. Frustrated by the taunting bellicosity surrounding his ships, Elliot ordered cannon fire against war-junks that were especially hostile that day.

However, the war began in earnest on July 5, 1840 when the British expedition captured Tinghai, capital of the Chusan archipelago that protrudes into the East China Sea, 100 miles south of the mouth of the great Yangtze and 120 miles from Shanghai. Commanded by Admiral George Elliot, cousin to Charles, the expeditionary force included 16 warships and four armed paddle steamers. It was not their speed that was decisive, it was their shallow draught and ability to move and tow other ships in a calm, up wind, or up tide.

The Chusan mandarins were painfully surprised; in their minds they had not harmed the British and were not responsible for what happened far off in Canton. Although they had performed their duty, several Chinese officials committed suicide because they knew that the Imperial Court would blame them. British officers found nothing more serious ashore than the men getting drunk from looted liquor.

On January 7, 1841, a British fleet seized the Bogue forts of Chuenpi, Wangton, and Big and Little Taikok, which guarded the narrow waterway leading to Canton. Five hundred Chinese were killed in a few hours with only 38 British wounded (Beeching, 1975; Inglis, 1976, p. 151; Fay, 1975). The British had little compassion for their enemies; there were many reports of barbarities inflicted on Britons captured when their ships went aground -- men and women were put in irons, confined in cages that were barely three and a half feet long, three feet wide, and two feet high, and exhibited in marketplaces (Inglis, 1976, pp. 155-156).

On March 6th, Major General Sir Hugh Gough occupied one of the forts overlooking Canton. His opponent being a habitual pessimist, General Yang Fang, past 70 and deaf but famed for vanquishing China's enemies, accepted an armistice; but conflict resumed with naval action. Hit by mortars, four heavy guns and a rocket battery, four more forts fell and everyone in Canton fled. Hostilities were suspended. A Chinese army of 45,000 lay uncommitted to the north and many thousands of armed peasants organized themselves as "Quell the British" Corps.

In one incident, a company of the Madras Native Infantry was caught in a thunderstorm just as the Chinese closed on them. The rain making it impossible for them to use their flintlock muskets, the Madras soldiers formed a square in water up to their knees. Encircled by thousands of Chinese, they were miraculously rescued by British Marines at the last moment, *ex machina deus* as in John Wayne films. The Marines were armed with the new percussion-lock musket that had been designed by the Brunswick Army. Although it remained in use until the Crimean War, the Brunswick musket was a very unsatisfactory weapon because of the inaccuracy and lack of range due to its smooth-bore barrel. The British Army would not have effective firing power until the rifled or grooved barrels were adopted that spun shots efficiently (Holt, 1964, p. 129).

China's defeats led to Elliot's agreement with Chinese officials on the Chuenpi Convention ceding Hong Kong and providing an indemnity of six million dollars for the destroyed opium. Chusan would be returned to China and all British prisoners would be freed. However, neither Britain nor China ratified the Convention. Trade resumed at Canton as the merchants returned to work. HK would become a great prize because of its magnificent deep-water anchorage and small, benign population, yet Lord Palmerston and the traders believed that Elliot had been overly lenient and that greater concessions were in order.

Palmerston replaced Elliot with Sir Henry Pottinger, a major general recently retired from service with the British East India Company in India at age 50. During his long service in the Company's army and as its Political Agent in Sind, he "forcefully represented British interests" and got what he wanted without delay. Restless in England, Pottinger grasped the offer of command in China and a salary of 6,000 pounds per year, double Elliot's. Arriving in Hong Kong in August 1841 with every advantage that comes from replacing someone deemed a failure, Pottinger mounted fierce hostilities against China; his "commanders who had to work with him, although they appreciated his combativeness after Elliot's humanitarian hesitations, had occasion to complain about his fondness for 'extraordinary powers and salutes' " (Welsh, 1993, p. 114).

With reinforcements from England added to Elliot's 4,000 British troops from India, Pottinger commanded a strong force of about 12,000 soldiers, some armed with the latest percussion muskets. His fleet included the *Nemesis*, the first iron sidewheel steamer to reach the China coast on her own power. With two swivel 32-pound guns, five six-pounders and a battery of lighter swivel guns, the *Nemesis* could maneuver freely but ponderously with its sliding keels, a flat bottom, retractable rudder, seven watertight compartments. Drawing only six feet, it could traverse shallow waters but was ponderous to steer. Pottinger's fleet also included a mighty ship-of-the-line, the HMS *Cornwallis*, with 74 guns, and many frigates, corvettes and transports (Beeching, 1975, pp. 149-150). In the year that followed, Pottinger's campaign up the China coast and the Yangtze River was so successful that many cities were captured, including Nanjing and Shanghai. In fact, the one-sided victories of 1842 and 1860 so shamed the Chinese that it still provokes strong emotions among many Chinese, though their ire is directed at the Manchus (Qing) for their ineptitude and loss of territory as well as the British.

The Treaty of Nanking was signed in the crowded great cabin of the *Cornwallis* on August 29, 1842, followed by a 21-gun salute with the Union Jack at the mizzen and China's yellow dragon flag at the mainmast (Fay, 1975, pp 362-363). In 1843 Britain was regarded as "the most favored nation," which granted her concessions which might be gained by others. In the Treaty of Wanghai the following year, the Americans obtained all the concessions the British enjoyed, and the French were permitted to have missionaries in China.

As Hong Kong became the chief nexus of the opium trade, over 70 British and American opium ships sailed in and out of the harbor in autumn 1845. The British Government worded its instructions to Treaty Port Consuls with care: it was neither their duty to help opium smugglers, nor to help the Chinese carry out their laws against the drug.

Sir Henry Pottinger returned to Hong Kong and assumed the post of Governor in June 1842. According to Welsh (1993, p. 145), the Governor was outranked in reputation and class by his General Officer Commanding, Lord Saltoun, the sixteenth Baron, and Major-General of the Grenadier Guards, who had been "described by Wellington himself as 'a pattern to the army both as a man and a soldier'. . . . (for) it was Saltoun who at Waterloo commanded the detachment of the Guards which held out in the garden of Hougoumont against everything the French could bring against them, and who personally received Cambronne's sword when he surrendered the Imperial Guard."

In one of those delightful coincidences which enhance British history, Lord Saltoun appears to have influenced the career of James Hope Grant, the commanding general that defeated Qing (Ch'ing, Manchu) China forces in the Second Opium War. For Saltoun, a great music aficionado, made Hope his Brigade-Major during the First Opium War mainly because Saltoun needed a quality cellist in his musical group (Beeching, 1975, pp. 279-280). Reaching staff rank, Hope's military skills and perhaps also his family relations to Lord Elgin, the Plenipotentiary of the 1860 expedition, brought about his appointment two decades after Saltoun's ears chanced upon him.

Hong Kong seemed unprepossessing -- someone described it as looking like a half-eaten Stilton cheese -- and there were fearful problems of lawlessness and ill-health in the early days. Predictions made four years earlier by the *Hong Kong Register* seemed to be coming true: "Hong Kong will be the resort and rendezvous of all the Chinese smugglers, opium smoking shops, and gambling houses will soon spread . . . the Island will be surrounded by floating brothels . . . ." The police were notorious for corruption and incompetence; many Americans and Europeans carried loaded revolvers. American and British seamen deserted their ships and joined Chinese pirates to get rich. It was said in 1845 that there were 25 respectable Chinese families and 26 brothels. But, worse than lawlessness, Hong Kong was beset by malaria and cholera (see pp. 153-155). What could be the impressions of a soldier posted there in the mid-19th century? Fortunately, a manuscript unearthed in 1978 provides some insight into a soldier's life in early HK.

A Soldier of the Queen: Hong Kong, 1850-1851

James Bodell was born in 1831, the son of an illiterate farm-worker knitter living in Leichestershire. He joined the 59th (the Leicestershire Regiment) at age 16, seeking money and adventure. Serving first in Ireland, he and the 59th reached Hong Kong after an appalling voyage of 235 days and an outbreak of cholera. Hong Kong had the reputation of being the worst possible place to be posted. His Regiment occupied the barracks close to the general hospital and two companies of the Royal Artillery.

Bodell (1982, pp. 56-59) wrote in his diary: "About half a mile towards Happy Valley were the sappers and miners . . . . on the hill above the cathedral were companies of the Ceylon Rifles. The total strength would be about 1,200." He continued:

> Each man had to provide himself with six suits of white clothing, pith hats and six hat covers in addition to the usual solder's kit and all this to be paid out of sixpence per diem. The first six months our Colonel thought of nothing but drill, heavy marching order, parade and four hours drill. About June the hospital became pretty full and the doctor had these heavy drills discontinued.
>
> During July, August and September we buried about 300 men. Everyone, native and European has this sickness. A man would appear in excellent health today and in a few hours became raving made with, as the doctors called it, remittent fever and in his grave the next day. My sore eye compelled me to go into the hospital in March, and I was tortured for several months by bad treatment. I became blind with my right eye. The new barracks was reported unhealthy and all the men were removed out of it.
>
> Several doctors arrived from England and these appeared to cope with the fever much more successfully than the old doctors. A Dr. Dickson took me in hand and instead of starving me he ordered one half fowl and half a bottle of Port each day and allowed me to exercise myself. In two weeks I left the hospital and my eye affected me for years. Poor Dr. Powell succumbed to the scourge, and died. I had an attack. If you had an attack and did not rally in 48 hours you would surely die. A John Preston occupied the next bed to me. One night about 8 o'clock the poor fellow commenced to eat bread and told me he had seen the good place and the bad place, and gave three loud cheers, and fell back in bed and expired.

With the fever and dysentery, the 59th Regiment within eight months after landing in Hong Kong could not furnish sufficient men to mount guard. These duties had to be performed principally by the Ceylon Rifles and Lascar Artillery. "Lascar" was considered a derogatory term since it was connected with laborers or coolies. A company of Lascar gunners was raised in India with the assistance of the British East India Company. Although paid much less than the British, Indian soldiers fought well in China. Energetic steps were taken to improve the men's health. Everyone took "barko"; bark of the cinchana tree which contained quinine, a malaria palliative.

Bodell reported that the medics were greatly puzzled by the epidemics that beset the soldiers in Hong Kong and felt the water was to blame. He said that two years after his regiment left Cork Barracks in 1849 only 62 remained out of 650 men. Those who were gone had died, deserted or declared "invalidated." "I did my best to get invalided by drinking vinegar, etc. to make me look pale so that I was sent to the Hospital Ship *Minden.* I went crawling up to the doctor, who said, 'My good man dress yourself. You are one of the healthiest men in the Regiment.' I retired crestfallen, my hopes of seeing Leicester vanished."

A new commanding officer, Lt. Colonel H. H. Graham, did much to improve conditions and by 1852 the Regiment was enjoying good health. By then Bodell was a sergeant, despite his having tried to desert. He subsequently lived in New Zealand and Australia, prospered greatly and returned to England twice, amazed with the improvements in his mother country.

More Opium Warfare

Warfare erupted again because China refused to honor her treaty obligations according to the foreigners' interpretations. Also, the British and French exaggerated incidents surrounding the Chapdelaine and *Arrow* affairs in efforts to get China's attention and embarrass her (see pp. 120-121). On October 23, 1856, the four Chinese forts below Canton were captured and dismantled. Next, the British Navy cannonaded Canton and Royal Marines searched the residence of Commissioner Yeh Ming-ch'en, Viceroy of Guangsi and Guangdong, whom they held responsible for the *Arrow* affair. Americans were as eager as the British to expand trade access, for concessions of the First Opium War were ignored and foreigners were still restricted to the old factories area. Mike Keenan, the American Consul in Hong Kong, watched the naval bombardment and brandished the Stars and Stripes before the enemy.

Although the British Navy controlled the Pearl River estuary up to Canton and sank junks at will, there were insufficient troops to hold the city. Reinforcements arrived from home despite heated debates in Parliament on the wisdom of further armed intervention. An Anglo-French expedition led by the 59th Regiment captured Canton. The expeditionary force was commanded by the experienced Lord Elgin, who was only 45 and a notable plenipotentiary with previous diplomatic successes in Jamaica and Canada where he had introduced responsible government. He had the face of a bewhiskered cherub, "his snow-white hair contrasting strongly with his sun-scorched face." Haunting him most of his life, most of his life, Elgin had his father's crushing debts to repay that came from the seventh Earl's passion for Greek sculptures.

Elgin sailed northeast. He was accompanied by the American and Russian Ambassadors, both of whom were ostensibly neutral observers but determined to secure their nations' share of any spoils that Britain and France might win. Arriving at the River Peiho leading to Peking, they captured the Taku forts and proceeded to Tientsin. Severely shaken by the forts' capture on June 26, 1858, China's officials signed the Treaty of Tientsin, which enabled foreign diplomatic missions to reside in Peking, opened more treaty ports to trade, making 16 in all, and agreed on an indemnity to cover British and French war expenses.

It was also conceded that representatives should be sent the following year to Peking to obtain the emperor's ratification of the treaty. As Peking delayed the visitation closer and closer to the deadline, what finally happened enkindled the Second Opium War.

Frederick Bruce, Lord Elgin's brother, and Admiral James Hope, the British naval commander, led the 1859 expedition. Upon their arrival at the mouth of the Peiho River, they discovered that the Taku forts had been rebuilt and an army of 50,000 commanded by the Qing Prince, Seng-ko-lin-ch'in, awaiting them. Hope was late in mounting his attack, and the Taku batteries opened fire with devastating effect. Disdaining cover in the warship leading his force, Hope was severely wounded. Transferred to another boat, he was wounded again. As the battle worsened for the British, Commodore Josiah Tattnall of the U.S. Navy ignored his country's neutrality declaring that "blood is thicker than water." He ordered his ships to tow the British reserves into battle and his sailors replaced British wounded and dead at their guns, but nothing could save the day (Graham, 1978, pp. 373-378).

Admiral Hope withdrew his fleet after losing four warships and 434 men. Victory over the "foreign barbarians" greatly enhanced Prince Seng-ko-lin-ch'in's prestige at court; but Britain and France were still determined that China should honor its treaty obligations and agreed that a combined force of 10,000 British and 7,000 French troops should be despatched to China as soon as possible.

Despite the 1859 Taku victory, the Qing Court was beset with internal unrest and its regular army was unable to exercise control over China's vast territory. Taiping rebels had broken the imperial troops near Canton, and Shanghai now relied upon British protection. To encourage the British to stay in Canton, its Governor-General gave them a lease of the Kowloon promontory, an area of only two square miles but very vital because it covered the northern approaches of Hong Kong harbor.

Lt. General Sir Hope Grant, a tall, dour, lean Scot (aforementioned cellist), became the military commander of the Anglo-French forces gathering in HK. Reporting to the Duke of Cambridge at the War Office on March 27, 1860, Hope wrote: "Kowloon will prove a much more healthy situation for troops. It also has excellent ground for artillery and brigade practice. I have accordingly encamped there the wings of the 31st and 99th Regiments, which keeps them from the temptations of the town, Victoria." Lord Elgin returned to HK as Plenipotentiary to lead the powerful armada to settle things once and for all.

Elgin sailed north on June 8, 1860. Grant and his staff paused at Shanghai for a few days. Lt. Colonel Garnet Wolseley, a future Field Marshal, reported on the dirt, filth and stench abounding everywhere. Hung around the walls in conspicuous places were small wooden cages containing human heads, some being the heads of pirates and those who had been convicted of assisting in the kidnapping of coolies by Americans and French.

All was in readiness for the retaking of the Taku Forts, including medical arrangements that had been deplorable in the 1853-56 Crimean War. The Allies sailed across the Gulf of Chihli towards the Taku forts where the British were repulsed the year before. This time, however, they veered northwards towards the town of Peh-tang eight miles from Taku. The landing party consisted of Brigadier Sutton's brigade hauling a nine-pounder and a rocket battery up the banks into firing range. As General Wolseley (1903) wrote:

> The first man to jump ashore and head up the mudbank was the brigadier, an old campaigner well known for his swearing propensities and famous as a game shot in South Africa. I shall never forget his appearance as he struggled through that mud. He had taken off trousers, boots and socks, and hung them over his brass scabbard sword which he carried over his shoulder. Picture a somewhat fierce and ugly bandy-legged little man thus accoutred in a big white helmet, clothed in a dirty jacket of red serge, below which a very short slate-coloured flannel shirt extending a few inches, cursing and swearing 'all round' at everybody and everything as he led his Brigade through the hateful mire.

"On reaching the shore," noted Robert Swinhoe (1861) of the Consular Service, "the Tartars retreated -- and the English army then advanced, the 60th Rifles to the right, and the Queen's on the left; the men struggled gallantly on through the vilest and most stinking slush, and in a few seconds the whole force was on the road." The Queen's (2nd Regiment of Foot) had joined the expedition from the Cape of Good Hope, while the 60th (the King's Royal Rifle Corps and today the Royal Green Jackets) had previously been stationed in India. That evening a party of the 60th and friendly Chinese entered Peh-tang to find four Chinese watchmen fast asleep and only a few wooden dummy cannon. Booby-traps were disarmed. Next morning, Peh-tang, noisome, smelly and surrounded by mud, surrendered to the French and British.

Ten days later the advance began towards the Taku Forts via Sinho and Tankku. Sinho was captured after British infantry and artillery subdued strong positions defended by Prince Seng-ko-lin-ch'in's Manchu cavalry. Brandishing outdated crossbows and swords against modern artillery, the Manchu cavalry were praised by Major-General Sir Robert Napier, who wrote: "They bore unflinchingly for a considerable time, such as fire as would have tried any troops in the world" (Yee, 1992, p. 61). Manchu horsemen fought gallantly as did the gunners, some of whom were tied to their guns by their legs to prevent them from fleeing. But they were no match for the invading forces. "It was common practice to murder the wounded," wrote a soldier (Swinhoe, 1861). "As the Sikhs rode past a prostrate wounded man, one would prick him with a spear's point, and if the unfortunate sufferer cried out or writhed under the pain inflicted, some of the party would dismount and deliberately saw his head off."

Sinho was a more formidable proposition than Peh-tang, but the Chinese fled leaving 45 outdated cannon behind. The attack on Taku was made by 2,500 British and 1,000 French as heavy guns from warships and six batteries of field guns hauled ashore engaged the enemy. Fortuitous for the aggressors, an eight-inch shell hit the powder magazine of the nearest fort and destroyed it with a huge explosion. Swift to take advantage, the combined navies moved closer and another lucky shot exploded a magazine in the northern fort. One by one, the forts were quickly captured with Anglo-French losses of 358 casualties -- far more than expected because of the spirited defense. Nevertheless, the expedition had achieved its first objective.

Friendly villagers inhabiting the countryside beyond the forts sold provisions at "twenty times the proper price." The troops and sailors were delighted to find ice that the Chinese had saved from winter and drank the ice melted or laid it beneath rugs on which they took cool siestas. As Lord Elgin commented, "A man scorns his gin if it is not well iced."

The march on Peking continued; it was an unequal struggle as the Chinese relied on antiquated arms and tactics that made much of bluff. They used a huge musket called a Gilgal which was serviced by three men, two of whom supported the Gilgal's barrel on their shoulders while the third aimed and fired it. Shooting a ball of about one pound weight, the weapon had the deadly tendency of blowing up in the soldiers' faces, which was lessened by reducing the amount of powder they fired. Chinese arms also included outdated crossbows, swords, and spears. In contrast, the Royal Artillery was equipped with six mortars and a mountain battery of twelve 12-pounder (weight of the projectile) howitzers; the siege train consisted of ten 8-inch (diameter of projectile) guns, ten 24-pounders, five 8-inch mortars and five 5.5-inch mortars. Two batteries were also armed with six more of the new 12-pounder Armstrong breech-loading field guns to be used against massed enemy troops.

During the Crimean War, artillery technology advanced considerably when it became possible to fire projectiles more accurately and further through the innovation of rifling, that is, grooving the bore of the gun to part a spin to the projectile, similar to spiral-throwing the American football. Sir Robert Armstrong produced a cast-iron projectile coated wtih lead and fired it from a rifled barrel. Not only did Armstrong's innovations dictate that the piece had to be breech loading but stresses forced upon the barrel by the spinning of projectiles meant that the barrel required much stronger engineering than could be produced by cast tubes. Despite its advances, the Armstrong cannon was clumsy and not always reliable. However, its grape shot devastated the Manchu cavalry and compelled the Chinese foot soldiers to flee.

Chanchiawan, the town near Peking, was given over to plunder and rape after its capture. Old soldiers with uneasy memories of the Crimean winter stole furs from pawnshops. Chinese women suffered most: one house broken into was full of females aged two to 50. Sticky tins of opium lay on the floor and the air stank of the raw drug. All of the women, disdaining dishonor, had done their best to commit suicide. "More of them, beating their breasts, condemned the opium for its slow work," reported a military interpreter. Fortunately, a sympathetic chaplain and army surgeon with a stomach pump saved all but one of them (Swinhoe, 1861).

Lord Elgin next advanced west of Tung-Chow towards Peking. On September 22nd, Prince Kung announced that the Emperor was willing to call off hostilities if the Allies agreed to return the Taku forts and leave China. Lord Elgin replied that his forces would not begin to discuss terms until all hostages, captured during the previous weeks, were returned. With French columns on the left and the British on the right, the advance on Peking continued.

On October 6, 1860, 3,000 French reached the Summer Palace which lay a few miles from Peking. The Palace was a Chinese fairyland -- 80 square miles of park containing 30 palatial imperial residences, some roofed with gold, and 170 other equally astonishing buildings, mostly designed by Jesuit missionaries. China's greatest treasure trove, the splendors of Summer Palace represented not only the Manchu dynasty, but China itself. Despite its magnificence, it was defended only by a helpless band of 480 imperial eunuchs, some of whom ran towards the French infantry, crying out in high pitched voices, "Don't come within the sacred precincts." They were shot down in cold blood while the rest fled. The Emperor had wisely departed for Jehol two weeks earlier.

To placate the aggressors, Prince Kung released some of the hostages who had been captured when sent to discuss surrender terms. Their barbaric treatment infuriated Lord Elgin. Although much loot had been taken from the Summer Palace, Elgin later ordered its complete destruction as a punitive lesson never to be forgotten. Popular to Britons later as the general they nicknamed "Chinese Gordon" and famed for his martyrdom at Khartoum, young Captain Charles Gordon followed orders when his First Division commanded by Major-General Sir John Michel was ordered to burn and devastate the Summer Palace. Gordon wrote to his mother, "(We) went out, and, after pillaging it, burned the whole place, destroying in a vandal-like manner most valuable property which would not be replaced for four million . . . You can scarely imagine the beauty and magnificence of the places we burnt. It made one's heart sore to burn them . . . " (Spence, 1969, p. 74).

Captain Hart Dunne of the Wiltshire Regiment found a very curious breed of small dog which was presented to Queen Victoria. It was Britain's first Pekingese, a lap dog. Aptly named "Lootie," it ran happily about Buckingham Palace until its death 12 years later.

The final objective was now the occupation of Peking. On October 9th, the British and French anxiously faced the city walls; Grant needed to bring the hostilities to a speedy conclusion before the harsh China winter set in. Peking's walls were 40' high and 60' thick. Moreover, the Chinese army, although defeated, was still a coherent force lying to the north of the city. Word was passed that the capital would be taken by storm if the Anting Gate was not surrendered by noon, October 13th. "At a quarter to twelve there was no sign of surrender," reported one soldier. "The guns were loaded and the mantlets cleared away, the 1st Royal Scots manning their prepared position. The chiefs waited with watches in their hands for the eventful moment when suddenly the huge gate opened signalling surrender. Our men and the French rushed in. Peking was ours" (Tulloch, 1903).

On October 24, 1860 Elgin marched into the Hall of Ceremonies with a large escort and left with everything he sought (see pp. 40-41). In Hong Kong, all of Kowloon peninsula up from the harbor to Boundary Road was ceded to Britain in perpetuity. The Treaty of Tientsin and Convention of Peking established friendly relations between England and China's Qing rulers for 40 years, whereby the latter also profited from the sale of opium imports and tea exports.

The Chinese people have always regarded them as "unequal treaties" and resented the loss of territory. As General Sir Hope Grant (Wolseley, 1869) reported:

> Kowloon was a spot which I was most anxious to gain immediate possession -- firstly because its occupation was absolutely essential for the defense of Hong Kong harbor and the town of Victoria; secondly because it was an open healthy spot, admirably suited for a camping ground. Thirdly, because at the conclusion of the war it would be a salubrious site for the erection of barracks, required for the HK garrison; and lastly if we did not take it, the French probably would.

Stonecutters Island was also ceded (now merged with Kowloon through reclamation; see Map 2), an important military base for 150 years and where the first contingent of People's Liberation Army (PLA) troops were barracked in 1997.

More Unequal Treaties, 1861-1900

One lesson of the Crimean War was that fixed land-based defenses had advantages over naval guns; Sevastopol's Russian defenses had inflicted serious damage on the Allied Fleet. Ships, firing from unstable and moving platforms, and with armament designed for action at close range, were very vulnerable to the fire of coast artillery. With everything else being equal, there was little doubt that well-sited coast batteries were a match for any seaborne attack. The Defense Committee of the Cabinet in London reporting in 1863 on defenses and armaments said: "Hong Kong is important as the only territorial possession of the British Crown in China. It is a refuge for our countryman, in case of emergency, and it contains considerable military and naval establishments. The trade, which it serves to protect, yields a revenue of at least five millions sterling at the national exchange. The harbor is a fine sheet of water approached by only two entrances, one of which is very narrow." The Committee recommended that artillery batteries should be established on Stonecutters Island, the western edge of Kowloon Peninsula, West Point or Possession Point, Kellett Island (off Central; subsumed by reclamation), and Lei Yue Mun or Lyemun (see Map 3).

This report was shelved when the Treasury hesitated to fund the proposals, but three years later, the Director of Ordnance reported: "The general state of our fortifications is good; they are armed with ten pieces of smooth-bore ordnance. There are in reserve 20 pieces of iron ordnance, including six 7-inch guns (the Armstrongs) and 57 pieces of brass ordinance. The magazines are generally in good condition, containing over 6,000 barrels of powder. The Field Artillery consists of three 12-pounder Armstrong guns with 120 rounds per gun." HK's artillery defenses continued to be reorganized and improved as lessons were learnt from wars elsewhere and as more sophisticated equipment became available. For example, after the Franco-Prussian War in 1871, twelve batteries were converted into field artillery for greater mobility.

Hong Kong remained an unattractive military posting because of problems with pirates, the police, public health and sanitation, the water supply and the colony's general administration. Moreover, there were two potential adversaries. Declaring war on Turkey in 1877, Russia succeeded in reaching Constantinople. After establishing its primary Pacific naval base at Vladivostok, Russia also reaped the same "most favored nation" benefits in China as enjoyed by the British, Americans and French. Closer to home, Chinese Customs harassed HK, stopping and searching all ships, claiming that China was losing revenue due to smuggling by HK-registered vessels. Against this troubling background, some proposed that the Hong Kong Volunteers, disbanded in 1866, be revived.

In 1877, HK's garrison consisted of 109 men of the Royal Artillery, 20 Royal Engineers, a battalion of infantry numbering 916 men, two Lascar companies of 176 Indians, and 18 in the Army Hospital Corps. This meager force brought about reactivation of the Volunteers in 1878. As the war scare eased, the Volunteers declined. Moreover the eccentric Governor, Sir John Pope Hennessy, fell out with the garrison commander, General Donovan, mainly over the question of sanitation. While the Governor insisted that local customs should be respected by right of China's long, continuous civilization, the General and most of the European community believed local sanitation problems were abominable (see pp. 175-179 & 225). Utterly incompatible, the two organized rival dinner parties on Queen Victoria's birthday in 1880 (Endacott, 1973, p. 178).

Four months after the next Governor, Sir George Bowen, arrived in 1883, a powerful naval squadron flying the Tricolor appeared in the harbor. Raising alarm, the French Hoche class battleships carried 13.4-inch guns weighing 75 tons each, clear testimony to gunnery advances. Many believed, correctly, that France, Britain's old enemy, had ambitions in Indo-China, now Vietnam. Brilliant when young (Rector of Ionian University of Corfu at the age of 26) but a pompous egotist in later life, Bowen travelled widely, such as taking the baths in Japan, and spent only 15 of his 32 months as Governor in HK (see 130-131). While relations with China went smoothly in what has been called Britain's 'informal empire,' the French and Russians aroused suspicions.

Lt. General J. N. Sargent now commanded the HK garrison and was one of the first to propose that the border with China be extended through the New Territories (opposed by Bowen). Energetic, well-acquainted with Asia through three tours, and a Francophobic, General Sargent reconnoitered the many bays about Hong Kong to find that enemy ships could devastate the colony at ease from many anchorages. His studies and proposals for new artillery defenses matched those of Sir William Crossman, an expert military engineer, who had designed fortifications for HK in 1881 but were never developed.

Sargent brought about the costly installation of 45 new guns, including eight 10-inch and twelve 9-inch breech loaders, with the maximum range of less than eight miles (9.2-incher firing 380 lb. projectile). Today, one of the 10-inch guns can be seen at Belcher's Gardens and a 9.2-inch gun remains at Hong Kong University in the garden of the Vice-Chancellor's residence (Rollo, 1992, pp. 54-67).

Although General Sargent successfully installed new artillery defenses, he and Governor Bowen continued to relate poorly and feuded. In the end, Bowen's connections through the Colonial Office proved mightier than Sargent's ties with the Secretary of State for War. To the regret of HK's senior civil servants who actually administered the colony, such as Colonial Secretary James Stewart Lockhart, Sargent was recalled home, where he wrote a book ridiculing Bowen and his supporters. See Welsh (1993) for more on "Fortress Hong Kong."

The Admiralty's Foreign Intelligence Committee decided that HK should be made secure from attack and independent of assistance from the fleet, since the colony was regarded now as vital to the Empire as a naval base and refuge for merchant shipping. Indeed, when the French squadron entered HK's harbor, most of the British squadron was away in northern waters with only three small ships in the colony. Governor Bowen had fears about Hong Kong's defenses:

> I am constantly urging on the Home Government that our position here is somewhat humiliating -- for the French have four ironclads in China, whereas we have only one and Hong Kong could be taken any day by a *coup de main* . . . the French could sweep our ships from the seas and bring 5,000 men in three days to seize Hong Kong. The English are defenseless although they have paid 20,000 pounds a year. If this money had been spent on fortifications, Hong Kong might now be as safe as Gibraltar.

The funds mentioned were a subsidy paid by the HK Government to the Imperial Government for maintaining the colony's defenses. However, no French or Russian threat to HK developed because the foreign powers chose to carve up Qing China. By 1885, France had consolidated her position in Tonkin and Annamand British trade interests were well-established in HK and the treaty ports. Other countries were also deeply involved in China's affairs -- the U.S. with her Protestant missions, Russia's trans-Siberian railway and mining interests in Mongolia and Manchuria; Germany's designs on Kiaochow [with chief city of Qingdao (Tsingtao) in Shandong (Jiaozhou) Province], and Japan was poised to take Korea.

Japan had occupied Korea in 1874 but withdrew after objections by the British Minister at Peking, Sir Thomas Wade. Destined to become Britain's leading sinologist and originator of the famed Wade-Giles system of romanizing Chinese, young Wade had been one of Lord Elgin's tough interpreters that Elgin characterized as "the uncontrollably fierce barbarian" (Yee, 1992, pp. 56-58).

When Japan overwhelmed China's fleet and army in 1895, the contrast between China's feudal and corrupt state versus Japan's Meiji modernization in one generation became vividly clear. Besides the ineptness of China's military, corruption at the highest levels deprived her ships and army of shells for their newly purchased Armstrong and Krupp guns. Harsher than treaties with Britain and other powers, the Treaty of Shimonoseki ceded Formosa, the Pescadore Islands, and an indemnity of 230 taels of silver (Walsh, 1993, pp. 315-316). China's indemnity to Japan in 1895 was ten times that paid to Britain after the First Opium War in 1842. Although the Treaty of Nanking ceded HK to Britain, the colony no doubt seemed puny compared to Formosa.

Therefore, Japan and Western nations competed for spheres of influence as China disintegrated. Yet, as each nation sought to carve out and protect its own interests, their collective wolfishness somehow helped to preserve China's integrity as a state. Before 1900, most of China's outlying tributaries had been lopped off: Britain in Burma, France occupying Indo-China; Russia was north of the Amur River, and Germany had Kiaochow.

To avert further disintegration, China reluctantly agreed in the 1898 Convention of Peking to concede more territory. From Boundary Road in Kowloon, HK's border was extended 25 miles to the northern shore of the Shun Chun River (see Map 2). Named the New Territories (NT), the land was leased for 99 years, unlike the rest of Hong Kong which had been ceded to Britain in perpetuity. That historic lease of the NT expired on June 30, 1997.

The NT became inestimably valuable. First, it enhanced the colony's defense; HK would have greater warning of any enemy coming by land. Secondly, agricultural land provided food. And years later, the NT provided reservoirs and land for housing developments, an airport, the container-port, and promoted Kowloon's expansion.

When the British took possession, many villagers resisted and some skirmishes occurred. On April 15, 1899, a company of Indians in the HK Regiment confronted 1,200 Chinese led by the Tang clan in Kam Tin who opened fire with entrenched artillery. The Volunteers arrived with maxim guns and the protesters fled after 200 Chinese were killed. Two weeks before Hong Kong's return to China on July 1, 1997, Law (1997) reported on New Territories villagers who discussed the "Tang war." Many said that they would rather 'forgive (the British) and forget the brief war.'

Early Years of the Twentieth Century

China's turmoil continued in the new century. The Boxer Rebellion of 1900 brought swift retribution from foreign powers. In frantic opposition to every-thing foreign, the Boxers murdered Christian converts and threatened Europeans and Chinese Christians whom they besieged in Peking's foreign compound. However, the siege collapsed after 55 days when a relief force of 20,000 men consisting (in order of size) of Japanese, Russian, British, American and French troops reached Peking. According to Seagrave (1992), his evidence portrays the seige as far less dangerous to the foreigners and characterizes the rescue forces as less heroic than historians have made it out to be. Seagrave wrote that British journalists resident in Peking fabricated their reports to unsuspecting editors of *The Times* for self-gain and nationalism, and the blunders and actions of the "rescue" forces fell into the realms of comic opera and greed.

After the Chinese Revolution of 1911 led by Dr. Sun Yat-sen, the numbers of refugees fleeing to Hong Kong increased dramatically. There was much discus-sion over the inadequate defenses of the colony, and some suggested that a rail-way be built around the south of the island so that trains carrying quick-firing guns could repel an enemy landing. As new, costly guns were placed on Stone-cutters Island and at Belcher's forts, the HK Government committed a staggering 20% of its annual budget to defense.

The First World War led to the withdrawal of British regular troops for service in Europe, leaving a seriously depleted garrison. The Royal Artillery occupied its war stations until September 1915 and the Hong Kong Volunteers initially manned block houses at strategic points in the hills above Kowloon. One Volun-teer (Bruce, 1991, p. 113) wrote:

> The whole Corps paraded every evening, and all Volunteers were ordered to be in uniform at all times with their rifles, equipment, and ammunition within easy reach. The 'Alarm,' a bomb detonated in the Naval Yard, was to be the signal to converge on the cricket pitch. This alarm never went off, but periodically the midday time signal, or an extra loud Chinese firecracker, brought perspiring gentlemen hurtling from their offices, feverishly donning equipment as they ran.

British and Chinese gave generously to British war charities and presented a Vicker FB5 aircraft to the Royal Flying Corps. Germans were interned. They were "our erstwhile friends, and quite ready to be effusively familiar," noted one Volunteer. "It was embarrassing for a zealous sentry to be hailed vociferously, as 'Good Old Bill' and asked whether he has remembered to load his rifle." Hand-ed tools to construct an earthen stage for a theater, the Germans tunnelled 180 feet beneath the wire. Their mass escape was foiled by a vigilant sentry and an Indian constable captured three escapees.

Of the powers that defeated Germany, Japan reigned supreme in Asia. As E. Suzuki, the Japanese Consul, put it to a cheering thong at the Hong Kong Club,

"Japan decided to extend her sphere of activity, sweeping the enemy away from the Pacific and Indian oceans in cooperation with the British Navy, and assisting in the enduring work in the Mediterranean, in addition to her latest efforts in Siberia." Although China had also participated in World War I alongside the Allies, the Versailles negotiators bypassed China's expectations of retrieving Kiaochow from Germany and gave it instead to Japan. Protesting the Versailles Treaties, the May 4th Movement of 1919 began a long boycott of foreign goods and demands for a new China. Chinese intellectuals and students also expressed disgust and hostility towards the ineffectiveness of their country's leaders. Nationalism grew apace and many Chinese increasingly focused on Hong Kong as another tangible reminder of China's past weakness.

By 1920, there was little enthusiasm or money in Britain for military matters. Moreover, the Naval Armament Limitation Treaty of the major powers had serious repercussions for Hong Kong; for it said that no changes were to be made to fortifications between latitude 30 degrees north and the equator, thus including Hong Kong but not Singapore. Governor Cecil Clementi reported in 1926 that:

> The naval and military forces at present available for the defense of the colony would not be able to hold any part of the New Territories against a powerful enemy, and that it would therefore be open to such an enemy to establish himself along the ridge and the hill range above Kowloon, which completely dominates HK harbor, and from which position he could direct fire upon the principal docks, forts, and naval and military establishments of the colony as well as upon all shipping in the harbour.

While HK was very vulnerable from the north, it was equally vulnerable from other directions if the enemy had air and sea supremacy. British defense forces were seen as inadequate, consisting of one flotilla of submarines, four sloops and five river boats, 3,000 regular troops and 600 Volunteers but no air force. Fixed armaments in the forts were barely sufficient to deter hostile ships; yet reminiscent of General Sargent (see p. 83) were simply too few to prevent enemy landings on the island and the pennisula concurrently.

Fortunately, China was preoccupied by internal problems, and relations with Japan were ostensibly good judging by the colony's welcome in 1928 to a large Japanese fleet of three battle cruisers, a cruiser and 16 destroyers. Six thousand Japanese sailors visited horse races, watched special cinema performances, enjoyed trips on trams and buses, and were presented with cigarette packets bearing crossed British and Japanese flags.

Relations between Britain and Japan eroded in time, especially after Britain and America forced Japan to modify her arbitrary demands for a predominant position in China. Also in 1922, Japan had grudgingly agreed that her capital ships would be no more than a third of the tonnage of the combined British and American fleets. A third humiliation for Japan came when Britain abrogated the Anglo-Japanese Alliance to develop her special relationship with America.

The Second World War and HK's "Lasting Honour"

In 1937, reviewing Hong Kong defense in detail, the British Chiefs of Staff concluded that in the event of war the colony would be untenable without reinforcements. Yet they decided that the existing garrison had to fight even to its demise in order to encourage Chinese resistance. Loss of HK's port facilities would be a grievous blow to China since 60% of its arms passed through HK. War with Germany in 1939 compelled the Admiralty to withdraw their major units to the Indian Ocean and reinforce the home and Mediterranean fleets. An alarming Japanese expeditionary force landing at Bias Bay only 35 miles from HK and Canton was captured. When France fell in June 1940, HK's isolation seemed almost complete, as Britain faced the necessity of keeping a powerful naval force in the Mediterranean, which left virtually no ships to defend HK and Malaya. With Holland's defeat, Japan rejoiced over its prospects of seizing the Dutch East Indies and its abundant oil, rubber, tin, bauxite and other resources. First, the Japanese looked to taking Hong Kong, Singapore and the Philippines.

Five months before Japan invaded HK, the Canadian-born Major General, A. E. Grasett, HK's general officer commanding, was posted home to London. Travelling via Ottawa, he briefed the Canadians on the need for reinforcements. Churchill was skeptical about sending Canadians to the colony: "It is a question of timing. There is no objection to the approach being made (to the Canadians for two battalions) as proposed; but a further decision should be taken before the battalions actually sailed." Two days before the small brigade with the Royal Rifles of Canada and the Winnipeg Grenadiers under Brigadier J. K. Lawson sailed from Vancouver, a brief arrived from London:

> The task of the Hong Kong garrison is to defend the Colony against external attack and to deny the use of the harbour and dry dock to the enemy. The threat: The Japanese are established on the mainland, are carrying out operations in the vicinity of the frontier, and are in possession of a number of air bases within easy reach of the Colony. They hold command of the sea and are therefore in a position to occupy the surrounding islands at will . . . .

Neither Canadian battalion was adequately trained for war; both had been stagnating on perfunctory garrison duties. Combat-ready Canadians were earmarked for Britain and the invasion of Europe. The two battalions reached HK on November 16, 1941 and made a good first impression as they marched through the city. Routed via Manila, their 212 vehicles would never arrive in time.

The church parade at St. John's Cathedral in Victoria on Sunday, December 7, 1941 was interrupted by an officer suddenly entering the church and whispering to Major General C. M. Maltby, Gen. Grasett's successor. With news suggesting that war was imminent, the entire HK garrison, including the multinational Hong Kong Volunteer Defence Corps, stood-to in battle positions.

On the mainland, beyond Kowloon, the 2nd Battalion of the Royal Scots, the

5/7 Rajputs and 2/14 Punjabis had been occupying trenches and pillboxes on the Gin-Drinkers' Line for four weeks. Behind them the Middlesex Regiment, the Volunteers and Royal Artillery manned coastal artillery and machine guns. Motor torpedo boats of the Royal Navy patrolled the sea approaches. Hong Kong was primed for war. At Pearl Harbor, 3,700 miles away that same Sunday morning, radar picked up the approach of many aircraft and a midget enemy submarine was sunk near the harbor. Yet inexplicably, the alarm was not raised.

At 8 AM, Monday, December 8th, without declaration of war Japanese aircraft attacked HK and destroyed the few, outdated RAF reconnaissance planes at Kai Tak Airport. Although the airstrip was badly damaged, gallant American and Chinese civilian pilots ferried people to Free China, about 275 in all from December 8-10, including the family of China's Finance Minister.

An hour after the Japanese attacked on the 8th, the Volunteer Field Engineers blew up the bridges on the border and the Punjabi covering force started a gradual withdrawal, imposing maximum delay and casualties on the enemy advancing out of China. Japanese tactics were to push on at the fastest possible speed, by-passing opposition which could be mopped up later; their ability to move rapidly and stealthily, especially at night, disturbed General Maltby.

On Hong Kong Island, theaters, cinemas and some restaurants still operated normally. The *South China Morning Post* on December 9th reported: "Hong Kong woke yesterday to find itself at war. This was a shock for all except those who listened to the radio all night."

At 11PM, Colonel Doi Techichi, leading three battalions, fell with devastating suddenness on the Royal Scots' 8th platoon holding the Shingmun Redoubt (200 meters south of the Shingmun or Jubilee Reservoir). The stronghold was on the west end of the Gin Drinkers' line, which ran along the mountainous area from Tsuen Wan along the Shing Mun River to Shatin (see Map 2). The line was so-called because it had been a popular picnic area. Throwing hand grenades into air ventilation chimneys, Col. Doi's infiltration teams entered the tunnels from which 18 of the Royal Scots reached the neighboring Rajput position. The last of the Royal Scots held out for a further eleven hours before "friendly fire" from a British shell destroyed their pill-boxes.

Having punctured a gaping hole in the Gin Drinkers' Line, Colonel Doi, to his dismay, was ordered on December 10th to withdraw immediately for he was in another regiment's sector. However, after Doi's achievement was recognized, his Japanese forces attacked in great strength. Of the four Royal Scots rifle company commanders, two were killed and the other two wounded in subsequent fighting north of Kowloon.

At midday on December 11th, General Maltby ordered the withdrawal of all troops to HK Island, which was carried out successfully without casualties. Dockyards, power station and cement works were all destroyed by the British and merchant ships were sunk. With the destruction of Kai Tak's runways, HK was now totally isolated. The battle on the NT mainland had not amounted to a major defeat, but numerous Royal Scots casualties and the speed of the Japanese advance boded ill for the future. There was no disguising the enemy's complete air superiority nor the accuracy of their mobile artillery which started firing across the harbor to destroy one pill-box after another. Without air reconnaissance, the British could not discover if the Japanese Navy would enter the fray.

At 7 PM on December 18th's exceptionally dark night, Col. Doi watched his 2nd Battalion silently embark in small collapsible assault craft. "Halfway across the harbor, our attempt had gone undetected because the grounded ships concealed our move," he wrote later. "But time and again the water was lit by flare of burning heavy oil in the storage tanks on the shore opposite." The attack fell at Lei Yue Mun (see Map 3), whereas General Maltby expected the main attack towards the northwest. Intriguingly, when the Japanese attacked Singapore, Lt. Gen. A. E. Percival expected them in the northeast instead of coming from the northwest!

As battalions of Japanese stormed ashore, stumbling over their wounded, they were machine-gunned by 5/7 Rajputs. Canadian Brigadier J. K. Lawson's West Brigade headquarters was at the strategically important Wong Nei Chong Gap between towering Mount Nicholson and Mount Butler (see Map 3). Situated in the island's center, the main lines of communication between East and West Brigades ran through the Gap. Canadian reserves, totally inadequate in numbers and training, had already been committed.

At 7 AM on December 19th, the Royal Scots, almost two miles to the northwest, received a desperate telephone call for help from Brigadier Lawson who said that his headquarters was surrounded. Responding, A Company, Royal Scots hurried in trucks up the narrow, winding road towards the Gap and came under heavy fire so that less than a dozen men reached Lawson, who went outside to fight it out. A Japanese machine gunner caught him in the open and he was seen to fall. His body was subsequently found by Colonel Shoji who said in tribute, "I ordered the temporary burial of the officer on the battleground on which he had died so heroically" (Lindsay, 1978, p. 130). Had Lawson not been chosen to command this brigade, he would certainly have reached high rank in the Canadian Army that participated in D-Day and played such a vital role in defeating Germany throughout 1944-45.

By December 19th, the Japanese were in possession of much of the high ground in the east of the Island. General Maltby asked Brigadier Wallis, commanding the Eastern Brigade, whether he should move the Royal Rifles of Canada to the west. The advantage of the proposed move lay in combining the strength of both East and West brigades to secure the Wong Nei Chong Gap. At his headquarters almost four miles to the east of the gap, Wallis appreciated the advantages but felt that the Royal Rifles, the only unit still largely remaining to him, was unable to move across that rugged, unreconnoitered country. Even highly trained, disciplined regulars that knew the area well would have found such a maneuver difficult if not impossible against such a formidable enemy. Instead, Brigadier Wallis withdrew to the south towards Stanley to join British forces enabling the enemy to continue their penetration between the two brigades, thus splitting the defenses with disastrous consequences. Despite valiant efforts, the brigades were never able to reunite. Wallis' Brigade, cut off near Stanley, could contribute little to the fighting.

A Company of the Winnipeg Grenadiers recaptured Mount Butler. "Grenades started to come over," recalled Private J. Pollock, "Company Sergeant Major J. R. Osborn kept throwing them back . . . ." Twice the enemy launched major attacks and were beaten off both times. The defensive positions became smaller as more soldiers were wounded. Osborn's calmness and courage had a steadying effect. He was a lean, granite-jawed, ex-able seaman who had fought in the Battle of Jutland before farming in Saskatchewan and enlisting in the Winnipeg Grenadiers. Although militia, the battalion had a small nucleus of regular non-commissioned officers.

"CSM Osborn and I were discussing what was to be done," wrote Sergeant Pugsley afterwards. "When a grenade dropped beside him, he rolled on to the grenade and was killed. I firmly believe he did this on purpose and so saved the lives of myself and at least six other men." Osborn was awarded the Victoria Cross, Britain's highest decoration for valor in the face of the enemy. A former British barracks in Hong Kong was named after him.

At 1:30 PM on December 19th, General Maltby ordered a general advance to recapture the key ground, but fire support did not materialize and the attacks were not coordinated, partly because Brigadier Lawson's death had not been taken into account. The Royal Navy's two motor torpedo flotillas, meanwhile, had been attacking Japanese light naval craft, shooting at Japanese positions and generally presenting a thorn in General Sakai's open flanks -- the sea, until most of the boats had been sunk or damaged on or about December 19th. Thereafter, naval forces largely fought as infantry as did the few Royal Air Force personnel.

Although British artillery inflicted many Japanese casualties, a series of disasters prevented their giving close infantry support. At Stanley Gap, gunners had been drawn into the infantry fight and "four medium 3.7-inch howitzers and two anti-tank guns were captured in the action," so wrote Colonel Doi Teihichi, who quickly put them into action on Mt. Cameron. "They were of considerable aid to my regiment." About then, British Fortress HQ received bitter reports that enemy artillery fire had become far more efficient; every round exploding instead of the customary one in three. Despite Japan's quality products today, Japanese shells often failed to explode in the battle for Hong Kong, such as a nine-inch shell that penetrated British Fortress HQ's plotting room but did not explode. The words, "Woolwich Arsenal," were plainly stamped on its case.

By December 20th, the exhausted, remaining troops of Western Brigade held an ill-defined and confused line facing east. Many hospitals were bombed and mortared indiscriminately; the servicemen's dependents and Chinese civilians alike faced a terrifying ordeal. Everyone waited in vain for Chinese troops rumored to intervene at any moment in the rear of the Japanese forces. A grim Christmas found the defenders in desperate straits after 18 days of fighting. They lacked rest, organization, supplies, mobile artillery, aircraft and much more.

General Archibald Wavell, commander designate of all Allied land, sea and air forces in the SW Pacific, was in no position to send Christmas greetings. After conferring with Chiang Kai-shek, Wavell's return to Rangoon coincided with an air raid during which he counted 17 bombs within 50 yards of his trench.

Later that day, General Maltby told Governor Young that further resistance was impossible. There was serious lack of water and ammunition and casualties were extraordinarily heavy, particularly among officers who had led from the front. Japanese soldiers were committing horrible atrocities against prisoners and nurses, plunging their bayonets into everyone in their frustration with the unexpectedly prolonged defense.

An unflappable Old Etonian, Sir Mark Young, like Maltby's staff officers, had forsaken the safety of underground bunkers and set a fine example of courage. Scornfully rejecting two earlier Japanese proposals that the British surrender the colony, he now agreed with General Maltby that further resistance was impossible and lives must be saved.

What went wrong? Why was Hong Kong defeated on its own ground? Students of the campaign find the speed of the Japanese victory astonishing, since they had no great numerical superiority in infantry. "Primarily this was due to the advantages which in such circumstances must always lie with the attacker. The defenders, too few in numbers and thinly spread, had no knowledge where the weight of the attack is to be anticipated. So it can only be expected that the assault, with the advantage of surprise, pressed forward in great strength at a few points, will succeed in breaking through" (Lindsay, 1978, p. 197).

Achieving a classic assault, the Japanese then pushed forward to capture the commanding heights dominating HK Island. Complete lack of air and sea support made defeat a foregone conclusion. Moreover, there being insufficient troops and deficiencies in equipment and training stemmed from the basic weakness of a democracy hoping above all else to avoid war. Other fundamental reasons for the defeat were: poor intelligence; a weak defense plan based on holding the Gin-Drinkers' Line with forces incapable of conducting a rapid, highly-flexible defense against a first-rate foe. Tactically, the defenders of HK were outclassed as were all Western armies throughout the early months of the Pacific War.

The Japanese 38th Division consisted of highly-trained troops with a wealth of battle experience after years of fighting in China. Out of 11,000 defending the colony, 2,113 were killed and 1,332 were seriously wounded in action. Many more would die in captivity. Still, political and moral reasons mandated that Hong Kong had to be defended and held as long as possible. Five days before the last shot was fired, Prime Minister Winston Churchill signalled to Governor Young, on December 21st, 1941: "The enemy should be compelled to expend the utmost life and equipment . . . Every day that you are able to maintain your resistance you and your men can win the lasting honour which we are sure will be your due." Churchill later wrote in his history of the war: "These orders were obeyed in spirit and to the letter . . . The Colony had fought a good fight. They had won indeed 'the lasting honour' "(Lindsay, 1978, p. 203).

Many Chinese would have been seriously discouraged from continuing their weary and interminable struggle against Japan if Britain had lacked the courage and determination to resist. Within weeks of their victory, although seriously weakened by casualties, regiments of the 38th Division were despatched to Timor, Java and Sumatra, where they ultimately suffered defeat by General Douglas MacArthur's armies in the savage New Guinea campaign.

The Hidden Years, 1942-1945

Although the fighting ended on Christmas Day 1941, British, American, and Canadian civilians were imprisoned to shift for themselves at Stanley Internment Camp -- 1,100 men, 1,000 women, 340 children and 80 infants. Morale gradually dissipated as everyone grew weaker fromhunger and hope of early release for most evaporated. In June 1942, 350 Americans were repatriated to be followed by Canadian civilians in September 1943.

Conditions for the more than 7,000 prisoners of war were very much worse. Their years of captivity at Shumshuipo Barracks and other camps fell loosely into four stages: First, the period of infections including wound sepsis, dysentery and a very serious outbreak of diphtheria; then came the period of deficiency diseases; next, the long period of slow decline which lasted until March 1945; and finally, five months of relative stability until Japan's surrender. Each was characterized by substandard nutrition including serious vitamin deficiencies.

The greatest single tragedy of the "hidden years" occurred in September 1942 -- 843 out of 1,816 British POWs were killed or drowned when the Japanese ship, the *Lisbon Maru*, shipping them to work in Japan was sunk by the American submarine, USS *Grouper*, near the Chusan archipelago. Armed and transporting Japanese troops, the *Lisbon Maru* bore no sign that she carrying POWs. The Japanese crew tried to prevent the POWs from escaping from the sealed holds and shot some in the sea, before orders changed and survivors were picked up from neighboring islands and the sea. Three POWs escaped into Free China to reveal the atrocity (Lindsay, 1981, pp. 150-160).

Some prisoners in Hong Kong were in touch with the British Army Aid Group run by British officers and assorted escapees in China. They were assisted by HK resistance groups consisting of dedicated, courageous Chinese. BAAG was led by Colonel Lindsay Ride, former commander of the HK Volunteers' Field Ambulance Medical unit. However, key Chinese couriers who smuggled information were arrested, tortured and executed in July 1943. This led in turn to the arrest of Colonel L. A. Newnham of the Middlesex Regiment, Captain D. Ford of the Royal Scots, and Flight Lieutenant N. B. Gray, who were finally shot on a beach after prolonged torture.

Supreme courage was also shown by Captain M. A. Ansari, 5/7 Rajputs, who was the only Indian officer left with Indian POWs in one camp. Also in touch with the BAAG, Ansari was the mainstay of resistance among the Indians -- only to be betrayed by another Indian. Captain Ansari was decapitated with others in a cruel and bloody affair. In 1946, King George VI approved the posthumous award of the George Cross to the four officers named in recognition of their most conspicuous gallantry. The George Cross is the highest recognition for courage which can be awarded in such circumstances. Each won it in the torture chamber when they never betrayed their comrades.

When American planes started to bomb Japanese positions and oil depots in July 1943, morale soared among the prisoners and internees. By now, facing starvation, unemployment, and reduced services, most of the Chinese had fled to their ancestral villages in China. The population fell below one million and by May 1945 only 600,000 remained. The Japanese bled the countryside and introduced Formosan rice to produce a heavier crop but it proved susceptible to destructive insects.

Although Hong Kong suffered in every way, life went on as in European cities under German occupation. It was not official Japanese policy to antagonize Chinese or Indian civilians, for there were vague plans for them to share in Japan's Greater East Asia Co-prosperity Sphere when the war ended. However, few Chinese trusted the Japanese, especially after their brutalities in Hong Kong and China. Collaboration was no greater than in occupied territories in Europe. When the Japanese restarted racing at Happy Valley, horses frequently collapsed during races due to their emaciated condition.

Unbeknown to those in Hong Kong during those "hidden years," the Japanese were losing the war. The Americans were defeating the Japanese at sea, on land, and in the air. With their secret radio codes and transmissions compromised and increasingly short of petrol and other essential supplies, the Japanese faced inevitable collapse. The British and Indian Army Divisions had recaptured Burma and were planning to retake Malaya and Singapore. According to most authorities (e.g., Fairbank, 1992, pp. 314-330; Tuchman, 1971), the Sino-Japanese conflict during World War II was secondary to preparations for China's civil war, which began in earnest soon after Japan capitulated.

Yet, China's collective contribution to the total war effort should be recognized. When the Pacific War began, Chinese forces had been fighting Japan since 1937. In December 1941, Japan had 22 divisions and 20 brigades engaged in China, compared with 10 divisions and three brigades which the Japanese used in its offensive against Dutch East Indies, Malaya, Hong Kong and Burma. When Japan surrendered, it had well over a million troops were in China, and almost 400,000 Japanese had been killed during the war (Young, 1963, p. 418).

Japan's Surrender. News of Japan's surrender reached the long-suffering POWs and internees on August 16, 1945. Their Japanese guards withdrew the following day and the Union Jack was raised. On August 29th, American planes air-dropped welcomed food, medical supplies and cigarettes.

Admiral Sir Cecil Harcourt arrived aboard his flagship, the cruiser HMS *Swiftsure*, on August 30th, and his proud fleet, including the carrier, HMS *Indefatigable*, and the battleship, *Anson*, anchored in HK Harbour. Of all the fleets that have visited the place, it must have been the most joyous and grandest sight of all.

Instead of the Japanese waiting to welcome Sir Cecil stood HK's Colonial Secretary (later Sir) Franklin C. Gimson. For when freed from internment, Gimson had had the foresight of stepping forward and claiming Hong Kong fromthe demurring Japanese: "As senior official of the Hong Kong government I will take charge of the administration" (Walsh, 1993, pp. 430-431). Gimson's timing prevented the possibility of HK's return to China during the hiatus awaiting formal surrender. Strongly opposed by Churchill, President Roosevelt, who had passed away before war's end, had talked of ending colonialism and turning HK over to Chiang Kai-shek.

Making use of his former enemies, Gimson maintained law and order and initiated essential services with the help of Japanese soldiers until Harcourt's arrival. While Britain's legal position for sovereignty over the Crown Colony of Hong Kong was strong, its military stance was weak. As General Carton De Wiart (1950, p. 272), who Churchill had sent to be Chiang Kai-shek's special emissary during the war, wrote: "British diplomacy may have been questionable at this time, but the choice of personnel was inspired, and the situation was saved by two men, Admiral Harcourt, who took the surrender and became the first postwar Governor of Hong Kong and General Frankie Festing, GOC Troops, Hong Kong" (Wilkus, 1991, p. 64). Thanking Gimson and other former internees for handling the Japanese and civic affairs until his arrival, Admiral Harcourt took the surrender and administered Hong Kong. On May 1, 1946, Sir Mark Young returned to resume his Governorship (see pp. 138-140).

Major General (later Sir) Francis Festing reestablished British military order in Hong Kong before returning to the War Office in 1946 where he had been when World War II broke out in 1939. Staying in touch with HK friends, particularly Jesuit priests, he found that the Jesuits were better informed about East Asian politics and issues than the British Intelligence Service. Extraordinary in scope and achievements, his military career included appointment as General Eisenhower's Assistant Chief of Staff (Organization & Training) at SHAPE, 1951-52 and later Field Marshal and Chief of the General Staff.

Early in the war, Festing's leadership and bravery gained high credit in Madagascar. He was promoted to major general commanding 36 Division in India which he led in the Arakan campaign in 1944. Later that year his division took over from the Chindits and fought their way through very difficult terrain in Burma to capture Maymyo, help clear Mandalay, and then on to Rangoon. Throughout these operations, Festing led his men from the front, even to the extent of taking over command of the lead unit when its commanding officer had been killed. Americans fighting next to the 36th in Burma grew to admire its gallant general.

According to Wilkes (1991, p. 60), General Festing accomplished much "to dispel the cloud of uninformed criticism that at one time threatened to darken Anglo-American relations. He also won praise and affection from the Chinese attached to his Division and this was to be great help to him when, on the Japanese surrender in August 1945, he was flown from India to Hong Kong to be General Officer commanding land forces."

Postwar Developments -- 1945-1975

The Gurkhas. Indian army units in Hong Kong were replaced by Gurkhas in 1947. The British-Gurkha relationship began towards the end of the 18th century after forces of the British East India Company fought the warrior Gurkha state of Nepal. By the end of the war, a healthy, mutual respect had grown up between the British and Gurkhas, and the British swiftly accepted the Gurkha suggestion that they would rather fight with the British than against them.

Ever since, the Gurkhas have more than proven their value to Britain in a tradition which begins with their selecting only the best recruits. During World War II, the Gurkhas fought bravely in North Africa, Italy, Greece and Burma with heavy casualties, especially in Burma and Italy. After the war, they served in many emergencies with the British, including Malaya, Borneo and the Falklands. But Hong Kong became their special home, since the sociocultural environments of Northern Ireland or with the British Army of the Rhine in Germany were judged unsuitable for their background.

The Gurkhas enjoy the reputation of being intelligent,excellent marksmen, well-officered, fit, and tough. In the mid-1990s the British Army faced major recruiting problems at home, whereas the Gurkhas continued to have far more applicants than needed. Despite their excellent reputation and lower cost than British units, when it came to disbanding many distinguished British regiments following the collapse of Russia and the Warsaw Pact, hard decisions had to be made and some very senior officers felt that the Gukhas should be disbanded instead. Now that they can no longer serve in HK, the Gurkhas confront greater uncertainities in the future.

Communist China. After World War II, there was no worrying activity across the border and the HK's defense forces included 25 Field Regiment, Royal Artillery, two Gurkhas and one British battalions. They expected a quiet tour. This peaceful interlude was shattered in 1949 by the increasingly warlike activities between the Chinese Nationalists and Communists. Francis Festing, now a Lt. General, was dispatched to Hong Kong again to take charge of a unified command of all sea, land and air forces; at that time a command unique in peacetime. Now the threat came not from Chiang Kai-shek's Nationalist armies but from the victorious Communists of Mao Zedong.

The British Government was concerned with the frailty of HK's defense position and reinforcements were rushed to the colony. What had been a garrison of 12,000 strong was soon increased to 30,000 with 2,000 Royal Marines in No. 3 Commando Brigade, two squadrons of Spitfire aircraft and a strong naval presence. Festing announced optimistically, "Although Hong Kong is a highly vulnerable target, it is in some ways relatively easy to defend. Fire will be very much concentrated which means it can produce a very much higher gun density which, when complete, would compare favorably with London during the height of the Blitz in the last war."

Thirty-six new camps were built, roads were constructed to deploy troops speedily, and the Royal Hong Kong Defence Force, i.e., the HK Volunteers, was reorganized. A new 40th Division was formed with a full regiment of anti-aircraft guns set in concrete and steel foundations. General Festing said that the defense preparations "were mostly hard work and bloody sweat."

The Communists reached the HK border by mid-October 1949 when the strength of the British garrison stood at 40,000 men. But the perceived threat diminished, which some historians argue that the British had exaggerated. In any event, HK's force level was gradually reduced, as units were despatched to fight in Malaya and then in Korea. Observation posts and gun positions, however, were manned in HK until 1955. See pp. 141-142 on HK's difficulties during the Korean War, such as the UN and U.S. embargoes against trade with China.

In 1951, compulsory service was introduced for all citizens of the United Kingdom and the Colonies between the ages of 16-60. This was greeted with mixed feelings by the Royal HK Defence Force. However, the Naval Reserve, the Home Guard and the Women's Services remained voluntary. In 1961, compulsory service was abandoned and the Volunteer contingents became truly voluntary again. During that year, the HK Defence Force started to be reorganized for a reconnaissance role. With intimate knowledge of the territory and people, the Volunteers were essential when Mao's Cultural Revolution spilled over into Hong Kong in 1967.

Confrontation. In May 1967, Communist organizations in Hong Kong sought to impose their will on the Government and the people by intimidating workers, fomenting work stoppages, by demonstrations and rioting, and by indiscriminate violence. Origins of the confrontation stemmed directly from the Cultural Revolution in China which inculcated among its adherents a fervent patriotism and blind admiration of Chairman Mao and his teachings. On June 24th, a general strike was called and 200 people attacked the police post at Sha Tau Kok (east end of NT border, see Map 2) with stones and bottles. On July 8th, a similar attack led to the police opening fire with gas and wooden baton projectiles, which was answered by heavy sniping and machine-gun fire. Armored cars and a detachment of 1/10 Gurkha Rifles arrived to assist the police, by then with five men killed and 11wounded. It was serious but at least it was not an invasion; no PLA regulars were involved and was organized and executed by nearby villagers.

The Army took over responsibility from the police for patrolling the whole of the border because of the continuing unrest. On July 12th, strong parties of police backed up by military units raided the principal Communist strongholds and seized home-made weapons and explosives. In August, indiscriminate bomb attacks began and continued to be an almost daily occurrence until the end of the year. Firm action had to be taken because serious violations of the law had been committed, not out of any support for Maoism or of any quarrel with Beijing.

There were three escalating phases of Communist provocations: (1) demonstrations to gain popular support, (2) work stoppages to paralyze the colony's economy, and (3) terrorism to undermine morale. The disturbances failed due to the great credit of the Hong Kong police and military (see pp. 144-145).

Supporting the local community. The British Army encourages its soldiers to help local communities when training and operations permits, and British and Gurkha servicemen engaged in many projects in Hong Kong over the years. For example, they performed engineering tasks, such as building roads or piers, installing electrical generators and wiring houses in remote villages, constructing playgrounds, providing training courses for youth leaders and projects to help the physically handicapped and underprivileged, and responding to disasters. On June 18, 1972, the Irish Guards worked all night saving lives after a typhoon collapsed a block of flats. Second Lieutenant J. C. Gorman won the George Medal after tunnelling seven hours under the debris to save a trapped Chinese.

A Soldier of the Queen, 1974-1975:
A Personal Glimpse

Soldiering in the Creggan area of Londondery, Northern Ireland in 1974 was a fairly traumatic, exhausting and occasionally, bloody affair. The overwhelming majority of the people in Northern Ireland want to remain part of the United Kingdom, but this did not deter terrorists of the Irish Republican Army. At that time, I commanded the Queen's Company, 1st Battalion Grenadier Guards.

During our first eight weeks in the Creggan, we were subjected to shooting incidents most days; we were mortared on April Fool's Day (!) and casualties were inevitable, but our constant patrolling at all hours paid off, as we successfully arrested a number of IRA snipers. Our commanding officer had served in Hong Kong during the 1966-67 emergency. While feeling that he lacked a free hand in Ulster, he had found few operational constraints in HK. Like Sergeant James Bodell 124 years earlier, I was posted from Ireland to Hong Kong. Yet unlike Bodell, I found the territory to be a haven of tranquillity and one of my happiest tours during 37 years of soldiering.

In his farewell address at West Point in 1962, General Douglas MacArthur expressed the sentiment of all true soldiers, especially those of us who did our best in Northern Ireland to keep the peace and save lives. He said: "The soldier, above all other people, prays for peace, for he must suffer and bear the deepest wounds and scars of war." In that spirit, therefore, the peace agreement reached on Good Friday, 1998 and subsequently approved by over 70% of the people in Northern Ireland was received with no less happiness than by those of us who served in Northern Ireland as humane guardians of peace.

The primary task of the British Armed forces in Hong Kong in 1974 was to be ready at all times to give instant support to the HK Government and the Royal HK Police Force when necessary (Lindsay, 1996, pp. 219-223). Lt. General Sir Edwin Bramall, later a Field Marshal and Chief of the General Staff, commanded the British Forces which consisted of 48 Gurkha Infantry Brigade at Sek Kong (center of NT, see Map 2) and 51 Infantry Brigade with its headquarters in Kowloon. The Grenadier Battalion, 600 strong with 294 wives, was based at Stanley Fort. The major part of the naval force was the permanently assigned HK Squadron consisting of the guardship, HMS *Chichester* and five patrol craft. Some 20 Royal Naval and Commonwealth ships visited Hong Kong in 1974.

The Royal Air Force Station at Kai Tak had its own radar and signal facilities. No. 28 Squadron with eight Wessex helicopters was used primarily for rapid deployment of troops and supplies. It also provided aircraft for search and rescue and a medical evacuation service from outlying areas to hospitals in Kowloon. Vulcan, Victor, Canberra and Nimrod aircraft of Strike Command used RAF Kai Tak for training flights from Britain.

The Grenadier Guards is the most senior infantry regiment in the British Army, having been formed in 1656 with the title of First Guards. It has fought in every major campaign of note, under famous commanders as Marlborough, Wellington, and Montgomery. During World War II, Grenadier armored and infantry battalions maintained the Guards' enviable reputation in North Africa, Italy, Belgium, France, Holland and Germany, and since then in Palestine, Malaya, Belize, the Falklands and the Gulf War. While justifiably famous for its colorful ceremonials, such as Trooping the Colour, the Grenadiers are primarily fighting soldiers, deriving their name in commemoration of their defeat of the Grenadiers of the French Imperial Guards at Waterloo.

As anticipated, our tour in Hong Kong proved to be very busy, exciting and enormous pleasure. Within six weeks of the Grenadier Battalion's arrival, the first of many counterrevolutionary war exercises took place. We were dropped, largely in four feet of water, by landing craft on Lantau Island where the new airport is located (see Map 2). Helicopter support enabled us to round up some mock enemy and the exercise ended with a battalion attack. The exercise being a tri-service affair, close liaison was quickly established with the Royal HK Police with whom internal security training was initiated. Army-police relations were excellent. Most of our senior ranks had served in Northern Ireland and were fully trained in dispersing hostile crowds or reacting to snipers, bombs or booby traps, skills that were not required during our tour in Hong Kong.

Within two months of reaching Hong Kong, most of the Battalion deployed on the border to observe and report on the Chinese Communist Army, as we then called it, and hand over to the police any illegal immigrants that we caught. The police were 40% understrength on the border and played a very small part. Each night our patrols lay in readiness to seize illegal immigrants who were often suffering from exposure, shock, malnutrition and thirst. We were told that they were seeking their fortunes in HK, rather than fleeing the PRC's ideologies. We arrested

95 men during our three weeks on the border and they were promptly returned to China. Then without warning, 4,000 Vietnamese refugees arrived on the MV *Clara Maersk* and we ran a camp for 600 of them; all friendly. We never anticipated that tens of thousands more, often in flimsy boats, would come in future years.

We were not confined to Hong Kong, far from it. Grenadiers trained for jungle warfare in Singapore and Borneo and occasionally served as the United Nations Honor Guard platoon in Seoul, Korea as part of an American Company. Adopting U.S. drill routines, the Grenadiers became familiar with such stirring commands as "Stand Slack, Soldier!" Visiting the Honor Guard in 1975, I was disappointed to find its role was entirely ceremonial. I found that the American rifles, handed from units of one non-U.S. nation to another, were shamefully rusty -- until the Grenadiers cleaned them properly.

If the North Koreans attacked, standing orders for the British contingent were to return to Hong Kong forthwith, by what precise means was unclear. This was hardly the case during the Korean War, 1950-53. For throughout that terrible war, a large British brigade fought bravely with American and other United Nations forces. It included regiments of the Gloucesters, Royal Ulster Rifles, Northumberland Fusiliers, Black Watch, and others. At the height of the Korean War, British Commonwealth Forces numbered 30,000 with soldiers from Australia, Britain, Canada, India, and New Zealand.

Although separation for Grenadier families usually averaged 12 days a month for training and operations, there was sufficient time for all ranks to travel far afield on leave, to enjoy sports and to benefit from a high standard of living in comfortable quarters. Company commanders lived in spacious residences overlooking the South China Sea. Considerable importance was attached to keeping the soldiers' families cheerful. My wife and I made good friends with a cross-section of Chinese from the influential members of the Hong Kong Club and Sheko to those of Stanley welfare organizations. Their hard work, friendliness and humor impressed us greatly.

By 1975, although the British Army was over-committed in many parts of the world as usual, steady financial cuts necessitated manpower reductions. Hong Kong force levels could not be justified and were gradually reduced over the following 22 years. The last of the Royal Artillery and Royal Armored Corps units were withdrawn in 1976; the Gurkhas were later amalgamated and the number of British battalions was reduced to one. Not all battalions enjoyed their tours in HK as much as the Grenadiers, for military life anywhere becomes largely a matter of leadership and morale.

Battlefields revisited. While in Hong Kong, I visited the sites of the battlefields which are well-illustrated by Keung & Wordie (1996). I was also able to walk the ground with among others, Colonel Sir Lindsay Ride, former Vice-Chancellor and Professor of the University of Hong Kong, who had commanded the aforementioned British Army Aid Group near Guilin, China.

Fortuitously, since many of the defenders of HK had been Canadians, my next posting was to Ottawa. Also, Canada had provided the prosecuting teams when Japanese war criminals were tried for atrocities committed in HK, and so I found the Japanese commanders' accounts of the HK campaign in Ottawa.

It was over a lunch of oysters at Boodles Club in St. James' Street, London, that my father, Sir Martin Lindsay, suggested I should write a book on the 1941 campaign. Having seen the ground in Hong Kong, found the Japanese records, and read through recently unclassified files at the Public Records Office at Kew, I could scarcely disagree. Also, I had interviewed over 100 veterans of the campaign across three continents. Thereafter, I was invited by successive commanders of British Forces Hong Kong to organize increasingly more sophisticated battlefield tours for the benefit of those serving in the colony. We were always accompanied by veterans who spoke movingly of their experiences, such as Jim Ford CB MC, who pointed out to us where the decimated Royal Scots had counterattacked Japanese battalions at the Wong Nei Chong Gap. His brother, Captain D. Ford, as mentioned earlier, had been awarded the George Cross after suffering torture and execution.

Colonel Tony Hewitt MBE MC described the long, heartening defense of Leighton Hill by the "odds and sods" of the Middlesex Regiment. Canadians told of the gallantry of the Winnipeg Grenadiers at the Gap which earned an extraordinary Japanese tribute to the survivors of the Battalion, which had been assessed earlier in Ottawa as being "not recommended for operational consideration" due to their lack of training. Survivors of the HK Volunteer Defence Corps, described where they fought -- and they fought everywhere, living up to their proud motto, "Second To None." Sadly, there were no survivors available from the Indian Battalions, since the Rajputs had 100% British officer casualties -- indicative of prolonged and courageous resistance.

And the Japanese? It was considered undiplomatic to invite them due to their shocking cruelty and atrocities against the nurses, wounded and Chinese alike. Instead, Gurkhas, dressed in Japanese WW-II uniforms, gave precise renditions of Colonel Doi and others on what happened and where. Colored smoke, machine-gun fire and charging Gurkha soldiers showed how the Japanese captured the Shingmun Redoubt (200 meters s. of Shingmun Reservoir; see Map 2). I like to think that Colonel Doi, who became the Chief Priest of Japan's General Temple in Urakable in 1952, would have loved it!

At the conclusion of the battlefield tours, while I was giving a critical summing up, a Canadian, playing the part of Brigadier Lawson who was killed at the Gap, would stagger in. Drenched in stage blood, he reminded us of what it was really like, fighting against impossible odds with outdated equipment and no aircraft. Elderly veterans had to be warned of Lawson's reappearance to ensure they did not suffer from heart attacks; such was the realism.

Unprecedented Prosperity -- 1976-1997

In December 1975, the respective administrations of Hong Kong and the United

Kingdom concluded a new Defense Cost Agreement whereby the garrison would comprise of four infantry battalions (one of them Gurkha), a Gurkha engineering squadron, five naval patrol craft and a RAF helicopter squadron.

The garrison costing $450 million a year, the HK Government met 50% of that in 1976-77, then 62 1/2% in 1997-8 and 75% in the third and succeeding years. The agreement led to the release of 250 acres of land occupied by the Services, which reverted to the HK Government. The Royal Navy continued to be responsible for search and rescue operations and worked closely with the marine division of the HK Police. A dramatic example of this cooperation occurred when Royal Navy divers assisted in recovering drug contraband from the sea worth nearly $100 million. Preventing illegal immigration, army patrols were regularly carried out in the more inaccessible areas of the NT and outlying islands. The Army also provided emergency fire-fighting units for hill and forest fires.

The Royal Air Force relinquished its station at Kai Tak Airport and moved to Sek Kong in 1978. Victoria Barracks was released the following year. Later, when equipped with Wessex helicopters, the RAF flew with a bucket holding 1.5 tons of water suspended underneath to douse hillside fires. Many dangerous fires in inaccessible areas were extinguished before they could become a major threat to life and property. In 1979, reinforcements were sent to Hong Kong due to the influx of illegal immigrants from Mainland China and refugees from Vietnam and the Army became responsible once more for patrolling the entire land perimeter of HK. The reinforcements included two Sea King helicopters, two SRN 6 hovercraft, an extra Battalion from Britain, two Gurkha companies from Brunei and more helicopters.

Mention should be given the HK Military Service Corps with a strength of 1,200 Chinese. Although a locally-enlisted force, the Corps was part of the British Army. The Corps consisted of full-time regulars filling roles as infantry, military police, interpreters, drivers, dog handlers, cooks, clerks, seamen and storeman. It played a big role in operations against illegal immigrants.

By 1981, Gurkha and British battalions were spending an average of 4 1/2 months a year on border duties -- thereby separated from their families and being over-committed. The border had become more difficult to infiltrate due to the increased deployment of surveillance devices, and HK police augmented this by combined operations involving surface vessels and observation platforms and a much improved, illuminated border fence. As more reinforcements arrived, units were able to take brief periods off for rest and training.

The policy was changed whereby illegal immigrants found anywhere in Hong Kong were returned to China. Hitherto only those picked up near the border were returned. Thereafter, the flow of illegal immigrants was much reduced; but two years later, battalions were still spending three months on the border each year. As significant numbers of illegals attempted to reach the colony in speedboats at night, Royal Navy helicopters used 65 million candle-power "nitesuns" to illuminate large areas and disorient speedboat drivers to facilitate capture.

One RAF or Royal HK Auxiliary Air Force helicopter was always on standby for territory-wide aeromedical evacuation. In May 1982, No. 28 Squadron carried its 1,000th casualty since assuming this commitment in 1972.

During Sino-British negotiations in the early 1980s, it was implicitly recognized by both Governments alike that HK would be untenable if split into two halves. There could be no question, therefore, of Britain retaining HK Island and the southern tip of Kowloon south of Boundary Street (which Britain possessed in perpetuity) when the New Territories were returned to China in 1997. The decision to return the entire territory was not a matter of controversy in the British Forces which were, as usual, over-committed in too many parts of the world, ranging from the Falklands to Northern Ireland and from Cyprus to the British Army of the Rhine in Germany. Regarded as an exotic and enjoyable posting, Hong Kong will be greatly missed.

British, Gurkha, and Chinese soldiers in Hong Kong carried the 7.62 mm L1A1 rifle. It was semi-automatic with a 20-round magazine and a combat range of about 300 meters, increasing to 600 m. as required. Its replacement was to be the 5.56 mm individual weapon which is shorter and has an optical sight. The general purpose machine gun was the 7.62 mm LTAZ with a fire rate of up to 750 rounds per minute. It could be vehicle-mounted and was to be replaced by the 5.56 mm light support weapon. Rifle companies also had the 51 mm light mortar for high explosives, smoke, and illumination. The Mortar Platoon had the 81 mm mortar with a range of 5,800 meters and a fire rate of 12 rounds a minute.

The Armed Forces in Hong Kong entered the 1990s in good heart and were as professional as ever. By now the multinational garrison numbered 11,000 men and women -- 8,500 military and 2,500 civilian support staff -- 38 % HK Chinese, 43 % Gurkha and 19 % British. The garrison's mission was to demonstrate sovereignty and safeguard the conditions which had helped HK to flourish -- thus underlining Britain's stated responsibility to the territory. The commitments included maintaining the integrity of the colony's sea, land and air boundaries, supporting police operations, and disaster and emergency relief.

Fifteen years before, plans existed for a fighting withdrawal from the border to Kowloon had the Chinese invaded. Such plans were quite unrealistic and were changed. Any fighting would in future largely be confined to the border, thereby saving civilian casualties. But there were no grounds to believe that the PRC would try and take HK by aggression, since Sino-British relations had been satisfactory. Even so, the garrison remained fully committed. Aided by Royal Navy ferries, the Army's landing craft once moved over 55,000 Vietnamese refugees to different locations while also providing a daily supply of fresh water to boat people on the Soko Islands (south of Lantau Island; see Map 2) -- a task entailing up to 14 hours at sea for the Chinese and British crews. Two years later, 100,000 Vietnamese were moved between locations. During 1990, servicemen were involved in 270 projects helping the local community -- from beach cleaning, repainting houses for the elderly to teaching handicapped children to swim.

In 1992, the Royal Hong Kong Police became responsible for the Sino-Hong Kong border once more, and the military garrison was reduced by a thousand and declined further as functions were transferred to civilian agencies. By 1993, the Army element consisted of one British infantry battalion and two Gurkha battalions supported by Gurkha engineer, signals and transport regiments. The Royal Navy moved three Peacock-class patrol craft to Stonecutters while Headquarters British Forces remained at the Prince of Wales Building, formerly called HMS *Tamar*. The Royal Air Force continued to be based at Sek Kong in the New Territories where it operated a squadron of Wessex helicopters. During the last two years of British sovereignty, the garrison dwindled to a strength of 2,600, comprising headquarters, an infantry battalion group, logistic support, naval patrol craft and Royal Air Force helicopters.

Nearly 50 years after HK's liberation from the Japanese, the Royal HK Regiment (the Volunteers) was disbanded, after a series of very moving parades. The light reconnaissance regiment of part-timers had existed in various forms for 141 years. I attended the farewell parades and like others felt that the Volunteers did not receive the publicity they deserved in the British and HK press. The same can be said for the parade at the Cenotaph, Hong Kong on 28th August 1995. It commemorated the 50th anniversary of the end of the Second World War and consisted of a special service in English and Chinese. The Service Detachments then marched past, led by 200 largely British veterans and members of the Royal British Legion who had come from England on a final pilgrimage.

In generations to come, I wonder if the HK Chinese will remember the British Services. Those few who come across the cemeteries containing the British, Canadian and Indian war dead will probably not know what it was all about. Nevertheless, the veterans and war widows can be confident that we will remember those who fell in Asia:

> When you go home,
> Tell them of us and say
> For your tomorrow,
> We gave our today.

It is heartening to know that the SAR Government is developing the HK Museum of Coastal Defense, estimated to cost HK$300 million. The Museum's opening is scheduled for 1999 and will occupy some 260,000 square metres at the Lei Yue Mun Fort in Shau Kei Wan (northeast tip of HK Island, see Map 3). The Museum is dedicated to promoting "public interest in and understanding of the history of HK's coastal defenses" (Defending the Seaboard, 1998).

First built in 1887 to protect the eastern approach to HK's harbor, the Lei Yue Mun Fort is one of the best preserved coastal fortresses. When built, it included a redoubt with 18 casemates and two 6-inch breech loading guns mounted on disappearing carriages. Over the years, Lei Yue Mun included barracks, tunnels, and launch facilities for the Brennan torpedo. However, according to Ko & Wordie (1996, p. 76), "Although the military installations at Lyemun had been installed and subsequently expanded over a period of almost six decades when they were finally put to the test (in December 1941) they were quickly proven to be ineffectual."

The handover. Tears flowed and eight bells tolled at a farewell for the Royal Navy in Hong Kong on April 13, 1997 as Britain closed its HMS *Tamar* naval base. "The White Ensign has just been lowered over this shore base, but the values that it has stood for will, I hope, remain in this place: respect for law and for person, trust, duty and service," said the popular British Governor of Hong Kong, Christopher Patten. "But there is no cause for thinking sad thoughts that there is dishonor in these endings. Nothing has melted away. There have been no defeats." HMS *Tamar* shut down 100 years to the day that a vessel of the same name first arrived in HK waters. Its closure ended a 156-year association between the Royal Navy and Hong Kong.

Before he flew to Hong Kong for the handover ceremonies, The Prince of Wales asked John Harris for information on the bravery of the Chinese who fought with the British in Hong Kong during World War II. With the Royal Engineers, Harris had fought with distinction in the defense of Hong Kong; as a POW, he became involved with the communications smuggled in and out of the camp by courageous Chinese of the British Army Aid Group, who were eventually caught and executed by the Japanese. The Prince of Wales was much impressed and highly moved by the bravery of the Chinese.

During the ceremonies, he delivered the Queen's message in the monsoon rain: "Britain is both proud and privileged to have been involved with this success story. Proud of the British values and institutions that have been the framework for Hong Kong's success. Proud of the rights and freedoms which Hong Kong people enjoy. Privileged to have been associated with the prodigiously talented and resourceful people of Hong Kong." As Hardman (1997) wrote: "His speech was as impervious to the monsoon as the band and a guard of honour from the HMS *Chatham* and the Black Watch. These last two British custodians of the place were joined by the Queen's Colour Squadron from the RAF, all standing to nose-dripping attention while that flag came down to the buglers' *Sunset*." Later at 12:50 PM on July 1, 1997, Prince Charles and ex-Governor Patten boarded the *Britannia* and sailed from Hong Kong, a Special Administrative Region of the People's Republic of China.

The Future

So much for HK's military past; what about its future? "By early 1997 there existed an unfortunate credibility gap for the People's Liberation Army amongst the Hong Kong Chinese," noted one respected historian in Hong Kong who wrote to me. "Those visiting China have seen the PLA in their environment and were not favorably impressed. There they were seen as scruffy and idle, almost criminal, something of the bully-boy and certainly not to be trusted or respected.

But this view is colored by the traditionally low opinion of soldiers in Chinese culture. Those posted at Hong Kong will need to prove themselves as having a meaningful role to play in Hong Kong as well as being conspicuously honest and untroublesome. We who continue to make our homes here hope that this will be the case."

In May, July and August 1996 Major General Bryan Dutton, the last Commander of British Forces in Hong Kong, met with General Lie Zhenwu, Commanding General of the PRC's People's Liberation Army. The high-profile meetings boosted public confidence. Dutton, who speaks some Mandarin, was under the impression that the PLA will rotate its very best conscripts through the garrison under the command of carefully selected officers, effectively demonstration troops. "They are a very different army," observed Dutton. "They are acutely aware of their international image; they want to use Hong Kong as a window on the world; these are the PLA's words to me. They want to use Hong Kong to rehabilitate the world's image of them. They said, 'We want to demonstrate to the world that we are a mature, modern, professional army, and Hong Kong gives us that opportunity'."

In April 1997, the London media reported that an advance party of 40 PLA soldiers, handpicked for their loyalty to the Communist Party, had arrived in HK to begin the takeover from the British garrison. The men were specifically selected for height and intelligence from a conscript army of more than three million. Wearing new uniforms and a badge featuring HK's bohinia flower, they possess state-of-the-art equipment, including a new rifle. Major General Zhou Borong, who led the advance party, spent a year at the Royal College of Defense Studies in London. The soldiers appear to have undergone strict training and were chosen carefully -- disciplined, tall, educated and mostly English-speaking. The media reported that they like nothing better than singing "I love you, Hong Kong" at karaoke parties.

It was reported that 3,000 Chinese frontier police have carried out a land and sea sweep to halt a suspected flood of illegal immigrants attempting to cross into HK. Prior to China's 15th Party Congress meeting in October 1997, all participants wanted to make sure that the handover was as successful as possible, especially since paramount leader Deng Xiaoping's greatest wish was to see the return of Hong Kong to China. By early 1999, as far as the army and naval changes were concerned the transition was progressing without incident.

It is not necessary to speculate here on the strength, location or roles of the PLA in Hong Kong in the 21st century. No doubt there will be various changes in PLA activities in future years. Over the last half century as the Empire withdrew, British servicemen have attended and participated in many farewell parades overseas and witnessed the Union Jack and their regimental flags being lowered for the last time at those sites. Usually there is justifiable goodwill and optimism, just as there is usually considerable pride in what the servicemen have achieved, often in difficult circumstances.

The British Army is proud of its military history and traditions, which include more in way of humanitarianism and peace than war. Obedient to the Crown, British forces defeated China in the 19th century. They also secured peace for HK as well as provided good services to the community for a century and a half. Surely, the Second World War in Hong Kong and East Asia helped to contrast the character of true soldiers from that of bloody, undisciplined brutes.

In *A Song of the English*, Kipling wrote what expresses the soldier's creed for maintaining peace,

> Keep ye the Law -- be swift in all obedience --
> Clear the land of evil, drive the road and bridge the ford.
> Make ye sure to each his own
> That he reap where he hath sown;
> By the peace among our peoples let men know we serve the Lord!

Hong Kong has enjoyed unprecedented prosperity and stability for many years: that is Britain's military legacy to their former colony. We hope and pray that the PLA in Hong Kong will meet the challenges with equal determination to do their duty whatever may lie ahead.

References

Beeching, Jack (1975). *The Chinese opium wars*. New York: Harcourt Brace Jovanovich.

Bodell, James (1982). Keith Sinclair (Ed.), *A soldier's view of empire 1831-1892*. London: The Bodley Head.

Bruce, Phillip (1991). *Second to none*. Oxford: Oxford University Press.

De Wiart, Carton (1950). *Happy odyssey*. London: Cape.

Defending the Seaboard (1998). Hong Kong: Provisional Urban Council and the Architectual Services Council, Hong Kong Government.

Endacott, G. B. (1973). *A history of Hong Kong* (2nd ed.). HK: Oxford University Press.

Fairbank, John K. (1992). *China: A new history*. Cambridge, MA: Belknap.

Fay, Peter W. (1975). *The opium war 1840-1842*. New York: Norton.

Graham, Gerald S. (1978). *The China station: War and diplomacy 1830-1860*. Oxford: Clarendon Press.

Hardman, Robert (1997, July 1). Flag of freedom. *The Daily Telgraph*, page 1.

Holt, Edgar (1964). *The opium wars in China*. London: Putnam.

Inglis, Brian (1976). *The opium war*. London: Hodder & Stroughton.

Keung, Ko Tim & Wordie, Jason (1996). *Ruins of war: A guide to Hong Kong's battlefields and wartime sites*. Hong Kong: Joint Publishing.

Law, Jim (1997, June 15). Villagers recall tales of Tang war with forgiveness in mind. *Hong Kong Standard*, Internet Edition.

Lindsay, Oliver (1978). *The lasting honour: The fall of Hong Kong*. London: Hamish Hamilton.

Lindsay, Oliver (1981). *At the going down of the sun: Hong Kong and South East Asia 1941-1945*. London: Hamish Hamilton.

Lindsay, Oliver (1996). *Once a Grenadier: The Grenadier Guards 1945-1995*. London: Leo Cooper.

Loch, H. B. (1870). *Narrative of events in China*. London: John Murray.

Mann, Michael (1989). *China 1860*. London: Michael Russell.

Rollo, Dennis (1992). *The guns and gunners of Hong Kong*. Hong Kong: Corporate Communications for the Gunners' Roll of Hong Kong.

Royal Archives, Windsor Castle, RA VIC/ADD MSSE/I 2681

Seagrave, Sterling (1992). *Dragon lady: The life and legend of the last empress of China*. New York: Knopf.

Selby, John (1968). *The paper dragon: An account of the China wars, 1840-1900*. London: Arthur Barker.

Spence, J. D. (1969). *To change China: Western advisers to China 1620-1960*. Boston: Little Brown.

Swinhoe, R. (1861). *Narrative of North China campaign*. London: Smith Elder.

Thorne, Christopher (1978). *Allies of a kind: The United States, Britain and the war against Japan*. London: Hamish Hamilton.

Tuchman, Barbara (1971). *Stilwell and the American experience in China, 1911-45*. New York: Macmillan.

Tulloch, Bruce (1903). *Recollections of forty years' service*. London: Blackwood.

Welsh, Frank (1993). *A history of Hong Kong*. London: HarperCollins.

Wilkes, Lyall (1961). *Festing: Field Marshal*. London: The Book Guild.

Wolseley, G. J. (1869). *Narrative of the war with China 1860*. London: Longman, Green, and Roberts.

Wolseley, G. J. (1903). *The story of a soldier's life* (Vol. 2). London: Longman.

Yee, Albert H. (1992). *A people misruled: The Chinese stepping-stone syndrome* (2nd ed., rev.). Singapore: Heinemann Asia.

Young, N. A. (1963). *China and the helping hand 1937-1945*. Cambridge, MA: Harvard University Press.

CHAPTER TWO

British Rule in Hong Kong:
From 1841 to The Sino-British Joint Declaration of 1984

Kenneth Topley

You have treated my instructions as if they were waste paper . . . . You have disobeyed and neglected your instructions . . . . you have obtained the cession of Hong Kong, a barren Island with hardly a House upon it. Now it seems that Hong Kong will not be a Mart of Trade . . . (though) it is possible I may be mistaken . . . .
Lord Palmerston, Foreign Secretary, to Captain Charles Elliot, April 1841

Beginnings

Captain Charles Elliot RN, then Superintendent of Trade and Plenipotentiary in China, declared Hong Kong to be British territory on January 20, 1841. Six days later, Commodore Sir J. J. Gordon Bremer made an unopposed landing on the island at Possession Point. Thereupon, Elliot declared that Hong Kong would be a free port and that the inhabitants would be treated in accordance with the laws and customs of China except that there must be no torture. However, neither London or Peking approved the Convention of Chuenpi that Elliot had negotiated after his victories over the forces of Qing (Ch'ing, Manchu) China.

As Welsh (1993, p. 114) put it, "Breathing flames of wrath at Elliot," Palmerston replaced Elliot and exiled him to Texas as Charge d'Affaires. Nevertheless, Elliot's acts and statements live on, for he was balancing Britain's desire for a secure trading base in East Asia and China's wish to restrict the movement of foreigners, whom they distrusted. Elliot thought that Britons con- fined to Hong Kong under British rule would cause little trouble, and if Chinese came to the island to live and work, their laws and customs should be respected. Although both sides rejected the Convention of Chuenpi, learned British judges have regarded Elliot's statement about respecting and observing Chinese laws and customs to be some way binding.

Lord Palmerston, the Foreign Secretary, wanted ports in China opened up to British trade and was prepared to go to war to get them. His objective was not to acquire more real estate for Britain. Sir Henry Pottinger, Elliot's successor, was instructed by Palmerston to prosecute matters with more vigor ("no shilly- shalling, no tender-hearted avoidance of casualties . . . ." Welsh, 1993, p. 115), and secure the opening of treaty ports for free trade. Although Elliot's Convention had not been ratified, the British did not leave Hong Kong. They were busy building and making themselves comfortable. They were also setting up a rudimentary government. For the merchants, the trouble with Canton had been the arbitrary as much as the restrictive nature of Chinese rule. Clearly, in Hong Kong the rule of law would be vital. Captain William Caine of the 26th Infantry Regiment was appointed magistrate. Those meriting punishment greater than 100 lashes or three months imprisonment were to be handed over to Captain Elliot.

Elliot's recall was announced on August 10, 1841 when Pottinger arrived with the news. Pottinger spent little time in Hong Kong, since his mission was to wage war with China in the north. He ordered that there should be no further land sales because a decision on Hong Kong had not been concluded; but Alexander Johnston, Elliot's and then Pottinger's Deputy, allowed land sales to proceed. Johnston was under great pressure from merchants, who wanted to enlarge and develop their holdings. The Deputy Superintendent also acquired property for himself (Welsh, 1993, p. 139).

When Pottinger returned to Hong Kong in February 1842 after defeating Qing China's forces, he found that much building and progress had been made despite his instructions. A Government Record Office had been built, Queen's Road had been completed and about 12,000 Chinese were living on the island. Pottinger had to acknowledge all of this and began to hint publicly that Hong Kong would remain permanently British and transferred his headquarters from Macau to Hong Kong. He reiterated Elliot's statement that Hong Kong would be a free port. When he was forced to alienate more land, commercial pressure had won again. Pottinger set up a Land Committee to deal with private claims and land for public use.

A change of government in Britain replaced Palmerston with Lord Aberdeen as Foreign Secretary. Aberdeen instructed Pottinger that there was to be no cession of land at China's expense. Pottinger explained as well as he could that he had no wish to create a colony, but development had gone too far for HK to be returned without great difficulties (see pp. 12-16).

Despite its reluctance, Whitehall ratified the Treaty of Nanking, which included Hong Kong's cession in perpetuity on January 4, 1843. The transfer of sovereignty was made on June 26th in HK soon after Lord Aberdeen's letter on the ratification reached Pottinger. The treaty also opened five ports to foreign trade -- Canton, Xiamen, Fuzhou, Ningbo, and Shanghai, where consular law would apply to British citizens. There would also be $21 million in indemnities. It was a bitter defeat for Qing China and resentment towards the "unequal treaty" has lasted to this day. Although Lord Palmerston's memory has much to answer for in lives expended and bitterness caused, without him there never would have been a British Hong Kong (see pp. 5-14).

As army generals dominate military histories, governors appear prominently in the 156-year history of British rule in Hong Kong. The nature of their work and responsibilities on the other side of the world from Britain tested and revealed their diverse backgrounds, personalities, and characters. Since communications between Britain and Hong Kong took three-four months one-way by ships before the telegraph was installed through Suez in 1871, governors were on their own and had to take charge. This chapter will discuss British rule in Hong Kong by reviewing its governors and their administrations from Pottinger to Youde. Chapter Seven covers Governors Wilson and Patten.

Early Governance: Law and Order

The Colonial Office created a structure to rule and organize Hong Kong. Pottinger was appointed Minister Extraordinary and Chief Superintendent of Trade as well as Governor of Hong Kong. Although London saw the roles as interrelated and best carried by one person, there were disadvantages. Negotiating with China, organizing trade, and governing Hong Kong were very different matters. Moreover, for the first two duties, Pottinger was responsible to the Foreign Office and for the last to the Colonial Office; HK's governors wore many hats until 1859.

At first, London viewed Hong Kong not as a real colony but more like the "factories" of the British East India Company, that is, a clubby hide-out for British merchants in an ill-kempt or ill-governed foreign country, where some of the comfort and security of home could be provided. A charter empowered the governor with extraordinary authority: (1) with the assent of the Legislative Council to make laws subject to disallowance by the Crown; (2) with the advice of the Executive Council to make grants of land and make temporary appointments to public office; (3) pardon convicted criminals (the Royal Prerogative) and remit or suspend fines; and (4) pass laws independently of the Legislative Council's assent if necessary. Instructions made clear that the island had been occupied, not for colonization but for diplomatic, commercial and military purposes and that unusual methods could be followed. Interestingly, from the legal point of view the doctrine of repugnancy would not be applied, since it was envisaged that legislation repugnant to British law might be needed. The legislature would have the power of levying taxes.

The powers of the Governor were great because he was regarded as the agent of the British Government, which did not trust merchants to treat natives fairly. Some municipal governance was envisaged in order to levy rates on property and pay for municipal and police services. China's laws and customs might supersede those of Britain in governing resident Chinese, except where a Chinese law was morally repugnant. Property and its succession were to be subject to British law. An annual budget was to be published of proposed income and expenditure

Table 2.1

The Governors of Hong Kong (1842-1997)

Sir Henry Pottinger, 1842-1844
Sir John F. Davis, 1844-1848
Sir S. George Bonham, 1848-1854
Sir John Bowring, 1854-1859
Sir Hercules Robinson 1859-1865
Sir Richard MacDonnell, 1866-1872
Sir Arthur Kennedy, 1872-1877
Sir John Pope Hennessy, 1877-1882
Sir George F. Bowen, 1883-1885
Sir William Des Voeux, 1887-1891
Sir William Robinson, 1891-1898
Sir Henry Blake, 1898-1903
Sir Matthew Nathan, 1904-1907
Sir Frederick Lugard, 1907-1912
Sir Francis H. May, 1912-1919
Sir Reginald E. Stubbs, 1919-1925
Sir Cecil Clementi, 1925-1930
Sir William Peel, 1930-1935
Sir Alexander Caldecott, 1935-1937
Sir Geoffry Northcote, 1937-1940
Sir Mark Young, 1941-1947
(Lt. General Rensuke Isogai, Jan. 1942-Jan. 1945
Lt. General Hisakasu Tanaka, Feb. 1945-Aug. 1945)
Sir Alexander Grantham, 1947-1957
Sir Robert Black, 1958-1964
Sir David Trench, 1964-1971
Sir Murray Maclehose, 1971-1982
Sir Edward Youde, 1982-1986
Sir David Wilson, 1987-1992
Mr. Christopher Patten, 1992-1997

and laid before the Legislative Council (Legco). The colony was to meet its own expenses; governors were to report their actions to London and their immediate superior, the Secretary of State for Colonies.

Supposedly, British subjects living in the treaty ports would be controlled from Hong Kong by laws for this purpose, but it was anticipated that it would be difficult to execute such laws in a foreign jurisdiction. The Chinese were to be governed by China's laws and mandarins would be stationed in Kowloon for that purpose. Chinese officials made much of the concept that Hong Kong was given as a place of residence for the British. Unhappy with this interpretation, the Colonial Office believed that it violated the Treaty of Nanking by according occupancy rather than sovereignty and provided no distinction between Chinese residents and visitors. Since the British would be exempt from Chinese courts, the Foreign Office thought the Chinese had a good case on the application of Chinese law and disagreed with the Colonial Office on this. Native visitors could be dealt with by a Chinese magistrate resident in Hong Kong and resident Chinese by a British magistrate administering the laws of China. Finally, London agreed that natives should be subject to Chinese law but left Legco to work out details.

A basic civil establishment was set up with a Colonial Secretary, Colonial Treasurer, Attorney-General, a Chief Justice and supporting staff, but the proposed post of Colonial Surgeon was disallowed on the basis of economy. Governor Pottinger was unable to institute Legco because eligible persons were limited.

Opium, property, and crime. Illicit opium smuggling was one thing; governing the drug terminus was another. The British Government set out its position on the question of opium in a despatch of January 1843. British opium smugglers were to receive no protection from the Hong Kong Government, and the colony must not become a smuggling center. If opium became legal, the Government would help to enforce suitable restrictions. The land situation was chaotic, for Elliot and Johnston had sold land on unclear terms. Chinese and Europeans held property without plain title and some merchants were making private reclamations to extend marine lots. Whitehall decided that no leases were to exceed 75 years and renewals were to be at the Government's discretion. Grants before June 26, 1843 were declared invalid.

To deal with these difficulties, Pottinger set up a Land Committee but members fell sick and a dispute over military lands arose. Merchants groaned over the new conditions, particularly the 75-year leases. Pottinger maintained that conditions for the original leases had not been complied with and the land should be re-entered and re-auctioned. Envisaging a large garrison, the army and navy demanded large areas of land; but Pottinger disagreed and said that Hong Kong was to be a center of commerce, not a military enclave.

Crime was rampant. Soldiers had been recruited as police but prove unsatisfactory, and Pottinger wanted a police force recruited and trained in England.

Captain William Caine, the magistrate, often patrolled the streets himself and meted out vigorous, some say vicious, corporal punishment on the spot. Merchants carried arms and employed guards. Away from the restraints of their home environs, lowly sorts came to the colony to make fast money, one way or another. For the very poor, prison was not unwelcome since they were fed. Rowdy Anglo-American seamen and deserters provided their own brand of mayhem. Anglican Bishop George Smith described Hong Kong in 1844-46 in terms of disgust (Endacott, 1973, p. 71): "The foreigners were hated for their 'moral improprieties and insolent behaviour,' . . . frequent street brawls brought discredit upon the British. Of the Chinese, Smith said, 'the lowest dregs . . . flock to the British settlement in the hope of gain or plunder;' where they are 'treated as a degraded race of people'."

In April 1843, Pottinger set up a Registry Committee to handle the registration of Chinese. It was to license shops and boatmen, control their charges, etc. Without a legislature until early 1843, Pottinger could not enact tax laws and was thus unable to raise badly needed revenue. When the Legislative and Executive Councils (Legco & Exco) began to function, the colony's first law was humanitarian -- to forbade slavery. Some of Pottinger's laws were disallowed in London for being loosely phrased and other reasons. Thus, it is hard not to sympathize with HK's first governor, who was on his own and required to refer all matters of weight to London with inevitable delays. The word was out that Hong Kong would become the center of Eastern trade and self-interest was the watch- word. In defense of the public interest, Pottinger was alone.

Frustrated, he resigned in July 1843; but was forced to stay until his successor arrived in May 1844. It is unnecessary to overdo our sympathy for Pottinger, for he became Governor of the Cape of Good Hope and later finally gained the job he really wanted, the Governorship of the Madras Presidency.

Sir John Davis Tries to Sort Things Out, 1844-1848

Sir John Davis seemed superbly qualified for the Governorship of Hong Kong, as he knew the Chinese and their language. He had been on the Amherst mission to Peking in 1816 and had been Chairman of the East India Company's Select Committee on China. However, he was no enthusiast for free trade. Among the many awkward matters that Pottinger settled prior to Davis' arrival was making the legitimacy of British rule in Hong Kong unequivocally clear, at least to the British.

Exclusive of 618 Europeans in the garrison, HK's population in 1847 was estimated to be 23,817 by Samuel Fearon, the first Registrar-General. With 595 Europeans (455 men, 90 women, and 50 children) and 362 Indians, the rest were Chinese. Thus, the colony's European community was quite small and people could get tetchy. Paralleling Pottinger's lament that London interferred too much, the Secretary of State for the Colonies (Secretary of State) denied Governor

Davis' early attempt to enlarge Legco and Exco on the basis that councils should be small to bolster the governor's authority.

No local taxes having been raised, the burden of HK's expenditures fell fully on taxpayers at home, which of course upset Parliament. The Home Government accepted that no colony could meet the totality of its expenses from the beginning and it covered defense costs and official salaries; but local revenues were to pay for public works. Davis could not levy import duties because Hong Kong had been declared a free port but land rents were possible and monopolies on opium and salt, for example, could be sold to the highest bidder. A wine and spirits tax was rejected, since as Davis pointed out it would have been the only tax to fall heavily on wealthier persons. Raising the most revenue, the Land Tax was very unpopular. Learning that speculators held many allotments on which they had made no deposits and had no intentions of building on, Davis thereupon required a 10% deposit on all sales. Nobody liked Davis' taxes and Whitehall continued to grumble about Hong Kong being an expensive colony.

Law and order remained a challenge. A British Superintendent of Police and two British inspectors were hired, but pay levels were too low to hire suitable constables. Drunkenness, corruption and inefficiency characterized the early HK police and remained so for some time, which is hardly surprising as police forces in Britain were a new institution and often not much better. Pottinger had proposed a registration system for Chinese residents in order to weed out criminals. Davis thought a universal system would be more just. After predictable protests from Europeans, the Chinese closed their shops and Davis modified his scheme so it applied only to those who could not produce $500, which largely meant the Chinese.

Sir John decided that the best way to deal with the Chinese was to follow Elliot's original proposal, i.e., allow them to be governed through their own people. An Ordinance of 1844 accordingly created peace officers who were to be elected and unpaid. They were to help with the registration scheme and pinpoint lawlessness in Chinese neighborhoods. Because it paid nothing and gave no attention to "face," the plan failed. The British learned that the Chinese took little interest in schemes without incentives.

Governor Davis had been asked to report on the Chinese Government's demand to try their own subjects. Davis thought that British law should apply, since the Chinese were, in his view, coming to the colony in large numbers to seek the protection of British law. The Supreme Court Ordinance of 1844 gave HK's courts power to punish natives in accordance with Chinese law. Davis concluded that the Chinese were too poor to pay fines and prison was no deterrent to them; hence the *cangue* (yoke hung around the neck) and caning were necessary, which displeased the Colonial Office. Although the choice between ruling the Chinese by British law and allowing English judges to apply Chinese law was not a happy one, British judges did mete out Chinese punishments. Thus, the principle of governing the Chinese by China's laws and customs was adopted only insofar as the Chinese managed their own affairs as in China. The problem remained of how to administer draconian punishments on China's model, and Davis proposed to deport Chinese to Australia but this was refused and a compromise of transporting prisoners to the Straits Settlements was finally adopted.

The Qing Commissioner complained about transportation (exile) and resumed demands that Chinese officials should try their own people. Governor Davis replied that no one was forced to reside in Hong Kong and that the Chinese in the colony must expect the same penalties and the same protection of the law as British subjects received. Chinese officials tried to arrest Chinese in Hong Kong and even to collect land rents; but after sporadic incidents, British law and courts prevailed. The Chinese were very surprised to see that the British meant what they said when Europeans were tried, flogged, and hanged, the first hanging being a seaman from HMS *Driver* in 1845 convicted of murder (Welsh, 1993, p. 166).

Davis like Pottinger never succeeded in getting Chinese authorities to legalize the opium trade. Taking advantage of the tacit acceptance of the illegal trade, Davis decided to raise revenue through an opium monopoly and allowed the import of opium for internal consumption, a device originated by Singapore. Not only did the opium merchants abhor the change and taxes, but the Colonial Treasurer Robert Martin objected to taxing an immoral activity in order to raise revenue. As the monopoly was difficult to enforce, Davis replaced it with a licensing system in 1847.

Rising lawlessness caused Governor Davis to decide that the police should be under his direct control instead of a municipal authority. Protesting the rate levied to pay for the police, the merchants petitioned Whitehall with a list of grievances. They complained of the excessive taxes and argued that Hong Kong served wider purposes than those of the individual merchants, notably the treaty ports and the British economy itself, and that very little of HK's expenses should fall upon the resident merchants. Declaring that it would have been cheaper to stay in Macau, the merchants said that a municipal body should decide what taxes were residually necessary. The then Secretary of State in 1845, William Gladstone rejected the merchants' petition. Permanent Under Secretary Sir James Stephen advised against municipal government on the grounds that the English minority could not be trusted with powers over the Chinese.

On April 4, 1846, Charles Compton, an English merchant resident in Canton, thrashed a Chinese fruit vendor. Davis fined Compton, but Chief Justice Hulme criticized the Governor's actions as "unjust, excessive and illegal." However, Foreign Secretary Palmerston wrote to warn Compton against fomenting problems with the Chinese and that if any deaths occurred from such actions that he could be prosecuted for murder. About a year later, two British sailors were beaten up in Canton and Davis fined their captain for letting his men roam about where they could be bullied by the Chinese. When Palmerston heard about this, he wrote a fiery letter to Sir John telling him that the Chinese could not be allowed to trample on British subjects, almost the reverse of his earlier scolding to Compton.

The chastised Davis turned about and mounted an attack up the Pearl River to bombard Canton, which Major-General Charles D'Aguilar and 1,000 soldiers handled vigorously by blowing up everything and spiking 827 cannon before Canton capitulated. Lord Palmerston approved. The Chinese, however, were extremely outraged; and half a year later, six young Englishmen were murdered in a village near Canton. Davis demanded that the entire village be severely punished and Canton authorities finally dealt with the chief culprits. Blaming Davis for upsetting trade, HK became thoroughly disgusted with their Governor.

Davis also faltered in testy bouts with his officials, especially the Chief Justice, John Walter Hulme, who drank heavily. The Colonial Treasurer, R. Montgomery Martin, was also a constant headache, forever writing to the Secretary of State to say that Hong Kong was useless and that Chusan would be better. Martin believed that the whole China policy was misconceived and that it was his job to right matters.

Davis and Chief Justice Hulme disputed who had the authority to administer the law in HK and whether Hulme could be called "His Lordship." In addition, Hulme's rules of the Supreme Court provided the Chief Justice six months vacation a year. In a rash letter to the Secretary of State, Sir John accused Hulme of habitual drunkenness and defying Legco with his extended vacation. A follow-up, informal letter on the same topic to the Foreign Secretary was treated by Lord Palmerston as official. Thus, much to Davis's chagrin, London ordered a public enquiry. Hulme was suspended after being found guilty, but the Home Government reversed the verdict and Hulme returned vindicated to his HK post.

Having resigned in August, Davis departed Hong Kong in May 1848 so disliked that the European community denied him any farewell. As Endacott (1973, pp. 63-64) wrote: "Yet (Davis) should not be condemned because of his unpopularity, which was partly the product of resentment at the failure of the colony to become the emporium it was expected to be: no Governor could have been popular." Davis's attack on Canton defines gunboat diplomacy. Mishandling the Hulme case, Davis turned a drunken buffoon into a hero. As for his unpopular taxes, he had little alternative in raising revenue. However, he arrogantly believed that his knowledge of Chinese was the mark of a superior man and he looked down on Europeans of the China Coast. Nevertheless, he lived in retirement for 47 years to the age of 95 and founded a scholarship for Chinese studies at Oxford, which awarded him an honorary doctorate in civil law.

Reviewing the Beginnings

So far, things had gone well or badly for Hong Kong in this initial period depending on one's viewpoint. Elliot, Pottinger and Davis would have said no doubt that they had done fairly well considering the difficulties -- perennial lack of funds, China's enigmas, shortage of capable and trustworthy colleagues, a population of native criminals and uneducated transients, and worst of all the Europeans, mainly British merchants, many of them well-off and influential with Parliament. Furthermore, the three pioneers were restricted in their actions by instructions from London, which frequently changed or arrived after action needed to be taken. From London's viewpoint, governors were always exceeding their instructions, spending money which was not theirs and quarrelling with all and sundry thereby creating headaches which London abhorred, especially when arising from clashes with China. On top of everything, nobody liked the opium trade except the merchants who had powerful allies and influence at home.

Merchants were disappointed that entrepot trade had not developed at Hong Kong as hoped and complained that taxes and restrictions were excessive. Objecting to the HK opium farm run by the Government, the merchants wanted the drug under their control. Used to the ways of colonialism and skilled at manipulating officials, only the Parsees seemed relatively happy. Governors, merchants and Whitehall might have agreed that early HK was a great absurdity. However, in less than a decade the first governors had secured British rule, established the principle of law and order without prejudice, initiated a tax system to provide revenue, founded a civil service, and fostered free trade.

The Estimable Sir S. George Bonham, 1848-1854

Samuel George Bonham was another British East India Company man. Reaching Hong Kong in 1848, he had been Governor of the Straits Settlements (Singapore, Penang and Malacca) for a decade and had solid hands-on experience working with Asian and European businessmen. He had the chance to improve a colony acknowledged to be floundering. On the minus side, he arrived with instructions to economize drastically and comply with the Report of a Select Committee of Parliament in 1847 which backed the merchants' charge that taxes were onerous.

Britain's Audit Department had discovered that a very heavy expenditure £23,000 was unaccounted for and it had to be put right. To cover debts while cutting costs, Bonham stopped all public works and forfeited his own salary for a year. On top of all this, London called for permanent curtailment of the civil service and abolished a number of senior posts, such as Treasurer and Registrar-General. The Colonial Secretary was to take over the Treasurer's duties in addition to his own., and at a reduced salary. Retrenchment fell hard on the police force and the naval and military establishments. Sir George Bonham cut expenditures in half over his six years.

Hong Kong's population nearly doubled, as China's devastating Taiping Rebellion raged and many Portuguese moved in after the murder of Macau Governor Amaral. Although HK's internal politics inevitably favored the merchants, they continued to complain that they were overtaxed and unrepresented. A former Company man himself, Bonham understood the merchants and how to handle them when they sought action on the Report of the Parliamentary Select Committee. Besides recommending tax relief, it called for some form of representative government. Gov. Bonham offered to hand over the police to municipal commissioners if they made up the difference between the police tax proceeds and the expense of maintaining the force. This would require more taxes which the merchants refused to accept. Bonham also suggested that two local residents be appointed to Legco and Exco and London accepted the addition to Legco. Bonham asked the unofficial Justices of the Peace to make nominations and merchants David Jardine and John Edgar joined the Council in June 1850, the first "unofficial" or civilian members of Legco. Jardine's appointment began a continuous succession of Legco appointees from the powerful firm of Jardine Matheson to 1919.

As for the civic participation of HK's people, Legco noted China's lack of a civil law tradition and decided to give headmen the power to settle disputes if the parties agreed. Their salaries would be paid from a special rate to be assessed by the Chinese themselves, and the plan was to apply only in districts which petitioned for it. Health was still a big problem and annual death rates of 20% for British troops were common, as compared to the Chinese death rate of around 1% (see pp. 153-154). After the Colonial Office rejected his proposal for a civil hospital, Bonham set one up in a house, which London was forced to accept.

When a devastating fire in the dry season of December 1851 destroyed nearly 500 Chinese houses, sheds were put up to house the homeless, food supplied and some local taxes remitted. During the reconstruction, opportunity was taken to fill in a creek with rubble and a new road layout was built on reclaimed land. Brick and stone were mandated as building materials. In April 1854, Bonham departed after resigning some time earlier. He was much more popular than previous governors, despite having to axe posts and costs. Clearly, he was more adroit in handling the merchants and probably the Chinese population as well, though they were in no position to complain.

During Bonham's six years as Governor, Hong Kong progressed apace in the calm atmosphere that he helped to develop. Unlike his predecessors, Sir George removed many irritating taxes and enjoyed the support of the merchants. Although trade continued to lag, he left Hong Kong in better shape financially. He showed the people that the HK Government would respond to their needs during the great fire of 1851. Wary of China, Bonham kept his distance and his administration avoided conflicts.

Sir John Bowring, 1854-1859: The Peace-Loving Warrior

The British Government was economizing again and Bonham's retirement opened the way for more savings. The long-serving WilliamCaine would become Lieutenant-Governor with less salary; as London thought that the importance of Hong Kong did not justify a governorship.

John Bowring was a poet, scholar, and peace advocate, a linguist and public accounts expert and honored by the courts of Europe and Siam for his trade mission successes. He was also politician, a former MP, schooled in parlimentary debate. When his business interests failed in 1847, his influential friends helped him to secure the post of Consul at Canton. In 1852 while Governor Bonham was on a year's leave of absence, Bowring filled in as Superintendent of Trade and Plenipotentiary without problems. On home leave himself in 1853 and most fortuitous for his ambitions, Bowring could put himself forward as Bonham's replacement with his old patron and friend, Lord Clarendon, just ensconced as Foreign Secretary.

Plans to shelve the governorship collapsed when it was learned that separating the office of Governor from that of Superintendent of Trade required new legislation. Thus, Bowring was appointed Governor in name but with little salary. When British interests required it, he was to have authority to intervene in the colony's affairs, but only then. Sir John had half Bonham's salary and was aggrieved. Residing in the newly-built Government House, he felt like a governor and insisted on presiding over Legco. Lord Palmerston agreed that the situation was "an administrative solecism," so in 1855 Bowring became Plenipotentiary, Superintendent of Trade and Governor as Bonham had been. Besides, he received the additional titles of Commander-in Chief and Vice Admiral of Hong Kong and was accredited to the courts of Japan, Siam, Cochin-China and the Corea. Indeed, the titles seemed to cap his life honors and achievements. Yet it was said that he was, "full of the importance of China and himself." Thus Caine stayed on as Lieutenant-Governor, his salary cancelled economies, and Bowring assumed a role for which he was poorly suited. Imbued with liberal ideas, it was not Bowring's merits that weighed in the balance but rather, his weaknesses, a high opinion of himself and absence of a firm character.

The great disaster of his governorship was the "Arrow" affair. A Chinese-owned craft registered in Hong Kong, *Arrow* was boarded and its crew imprisoned on a charge of piracy in Canton in October 1856. Bowring demanded their release and issued an ultimatum. With no satisfactory response, Bowring launched an assault on Canton. His action was furiously attacked in Parliament, which caused the Government to fall, demonstrating the impact of mismanagement in a small and distant colony. A general election returned Lord Palmerston's Whig party to power. Ironically, the peace advocate sparked the Second Opium War, 1856-60, which changed China forever.

Lord Elgin was sent as Plenipotentiary to China in July 1857 replacing Bowring in that role. Although Whitehall was prepared to support Bowring, they did not trust him when it came to decisive issues (pp. 76-81 discuss the Second Opium War). We cannot blame Bowring for everything. Much more was at stake; for long the merchants had sought the right provocation to compel China into granting maximal trade rights. The Middle Kingdom's defeat and the Treaty of Tientsin ratified by the Convention of Peking in 1860 led to the legalization of opium imports, British and other foreign legations in Peking, and the right of foreigners, including Christian missionaries, to reside, trade and travel in China, and extraterritoriality, the right to be tried by their own laws. For Hong Kong, a direct consequence of the Second Opium War was the concession to Britain of the Kowloon peninsula as far as Boundary Road and of Stonecutters Island in the harbor. Other results affected Hong Kong goverance significantly. After Bowring left in May 1859, no future HK governor was appointed plenipotentiary and the duties of the superintendent of trade were given to the British Minister in Peking. Henceforth, governors would be responsible solely to the Colonial Office.

During the hostilities, Hong Kong suffered Chinese countermeasures. An embargo on exports of food to the colony was ordered and Chinese residents were called upon to join the struggle against the foreigners. In 1857, arsenic in the bread from a well-known Wanchai bakery poisoned 400 Europeans, but the dose was so severe that they vomited and recovered. Lady Bowring, however, did not recover and returned to England where she died in 1858. Bowring arrested the bakers and introduced harsh legislation; his wife's health was agonizing but so was the fear of civil disobedience. After he refused to allow the execution of suspects without a trial as the European community demanded, the chief suspect was acquitted by a British jury for lack of evidence (see p. 35). Because of the tense and bitter climate, many more Chinese departed HK for California and Australia than before (Endacott, 1972, pp. 93-94).

Sir John could see that the outstanding weakness of the HK Government was the unsatisfactory nature of its personnel. He recommended formation of a "Cadet" scheme to recruit young university graduates in Britain on the basis of a competitive examination; the cadets would be required to learn Chinese and offered a decent salary and career. Adventurers are useful at the start of an enterprise, but their uncertain ways and unreliable temperament ill-suited a professional civil service. At that time, Britain had little notion of a career civil service. It was only in 1854 after the acceptance of the Northcote/Trevelyan report that recruitment by patronage was abolished in Britain and recruitment by competitive examination began. Similar arrangements had been instituted earlier in India under the aegis of the British East India Company. In China, a powerful and tightly organized civil service had been in place since the Tang dynasty (618-907) which selected scholar-officials by written examinations. Bowring's cadet proposal did not appeal to London at first and it was left to his successor to carry through this vital reform. However, he did succeed in getting the consular service to adopt the cadet scheme including training in the Chinese language.

Bowring foresaw that the Chinese people themselves would be the source of HK's future prosperity and he wanted them to be properly treated and protected from extortion. He wanted to broaden Legco's base and give the vote to all holders of Crown land irrespective of race. He proposed a waterfront highway and other major public works; he saw that sanitary conditions needed to be dealt with seriously; he promoted schools for the Chinese; and he wanted a botanical garden. Bowring got the garden. Those he tried to help sometimes opposed him. The Buildings and Nuisances Act of 1856 was opposed by the Chinese because they resisted interference in their way of life. Nor were Chinese willing to give evidence when Bowring set up a commission to enquire into illicit fees demanded by civil departments and business; for it was commonplace to pay a fee in order to see a public official in China. Nor did the Chinese support his move to control gambling. Sir John wanted to license gambling houses but London would not permit it. The licensing of brothels was agreed to but the Chinese opposed and the ordinance was not applied to them. There was some success in bringing the Chinese into the wider community. The Secretary of State agreed that Chinese might be appointed as Justices of the Peace and allowed to serve on juries and qualify as legal practitioners but these reforms took time to become effective.

The 1849 discovery of gold in California led to large-scale, Chinese immigration and conditions on the coolie transports were atrocious and often deadly. Enforcement of the Chinese Passenger Act of 1855 led to the trade moving to Macau and other ports. With a knack for instituting new posts with worthy titles, Gov. Bowring established important governmental activities. The Inspector of Schools and the Inspector of Nuisances foreshadowed an Education Department and a much needed Sanitary Department. Bowring resurrected the post of Registrar-General and gave it the resounding title, Protector of Chinese, which later became the Secretariat For Chinese Affairs.

It is clear from all this that Hong Kong was beginning, even if with some reluctance, to take its Chinese population seriously but not in the manner originally envisaged. Captain Elliot had pledged that the Chinese could be governed through their own laws and customs by their village elders (see pp. 173-174); but this was impractical as the population swelled during the Taiping Rebellion -- from 38,000 to 85,000 in 1853-59. The good news of the increase was that more gentry were arriving.

Bowring's downfall came, not from starting a war with China and bringing down the Tory Government but from his Registrar-General, D. R. Caldwell. Born in St. Helena, Caldwell was of mixed parentage and married to a Chinese Christian; he had an excellent command of colloquial Cantonese. Possessed of considerable talents, he understood the people with whom he was dealing -- too well it might be said. Unfortunately, Caldwell's nemesis was at hand when T. C. Anstey was appointed Attorney-General in 1854. He had been a MP, was a Roman Catholic convert and a vigorous critic of all and sundry from a high, moral standpoint. Caldwell became his chief target; indeed, he had something to shoot at -- brothels, bribes, pirates. Surely, Caldwell knew much about all of these, for he had proved himself invaluable in his previous role as Assistant Superintendent of Police. He had many informers who had to be paid, and the money did not come from official funds. It would not be the last time that the HK police had to face this accusation, or for the colony to face this dilemma. Should there be compromise with criminals and the Chinese way of doing things? If so, Caldwell personified compromise.

Caldwell was forced to face an official enquiry, but only on the more trivial charges was he found at fault. Anstey was now accused of bringing unsubstantiated charges against Caldwell and suspended, and then with the agreement of the Colonial Secretary of State, dismissed. But that was not the end of it, for a local editor alleged that Dr. W. T. Bridges, the Acting Colonial Secretary, himself a barrister, had destroyed evidence against Caldwell when the house of a man accused of piracy was raided. Bridges failed in his suit for libel.

All this and more had to be explained to the Secretary of State, who in turn, had to explain it to the House of Commons which found the HK situation ridiculous if not shameful and disgusting. As is usual with scandals, the work of government ground to a halt while the scandal was dealt with. A new Minister to Peking arrived to take over relations with China and Bowring was permitted to resign. In appreciation of his efforts on their behalf, representatives of the Chinese population presented him with gifts on his departure in May 1859.

Yet Bowring's departure was destined to be uncomfortable. On his voyage home, Bowring's ship, the *Alma*, struck a rock in the Red Sea and the ship's complement was forced to spend three days on a coral reef. Comfortably active in retirement, "not very long before he died in 1872 at the age of eighty, Sir John could be found lecturing an audience of three thousand in his native town of Exeter" (Welsh, 1993, p. 223).

Sir Hercules Robinson as Governor, 1859-1865

Robinson was rushed to replace Bowring by a nervous Colonial Office, fearing a complete breakdown in the administration. Sir Hercules was only 35 years of age; he began his career in the army and then became Governor of two small colonies in the West Indies. Within a year the old team had been replaced and his own men arrived to fill the civil posts. The exception was William Mercer, the Colonial Secretary.

The first thing that Robinson needed to deal with were the cases of Daniel Caldwell, the Registrar-General who had responsibility for Chinese affairs and Charles May, the Superintendent of Police, both under suspicion for corruption. The enquiry was held in public by Exco and dragged on for more than a year. Caldwell tried to resign and refused to cooperate with the enquiry. Chinese witnesses would not testify and records had been destroyed. The final verdict exonerated May completely, but Caldwell was found unfit for public service because of his close association with the known pirate, Wong Ma-chow. Dismissed under protest, Caldwell remained in Hong Kong, as we shall see.

Bowring's cadet scheme was now accepted by the Secretary of State and the first three cadets arrived in Hong Kong in September 1862 and began to study Chinese. A professional civil service was underway to replace adventurers and transfers from the armed services. Also in 1862 a Police Ordinance was passed, police pay was raised, and the force was reorganized with a promotion schedule.

It was clear to Robinson that although good pay and organization would not guarantee an honest and effective police force, at least these were essential preconditions. As government revenue tripled during Robinson's term, yearly costs of £25,000 for the police was not the burden it would have been in the past. However, much to Robinson's and Legco's fury, London seiged the opportunity to require a £20,000 defence cost contribution.

To meet the growing needs of trade, banking institutions developed and Hong Kong issued its first postage stamps in 1862. A new jail was completed in the same year but proved too small and a convict hulk was moored off Stonecutters Island. Crime was still a great problem but the introduction of street lighting in 1865 helped. Trees were planted in the streets, a clock tower was built as well as a central school, a central police station, and a new hospital. Hong Kong was becoming modern as its 25th year neared.

A difficult area to make progress, sanitary conditions were still a cause of anxiety. Colonial Surgeons uniformly lambasted the Government over sanitary conditions and not giving adequate attention to drainage and sewage. Fear of cholera led to the appointment of a Sanitary Committee, which reported that the drainage system was woefully inadequate but detailed proposals were slow to come. Since Hong Kong had grown too fast and with insufficient forethought, remedies would be expensive. One major advance was made when a reservoir was built at Pokfulam on the west side of the Island and its water was delivered by conduit to the city. When this important step in promoting health and sanitation was completed in 1864, demand had much increased. No stable conditions for health could be established without an adequate and reliable water supply.

Legislation in Hong Kong was brought more into line with that in Britain in fields such as bankruptcy. Imprisonment for debt was abolished. Judicial reforms and a new Court of Summary Jurisdiction made debt recovery simpler. In hiring two more police magistrates, their knowledge of Chinese was thought to be more important than formal legal qualifications. Bowring once exclaimed, "We rule in ignorance, they obey in blindness."

Robinson also wanted to narrow the communication gap and counter the endemic rumor-mongering. *The Daily Press* printed a Chinese edition but it thoroughly confused the Chinese by its attacks on the Government, which would have been prohibited in China and did not appear at all proper. Robinson brought out a Chinese issue of the *Government Gazette* as well as official announcements to explain civic measures and report on legal cases and summaries of European news. While Bowring wanted Chinese and Westerners to live in the same areas, Robinson did not think this was feasible and that relations would be better served if they lived separately and only communicated as needed.

Robinson proved to be an efficient and shrewd Governor. By and large, he saw correctly what could be done and what not, and moved with energy on measures that seemed practical. Improved commerce benefited his and Bowring's administrations. The increasing Chinese population brought social and administrative problems but it also expanded trade. Great numbers of emigrants shipped off to North America, Australia and to Malaya and they demanded Chinese goods in their new habitats. The Convention of Peking legalized the opium trade and more Chinese ports were now open to foreigners. In 1864, shipping through the port of HK exceeded two million tons compared to 200,000 tons when Bonham arrived 16 years earlier. As Chinese merchants prospered, the news spread throughout South China that Hong Kong provided secure conditions for making money and for living. Of course, it was under foreign rule but so was China itself, although the Manchus (Qing) had been in control for two centuries and had themselves become largely sinified. At any rate, although few Chinese planned to spend their whole lives in Hong Kong, they were staying longer and returning to China only after they had made their fortunes.

Robinson's Governorship was very successful; he left satisfied that he had fulfilled much of what Bowring had imagined. He became Governor of Ceylon, had a successful colonial career in Australia, New Zealand and South Africa and was eventually raised to the House of Lords.

Sir Richard MacDonnell as Caesar, 1866-1872

An able and energetic Irishman with experience as Governor of South Australia and three other colonies over 20 years, Sir Richard arrived to assume his last posting before retirement. With little to lose, he decided to follow his own mind and intimated as much to the Colonial Office (Welsh, 1993, pp. 237-239). Upon arrival, he found the colony in the midst of a serious recession. Six out of eleven banks failed; Dent and Co., the great opium rival of Jardine & Matheson, had failed. Land sales, that reliable barometer of HK's well-being, had plum- meted. Government accounts of 1865 showed a huge deficit of $95,000, which caused the military contribution to be delayed. McDonnell raised a loan of $80,000 from the Hongkong and Shanghai Bank on eight percent terms versus the regular 12%. Complaining for long that governors were overly controlled by the Colonial Office, the merchants wanted someone who would govern in their interests. MacDonnell changed their minds.

McDonnell probed everything and all government departments. He was one of those colonial governors who assume until the contrary is proved, that what is being done at present is either entirely wrong or if right, being done incompetently or without sufficient vigor and resource. He rapidly devised a raft of reforms which he pushed through over local and Colonial Office opposition. HK was on the whole impressed, maybe in part because the Colonial Office was taken aback. MacDonnell introduced a Stamp Ordinance to meet the financial deficit. There would be a charge on all official documents including bank notes, which was bitterly opposed but became law with amendments. The mint, unwisely set up by Robinson, was closed and its machinery sold to Japan. The Chinese were happy with silver by weight and not prepared to pay the minting charge.

MacDonnell attacked piracy boldly on several fronts. He set up a special piracy court and authorized the Registrar-General to call Chinese inhabitants to his office to prosecute enquiries. Householders were held responsible for everyone living in their residences. District watchmen, paid for largely by the Chinese, were made responsible to the Registrar-General. Junks were brought under close control for registration, anchoring, arms, and movement in or out of colonial waters. When MacDonnell wanted to disarm junks, the Canton Viceroy cooperated to the extent of a proclamation disarming all fishing boats but went no further. Combatting pirates, Sir Richard ordered marine police to inspect junks and took the precaution of having a Chinese magistrate on board to cover his legal position. However, the Supreme Court would not convict captured pirates on the ground that action outside colonial waters was the responsibility of the Royal Navy. The piracy court failed because of insoluble problems due to the lack of any compromise over the traditional precedence of naval members. Though far from being eradicated, piracy's back was broken and would never be the same again.

Piracy required a more efficient and less corrupt police. McDonnell saw gambling as the big problem to tackle. The gambling houses could afford to pay off the police and if necessary to ward them off. As Chinese pastimes in this era did not include sports as Westerners understood them, gambling was their favorite recreation. Horse-racing, of course, would become the favorite Anglo-Chinese recreation and helped to satisfy the partiality of many in HK for gaming and risk. Sir Richard's answer to big gambling and its ties to piracy was to legalize gambling, for it would then be in the interests of licensed gambling houses to suppress competition. But Whitehall did not wish to be criticized in Parliament on this issue. Not one to surrender easily, McDonnell then tried to suppress gambling, terrorizing police, gambling houses and householders alike; though partly successful at first, he was forced to seek another route.

He then went for the heroic measure of licensing gambling. Surprisingly, the Secretary of State agreed but said that the license fees must not exceed the cost of the extra policing needed. This was to keep intact the principle that government must not be seen to be gaining monetarily from immoral activities. Sir Richard managed to get around this rider with obscurely worded legislation in Hong Kong: "Let the money be thrown into the sea as soon as it is paid, but do not let the hold which it gives the Government over the licensees be abandoned." The system worked and gambling and police corruption appeared to be under control. Caldwell, who had run into trouble during Bowring's time reappeared as liaison officer for the gaming houses. Effective and well-paid at $20,000, almost equal to the Governor's salary, Caldwell's role epitomized the sinfulness of the licensing scheme, as it appeared to the righteous of Hong Kong.

Ill-health caused Governor McDonnell to take extended leave. In his absence on January 1, 1871, the Chief Justice and the garrison general acting as governor conspired with a group of missionaries, called the "Moral Six," and closed the houses and ended the licensing system. Recent legalizing of off-course betting in special shops run by the HK Jockey Club has moderated illegal gambling and has aided charitable projects, e.g.,The Centre for Performing Arts.

McDonnell struggled mightily to reform the Police Force. On his arrival, he assured the Secretary of State that he had never seen in any colony a body of men so ineffective in proportion to their number, or so corrupt generally, as the Royal Hong Kong Police Force, consisting of 89 Europeans, 377 Indians (chiefly Bombay sepoys) and 132 Chinese. MacDonnell substituted Scottish for English constables and Sikh for Bombay constables as well as introducing good conduct pay, promotion prospects for Chinese constables, more police stations with telegraph intercommunications, and the establishment of a Police School. No sooner had Sir Richard gone on leave than the complaints about the police recurred.

In matters affecting piracy, gambling, and crime, wrongdoers and police were genuinely fearful of Gov. McDonnell. Substituting the cat-of-nine-tails whip for the cane, he saw to it that prison conditions were made extremely unpleasant and he ensured that punishments of all kinds were rigorously imposed. It was his personal vigilance and presence which were feared and criminal activity declined. Gambling licensing proved very lucrative and funds went to Chinese welfare, such as helping to establish the Tung Wah hospital foundation for the use of destitute and dying Chinese. Widely supported by the community, the Tung Wah would become a respected institution and its directors became honored community leaders (see pp. 163-164).

McDonnell retired in April 1872. A vigorous and reforming Governor, he raised respect for the Government in the eyes of Chinese and Westerners alike.

Kennedy Carries On, 1872-1877

Kennedy was a genial Irishman of great experience in colonial governance but had no knowledge of China and was in no hurry to deal with Hong Kong issues. MacDonnell had set up a Police Commission which reported soon after Kennedy's arrival with recommendations that more men, better pay and conditions were needed but there was disagreement about Chinese policemen. With 30 years as Police Superintendent and Magistrate, Charles May took the view that Chinese policemen were useless. Kennedy waited a year before deciding that Chinese police must provide the backbone of the future HK police force. Although results were not immediate, it was clearly the right course for the long run. While approving a Chinese police force, Kennedy also ordered thirty Scottish policemen as insurance.

A great typhoon swept Hong Kong in September 1874 and much labor and expense went into dealing with the damage. Hundreds of Portuguese families moved from Macau to Hong Kong because their homes had been destroyed. One constitutional development is worthy of mention. Infuriating the military, the arrangement whereby the General Commanding acted in the absence of the Governor was changed in favor of the Colonial Secretary. The argument for this change was that the senior civil official was more knowledgeable about current issues than the general and second, it made good use of the opportunity to test the abilities of one who might be a candidate for a governorship. In fact, the change was triggered by General Whitfield who, in the absence of Governor McDonnell, in addition to reversing the Governor's policies was accustomed to address letters as General Commanding to himself as Governor and vice versa.

Kennedy was the first Governor to invite Chinese to Government House. Britons did not like it much but he persisted. He also encouraged the Chinese to bring grievances to him directly. The Directors of the Tung Wah Hospital now formed the habit of waiting on the Governor once a year. Their first request was that he should pass an ordinance punishing adultery in the case of Chinese women, which Kennedy passed on to the Registrar-General. In March 1877, Sir Arthur left Hong Kong to become Governor of Queensland.

Sir John Pope Hennessy, "He Himself," 1877-1882

Appropriate perhaps for an inspector of schools, Eitel (1895) closed his history of Hong Kong by giving marks to the various governors. He concluded that "It is remarkable how little really depended upon the character, wisdom and energy of these exalted individuals." But then Eitel was an Hegelian who believed that history had a trend and that Hong Kong had a destiny. When he reached the ninth governor, Eitel wrote:

> As to Sir J. P. Hennessy, the less said the better. His acts speak powerfully enough. The centre of his world was he himself. But with all the crowd of dark and bright spirits that were wrestling within him, he could not help doing some good and the Colony emerged out of the ordeal of his administration practically unscathed. No, what makes or mars the fortunes of Hong Kong is not the wisdom or foolishness, the goodness or badness of its Governors. There is an indomitable vitality within and a Supreme Governor above this British Colony, and these powers irresistibly push on and control the evolution of Hong Kong until destiny be fulfilled in accordance with a plan which is not of man's making.

Like Bowring, Hennessy had been a politician and MP. It was only through the personal intervention of then-Prime Minister Benjamin Disraeli that Hennessy received his first post as governor, which was at Labuan, a 38 sq. mi. island off North Borneo where Japan surrendered to Australia in 1945. Sir John had advanced ideas and enjoyed raising bothersome issues, particularly the handling of criminals. He criticized the penal system of Hong Kong -- no separation of hardened criminals from young offenders and excessive branding, flogging and deportation. The European community thought the Governor's policies altogether too lenient, held indignation meetings on the cricket club ground and petitioned accordingly. Many years later, when zealous policemen chased a robber through central district and gunned him down, Chinese bystanders applauded but the consensus in the cricket club bar was that the police had gone too far. Sir John received the support of the Chinese community which saw a pro-Chinese Governor being attacked. After much delay, the Secretary of State upheld Hennessy's views on the treatment of criminals. Lawlessness was real and some crimes were well-organized. Eitel (1895, p. 542) wrote of one robbery: ". . . from 40 to 80 armed burglars attacked a shop in Winglok Street, when these marauders took forcible possession of the thoroughfare, held it for some time against armed police and finally escaped with their booty in a steam launch." Eitel went on to say that a rumor spread among the Chinese population that a pirate fleet was planning to attack and sack the town. Reflecting the lawlessness of the times, the police actually took appropriate precautions.

Hennessy wanted to govern in a manner respectful of Chinese opinion and custom. He had already angered the foreign community by his support for extending the areas in which the Chinese were permitted to live. He now faced a dilemma. Sir John Smale, the Chief Justice, ruled that the custom of indentured girls or *mui tsai* was slavery and therefore illegal under British law. There was no doubt that this was an old Chinese custom and there were cases of mistreatment. The Chief Justice had, however, confused the issue with that of kidnapping for immoral purposes. The whole matter was debated in the House of Lords which concluded that the Chief Justice was wrong to intrude on Chinese ways. Good came of the debate, however, as the Chinese community formed an anti-kidnapping society, the Po Leung Kuk, which endures as a valuable charitable society for the humane interests of women and girls to this day.

Hennessy was the first to appoint a Chinese to Legco, Ng Choy, a lawyer born in Singapore. Ng would become China's first Ambassador to America. Although the appointment was only temporary, it was a significant step forward. If the Colonial Secretary of State had had more faith in Hennessy, the appointment of a Chinese might have become permanent. In 1878, Sir John also reorganized the Volunteers, a civilian militia (first in 1854 by Bowring and Caine), when Russian military action threatened. The civil hospital was built in 1880. So much for Hennessy's virtuous acts.

We need not linger over Hennessy's many betises, such as his long feud with a barrister whom he suspected of having an affair with his wife half Hennessy's age (Lethbridge, 1983). He related poorly with officials and the military and public works did not progress (see p. 226). To everyone's despair, he thought water supplies were sufficient and praised the Chinese "dry earth" sanitation system. Neglecting despatches from the Secretary of State, Hennessy once left 39 unanswered.

Nevertheless, his quarrel with the military over unsanitary conditions brought Osbert Chadwick, a highly competent engineer, to Hong Kong. Chadwick's report of 1882 laid the foundation for sanitary reform and led to the formation of the Sanitary Board, which became the Urban Services Department (see pp. 157).

British colonial policy held to non-discrimination between races and Hennessy attempted to implement it by treating H.M's Chinese subjects "on terms of perfect equality with the other residents in the Colony," but his manner of going about this provoked the very hostility among Europeans that he was trying to dispel. Hennessy became Governor of Mauritius where he provoked hostility as he had in Hong Kong, Labuan, the Gold Coast, and the Windward Islands.

Sir George F. Bowen, 1883-1885, and Sir William Des Voeux, 1887-1891: Absent Presence

Bowen and Des Voeux, the next two governors, were uninspiring. While their terms span the eight years of 1883-1891, they were absent from Hong Kong for about five of those years largely for reasons of ill-health. All was not lost, for a competent civil service had developed thanks to the cadet scheme. Des Voeux said that when first in Hong Kong he was agreeably surprised to find that any correspondence which required his attention was accompanied by a digest of the history of the issue and a well-considered draft reply. The HK Government now had momentum and governors could take advantage of an efficient machine.

Acting appointments were an important component of colonial life, particularly in Hong Kong until the jet aircraft era. Governors went on leave. The one-way sea voyage took a month. Someone had to do their work meantime. In early times this was usually the Commanding General. In Kennedy's time, as related earlier, this duty was transferred to the Colonial Secretary. During the Governorships of Hennessy and Bowen, Sir William Marsh, the Colonial Secretary, was in command for well over two years and did very well. In a later era, the fluent and able Claude Burgess was an impressive *locum tenens* in Sir Robert Black's absence. Still later, there was a scandal when Kenneth Kinghorn was appointed Chairman of the Urban Council and promptly went on ten months accumulated leave. Shorter leaves by air were promptly introduced.

The government machine, however, was not programmed to handle external threats, such as the Sino-French war of 1884-85. The bombardment of Fuzhou by French ironclads showed the vulnerability of HK's defenses and there was a good deal of panic in the acquisition of howitzers of sufficient calibre and range to defend the island (see pp. 82-83). A loan of £200,000 was raised in London for colonial defense. Bowen found it expedient to go off to Japan for his health. The HK Government unwisely decided to prosecute strikers who refused to load French ships in the harbor, which led to riots and troops were called to support the police. Parliament criticized Bowen's action in strong terms.

Sir George deserves credit for some sound constitutional changes. It was decided that at least one member of the Legislative Council should always be Chinese and that Legco's Finance Committee should comment on the budget estimates before they were sent to the Secretary of State. Municipal tax rates were to be decided by Legco, not Exco as before. Perhaps most importantly, Bowen stated that it should be a constitutional principle that the official majority "should not be used to control an absolutely united unofficial minority, especially on financial questions." In other words, the Governor and his officials should not use their *ex officio* majority in Legco to ram through any measure which the people's representatives opposed en bloc, most particularly if money was involved.

When an attempt was made to implement some of Chadwick's recommendations for housing space, drainage, ventilation, and lighting, property owners resisted, since improvements would cost money and the Chinese complained against being forced to live as Europeans decided. A rather thin Ordinance was passed; but when Des Voeux arrived in October 1887, a petition against it signed by 47,000 Chinese awaited him. Predictably, nothing much was done in his time. Dr. Patrick Manson and others started a College of Medicine that would become famous (see pp. 167-169). Public works recommended by Chadwick went ahead, including the Ty Tam reservoir, a new central market, new main drains and sewers, and reclamation of swamps at Causeway Bay and Yaumati. Opportunity to move the Tamar Naval Base out of town central during extensive reclamation was lost when Governor Des Voeux decided it was too expensive.

Sir William Robinson, 1891-1898, Plague Fighter

Sir William Robinson inherited the whirlwind in the form of the Bubonic plague of 1894 (see pp. 175-179). Robinson was very much a Colonial Office man, since he began work there as a clerk at the age of 18 and rose exceptionally to the rank of Governor in the Bahamas.

In 1892, British officials were forbidden to own property in the colony other than for their own occupation and were also forbidden to engage in trade and own shares in local companies (Endacott, 1973, p. 226). Two years later, a constitutional change was sought for the "common right of Englishmen to manage their local affairs." The aim was to put a majority of British subjects on Legco. Lord Ripon, the Secretary of State, was cautious, for he feared that a small oligarchy could dominate the place, leaving 98% of the population underrepresented. It was decided that two unofficials would be added to Exco and an additional Chinese to Legco.

When Philippine nationalists became active in Hong Kong, London warned Sir William not to let them plot against Spanish control of the Philippines. In 1896, Robinson issued an exclusion order against Dr. Sun Yat-sen, a graduate of the HK College of Medicine for conspiracy against the Qing Government in Canton (see p. 60). Later that same year, Dr. Sun was kidnapped in London and held in the Chinese legation. With the help of an English servant working at the legation, he managed to pass a message to Dr. James Cantlie, Dr. Sun's former mentor at the College of Medicine. After Cantlie (1899) persuaded the Foreign Office to secure his release, the affair was widely reported and made Dr. Sun famous overnight. Parliament asked why it was that London treated Dr. Sun as a patriot, yet he was *persona non grata* in Hong Kong (Welch, 1993, p. 338).

Sir Henry Blake, 1898-1903, New Territories; Sir Matthew Nathan, 1904-1907, The Engineer

The Sino-French war of 1884-85 put Hong Kong on the alert. Now that France controlled Tonkin (Vietnam), what was to stop her from planting the Tricolor on the southern provinces of China? Russia and Germany were also ambitious in East Asia. It was feared that all of this would lead to a scramble for China's territory, a fear that came true when Japan's modern navy and army subdued China overnight and carried off Formosa and more (see p. 84). Germany took over Kiaochow (Jiaozhou) in Shandong Province in 1898. So HK wondered how it could ward off possible foreign attack.

The answer from successive generals commanding HK's garrison was to acquire more territory on the mainland north of Boundary Road. This was not something that Whitehall wanted but finally realized it had no choice. Accordingly, when negotiations were begun, the Chinese were shocked by the size of the requested area, about 355 square miles; but the British said it was made necessary by the latest developments in long-range artillery. Lord Arthur Balfour, Conservative leader in Commons, preferred a lease for an indefinite period determinable by mutual agreement but agreed to the terms (Welsh, 1993, p. 324).

The New Territories (NT) lease for 99 years starting from July 1, 1898 was finalized when the British conceded to China's demand that the walled city in Kowloon remain Chinese territory. Built after 1842, the tiny enclave mushroomed into a monstrosity after the Korean War and was finally demolished with Beijing's approval during Gov, Wilson's tenure.

Agreement with China on the NT lease was one thing; implementation was another. Villagers burnt down police sheds. Still new, Gov. Blake visited the Canton Viceroy and obtained the promise of protection by 600 soldiers for survey parties. However, when the police were attacked by a mob and forced to flee, Chinese soldiers supposedly sent to provide protection did nothing. With artillery support, 1,000 Chinese soldiers attacked a landing party seeking the site of a future military camp. Stewart Lockhart, the Colonial Secretary who handled civil arrangements for the handover, immediately raised the Union Jack to establish the right of British troops to be in the NT. Later, about 2,600 Chinese advanced in three lines, waving banners and shouting loudly. The action was soon over.

Blake had his share of international political problems. His predecessor's ban of Sun Yat-sen from the colony raised awkward questions. Dr. Sun's kidnapping and heroic rescue made him a hero in London and enhanced his fame worldwide as the leader of the Chinese revolutionary movement. Such contradictions between public sentiment in Britain and actions of the HK Government were not infrequent throughout the colony's history. Although Whitehall regarded the Qing regime as a friendly government, to which it had treaty obligations, Governor Blake was personally sympathetic to the aims of the Chinese revolutionaries, which included setting up a Southern Chinese Republic. Blake thought that such a republic would be less anti-foreign and continued to support the Southern revolutionaries until Austin Chamberlain, the Colonial Secretary of State, ordered him to desist.

One insurrection after another took place in Canton with no success. When assassins from Canton killed one of the plotters by gunfire in HK, Blake protested. Canton officials responded by executing the killer after they had rewarded him and sent Blake a list of revolutionary suspects in HK. Vigorously denying that they were implicated, Sir Henry gave the leading suspect police protection.

Blake left in 1903 to become Governor of Ceylon. Keeping an eye on Hong Kong, he complained furiously to the Colonial Office when Francis May, the acting Governor, whose authoritarianism had been restrained by Blake, introduced a Peak Reservation Ordinance. It meant that only Europeans could live on the choice real estate of Victoria Peak towering above HK. May made it more palatable to the Colonial Office by the rider that The Governor in Council might exempt any Chinese from the Ordinance.

Blake's successor, Sir Matthew Nathan, did not attempt to undo the Peak Ordinance. In fact, he worked well with May with whom he shared a strong distaste for Chinese revolutionaries. Nathan had been an army engineer and took an immediate interest in roads and railways. Nathan Road, the broad thoroughfare running due north from Tsimshatsui (see Map 3) at harbor-edge through Kowloon is his obvious memorial. In his time it was known as "Nathan's Folly" but was later termed the "Golden Mile." He also gave much time and effort to get the Kowloon/Canton railway (see Map 2) financed and built and was thought to be overly immersed in the scheme's details. Though started during his time, the KCR did not reach the border until five years after Nathan left HK in 1912 and has promoted Kowloon's development ever since.

In HK only three years, Nathan was sent to Natal in South Africa. His stay in may have been shortened by the eagerness of his successor's wife, once colonial editor for *The Times* and an enterprising, well-informed woman with connections. Nathan's bachelor status made it possible for Colonial Secretary May's wife, Helena, to be the colony's first lady and social leader. According to Hoe (1991, p. 209), Hong Kong perceived Flora Lugard as the "good woman" the community desired above all else.

Sir Frederick Lugard, 1907-1912: On Leave from Africa

Famed in British colonial history, Lugard's name is primarily associated with the creation of Nigeria. He came to Hong Kong with enormous experience of working in desolate places where his successes were legendary. His tasks in Hong Kong were somewhat different. He wrote to his brother that he felt "horribly circumscribed." "My role is . . . to endure fools gladly, to sign my name perpetually and to agree to the faultless suggestions of the Honourable the Colonial Secretary." He looked back with deep longing to "the man's work I had to do in Nigeria" (Perham, 1960, p. 287).

His biggest task was to deal with the effects of the Chinese Revolution. Hong Kong was the center of revolutionary activity in South China, and coups launched in Canton had been hatched in Hong Kong. The successful uprising overthrowing the Qing Dynasty finally came in Wuchang in Hupei on October 10, 1911 when a number of army officers plotting revolution learned that they had been discovered and were forced into a premature coup. Qing rule ended after uprisings in other provinces succeeded, and Dr. Sun's Kuomintang Party assumed power. China's ultimate fate was by no means clear, and Lugard trod carefully amidst boisterous celebrations in Hong Kong. When a large number of criminal ruffians from Canton used the celebrations to loot, obstruct the police, and incite anti-foreign agitation, Lugard warned that HK laws had to be respected. As the commotion continued, streets quieted down after he sent army patrols into the worst areas and authorized magistrates to inflict summary floggings under draconian emergency legislation.

Although it was Whitehall's policy to support the failing Qing regime, Lugard's immediate concern was to maintain good relations with whomever happened to be in power in Canton. His attempts to do so annoyed the Foreign and Colonial Offices who thought that Lugard was usurping the functions of the British Consul-General in Canton. Lugard also had to apologize to the British Minister in Beijing for trespassing on his turf (Perham, 1960, p. 369).

Lugard then faced a highly inconvenient, very Hong Kong kind of problem. Pressure had been building in Parliament to make the opium trade totally illegal. After Qing Empress Dowager issued an edict to eliminate the production of opium over ten years and to close all opium dens, the British and Indian Governments agreed to reduce and eliminate the export of opium to China over the same period.

As revenue from opium was about 30% of the HK Government's income, this was hard enough, especially in the short run. Worse came during debate over a motion in Parliament that there should be a speedy end to the licensing of opium dens in HK and the Straits Settlements. A newly appointed Under Secretary of State informed Parliament that he had instructed the HK Governor that immediate steps must be taken to close all opium dens. Furious and frustrated because of the sudden revenue shortfall, Lugard made an inspection of the dens and said that they were better described as divans and rationalized that they were more salubrious than public houses in Britain. The budget crisis was settled by a temporary grant from Whitehall and higher taxes on liquor, perfume and tobacco.

Lugard's name is most remembered and deservedly so for organizing and promoting the establishment of the University of Hong Kong (see pp. 228-230). His biographer, Perham (1960, p. 372) avers, "His first contribution was his character. It is difficult for those who have not lived in a Colonial society, especially one of mixed races, with all their suspicions of each other and of a semi-autocratic government, to realise the immense importance of integrity in the man at the top." In March 1912, Lugard returned to complete the unification of Nigeria and from thence, he enjoyed 26 years of active retirement before he died in 1945.

Sir Francis H. May, 1912-1919, The Police Chief

Lugard's successor was Francis May, Captain Superintendent of Police in Blake's time and Colonial Secretary in Nathan's and a hard-nosed Officer. Administering the Government after Nathan's departure. May was the first HK cadet to obtain a governorship. Governor of Fiji, he was recalled to Hong Kong. Just arrived in the colony, he was on his way to the City Hall to be sworn in when he was shot at by a man in the crowd, who was confused by an ambiguity in Cantonese. As Fiji and South Africa were both referred to at that time as *Fei Chau*, the would-be assassin assumed that May had been associated with the British ban prohibiting indentured Chinese labor into South Africa, a policy designed to protect the Chinese from exploitation.

May was not a good choice to head Hong Kong affairs. It is not clear that he ever adjusted to the fact of the Chinese Revolution, which had taken place during his absence. His idea of an eternal, never-changing China and low regard for the Chinese in general as shown by his opposition to their becoming policemen, "useless, physically and morally" (Endacott, 1973, p. 160) were too firmly fixed. Welch (1993, p. 359) suggested that May reached his level as Captain Superintendent of Police, when he was instrumental in reforming the HK Police Force in a thoroughgoing way. In charge between governors, Colonial Secretary May was often "rash and ill-considered," and he lacked the polish and aplomb to "face down criticism."

The tramway boycott of 1912 was awkward enough. While Canton coins had been accepted for long, when they lost value the Hong Kong Tramway insisted on fare payments in HK currency. Perceiving the change as an insult to the new Republic of China, the public boycotted the Tramway. May countered with a punitive Boycott Prevention Ordinance that London sharply criticized for its harshness. Lasting more than two months, the boycott caused ill-feeling on all sides.

Opium became a point of dispute again, as Parliament vigorously attacked its continued sale by the HK Government. May tried to address the furor by dropping subcontractors and having the Government take over the opium monopoly itself. He claimed that it was the first step of a long-term program to ban the drug completely. Despite Parliament's admonitions against the narcotic, by 1918 opium revenue was nearly *half* the income of the HK Government, a fact that was hidden away in HK's accounts and unknown to Parliament.

A timely gift of $5 million was made to the British Government to help in the huge costs of the First World War. From 1914-1919, opium netted more than $25 million (Welch, 1993, p. 365). After a slight stroke, May returned home in September 1918. The HK Government continued to sell opium up to its surrender on

December 25, 1941 (See pp. 36-37 of the Overview).

Sir Reginald E. Stubbs, 1919-1925, Strike-Breaker

Stubbs arrived a year after May departed. Highly qualified academically and the son of a famous bishop and church historian, Sir Reginald spent 13 years in the Colonial Office, where he had been a thorn in Lugard's side. He transferred to the Colonial Service and served as Ceylon's Colonial Secretary. The British Representative in Peking upset Stubbs by proposing that in the interests of Anglo-Chinese relations the New Territories should be returned to China, but Lord Curzon, the Foreign Secretary, did not agree. However, Stubb's efforts to help the Canton Government secure its share of the revenues from the China Maritime Customs provoked a sharp rebuke from the Foreign Secretary.

Stubbs was faced with two very well-organized and effective strikes in successive years. The first was in 1920 by the Engineers Union when employers dismissed the union demand for a 40% increase in wages to meet the increased costs of living. The engineers, all 8,000 of them, departed for Canton and the employers capitulated. The next year the Seaman's Union tried similar but extended tactics, and early in 1922, the seamen departed for Canton taking with them coolies, domestic servants and others to the tune of 120,000. Pressured by employers and "responsible Chinese opinion," the HK Government tried repressive measures, emergency regulations, and even raids on the Seamen's Union headquarters. Chinese were forbidden to leave the colony, a measure that led to five deaths when a Sikh policeman fired on a crowd trying to cross the border. The seaman won what they wanted and Stubbs was left in a quandary.

Worse was to come. One of HK's most dangerous and damaging events, the General Strike and Boycott of 1925-26 followed Anti-Japanese demonstrations in Shanghai on May 30, 1925. Anxious International Settlement police commanded by a British officer fired on the crowd and eleven demonstrators were killed. Retaliatory strikes were called in Shanghai and in Hong Kong. Three weeks after the Shanghai tragedy, nervous Anglo-French troops fired on demonstrators at Shameen, the old foreign compound in Canton, causing 52 deaths, some only youth. Fury in Canton overflowed into Hong Kong and there were calls for war against Britain, for nothing stirs the Chinese more than martyrdom (Yee, 1992, pp. 144-159).

Although anti-British sentiments were nothing new in Hong Kong, this was on an unprecedented scale. Most of HK's labor force departed with their families for Canton where well-financed left-oriented organizers attended to the needs of 250,000 people. Unable to obtain aid from the West, Sun Yat-sen had sought Russian assistance to organize the next stage of his revolution. He feared that the independent growth of the Chinese Communist Party under Soviet control would be more dangerous than collaboration. Russia sent Dr. Sun talented advisers, the most important being Michael Borodin, who arrived in Canton in October 1923 and reorganized Dr. Sun's party on Soviet lines. The Soviets helped to organize a military academy in Whampoa, and Chiang Kai-shek, who had received brief military training in Moscow and Japan, was put in charge. Zhou Enlai, a future PRC Premier, was deputy head of the political education department. When Sun Yat-sen died unexpectedly on March 12, 1925, Chiang gained power and worked with the communists until 1927 when he turned sharply against them. Mao Zedong would take his revenge in 1949 when he defeated Chiang's armies and conquered the mainland. During the 1925-26 General Strike and Boycott, however, the KMT and CCP worked together against the British.

The Stubbs Government responded to the massive strike by organizing volunteer services and food supplies, guaranteeing Chinese banks which were under threat of runs, and gaining the support of the Tung Wah Hospital Committee. Strikers began to return to Hong Kong by the end of July. However, the boycott of British goods and ships was "savagely damaging to Hong Kong" (Welsh, 1993, p. 372). As usual, Stubbs had to deal with a Foreign Office which saw things differently from the governor on the spot. Whitehall did not contemplate military action, which would have infuriated the Chinese further.

The nine-power Washington treaty of 1922 required the powers to respect the political independence of China and its territorial integrity. Stubbs wanted to offer Peking $3 million if it would convince Canton to lift the boycott, but London disagreed. Stubbs then persuaded the Tung Wah Board to use $50,000 of its funds to mount a coup in Canton, which failed and created great embarrassment. The Colonial Office later reimbursed the Tung Wah. The boycott lasted another year after Stubbs departed in October 1925.

Sir Cecil Clementi, 1925-1930

Clementi was very different from Stubbs. Although equally capable academically, he knew much more about China and the Chinese. Beginning his career as a HK cadet in 1900, he had travelled extensively on his own in China, largely on foot. He subsequently spent 12 years as a colonial officer in British Guiana and Ceylon. Where Stubbs was irascible, Clementi was thoughtful and open-minded. He quickly reestablished communications with Canton, the Foreign Office, and the British Minister in Peking and was sensitive to the growing nationalism in China. Since the boycott was being orchestrated from Canton, Clementi knew that action in Hong Kong alone would have little effect. Yet with much help from Robert Kotewall, the Chief Clerk, he worked to mobilize public opinion and morale, starting a newspaper with public funds so that communist propaganda was met with counter-propaganda. The Colonial Office tried to restrain Clementi fearing that he could agitate the Chinese further.

Governor Clementi realized that he had to wait on events and decisions in China and sit out the storm without loss of nerve. Chiang's increasing power and his desire to concentrate on defeating the Communists finally led to the raising of the boycott in October 1926. Hong Kong could breathe more easily.

Clementi brought about some judicious constitutional reform. British business still wanted an unofficial majority in Legco, excluding the Chinese, but their petition was turned down again. The Governor believed that any serious constitutional development should be in the direction of giving more power to the overwhelming body of the population. On the other hand, it was argued that the HK Chinese still looked to China as the center of their cultural and political loyalty, a democratically elected government in Hong Kong would be swayed by events on the mainland and nationalist sentiments. Governor Clementi increased the number of unofficials in Legco and appointed the first Chinese to Exco in 1926, Sir Shouson Chou, who was HK born and had worked in the Imperial and Republican governments. Chou was instrumental in the start of Clementi's anti-communist newspaper.

The Thirties

Much to Hong Kong's regret, the Colonial Office unexpectedly transferred Clementi to the Straits Settlements as Governor where a crisis was brewing. He was succeeded respectively by Sir William Peel, Sir Andrew Caldecott and Sir Geoffry Northcote. It is agreed by commentators as diverse as poet W. H. Auden and Alexander Grantham, a cadet at the time and a future Governor, that Hong Kong was a dull and stuffy place in the 1930s, a colonial backwater, in part because Shanghai was where the action. China was much more interesting. While the Long March was taking place in 1934-35, Sidney Caine, the first Financial Secretary, was introducing income tax but not before the Secretary of Chinese Affairs had taken careful soundings of the public. Revenue from opium had become minimal, and the business community was dissatisfied with the Government as usual.

Although Japan had annexed Manchuria in 1932, China was progressing and Chiang consolidated his power across the country. In 1937 China fell into turmoil after Japan mounted the Sino-Japanese War. Except for an increase in population to over a million in 1938 and a boost in the HK Government's revenue from opium sales (see p. 37 of the Overview), Japan's aggression had little bearing on Hong Kong at first; but in time its effects would be devastating..

The Second World War and the Occupation

Sir Mark Young arrived in Hong Kong in September 1941. Although a Ceylon cadet, he had been posted elsewhere but East Asia for 13 years. He was Governor of Tanganyika before coming to Hong Kong. On December 7th, Japan's unexpected attack on Pearl Harbor was soon followed by aggression on Hong Kong. Churchill had hoped that the garrison could resist for a month or more, but Sir Mark surrendered the colony on Christmas Day when commanding general C. M. Maltby informed him that it was futile to continue (See pp. 87-95).

Initially, Governor Young was separated from other prisoners and held in Room 366 of the plush Peninsula Hotel. He had showed much courage and coolness during the fighting, such as walking through the streets under shell fire to help maintain morale. For more than four years until the war ended, prisoners and the population at large were very badly treated. The Colonial Secretary, Franklin Gimson, had only arrived in HK on the very day the Japanese attacked. During the years of detention at Stanley, Gimson did what he could to organize the civilian prisoners.

Fortunately, for most of the war, the Japanese kept Hong Kong under a separate administration. They could have incorporated it into and administered it as part of the Guangdong province and HK's identity might then have been lost or at least diminished. This was important because it was uncertain that Hong Kong would remain British after the war, as President Franklin D. Roosevelt had spoken of returning Hong Kong to China. Even the British Foreign Office did not visualize a British reoccupation (Welsh, 1993, pp. 424-425). Churchill of course firmly intended that Britain would retain the colony, and the Colonial Office argued that Britain had a responsibility for the HK people, who were British subjects. The Americans finally agreed that the British should receive the Japanese surrender and that British forces should be the first to enter Hong Kong (see pp. 93-94).

Lt. General Rensuke Isogai, a serious student of Chinese classics and art, was military governor from early 1942 to January 1945. The present-day Government House was largely built during his administration. Upon Isogai's recall to Japan, Lt. General Hisakasu Tanaka, commanding the 23rd Army with headquarters in Canton, assumed the role of governor. However, as Japan's defeat approached in 1945, Tanaka had no time for HK as he prepared for an Allied offensive, which in his sector never came. After the war, Tanaka was tried and executed for war crimes, but evidence against Isogai was not strong enough to hang him. He was released from prison in 1952 (Spurr, 1995, pp. 184-201).

Hong Kong's Rehabilitation

After Japan surrendered on August 14, 1945, Admiral Sir Cecil Harcourt sailed for Hong Kong with a Royal Navy flotilla. Meanwhile, Colonial Secretary Gimson had taken charge of HK's administration. Harcourt arrived with plenary powers and took over from Gimson on August 30th. David MacDougall, HK's Chief Information Officer who made a daring escape just before the surrender of Hong Kong on Christmas Day 1941, had been assigned to head a HK Planning Unit in London. When Admiral Harcourt took the official surrender on September 16, 1945, MacDougall stepped ashore in the brigadier's uniform of the incoming military government. He and his team of fellow civil servants also in uniform had prepared rehabilitation plans and knew what priorities to tackle. Law and order needed to be established and food and water supplies organized. They bought food in bulk all over Asia. People needed shelter and work, the economy had to be rekindled, and health services and basic welfare for the destitute had to be provided. The Japanese had left Hong Kong in disgusting shape and this also provided the returning British an opportunity to show what they could do. Everything went so well that price controls on foodstuffs could be dropped by November 1945 and free enterprise was reinstated. American firms provided credit to Chinese merchants so they could get started. The Hongkong and Shanghai Bank also played a crucial role in lubricating the economy. MacDougall and Co. began to turn Hong Kong around.

Governor Young's plan. On May 1, 1946, Sir Mark Young returned from recuperation leave to resume his interrupted Governorship. He announced on his arrival that "a fuller and more responsible share in the management of their own affairs" would be given to the inhabitants of Hong Kong. He presented a plan to change the constitution of the territory. It was the first time that Hong Kong had been referred to as a "territory," so that was significant in and of itself. Clearly, the incoming Labour Government had a different attitude towards colonies than its predecessors. The gist of Young's plan was to give substantially greater powers to a Municipal Council and to elect two-thirds of its members with half of them being Chinese. Voters would not need to be British subjects. The rest of the members would be elected by representative institutions. Legco would be evenly divided between unofficial and official members, and the Governor would have a tie-breaking vote. After much local discussion, agreed proposals were promptly sent to London, where they sat. Sir Mark retired in May 1947. The Japanese had mistreated Governor Young and his health had not recovered.

Sir Alexander Grantham, 1947-1957

"The fundamental political problem of the British Colony of Hong Kong is its relationship with China and not the advancement to self-government and independence as is the case with most British colonies," thus said Grantham (1957) in his autobiography. It seems clear that Gov. Grantham was behind the demise of Young's plan. Whether he was right or wrong is a moot point today. Certainly Hong Kong has prospered as he expected and widespread demand for democratic reform began only after the Sino-British Joint Declaration of 1984 was signed.

Since Sir Alexander set the tone of post-war Hong Kong, it is important to understand the man and his thinking. His initiatives and response to events helped to bring modernity into what was once a colonial backwater, yet his changes were just an updating of pre-war colonial Hong Kong, hardly in tune with the socialistic and egalitarian waves sweeping postwar Britain. The Governor believed that Hong Kong was politically fragile and that China's past political form suggested an uncertain future for both China and Hong Kong. He thought that the place was tough enough to govern without the job being made impossible by by introducing democracy. Governor Grantham thought that democracy sounds good when you are talking about it but when you think more deeply about its implications for HK with its diverse loyalties, one would have second thoughts.

Nevertheless, with Grantham's support a modified version of the Young Plan went before the British cabinet in May 1952 and was agreed upon. Before it was made public, however, Grantham received a visit from the senior unofficials who said that the plan's implementation would be disastrous (Grantham, 1957, p. 112). The Colonial Office were horrified, but Oliver Lyttelton, the Colonial Secretary of the Conservative Government, had no difficulty in persuading the cabinet to reverse its position, since it interested the British electorate very little anyway. This was the only chance of introducing an element of democracy in HK without the risk of confrontation with China and was not to recur.

As Grantham (1957, p. 138) said, it was not so much that the new Government of China was communist but that it was strong and at some stage would want HK returned. Grantham believed that since HK would not last forever as an entity outside of China, it had a better chance of lasting longer and would be in better shape if there was no experiment with democracy. Further, he thought that the enterprise of a benevolent autocracy in HK lasting until 1997 was worthwhile from everyone's point of view.

Governor Grantham influenced Hong Kong's future direction significantly. A Sandhurst and Cambridge graduate, he received further preparation as a HK cadet for 13 years before tours in Africa, West Indies and Fiji. He was concerned with the welfare of the people but mindful of British interests and one who sought out practical men who would find practical solutions to problems. Grantham believed strongly in free trade, low taxes, and modest budgets. He knew China and its leaders and had studied Chinese in Canton but did not consider himself a Sinophile believing that Westerners who went too far were neither European or Asian.

When Mao conquered mainland China in 1949, all of the defeated KMT did not go to Taiwan with Chiang. A million refugees poured into HK doubling the population almost overnight and brought immense social problems in housing, welfare and education. They also brought political problems since many were KMT supporters. Mostly from neighboring Guangdong province, they were culturally attuned to HK, spoke the dialect, and many had relatives in the territory.

Since 1841, Chinese had been permitted to cross the border into HK and back without restraint. In 1950, the Grantham administration decided that this policy could no longer be maintained and closed the border, a very big step that led to a marked divergence of the way of life on both sides of the border. Also of great significance for Hong Kong, the Korean war broke out in June 1950 and lasted three years. [Editor: Records revealed in 1999 that Whitehall became so alarmed with the PRC in 1951 that it instructed Grantham to plan a possible retreat from HK, called Plan Cinderella (Macklin & Pegg, 1999).] HK's economy was seriously damaged by the United Nations embargo on the export to China of strategic goods. Bad went to worse as the United States extended the UN stand to a total embargo on every kind of trade with China. China trade being the lifeblood of HK's economy, these uncontrollable events were disastrous.

Before the mainland was conquered, Shanghai's leading manufacturers decided that they would do better in Hong Kong and transferred their factories with the machinery, skilled workers and management to establish a modern cotton spinning industry in the territory. Hong Kong thus had a new, sophisticated elite that was highly educated, English speaking, and aversive to learning Cantonese. The territory had had industries from before World War II but never on this scale. With the change of flag in China in 1949, the whole of its missionary and foreign welfare dispensing industry moved to HK en bloc where it performed valuable work and became a vocal lobby.

Hong Kong became sensitive to the oft-stated charge that it existed only for the benefit of the rich and the near rich. It was a claim that was clearly tested on Christmas day 1953 when a great fire at Shek Kip Mei north of Kowloon destroyed 50,000 squatters' homes. Except for the New Territories, all land in HK belonged to the Crown unless it had been specifically alienated. The one thing that Grantham's Government was determined not to do was to have refugee camps on the Palestinian model and let them become centers for KMT organization. This meant letting people build huts where they wanted. At least the police could control squatter towns. The simple plan defused the political and housing crises temporarily.

Some attempts at resettling squatters had been made in "cottage areas," pleasant enough but hardly scratching the surface as squatters numbered in the hundreds of thousands. In the past when large numbers flooded into HK, most returned to China after the crises subsided. Now that China was communist and unlikely to change soon, the situation was different. The Governor's answer was to select Ronnie Holmes (HK crises were usually met by appointing a man not a committee) to head a new Department of Resettlement. Holmes had distinguished himself during the war by escaping and serving with the British Army Aid Group in which he played a leading role. The plan was not to allow the squatters to rebuild on site but to allow them, with a promise of permanent resettlement later on, to rebuild their huts on a nearby area and use the vacated space to build a resettlement estate in seven-story blocks with 2,000 persons per acre. This was the beginning of HK's continuing public housing program, which has not only transformed the landscape but also the political tone of Hong Kong by providing the people with their own homes.

On the KMT's Double Ten celebration of the 1911 Revolution, October 10, 1956, a great riot erupted at Shek Kip Mei. By this time it was a resettlement estate housing 50,000 people in seven-story blocks peacefully enough. But on that great festival day when Nationalist flags were everywhere, a uniformed officer of the Resettlement Department tore down a paper KMT flag pasted up on one of the blocks. The rioting lasted for some time before it could be brought under control and 59 lives were lost. Away at the time, Grantham quickly flew back and assumed responsibilities from the hapless Colonial Secretary.

Grantham summed up HK's situation vis-a-vis Mao's China as being altered completely; the idea that Hong Kong could stay under British rule indefinitely was fantasy. The new regime was powerful and it was vehemently anti-Western, anti-British, and anti-Hong Kong. In such circumstances what were the guiding principles? Between the extremes of appeasement and provocativeness, a consistent balancing act had to be maintained to handle any number of incidents such as, the closing of a communist school, the deportation of an agitator or the prosecution of a communist newspaper for an especially seditious article. "We had to take a decision in the light (often obscure) of such facts as we had before us, and of our estimate or guess of the probable consequences of the course of action we proposed to adopt. All I can say, in retrospect, is that we managed to get by" (Grantham, 1957, p. 139).

Indeed, Sir Alexander retired in December 1957 after an arduous and productive decade. He left Hong Kong far more prosperous than when he arrived, but his views and actions inhibiting the introduction of democratic reform in Hong Kong will be subjected to fresh examination as time passes.

Sir Robert Black, 1958-1964
and Sir David Trench,1964-1971

Black started his career in Malaya and had been a prisoner of war in Japan. "I know all about planting rice," he remarked dryly when shown an art film on rice cultivation in Japan. He had been Grantham's Colonial Secretary before becoming Governor of Singapore. More liberal than Grantham, Black's leanings were tempered by his able Colonial Secretary Claude Burgess and decidedly brilliant Financial Secretary John Cowperthwaite. Although the Colonial Office wanted HK to be more welfare-minded and generally to be more like Britain, this was difficult to achieve because the whole ethos of Hong Kong was opposed to the welfare state.

Hong Kong and its administration had developed its own way of life. In 1958, the Colonial Office "granted financial independence," which meant that the HK budget was no longer subject to scrutiny in London (Rabushka, 1979, p. 3). In spite of its political fragility, Hong Kong was moving ahead but what was its destination? HK's economy had taken off and everything else could tag behind to be taken care of later. Cowperthwaite correctly gets much credit for the territory's economic success, on which everything else depended. It is important to realize that Hong Kong was already set on the course he was steering; it had been a free port with low taxes and no public debt for a long time.

What Cowperthwaite did was to add systematic expression and justification to those practices. At the heart of this was the belief that governments do not know better than markets and businessmen when it comes to commercial and financial decisions. Hong Kong maintained and practiced free enterprise philosophy at a time when the whole world was headed in the opposite direction. What is more the practice was defended with the utmost vigor against all opposition. Budget proposals were examined with extreme care, which was in the 1960s very valuable because HK had not yet learned to spend money well.

New educational institutions were developed to meet new and greater societal needs. A notable achievement of the Black era was the foundation of the Chinese University (see pp. 258-259). Steps were also taken to address questions of Chinese marriage that related to concubinage. A marriage ordinance was eventually passed in 1971 which recognized Chinese traditional marriages up to that date but not thereafter.

When Trench arrived in 1964, great things were expected of him. However, he turned out to be unexpectedly cautious. Sir David started his career in the Solomon Islands in 1938 and was awarded the Military Cross for work behind enemy lines during World War II. He spent most of his postwar career in the Secretariat, the HK Government's nerve center of top administrators, apart from a spell as Commissioner of Labour, where he had displayed great energy and a welcome disregard of sacred cows, such as refusing to speak to communist trade unions. He returned to the Pacific as High Commissioner, the post that Grantham had held, before becoming Governor of Hong Kong.

Trench certainly knew the Secretariat well, but he may have had too much respect for its wisdom. When his attempts to reform were resisted, he understood the counter arguments too well. One cadet suggested that "he would have been better as Colonial Secretary. You can get things done better from there." Trench was essentially a doer but a frustrated one. When he tried to amalgamate the Departments of Housing and Resettlement, a thousand arguments said it would be impossible or at least unwise. Another difficulty was that Cowperthwaite was so much brighter and incisive than department heads and other secretariat officers that even good ideas often got short shrift. In Keynes' memorable words, "It is the Treasury's job to turn down good schemes. Bad schemes should never get anywhere near the Treasury."

Yet there are limits. A testing point for Hong Kong came in 1967. There had been a riot in 1966, which caused one death and led to a public enquiry, for no apparent reason -- social discontent, a long hot summer, not enough outlets for youthful energy were suggested. A rise in first class fares on the Star Ferry was the ostensible spark. Mao's Cultural Revolution was just getting started. Like Hitler, Mao Zedong knew how to bring the worst out in people. In 1967, the Cultural Revolution (CR) hit HK hard with strikes by every communist-controlled union, including the public transport unions. The walls of Government House were plastered with abusive posters and noisy, well-rehearsed demonstrations were held there. Marchers in the streets flourished Mao's little Red Book. The communist press poured out a stream of virulent threats against the British. Primitive bombs, many made in communist schools marked "fellow countrymen, keep away," were left all over Hong Kong.

The vast majority of the population was unimpressed. Press advertisements representing over 900 groups supported the Government, including district associations, family associations, sports clubs, martial arts schools, commercial associations, etc. The Students Union of the University of Hong Kong published a notable protest against this attempt to bring down the HK Government. The Government proved itself skillful at counter-propaganda; and "the police showed great courage and determination, losing ten killed and many wounded, while continuing to act with disciplined restraint: 'Hong Kong neither bent nor broke before the storm' " (Welch, 1993, pp. 468-469). Derision followed loudspeaker calls from the Bank of China, such as, "Chinese policemen, lay down your arms or turn them on your European officers." Regular buses stopped but were quickly replaced by free enterprise and private minibuses.

The outcome was a deeper appreciation by the Government of the qualities and loyalties of the HK people, who themselves saw the Government as working for the stability and prosperity which they wanted. It seemed that Hong Kong was developing a true sense of community to replace colonialism. Pressure was put on exclusive clubs to admit Chinese members. Socially and otherwise, Hong Kong would never seem the same again.

When the British embassy in Beijing was burned down during the mayhem, the Foreign Office blamed Trench's refusal to release Chinese journalists arrested in the disturbances in Hong Kong. Meanwhile, in London, an official of the Chinese embassy attacked a policeman with an axe at the front door of the embassy. The effect of these developments was to reinforce the people's common-sense belief in and commitment to law and order. That was a great departure from 1948 when the police restrained a KMT-instigated riot in Kowloon's walled city and one rioter was killed. In protest, the British Consulate in Canton was sacked and burned with student support.

Sir Murray Maclehose, 1971-1982

Departing toward the end of 1971, Trench was replaced by Sir Murray Maclehose. He was the first of three successive governors from the Foreign Office. The Colonial Service had not exhausted its governor material, but Britain was running out of colonies in which they might receive suitable preparation. So there was a certain inevitability about such an appointment and it had been widely expected. There was a feeling in HK that things had not moved as fast as they should have. Postwar British Governments had thought so too, except that their view of progress and the HK community's were somewhat different. So Maclehose arrived with a plan and maybe a hit list of obstructive officials who had to be dealt with.

As for the plan he was always eager to spend money. Fortunately, Hong Kong itself was already getting much better at spending money carefully but in large quantities through such devices as the Public Works Programme, in which every project was assigned a priority and its cost carefully estimated. Costs and priorities were kept under continuing review. An early Maclehose innovation was to bring in the management consultancy firm, the MacKinseys, to examine the Government's machinery. The most notable change was to the Secretariat, the top echelon of officials. The post of Deputy Colonial Secretary, through whom all important government business passed, was abolished; secretaries were to cover the broad policy areas. The change speeded up business without causing noticeable harm, but it drew serious thinking about new policy into the Secretariat and away from the departments where it had largely lain before. As the departments were closer to the grass roots than the Secretariat officials, this was a mixed blessing. A mechanism of annual operating and long-term plans was also introduced but gradually faded away when it was found that the Civil Service was performing well.

Instead of extensive study and discussion on the issue of public housing, Maclehose took it upon himself to decree a ten-year plan which was impressively carried out. Against the advice of cynics, he risked his reputation on the successful "Keep Hong Kong Clean" campaign, which brought new standards of cleanliness to HK streets. Educational funds and opportunities were greatly increased (see Chapter Five). Because of unforeseen tunneling problems, the Mass Transit Railway, a massive private project underground, became more costly than expected and public funds were committed. The result is an excellent facility which transformed public transport. Trade was generally good, markets and finances buoyant, and the reserves increasing. All was right with Hong Kong.

Perhaps his most challenging project, Maclehose determined to combat corruption. His predecessor, Governor Trench, did little with HK's bug-bear. In 1973, world-wide publicity was given the escape of Police Chief Superintendent Peter Godber from Hong Kong after being accused of taking millions in bribes. The shock of Godber's case was great because he had distinguished himself during the 1967 riots; evidence against him was gained when a party of raw constables from the Police Training School was used to break into his safe. The high-stakes scandal helped to provoke a huge wave of indignation against corruption that finally led to the establishment of an Independent Commission Against Corruption (ICAC) that continues to combat syndicated crime independently of the police today.

The Governor appointed Sir Jack Cater (later the Colonial Secretary), to direct the ICAC with Sir John Pendergast as Chief of Operations. Pendergast was famed for his colonial police work combating Kenya's Mau Mau in the 1950s and in Palestine. They uncovered rampant corruption. The ICAC's effectiveness became apparent when "Policemen were arrested in veritable droves -- fifty-nine sergeants from a single division, one Senior Superintendent dead by his own hand, and three British Superintendents in custory -- as investigations revealed highly-organized corruption on an enormous scale" (Welsh, 1993, p. 492). Corruption was found to be so pervasive that an amnesty for past crimes, except the most heinous, had to be declared.

Because Hong Kong was ripe for change, Governor Maclehose succeeded over a wide field when his predecessors seemed to accomplish less. No longer a provincial backwater, Hong Kong was maturing and becoming sophisticated. People travelled abroad and began to care what other people thought of them and their community. Also, HK's income and resources were fast outstripping expenditures, so the expression, "We can't afford it," rang less true than before. Maclehose bent the civil service not only to his will but over to his side. He arrived with a plan but it was a flexible plan and he was able to carry it out. He made the most of what his predecessors had accomplished in developing HK's infrastructure, financial strength, and education system.

There was one big snag. The New Territories lease would expire in 1997, and bankers were adamant that the matter had to be settled. Money cannot be loaned against an indefinite future. There were of course other possibilities. One was for Britain to annex the NT. This could be done at the stroke of a pen if the two governments could agree, but it was unbelievable that the PRC would accept this idea. Another possibility was to ignore the question altogether until the Chinese brought it up. China had already persuaded the United Nations that Hong Kong had been ceded through an unequal treaty, one that China did not recognize. Also, Beijing had stated many times that the question of Hong Kong and Macau were questions to be settled by China and the occupying power when the time was ripe.

People on both sides maintain that the British were foolish to raise the question and that Hong Kong could have gone on happily without any notice being taken. Some say that the whole matter could have been settled in the Chinese way, that is, by some informal, discreet chat and money passing, which even if remotely feasible could never be explained to Parliament. In any case, MacLehose went to Beijing in the spring of 1979 and Deng Xiaoping, the PRC's paramount leader, raised the question himself. Maclehose came back having been told by Deng that there was no question of extending the lease but that HK investors could put their hearts at ease. "China would respect Hong Kong as a special case" (Cradock, 1994, p. 166). In conversation with former PM Sir Edward Heath in April 1982, Deng went further, asking whether the British would not accept "a solution on the lines of the nine-point plan for Taiwan. HK would remain a free port and international investment center. It would be run by HK people and would become a special administrative region of China" (Cradock, 1994, p. 171).

Unfortunately, at that time PM Margaret Thatcher was engaged in the Falklands War and there had no time for HK issues. Thus, Deng's initiative was set aside.

Sir Edward Youde, 1982-1986, The Good and True

Maclehose retired as Lord Maclehose, the first Hong Kong Governor to be raised directly to the House of Lords. His replacement was Sir Edward Youde, No. Two in the Foreign Office, a position quaintly titled as Chief Clerk. Although he did not complete his degree at the School of Oriental and African Studies, Youde became proficient in Chinese after becoming seconded from the armed forces to language studies at Cambridge. After joining the Foreign Office in 1947, he was appointed to the Nanjing embassy in 1948 as third secretary. Youde gained fame during the HMS *Amethyst* crisis of 1949 when at great personal risk the 24-year-old diplomat sought the release of the last British gunboat from the PLA on the Yangzi (Murfett, 1991). Youde was thoughtful and even-tempered and determined to do his best for Hong Kong. Well-respected in China where he had served as Ambassador, Youde quickly won HK's heart.

When negotiations began in 1982, Prime Minister Thatcher tried to stand upon China's treaty obligations but Deng Xiaoping replied scornfully. The British would have liked to retain HK's administration and thereby preserve confidence in the territory even if they had to surrender sovereignty, but they had no strong cards to play. Force was out of the question, since American support would be required and would not be forthcoming. Of course, China had a lot to lose if they took over and made a mess of things. Not only would China lose a valuable economic asset, but the world was poised to see the magic territory become another communist slum.

Yet if China was to take over it was hard to imagine a better deal than the "one country, two systems" formula that Deng Xiaoping devised for the 1997 transition. The Sino-British Joint Declaration says that Hong Kong will enjoy capitalism for 50 years, main- tain its own legal system including its own court of final appeal, and have the rights of free speech, press, assembly, and academic freedom. HK will have financial independence and no defence costs. The difficulty was believing it. There surely will be competitive pressure from Shanghai, which remembers the time when HK was just a backwater and Shanghai was China's leading commercial center.

The history of the Chinese Communist Party and of China generally did not inspire confidence that the PRC would uphold the Declaration. Many sticky points awaited negotiation and agreement and Youde labored tirelessly to effect the best for the territory. As for "the rule of law," China never had a system of clearly stated laws and an independent judiciary. Laws were always interpreted to suit the purposes of those in power.

The HK people were not overly happy, but there was nothing that they could do about it and it could be worse. Actually, there was one thing that they could do and that was to emigrate and this they did in large numbers to Canada and the USA. Fortunately, some returned to Hong Kong once they had fulfilled their residency qualifications and gained their foreign passports.

Youde was in the difficult position of not only having to govern Hong Kong but also to act as Whitehall's representative in its relations with China. The two roles were hard to handle; Youde was not allowed to forget Britain's wider interests in the world beyond the territory. Sir Edward was determined on two things: (1) He wanted to improve educational opportunities and he initiated the founding of the University of Science and Technology and (2) He was determined to set Hong Kong firmly on the path to democracy. On the second, he had great difficulties; for the Foreign Office thought it had done well to achieve a good agreement with China, and they did not wish to lose it all by pressing for democratic arrangements which China would oppose.

While in Beijing on yet another round of negotiations in 1986, Youde died of a heart attack. His character and dedication epitomized the best in British rule and his tireless efforts were greatly appreciated by the HK people, who were much grieved by his passing and gave generously to a foundation that Lady Youde administers in the SAR.

The Governors and the People

The story of Hong Kong's development is more than the sum of its governors and their administrations. All the same, there is a thread that runs through the long sequence of 156 years of British rule. It is too early to undertake a revised theory of imperialism or an audit of the colonial experience, but given that Great Britain took responsibility for Hong Kong and the people who came to live there, the question is, how did British rule meet this responsibility? This question can be answered, in part at least, by reviewing the governors made responsible for this trust. Throughout such a review, one is tempted to ask, Would I have done better in that position?

So what did British Hong Kong mean to the people who lived and worked there? To the Chinese, it was always an alternative to living in China. There were three evils from which to escape -- poverty, chaos, and persecution, often simultaneous. Natural disasters in China were on a scale beyond the capacity of its regimes to manage. Population pressure during the 19th century was extreme, and the Taiping Rebellion and other uprisings led to emigration on a large scale. Religious persecution was a factor for converted Christians and Buddhist sectarians. After 1949, KMT supporters fled the mainland, many to HK rather than Taiwan.

What did they seek and find? To settle in HK was convenient linguistically, gastronomically, and socially, and many passed through on route to remote destinations and returned. They were among their own people. Business and job opportunities were probably better in Hong Kong than in Australia, say, once the gold rush was over. Close to the mainland, they could travel back and forth for business and to visit relatives and attend schools. A Chinese way of life was possible in HK; families could raise their children as Chinese and native amusements and recreation were available (see Overview on the CSS). On the whole, the HK Government left them alone. As time passed, the people expected more from the Government in terms of education, housing, and medical treatment. Institutions became more sophisticated and patterned on foreign models, as in higher education and financial markets. After the border was closed in 1950, HK and its neighbor went their separate ways until Deng opened the adjacent Shenzhen Special Economic Zone in the mid-1980s for foreign investments.

In 19th-century HK, Chinese and other Asians did not expect to be treated as equals; but increasingly with the rise of wealth, education, and nationalism, expectations changed. Gradually, the gap was narrowed, especially with the accelerated "localisation" policy after the Declaration. Chinese residents and expatriates had similar life expectations and were generally judged by their merits and abilities. In spite of political uncertainties, overcrowding and pollution, many Chinese and non-Chinese find HK to be a desirable and stimulating place to live and work.

The first three in charge of Hong Kong, Elliot, Pottinger, and Davis, struggled with a chaotic situation. Davis brought some of his troubles upon himself. The three as well as those who followed them had great difficulty with instructions from Britain, which seemed to change inconveniently. They did get the place started and something like the rule of law in place, even though it took draconian means at times.

Bonham calmed things down in spite of having to save money to an extraordinary degree. Bowring was a disaster, although he had some good ideas. Hercules Robinson sorted out Bowring's mess with energy and used some of his better ideas. MacDonnell showed great energy and fortitude in fighting piracy and corruption Kennedy did nothing wrong and some things very right, such as inviting Chinese to Government House. Hennessy was another disaster with good ideas, which he could not articulate and put into practice. Bowen was not bad, though more pompous than others and often absent. Des Voeux and William Robinson were both mediocre. Blake took over the New Territories. Nathan built a prominent road and helped to start a vital railway. Lugard saw Hong Kong through the Chinese Revolution of 1911 and started the University of Hong Kong. May should have remained as colonial secretary or as commissioner of police. Stubbs struggled with a tumultuous general strike. Clementi sorted out Stubbs' problems. Peel, Caldecott and Northcote left little impression, for they governed when HK was a colonial backwater overshadowed by Shanghai. Young symbolized suffering under Japanese oppression and left a plan for democratic development which was never implemented nor forgotten.

Grantham saw Hong Kong through the communist takeover of China. Black founded the Chinese University of Hong Kong, and Trench saw HK through the Cultural Revolution. Maclehouse used HK's new resources to develop social services, integrate infrastructure, and combat corruption. Maclehose did great work standing on the shoulders of his predecessors, who built up the human and financial resources which he exploited so skillfully. Youde founded a third university and sacrificed himself for democracy. Chapter Seven covers Governors Wilson and Patten at length.

It would be unfair to rank them in order of achievement, since so much depends upon the circumstances they faced and the resources they commanded. For different and contradictory reasons, I single out Elliot, never formally governor, MacDonnell, Grantham, and Youde as exhibiting the qualities of energy, determination, coolness, and integrity which a colonial governor needed in British Hong Kong. On the whole, the governors were a decent lot and most of them suited their time. Spurr (1995) includes the portraits and photos of many governors as well as photos of Hong Kong across the years.

References

Cantlie, James, & Jones, C. Sheridan (1912). *Sun Yat Sen and the awakening of China.* New York: Fleming H. Revell Co.

Endacott, G. B. (1973). *A history of Hong Kong* (2nd ed., rev.) Hong Kong: Oxford University Press.

Grantham, Alexander (1965). *Via ports.* Oxford: Oxford University Press.

Hoe, Suzanne (1991). *The private live of old Hong Kong.* Hong Kong: Oxford University Press.

Lethbridge, H. J. (1983). Foreword. In reprint of E. J. Eitel (1895). *Europe in China.* Hong Kong: Oxford University Press.

Macklin, Simon & Pegg, Jo (1999, February 22). UK had plan to abandon colony. *South China Morning Post,* Internet Edition.

Murfett, Malcolm H. (1991). *Hostage on the Yangtze: Britain, China, and the Amethyst crisis of 1949.* Annapolis, MD: Naval Institute Press.

Perham, Margery (1960). *Lugard: The years of authority 1895-1945.* London: Collins.

Rabushka, A. (1976). *Value for money: The Hong Kong Budgetary Process.* Stanford: Hoover Institution.

Spurr, Russell (1995). *Excellency: The governors of Hong Kong.* Hong Kong: FormAsia.

Welsh, Frank (1993). *A history of Hong Kong.* London: HarperCollins.

Yee, Albert H. (1992). *A people misruled: The Chinese stepping-stone syndrome* (2nd ed., rev.). Singapore: Heinemann Asia.

CHAPTER THREE

Hong Kong's Health and Medical Services

Gerald Hugh Choa

The present is the opportunity for Hong Kong to take up a manifest long-neglected duty: to become a centre and distributor, not for merchandise only but also for science. I do not doubt our ultimate success, and when we succeed we shall not only confer a boon on China, but at the same time add to the material prosperity of this Colony. From Sir Patrick Manson's address at the Inauguration of the Hong Kong College of Medicine on October 1, 1887.

Origin and Development

Before 1841, Hong Kong Island was inhabited mostly by fishermen. Perhaps as many as 3,000 took shelter in huts built on the beaches on the south side of what is Shaukiwan, Stanley, Tai Tam and Abderdeen today. They did not seem to have health problems; but even if they did, no records would have been kept. British troops landed in January of that year on the north shore and soon found "this barren island with hardly a house on it" as described by Lord Palmerston, then Foreign Secretary, to be truly a white man's grave (see pp. 75-76). Mortality was exceptionally high as revealed by official statistics. In 1843, between May and October, 24% of the garrison and 10% of the European civil population died of what was called Hong Kong Fever. In later years the situation was no better. In 1850, it was reported that 136 out of 568 soldiers in one single regiment or 24% died of the same cause. In 1860 and 1871, the death rates among the European population were given as 64.8 per 1,000 and 30.3 per 1,000, respectively.

By comparision, mortality among the Chinese was remarkably low at 1.14% in 1848 and 0.61% in 1849. The unhealthy environment and climate were held responsible for the prevalence of deadly diseases (Eitel, 1895; Wright, 1908).

A Colonial Treasurer (nowadays Financial Secretary), R. Montgomery Martin, described the conditions in Hong Kong in a letter he sent home in 1844 as follows: "The formation of the island was of rotten granite and the material excavated in the course of building operations appeared like a rich compost: it emitted a foetid odour of the most sickening nature and at night must prove a deadly poision." Similarly, a doctor wrote that "the geological formation of Hong Kong is found to consist of strata which quickly absorbs any quantity of rain, which it returns to the surface in the nature of a pestiferous mineral gas." Another doctor, in describing this poisonous vapor, claimed that it had a depressing effect on mind and body, which undermined even the strongest constitution. The rains also helped to fill the swamps and marshes which became perfect breeding grounds for mosquitoes and other insects responsible for the prevalence of disease.

Settlers found the climate to be subtropical, temperate for half a year but hot and humid in the summer months between May and October, during which hurricanes known to the Chinese as typhoons would occasionally hit the area or pass close by, bringing devastatingly gusty winds and heavy downpours. The first recorded storm struck in July 1841, causing much damage to ships and the flimsy structures that were built on undeveloped and undrained grounds. Life indeed was extremely difficult for the Europeans who had to suffer from the environment and disease, but R. Montgomery Martin said in his letter that the Chinese never deemed HK as especially injurious to health and fatal to life.

Hong Kong Fever must have been malaria and its high mortality was probably due to the malignant *tertian* type. Its transmission by the *anopheles* mosquito, which Sir Ronald Ross discovered in West Africa in 1897, was not then known. Among the many who succumbed to the disease was the most promising government official at the time, John Robert Morrison, son of the pioneer missionary, Dr. Robert Morrison, who died before the curtain rose on Hong Kong (see pp. 219-220). Fluent in Cantonese, which he learned as a boy at his father's side, John Morrison served as interpreter for the British Superintendent of Trade. When he died in 1843, at the age of only 29, he was Colonial Secretary designate.

While the army and the navy promptly established medical services for their personnel, the civilian population was uncared for until the Governor, Sir Henry Pottinger, appointed a Colonial Surgeon in 1843, thus inaugurating a Government medical service. The Home Government did not approve of the appointment at first, insisting that lower grades of civil servants should get treatment from private hospitals and pay for themselves.

Operating from a dispensary, the Colonial Surgeon's duties included treating government officials and employees, their dependents and other nationals, but not the indigenous Chinese. There was a rapid turnover of Colonial Surgeons over the first five years. The first occupant was Dr. Alexander Anderson, a year later he was succeeded by Dr. F. Dill, who wrote the first Colonial Surgeon's report for the year 1845. The first volume of Colonial Surgeon's Reports for the first 15 years, 1845-1859, has survived and is kept in the Government Archives. The reports were written in black ink on foolscap papers; and after 100 years, the words read clearly. Dr. Dill painstakingly tabulated the number of cases of many diseases he had seen during the year 1845: 71 cases of ague fever, 60 cases of intermittent fever, 71 cases of diarrhoea and 51 cases of dysentery among other frequently occurring ailments. He blamed the mortality on "the constant exposure to the vicissitudes of the climate, the intemperate habits of the individuals, and the temporary dwellings erected on the damp soil." Dill himself died a year later and was succeeded by Dr. Peter Young who was replaced by Dr. William Morrison after only one year. Morrison remained in office for seven years and the situation stabilized.

In 1873, Dr. P. (Phineas) B. C. Ayres took over and served for 24 years, the longest period on record. Dr. Ayres' annual reports repeatedly criticized the insanitary conditions in the native quarters and called for the reform of buildings and drains but found no encouragement or support. In the end, it fell on him to lead the fight against the great Bubonic Plague Epidemic, which broke out in 1894 during the last three years of his tenure. More on the epidemic later.

After Dr. Ayres, the title of Colonial Surgeon underwent several changes -- Principal Civil Medical Officer in 1897, Director of Medical and Sanitary Service in 1936, Director of Medical Service in 1938, and finally, Director of Medical and Health Service in 1952. The titles reflect the duties of the holders.

The Principal Civil Medical Officer's duties included administration of the medical and sanitary departments, inspector of hospitals, port-health officer and superintendent of the Government Civil Hospital. The Directors were full-time administrators without clinical duties. With the appointment of a Director of Medical and Health Services in 1952, a Medical and Health Department was established. It was divided into two divisions: a medical division for administering hospital services and a health division for administering health services with the exception of environmental hygiene which then as now is the responsibility of the Urban Service Department under the Urban Council. In December 1990, a Hospital Authority was established as an independent body to take over the administration of government and Government-subvented hospitals from the Medical and Health Department. This restructuring put the administration of health services under a Department of Health headed by a Director of Health.

In 1952, Dr. K. C. Yeo became the first Chinese appointed head of the Service and also the first Director of Medical and Health Service. Dr. Yeo, a HK University graduate,· spent his entire working life in Government service and was Director from 1952 to 1958. Aged over 90 years now, he has been living in happy retirement in England since leaving office.

In HK's long succession of diligent and often heroic medical leaders, the most memorable and remarkable personality was undoubtedly Dr. P. S. (later Sir Selwyn) Selwyn-Clarke. He arrived in Hong Kong to assume the post of Director of Medical Service in 1938. He turned out to be an able, energetic and forceful administrator with much compassion for the indigenous sick and poor. His wife, Hilda, also became actively engaged in raising funds for local charities as well as the China Defense League. The League had been established by Mme. Sun Yat-Sen, then living in Hong Kong, and others for relief work in war-torn China.

Japan began its occupation of Hong Kong on Christmas Day 1941. Colonel T. Eguchi of the Japanese Occupation Forces took over the administration of the Medical Department. From 1942 to 1945 Hong Kong became a dead city; its once busy harbor was devoid of ships except for those that had been sunk, the economy came to a standstill, and public utilities and services were greatly reduced. Because of short supplies, rice was rationed from six ounces per person daily to four towards war's end. The Chinese departed for the mainland in a steady stream, resulting in a population decrease from 1.6 million to about 600,000. Under such circumstances, fortunately there were no epidemics and the incidences of infectious diseases remained normal. This was due to the Japanese being aware of the situation and the efforts of those working in the Anti-Epidemic Bureau of the Medical Department, to which Selwyn-Clark was assigned and K. C. Yeo was attached throughout the occupation.

The Japanese allowed Dr. Selwyn-Clarke freedom of movement for about 16 months, which he used to work tirelessly to obtain food and medicine for the Stanley Camp internees. He and his wife even managed to confiscate a dental chair from a godown and smuggle it into the Camp. His activities aroused the suspicions of the Japanese, who accused him of spying and passing on information and put him in solitary confinement for 19 months. Interned in Stanley, Mrs. Selwyn-Clarke and their daughter were reunited with her husband a few months before the war ended. They survived their ordeal weaker in body but not in spirit; after recuperation leave, Dr. Selwyn-Clark resumed his post as HK's Director of Medical Service.

In 1947 Selwyn-Clarke was appointed Governor of the Sychelles Islands, the first time in the history of the Colonial Service that a professional officer was made Governor. He received a knighthood on retirement. In his autobiography, *Footprints* (1962), he wrote that he forgave the Japanese for what they did to him because he found at least one humane person among them. This was Reverend John Kiyoshi Watanabe, a Lutheran minister in civil life conscripted into the Japanese Imperial Army and serving as an interpreter. He also risked his life to help British prisoners of war and European civilian men, women and children in the detention camps. It was to him that Sir Selwyn dedicated his book. While presumably Watanabe escaped punishment since *Footprints* gave no details, his wife and daughter perished in the 1945 bombing of Hiroshima. True to his magnanimous nature, Sir Selwyn bequeathed his body to the Anatomy Department of his teaching hospital, St. Bartholomew's of London for students to dissect. He died at age 83 in 1976.

Health Services

As early as 1843, in view of the heavy toll of lives taken by disease, a Committee of Public Health and Cleanliness was appointed with authority to enforce sanitary rules among all classes of the community. Although some health ordinances were enacted, the Colonial Surgeons were not satisfied and continued to warn of the danger of epidemics. Consequently, Osbert Chadwick, an associate member of the Institute of Engineers and a public health expert, was sent to Hong Kong in 1881 to investigate the overcrowded and unsanitary conditions. Chadwick's 1882 report recommended the removal of refuse and improvements in water supply, building construction, drains and sewers and the supervision of scavenging and night-soil removal.

To implement the recommendations, a Sanitary Department was created under a Sanitary Inspector. A Sanitary Board was also constituted to deal with matters concerning public health. The Surveyor-General (Director of Public Works today) was appointed chairman, with the Registrar General (in charge of Chinese affairs) and the Colonial Surgeon as the other two members. However, very little was accomplished until a cholera epidemic in 1883 warned the Government against further delay. In 1886 the Sanitary Board was reconstituted with the Registrar General as Chairman and additional members including two prominent physicians, Drs. Patrick Manson and Ho Kai (more later). The Colonial Surgeon was relieved of his duties as health adviser and a medical officer of health was appointed. A draft Public Health bill was introduced in the Legislative Council (Legco) in May 1887 to give the Board the power to make or amend by-laws relating to many sanitary measures, some of which would improve the living conditions of the Chinese, such as laying down standards of space, drainage, and ventilation.

The measures were hotly opposed by Chinese property owners whose self-interests made them afraid that they would suffer financial losses if their houses had to be demolished and rebuilt. Taking their side, the Sanitary Board's Chinese member, Ho Kai, also raised objections when the bill was debated in the Legislative Council. Strange enough for one who had been educated abroad, Ho Kai said that it was a mistake to treat the Chinese as if they were Europeans and argued that the proposed standards would diminish available building space and drive up rents. The bill went through several amendments over time. In the end, an emasculated version of the original was eventually passed by Legco in September 1887. Chadwick's second visit in 1890 raised the Government's stake; for without precedence, Governor Sir William Des Voeux had Chadwick appointed temporarily to his cabinet, the Executive Council.

Eventually, the decades-long Bubonic Plague Epidemic broke out in 1894 and proved to be a watershed for Hong Kong. Faced with the fiercesome plague, the colony was finally given a thorough cleanup and effective health legislation and control measures were enacted to make Hong Kong a much healthier place. The Sanitary Board became the Urban Council in 1936.

Because scientists knew very little about diseases in the 1890s, it was difficult to introduce specific measures to improve public health. Early attention was given the possibility of diseases being imported by ships and spread by seamen and passengers. A port health officer was first appointed in 1868, a post that was held by a private practitioner or a Government doctor, whose duty was to inspect all ships coming into the harbor and examine everyone on board. As expected, ship owners blustered when their ships were quarantined after suspicious cases were found. The longer the quarantine the louder they protested. However, vigilance was maintained and inspections worked well especially after the post of port health officer became full-time.

Colonial Surgeons in the 19th century reported that the diseases commonly found were: malaria, cholera, dysentery, smallpox, phthisis or tuberculosis, leprosy and nutritional disorders. Since then, the situation has changed dramatically. Cases of malaria today, which once caused many deaths in the early years, are usually imported. From 1986 to 1995, 1,923 malaria cases were reported, of which only 25 were of indigenous origin. Immigrants from China and Vietnamese refugees are occasionally detected with malaria.

Another dreaded disease, cholera is also under control but has not disappeared altogether, as there were 100 cases between 1991 to 1995. Until recently, pulmonary tuberculosis was a serious problem. During the particularly bad year of 1951, the notification rate was 689 per 100,000 and the death rate 207 per 100,000. Introduced in 1952, B.C.G. vaccination achieved a 98% result among newborn babies. In addition, effective drug therapy abecame available and the incidence of tuberculosis declined. The latest figures for 1995 were 100.97 per 100,000 notified cases and 6.8 per 100,000 deaths. Even more remarkable is that the mean age at death was 71 years and no deaths occurred under the age of five.

Before World War II, leprosy patients were sent to a colony in Sek Lun, a village near Canton. After the War, a settlement on the island of Heilingchau was maintained for some years but eventually closed as the incidence of the disease gradually fell during the last two and a half decades. Only 15 cases were reported in 1995. Nutritional disorders, commonly Vitamin B deficiency, manifested as beriberi and pellagra, were last seen among refugees who fled Canton after its occupation by the Japanese in the late thirties and then among the local population after Hong Kong was captured. As socioecomonic conditions steadily improved after the war, nutritional disorders gradually declined and disappeared.

Modern methods of prevention and control of contagious diseases have been introduced with remarkable success as they became available. Nowadays babies are given a program of immunization against nine childhood infections: BCG, smallpox, diphtheria, tetanus, whooping cough, measles, rubella, poliomyelitis and hepatitis, entirely free of charge. As a result, no cases of diphtheria, poliomyelitis, whooping cough and smallpox had been reported during the period of 1990-1994. Older children receive another dose of B.C.G. on entering Primary One. A school medical service in which private practitioners provided low-cost care to schoolchildren has been replaced by a student health service with emphasis on health promotion and disease prevention.

Two relatively new diseases threatening the community are AIDS and hepatitis. The general public is warned of the danger of contracting hepatitis A by eating food and particularly seafood contaminated by the virus. It is hepatitis B which gives rise to concern. It has been found that about 10% of the population are carriers of the virus, which is introduced by transfusion of blood and blood products, a dirty needle shared for instance by drug addicts and sexual or other body contacts. As the aftermath of chronic hepatitis B is cirrhosis and cancer of the liver. Since the latter is the second most common maligment tumor on the register, much attention has been paid to prevention and public education. Started in 1988, all new born babies are immunized against hepatitis B.

Auto-Immune Deficiency Syndrome (AIDS) raised its ugly head in 1986. It is estimated that there may be as many 3,000 HIV positive cases, those whose blood shows evidence of infection by the virus. Compared with the U.S. and other regions in South East Asia, HK's figures are relatively small. The actual number of serum positive had been increasing from 53 in 1986 to 520 in 1994, among them were 130 clinical cases of AIDS disease. The latest figures as of June 30, 1996 were 702 HIV cases and 214 AIDS cases, according to the *Public Health & Epidemiology Bulletin* of August 1996. To combat the disease,an Advisory Council on AIDS has been constituted with three main committees: Scientific, Education and Publicity, and Services Development.

Related to AIDS are other sexually transmitted diseases and drug addiction. Of those attending the social hygiene clinics for sexually transmitted diseases, most are in the 20 to 40 age groups. Similar to other developed countries, the commonest diseases are non-specific infections of the urethra followed by gonorrhea. Syphilis is no longer the commonest infection, the latest figure being 2.19% of the attendance. Health promotion activities are delivered by teams using videos and face-to-face interviews in the clinics which adopt an open door policy without referral.

Drug addiction has been a problem in Hong Kong from the beginning of its history, in fact, it was the so-called Opium Wars which led to its cession. Once openly sold to addicts by "farms" enfranchised by the HK Government for revenue (see pp. 36-37 & 134-135), opium has been gradually replaced by heroin. Heroin's administration by inhalation or injection is simpler but is perhaps even more dangerous and harmful. The Medical & Health Department introduced a methadone maintenance program in 1972. The total number of patients registered for methadone and attending the clinics was 10,006 as of December 31, 1995 and the average daily attendance was 7,002. A typical addict, according to a survey conducted three years after the program was started, was a man aged between 20 to 30 years, who began the habit between 15 to 19 years, had a job as laborer, hawker, factory worker, etc. and first took the drug because of curiosity, sex, fatigue, illness, and frustration. The Society for Aid and Rehabilitation of Drug Abusers has operated a detoxification program since 1963 on the island of Shek Kwu Chau where addicts volunteer to be confined.

Today, the state of health in Hong Kong is excellent as can be seen in vital statistics figures. The average life expectancy at birth has gradually increased to reach 76 years for males and 81.5 for females in 1995. The infant mortality rate at 4.4 per 1,000 births is second in Asia outside Japan and one of the lowest in the world, and so is the maternity mortality rate of 7.3 per 100,000 birth. Principal causes of death are the same as in the developed countries, namely, cancer (31%), heart disease (16%) and strokes (11%).

Cases of humans infected by the influenza virus H5N1, which normally affects chickens and other poultry, have occurred in Hong Kong. The first case reported was a 3-year-old boy in May 1997. Subsequently, more cases were discovered and up to December 1997, altogether 18 cases became known. This outbreak of Chicken Flu as it has become known attracted world-wide attention, because it was the first time the virus H5N1 was found to be capable of being transmitted to human beings. As authorities were concerned that there may be far-reaching implications for the rest of the world, they reported the incidence to and sought assistance from the U.S. Center for Diseases Control. They also took the drastic measure of slaughtering all chickens in the territory and banning their import from neighboring sources until no further cases were reported after two months.

Dental Services

The first dentist to practice in Hong Kong was Dr. Herbert Poate, an Englishman who qualified at Pennsylvania University, U.S.A. in 1878. Nine years later, he was joined by an American, Dr. J. W. Noble, also a graduate of Pennsylvania. Dr. Noble took an interest in medical affairs in Hong Kong and became a member of the HK College of Medicine and the Planning Committee of the University of Hong Kong. The Poate-Noble practice provided free service at the Alice Memorial Hospital (Walker, 1984).

A dental service is administered by the Department of Health today. Fluoridation of the water supply to protect dental caries among the people was introduced in Hong Kong in 1961, resulting in the decreased incidence of tooth decay. The Government's policy is to provide an essentially preventive and protective oral health care, together with curative dental service to special groups and emergency dental services to the general public. A School Dental Service was started in 1980 after establishment of a school for training dental therapists. The Service has benefited 80% of the primary-school population. Both the School Dental Clinic and the School for Dental Therapists are named after Sir Shiu-Kin Tang, the philantrophist who donated substantially to the building cost of the MacLehose Dental Centre on Queen's Road East in which the two are housed. The University of Hong Kong established a Faculty of Dentistry in 1981, which uses the Prince Philip Dental Centre on Hospital Road as its dental teaching hospital.

Medical Services

Since World War II, medical care for the general public in Hong Kong is delivered by a three-tier system. Patients first attend a general clinic which can be found in many localities in the territory. If necessary, they are referred to a specialist for consultation in a specialist clinic situated at various urban areas. For further treatment, they are admitted into a hospital. Accident and emergency cases are admitted directly. Public hospitals are of two categories: government and government-subverted, all, as mentioned earlier, under the Hospital Authority. Charges are kept at minimal levels affordable by the general public; in hardship cases, fees are either reduced or waived after assessment by a medical social worker. No one in Hong Kong is denied treatment because of any inability to pay.

The Hospitals

Some of the older hospitals have a very rich past. Their stories are well worth telling as they illustrate the humanitarian progress of and devotion to medical services in Hong Kong.

(a) Hong Kong Missionary Hospital, 1843. Protestant missionaries began to arrive in Macau in the early part of the 19th century. Among them were medical doctors whose motto was "Heal the Sick"; their objective was to evangelize the people while treating their ailments (Choa, 1990). The missionaries intended to go to China but were unable to do so because foreigners were not allowed to enter the country, although merchants were permitted to stay in the so-called Factories District in Canton during the trading season. Dr. Robert Morrison was the first to arrive in 1809. A Doctor of Divinity, not medicine, he set up a clinic in Macau that was operated by surgeons of the British East India Company as charity work. Next came Dr. Peter Parker, the first medical pioneer, who opened a hospital in Canton and another in Macau. Then came Dr. Benjamin Hobson in 1839, who was advised by the Medical Missionary Society to move the Macau hospital to Hong Kong after it was declared a British colony.

The first hospital in Hong Kong, which Dr. Hobson built and opened on June 1, 1843, was situated on present-day Morrison Hill in the Wan Chai District. In its first year of operation, the hospital had 3,348 outpatients and 556 inpatients. Those figures were quite impressive, in view of the prejudice against what the Chinese called "Western medicine." More will be said about Dr. Hobson later on. In 1848, he was succeeded by Dr. H. J. Hirschberg who enlarged the mission by opening a dispensary in Kowloon which was then Chinese territory. With no replacement after Hirschberg was transferred to Amoy, both the hospital and the dispensary were closed.

(b) Seaman's Hospital, 1843. The Seaman's Hospital was opened on Morrison Hill in August 1843. A Parsee merchant had originally offered to donate $15,000 to build it, but he never paid it because his business failed. Jardine Matheson & Co., however, came to the rescue with a donation of $20,000 and a further $2,000 was raised by public subscriptions. Seaman's first superintendent was Dr. Peter Young who became the third Colonial Surgeon in 1846. The cost for the hospitalization of sailors was defrayed by charging the shipping companies employing them. British subjects residing in Hong Kong were granted admission to this hospital and their bills were paid by the Government. Officials and civil servants also used the hospital as the HK Government did not have a hospital of its own. Eventually, the Seaman's Hospital had to close because it ran into financial difficulties in 1873. As the Royal Navy in Hong Kong had been looking for a shore-based hospital, the Seaman's was sold to the Admiralty by Jardine Matheson & Co. for the price of $36,000. After the main building was refurbished and new ones added, this Royal Naval Hospital was used up to the battle for Hong Kong in December 1941.

(c) Government Civil Hospital 1850 and other Government Hospitals. A Government Civil Hospital was not established by the HK Government until 1850. Similar to the appointment of the Colonial Surgeon, the Home Government was very reluctant to give approval, again on economic grounds, and instructed: "Provision (of a hospital) could be helped from Colonial funds only if the resources were sufficient, private benefaction would do the rest and the institution would be able to maintain itself." In the first year, 222 patients were treated with 18 deaths, and a year later 245 patients were treated with 36 deaths. Apparently, only so-called first-class patients were treated in this hospital, meaning paying Chinese and European nationals. The daily charge was $1, a very large sum of money in those days. When Government Civil Hospital was destroyed in a typhoon in 1874, a vacant hotel was taken over as a hospital, which in turn was destroyed by fire in 1878. Finally, in 1880 a proper hospital was built on Hospital Road; and this was the Government Civil Hospital, known also as the Sai Ying Pun Hospital which continued to function until 1937, when the Queen Mary Hospital was opened. The old building became an infectious disease hospital before it was torn down to be replaced by the present-day Prince Philip Dental Centre.

By 1881, there were other Government hospitals: a smallpox hospital on Kennedy Town, a Lock Hospital (for the treatment of venereal disease) and an Asylum, the buildings of which are still standing on Hospital Road and Western Street. In 1903, to commemorate Queen Victoria's Diamond Jubilee, a hospital for women and children was built on Barker Road on the Peak. It does not exist anymore but its foundation stone has survived, situated below the chief secretary's residence. In 1922, a small hospital with the object of providing a much needed maternity service and establishing a training school for Chinese girls as midwives was opened in October. Named the Tsan Yuk, it was situated at the corner of

Western Street and Third street in the Sai Ying Pun District. In 1952, the foundation stone for a new Tsan Yuk Hospital on Hospital Road was laid, and its opening ceremony was performed in 1955. The first Government general hospital in Kowloon was situated in Lai Chi Kok, which became an infectious disease hospital in later years. The Kowloon Hospital was opened in 1925 and the Queen Elizabeth Hospital in 1963. In 1961, a hospital for mental patients, known as the Castle Peak Hospital, was completed, thus closing the old Asylum buildings on Hospital Road which had become totally unsuitable by modern standards.

After the Queen Mary and the Queen Elizabeth, two more Government regional hospitals were opened, the Princess Margaret in Kwai Chung in 1975 and the Prince of Wales in Shatin in 1984. The Princess Margaret never had a proper opening ceremony, since it was requisitioned on short notice to receive the first boatful of Vietnamese refugees arriving on May 25th (see pp. 99 & 102). Coincidentally, the Queen, Elizabeth II, was visiting HK at the same time.

(d) The Tung Wah Hospital, 1872. Many Chinese who were dying would refuse admission to the Government Civil Hospital because of the fees and native faith in traditional ways and medicine. Since the overwhelming majority of the population were transients from China, most of the terminally sick and wounded did not have relatives at hand to care for them and transport the dead back to their home villages for proper memorialization. Since the foreigners had never encountered such a problem before, the Government did not have a satisfactory solution for very long. A charitable hospice, an *I Tze* or Free Charitable Temple, was established in 1851 in the Tai Ping Shan District where the dying could languish away. The scene inside defied description: the barely living and the dead lying side by side and huddled together in unbelievable squalor and filth. Although the authorities were shocked, which they should have been, a remedy required something innovative and would take time to decide upon and fund.

Finally, a creative idea was proposed in 1869 for a hospital that would treat Chinese patients with native medicine and practices and provide hospice needs. Governor Sir Richard Macdonnell readily approved the project which became the first institutional fusion of Chinese and Western traditions in Hong Kong. The Chinese Community raised more than $40,000 and the HK Government gave $15,000, a free piece of land and a grant of $100,000 from the Gambling Fund as a capital fund. After the foundation stone was laid in 1870, the Hospital opened two years later with the name of Tung Wah (Sinn, 1989). Although it was called a hospital, patients were treated by practitioners of traditional medicine. Other charitable services were provided, such as relief after typhoons and floods, provision of free passages for the living, and coffins for returning the dead to their native villages. An annually elected Board of Directors was responsible for Tung Wah's management and raising funds for its expenditures. More on Tung Wah Hospital later on. Other hospitals were added to form a Group of Tung Wah Hospitals: the Kwong Wah Hospital in Kowloon in 1911 and the Tung Wah Eastern in the Eastern district in 1912.

(e) The Alice Memorial Hospital, 1887. After its Hong Kong Missionary Hospital was forced to close in 1853, the London Missionary Society curtailed its work. Twenty-eight years later in 1881, the Society made a new beginning by opening a dispensary in the notorious, plague-stricken Tai Ping Shan District with Dr. William Young in charge. Then it was proposed that a hospital should be built. In 1882, the first HK Chinese to qualify in medicine as a doctor of medicine returned from Aberdeen University. Also called to the Bar at Lincoln's Inn as a barrister, Ho Kai , later Sir Kai Ho Kai, decided to practice law instead of medicine; as he soon found that there were more legal clients than patients. He also began to take an active role in public affairs.

Sadly, his wife, an English lady by the name of Alice Walkden, died in 1884. To commemorate her, Ho Kai offered to pay for the cost of building the Hospital which would be known as the Alice Memorial. A site was purchased on Hollywood Road for $22,000 to which the London Missionary Society contributed $14,000 and the balance raised by public subscription. Mr. E. R. Belilios, a bullion broker, made a further gift of $5,000, the interest from which was to be used for medicine. After the hospital opened in 1887, treatment for both in- and outpatients was entirely free. As it was the teaching hospital for the HK College of Medicine, more will be said about the Hospital and Ho Kai later on.

In 1893, the London Missionary Hospital opened another hospital on Bonham Road, known as the Nethersole Hospital in commemoration of the mother of Mr. H. W. Davis, an accountant. It was mainly for women and children. Later, another two hospitals were built on the same site: The Alice Memorial Maternity Hospital and the Ho Mui Ling Hospital, named after Ho Kai's sister, Ho Mui Ling, who was the wife of Ng Choy, the first Chinese barrister to practice in Hong Kong and the first Chinese member of the HK Legislative Council. Using the name of Wu Ting Fong (many Chinese have used different names for various roles), he became the Republic of China's Foreign Minister and Ambassador to America. Eventually, all four hospitals were merged into one, with Alice Memorial leaving its Hollywood Road site to become the Alice Ho Miu Ling Nethersole Hospital, popularly known as the Nethersole. The entire Nethersole complex was demolished in 1994, and a new Nethersole Hospital has been built at Fanling in the New Territories which became operational early in 1997. During its construction, the Nethersole continued to function by merging with the Pamela Youde Eastern Hospital in Chai Wan, a Government hospital which opened in 1994.

(f) The Hong Kong Sanatorium and Hospital, 1926. Four years before its founding in 1922, the Hong Kong Sanatorium and Hospital was a private hospital named the Yeung Wo Hospital. It was originally established by a group of senior Chinese doctors; Dr. Kwan Sum-yin, of the second class of graduates from

the HK College of Medicine; Dr. Jeu Hawk, who was trained in the U.S.; Dr. Wan Man Kai, a graduate of the Tientsin Medical School; and three other licentiates, Drs. Ho Ko Tsun, Ma Luk and Wong Cheong Lam. It served Chinese patients who preferred to be treated by their own doctors in a private hospital instead of the Goverment Civil Hospital.

In 1926, management of Yeung Wo Hospital passed to Dr. Li Shu Fan, who was a 1908 graduate of the HK College of Medicine. Dr. Li also took the degree of M.B.Ch.B at Edinburgh in 1910 and was elected a fellow of the Royal College of Surgeons of Edinburgh in 1922, the first from Hong Kong. He had a colorful career after he returned from abroad. At a relatively young age, he was Dean of a medical school and a Minister of Health in the Canton Government. Entering private practice in Hong Kong, he was asked to take over the Yeung Wo which was not doing well financially. Changing the name to the Hong Kong Sanatorium and Hospital, Dr. Li built extensions at the same Happy Valley site where it remains today and added more facilities such as a modern operating theater, he himself being a chest surgeon. Dr. Li Shu Fan's (1964) autobiography includes many amusing stories of his professional as well as personal life.

In recent years, under his brother, Dr. Li Shu Pui, the hospital has been renovated and redeveloped in phases to become the largest private hospital in Hong Kong. At the time of this writing, Dr. Li Shu Pui is 94 years old and still full of energy, running the Hospital as Medical Superintendent and performing some clinical work everyday. He also manages the Li Shu Fan Foundation, which was set up by his late brother for medical philanthropy, an example being the new Li Shu Fan Block for the Hong Kong University's Faculty of Medicine.

(g) The Ruttonjee Hospital, 1949. After resumption of British Administration in 1945, the Naval Hospital was so dilapidated that the Admiralty Board decided to give it up. And so begins the story of the Ruttonjee Hospital which was established after extensive renovation and reconstruction of the old buildings (Humphries, 1996). Its benefactor, Mr. J. H.Ruttonjee, who donated $2 million to help complete the project, placed it under the management of the HK Anti-Tuberculosis Association. The territory's past problems with tuberculosis have been discussed. The need for vigorous action against TB was clearly indicated; hence the formation of the charity and the building of a hospital for the treatment of all tuberculosis diseases. Mr. Ruttonjee's compassion towards TB patients was aroused by the loss of his only daughter, who succumbed to the disease as a result of deprivation during the Japanese occupation.

Geographically near the HK Sanatorium and Hospital, Ruttonjee became fully operational in 1949 and was staffed by members of the Order of St. Colomban, including doctors, nurses, radiographers, etc. Fortunately for Hong Kong, the sisters, whose plans were to work in China, were diverted to HK because the Mainland was torn by civil war. Two physicians, Dr. Mary Gabriel Mahoney and the late Dr. Mary Aquinas Monahan, received many awards for their contributions to the Medical Research Council trials on various anti-TB drugs and treatment regimens. Operating as a general hospital, a new Ruttonjee can be found on the original site. The incidence of TB has subsided to such an extent that a special TB hospital is no longer needed, yet another reminder of the progress that has been made in medical and health care in Hong Kong.

(h) Other hospitals. While an exhaustive list of all hospitals in Hong Kong is not intended here, a few more deserve mention. On Bowen Road, buildings of the British Military Hospital constructed nearly 100 years ago still stand and are now used by schools and voluntary agencies. On the Peak is the Matilda Hospital, having been there since 1907. It commemorates the wife of Mr. Granville Sharp, who willed that the hospital should serve destitutes of any nationality, except Portuguese and Chinese, a prohibition which is irrelevant today since there are no Portuguese or Chinese destitutes. The Catholic Church built St. Paul's Hospital in Causeway Bay in 1917, which is managed by the French Sisters of Charity. For some years after World War II, Dr. A. M. (later Sir Albert) Rodrigues was its Superintendent. He also found time to serve on both the Legislative and Executive Councils. Well-respected and admired for his services to the community, he is now retired. In 1964, the Church also built the Caritas Medical Centre in a populous district of Kowloon, where hitherto no hospital service was available. The London Missionary Society also extended their work by building the United Christian Hospital in the crowded industrial district of Kwuntong in 1973 to fulfill the needs of a sizable, growing population.

The Nurses

Proper nursing care as we understand it today came late to the hospitals in Hong Kong. The scene in any of the early hospitals could not have been too different from what Florence Nightingale confronted about the same period in the Crimea War of 1854-1856. When the Government Civil Hospital was opened in 1880, two European wardmasters were appointed but they were reputed to be beachcombers and fell into disgrace. There were Chinese male attendants, one of whom rose to become the first Chinese Wardmaster and worked for 25 years. In 1888, five French Sisters of Mercy were appointed but for various reasons they served for only a year. In 1890, it was recorded in the Colonial Surgeon's Annual Report that "Miss Eastmond the Matron with five trained nurses do the greatest credit to the Hospitals from which they came and by their skill and kindness have earned the good will of all with whom they came into contact." This praise led to the beginning of the Government Nursing Service.

Towards the end of 1891, Mrs. H. Stevens was appointed Matron of the Alice Memorial Hospital. She found a Chinese lady and a helper serving as nurses but the two knew little about nursing. At that time, recruiting intelligent and educated local girls to take up nursing was hard, as it was considered beneath their dignity to perform lowly chores and to be in contact with men. It was not until the end of 1893 that Mrs. Stevens finally found a willing and suitable candidate,

A. Kwai, who became the first trained nurse in Hong Kong. A second probationer was recruited in 1895 and two years later Mrs. Stevens reported that she could have as many as she could train.

The Midwives

When the Alice Memorial Maternity Hospital opened in 1904, Dr. Alice Sibree, probably HK's first woman doctor, an obstetrician and gynaecologist, was appointed to the staff. Known later as Mrs. Hickling, she started training midwives with three students. Nurses were sent to her from the Government Civil Hospital for training in midwifery. As a result, sufficient midwives were available when the Tsan Yuk Hospital was opened to provide midwifery training. Thereafter, other hospitals, government and private, offered training in nursing and midwifery; and the professions became popular to many girls seeking work after leaving school.

Medical Education

Earlier mention was made of the Protestant medical missionaries who arrived in South China early in the 19th Century and that Dr. Benjamin Hobson was the Superintendent of HK's first hospital. Besides healing the sick and spreading the Gospel, they planned to initiate medical education in China so that there would be Chinese doctors who could treat their own people. Hobson took on pupil assistants at the Missionary Hospital and went one step further by proposing the establishment of a medical college in Hong Kong. This he did at a meeting of the Medico-Churugical Society of China which local practitioners formed to discuss clinical and other problems (Rydings, 1973). He proposed an application to the Government for a site to build the college, which had to be abandoned because of insurmountable difficulties. Proficient in Chinese, Hobson was the first to write and translate medical textbooks; therefore, Dr. Hobson can be credited with starting medical education in Hong Kong.

Hong Kong College of Medicine for the Chinese, 1887. Forty-five years into British administration, the Hong Kong College of Medicine for the Chinese was established in 1887. The words, "for the Chinese," indicated that the College was founded to train Chinese as Western doctors, who were needed as the Government had organized a medical service for the general public. Meant to train doctors for China as well as Hong Kong, the College received the blessing of the most powerful Mandarin of the day, Li Hongzhang, who consented to be named the College's patron. Personal experiences with Western medicine had convinced Li of its value, for after his wife's condition was declared hopeless by native healers, a medical missionary cured her.

The College founders were private practioners who treated patients without re-

muneration at the teaching hospital, the Alice Memorial. Indeed, it was only because the Alice Memorial, which opened the same year, was available as a teaching hospital that the College could have been established at all. Most prominent
among the founders were Drs. Cantlie, Ho Kai, and Manson. By coincidence, all
three were medical graduates of Aberdeen University.

In addition to his law practice and teaching at the HK College of Medicine, Ho
Kai held many public offices as a member of Legco. He was the second Chinese
appointed to Legco after the departure of the first, his brother-in-law Ng Choy.
Ho Kai remained in Legco for a record 24 years. Furthermore, he was also active
in Chinese politics and wrote articles supporting the Reform Movement calling
for the revitalization of the moribund state of the Qing Dynasty and won wide
acclaim for the depth of his political thoughts (Choa, 1981, p. 134). After the Reform Movement failed, Ho Kai reversed himself and worked to help his former
student, Dr. Sun Yat-Sen, and other revolutionaries to found the Republic of
China.

Dr. (later Sir) Patrick Manson was posted to Formosa in 1866 as a medical officer in the Chinese Imperial Customs Services. Four years later, he was transferred to Amoy where he had the opportunity to research the disease *elephan-
tiasis*, which was common in the region. As a result, he contributed significantly
to tropical medicine by finding that the parasite *filaria* was transmitted by the
culex mosquito to the human body. This discovery was reported in 1877, well
before it was learned in 1897 that the *anopheles* mosquito transmits malaria. In
1883, Manson left China to enter private practice in HK and returned to England
six years later and founded the London School of Tropical Medicine and Hygiene in 1897 as a research and training center. Earning many awards and honors
during his lifework, Dr. Manson is acknowledged as the Father of Tropical
Medicine.

However, one lasting contribution is perhaps not well-known, which is that
Manson founded the popular Hong Kong Dairy Farm Co. to provide fresh milk
for the European population of his day. Dr. J. W. Noble, the American dentist
mentioned earlier, was Chairman of Dairy Farm's Board of Directors.

Dr. (later Sir) James Cantlie (Stewart, 1983) came to Hong Kong to join Manson's practice in 1887, at which time Manson was already thinking of leaving
Hong Kong. After spending ten years serving in the Alice Memorial Hospital
and teaching at the HK College of Medicine, Dr. Cantlie returned to England in
1896 and joined the Charing Cross Hospital staff as surgeon. He became Manson's ally in founding the London School of Tropical Medicine and on his own,
Cantlie founded the (later Royal) Society of Tropical Medicine. During World
War I, Dr. Cantlie worked diligently to help organize the Red Cross, St. John's
Ambulance, Voluntary Aid Detachments, and the Voluntary Medical Staff Corps,
the latter to provide first-aid, nursing care and treatment for the wounded. For
such outstanding services, he was knighted.

Before he returned to England, Manson was elected the first dean of the HK
College of Medicine (Manson & Alcock, 1927). In his 1897 inaugural address, he

said, "the object of course is the spread of medical science in China, the relief of suffering, the prolongation of life and as far as hygiene can offer the increase in comfort during life." Manson taught internal medicine at the College, Cantlie surgery and Ho Kai medical jurispudence.

Other clinical teachers included Dr. William Hartign, diseases of women and midwifery, Dr. J. C. Thomson, pathology and Dr. G. P. Jordan, public health (more on Jordan later). The course of study was five years to be taught in English. At the end of the course and after a number of professional examinations, graduates were awarded the diploma of Licentiate of Medicine and Surgery College of Medicine for Chinese (L.M.S. C.C.).

The first students assembled six months after the Alice Memorial became operational in 1887. Each affording the tuition fee of $60 a year, 12 students were in the College's first class, among them the College's most illustrious and famous alumnus, Dr. Sun Yat-sen, founder of the Republic of China. He proved to be the top student of the class, scoring the highest marks in all examinations throughout the course, at the end of which only he and one other student, Kong Ying Wah, graduated in 1892 (Lo, 1967). This is not the place to present even a short biography of Dr. Sun, but it should be mentioned that he practiced only two years in Macau and sacrificed a worthy medical career to devote the rest of his life to the Revolutionary Movement and establish the Republic of China (Choa, 1992). The remarkable story of his rescue by his former teacher, Dr. Cantlie, when he was kidnapped and imprisoned in the Qing China legation in London is too well-known to be repeated here. Perhaps lesser known was Sun's acknowledgment of his debt to the British in his address to the Students Union when he visited the University of Hong Kong in 1923, saying that it was in HK that he learned about democracy (see p. 45). His co-graduate, Kong Ying Wah, returned to Borneo and never practiced in HK. The first graduate (1893) of the College to practice in Hong Kong was Dr. Kwan Sum Yin.

Dr. Manson left Hong Kong in 1889, two years after the College opened and was succeeded as dean by Dr. Cantlie who presented the two graduates at a ceremony held in the City Hall in July 1892. His address reminded the gathering that "we (the teachers) who had taught them without pecuniary award or extraneous help freely, now hand over our offspring to the great empire of China where science is not yet known." Dr. Cantlie also expressed the hope that "the greatest effect of the work done in the College will be beyond this small island and extended to the treaty ports where human suffering can now be relieved by the most advanced methods known to the healing art."

In 1905, some reforms were introduced into the College, notably the deletion of the three words "for the Chinese" so that students of other nationalities could be admitted. The first non-Chinese student to graduate from the College was Dr. E. L. de Sousa from Malacca. Other foreign students were mostly from Malacca, Penang, Singapore and Ceylon. The HK College of Medicine was dissolved in 1915 when it was absorbed into the Faculty of Medicine of the newly-established University of Hong Kong. Its record cannot be regarded as impressive, for of the 128 students admitted only 51 graduated during its 22 years of existence. However, its high humanitarian ideals and far-reaching pioneering activities cannot be understated, especially in combining Western medical knowledge and Chinese needs and students for the betterment of HK's health services.

The University of Hong Kong, 1912. With strong community support for the idea preceding his arrival, Governor Sir Frederick Lugard, a farsighted adminis-trator, officially proposed the founding of a Hong Kong university in 1907 (see pp. 228-230). Sir Frederick as well as the gentry saw the great need for a univer-sity to satisfy two importants goals: (1) prepare local students for the professions that a growing, vibrant city required and (2) promote East-West interchange by introducing modern science into China and Asian philosophy into English-speaking societies. Community leaders responded generously to Lugard's call for donations, the largest of which was made by Sir Hormasjee Mody who gave $150,000. Ho Kai again played a vital role on the preparatory committee, active-ly soliciting donations, writing the constitution and arranging for the transfer of the College of Medicine to the University of Hong Kong (HKU), which opened in September 1912. Medical education was thus raised to university level in Hong Kong (Endacott, 1973, pp. 282-283 & 296).

The Faculty of Medicine offered a six-years course of study leading to the degree of Bachelor of Medicine and Bachelor of Surgery (M.B.B.S), which soon gained recognition by the General Medical Council of the United Kingdom (Ride, 1962). The M.B.B.S. is the basic qualification similar to the M.D. of other countries, whereas the M.D. in the British system is a higher postgraduate degree taken after further study and examination. The Government Civil Hospital in Sai Ying Pun became the medical faculty's teaching hospital.

First to graduate was Dr. G. H. Thomas, who had completed the College of Medicine course in 1912 but desired the HKU degree. Thomas worked in the Medical and Health Department until retiring as its Deputy Director in 1949. Afterwards, he continued to work at Tung Wah Hospital as a visiting surgeon until he completed 50 years of career service. Dr. Thomas was so versatile that he taught almost every clinical subject in the curriculum as a part-time HKU lec-turer. He was the first to obtain the higher degree of Doctor of Medicine (M.D.) from HKU and was also the first from the territory to be elected Fellow of the Royal College of Surgeons of England (F.R.C.S.) without examination. Dr. Thomas enjoyed telling the following amusing story about his graduation:

Three licentiates of the College of Medicine including me were admitted as advanced students eligible for the degree of M.B.B.S. after a period of two years of further study at the University. At the end of the prescribed two years, seven candidates presented themselves for the final examination. Lavish preparations including a banquet had been made for the first degree conferring ceremony in which the Chancellor and the Vice-Chancellor would officiate, but alas, it ap-peared that none of the seven applicants had been found worthy of the degree. Faced with the awkward situation, the authorities decided to produce one candidate for the ceremony according to plan. I believe that they selected me on the mistaken assumption that I, who was already holding the post of medical officer at the Tung Wah Hospital since 1912, would probably be the one calculated to do the least harm to the community. I firmly believe that this is the true story that I, in May 1914, obtained the coveted but undeserved distinction of being the first graduate of the Hong Kong University.

While all found Dr. Thomas' story amusing, knowledgeable people of course did not believe the details.

As at the College, early medical instruction at HKU was given by private practitioners. The first dean was Dr. Francis Clarke, a principal medical officer in Government Service. Named Chair of Physiology in 1913, Dr. G. E. Malcolmson was the first, full-time professorial appointee. Dr. Clarke held the title of Professor of Medical Jurispudence. In 1914, the Chair of Anatomy was filled by Kenelm H. Digby, who later became Professor of Surgery. Greatly admired as a teacher by his students, Dr. Digby worked at HKU for over 30 years and survived internment during WW II. Later, Dr. Wong Chung Yik, who graduated form the College of Medicine in 1908 and then studied at Edinburgh, became HKU's first Chinese professor and held the Chair of Pathology from 1920 to 1930 (Evans, 1987).

From its founding to the outbreak of the Second World War, HKU's Faculty of Medicine progressed uneventfully. Some suggested that it should be disbanded because its purpose of supplying China with doctors was not being fulfilled and the fact that graduates found it difficult to make a living because Hong Kong had too many practitioners. Fortunately, the Faculty was not disbanded.

Meanwhile, the University ran into financial difficulties which generous support from the Rockefeller Foundation in the U.S. resolved. There was no organized training program for graduates. Each professor had under him a first and a second assistant, equivalent to senior lecturer and a lecturer nowadays. Usually, the second assistant was appointed after a year or two as a clinical assistant. Two or three years later, he would succeed the first assistant who would have entered private practice and then he himself would follow the same path after another two or three years. Four members of the staff appear to have benefited by further training abroad that Rockefeller Foundation travel fellowships made possible -- Drs. S. W. Phoon in surgery, T. Y.Li in medicine, D. K. Samy in obstetrics and gynaecology, and M. B. Osman in pathology. No significant research was done owing to the lack of funds and perhaps initiative as well.

World War II. Hong Kong was occupied by the Japanese from December 1942 to August 1945 when the University ceased to function altogether. The day after war broke out, a meeting of the Academic Senate was held at which it was resolved to award wartime degrees to all students in their final year without further examinations, including the M.B.B.S. for all final-year medical students. Shortly after the occupation commenced, many medical students departed HK and made their way to what was then known as Free China. Fortunately, Gordon

King, Professor of Obstetrics and Gynaecology and Dean of the Faculty, had made a dramatic escape from Hong Kong himself and was available in China to assist those students. Dr. King placed the students in medical schools in China so that they could continue their studies -- Lingnan University in Guangdong, Hsiany-ya Medical College in Kweiyang, Shanghai Medical College in Chung-king or Chongqing, and the West China and Cheelo Universities in Chengdu.

When British rule was resumed in Hong Kong after the war, some of the medical students had completed their studies in China; on their return, they plunged themselves into the rehabilitation of the medical and health service. Had there been a hiatus without this pool of wartime graduates, HK's medical services would have been slow to recover. Thanks to the foresight and courage of Gordon King and the persistence of the students, the community enjoyed far better medical services than deemed possible.

Dr. King returned to his former posts as professor and dean. He was one of the last of that breed of Protestant medical missionaries who worked in China. He served on the staff of Peking Union College and Cheeloo University, both Christian institutions, before going to Hong Kong in 1938. After he retired in 1956, he was succeeded by the University's first female professor, also the first HKU M.B.B.S. to hold a chair, Dr. Daphne Chun.

Besides Gordon King, another British professor, Lindsay T. Ride of physiology, made an even more dramatic escape from the POW camp in Shamshiupo, literally under the noses of Japanese guards constantly patrolling the compound. Commissioned as a major in the Hong Kong Volunteer Regiment in charge of the Field Ambulance Brigade, Dr. Ride was captured by the Japanese after the garrison surrendered on Christmas Day 1941. Smuggled into China after breaking out of prison with the daring help of Chinese, Dr. Ride assumed command of the British Army Aid Group, a unit organized to gather intelligence and to assist POW escapees from HK (see p. 92). Returning to Hong Kong after the war as Sir Lindsay Ride, he became Vice-Chancellor of HKU (same as university president in the U.S.; governor and chief executive are titular chancellor) from 1945 to 1964.

There were casualties among the medical staff, notably Prof. R. C. Robertson of Pathology who, unable to endure the hardship and indignity of internment, took his own life by jumping from the Pathology Institute's roof on Caine Lane.

By the autumn of 1948, the Faculty of Medicine was functioning again and so began a new chapter in its history. A new staff assembled in the postwar momentum, together they planned a new teaching program to include research and postgraduate training.

The brightest star among them was undoubtedly A. J. S. (Alec) McFadzean, the Professor of Internal Medicine, who came from Glasgow. Appointed at the relatively young age of 34, he spent 25 years at HKU until his retirement in 1974. By dint of hard work and sheer determination, he built a department that became internationally renowned for its quality of research. Of the galaxy of those that he trained, many became chairs of medicine as more were founded. The best catch was a veteran who had already held pathology chairs at Chinese universities and was internationally famed, Professor Hou Pao Chang. An authority in Chinese classics as well as pathology, Dr. Hou trained many HK pathologists, a difficult task as the subject matter was by no means popular with local students in those days.

Another veteran coming from China was Leslie Kilborn, also a medical missionary as was Gordon King. Dr. Kilborn had been Professor of Physiology and Dean at the West China Union University that British and Canadian missionaries diligently operated in Chengdu for many years. To complete the list, the Chair of Surgery went to F. E. Stock from Liverpool and Anatomy to S. M. Banfil from Canada, shortly replaced by Francis Chang from Singapore.

Chinese University of Hong Kong. A more recent event was the establishment of a Faculty of Medicine at the Chinese University of Hong Kong. In 1973, the Government published a White Paper, titled, "The Further Development of Medical and Health Service in Hong Kong," which recommended that HK's annual intake of medical students be increased by 100 in order to fill vacancies anticipated in future years. As HKU was already at full capacity and further physical extension would be difficult, the University Grants Committee decided to establish a second medical faculty at the Chinese University of Hong Kong (CU), itself only founded in 1963 (Choa, 1970, 1992, & 1994).

As the new Faculty of Medicine admitted its first students in 1981, unexpectedly, history repeated itself. It will be recalled that the HK College of Medicine's teaching hospital was the Alice Memorial, which later evolved into the Nethersole. When CU medical students were ready to begin clinical studies in 1983 at their designated teaching hospital in Shatin, the Prince of Wales, its construction had not been completed. Arrangements were then made for tempory use of the United Christian Hospital in Kwuntong, in fact a sister hospital to the Nethersole, both being under the management of the London Missionary Society. The change caused many to fondly recall the story of the College of Medicine and the Alice Memorial Hospital in the 1880s.

To summarize, the history of medical education in Hong Kong can be divided into four periods: *1.* 1887 to 1915, founding and work of the HK College of Medicine; *2.* HKU, 1915 to 1941; *3.* war years of 1941 to 1945 when HKU medical students continued their studies at medical schools in China; and *4.* postwar rehabilitation and Chinese University's Faculty of Medicine.

Western versus Chinese Medicine

On February 1, 1841, a joint manifesto written in Chinese in the names of Captain Charles Elliot, Plenipotentiary, and Commodore Sir James Bremer, Commander-in-Chief, addressed the inhabitants of Hong Kong. It contained the following passages:

The inhabitants are hereby promised protection, in Her Majesty's gracious name, against all enemies whatever, and they are further secured in the free exercise of their religious rites, ceremonies and social customs, and in the employment of their lawful private property and interests. They will be governed, pending Her Majesty's further pleasure according to the laws, customs and usages of the Chinese . . . .

It was the 20th year of the reign of Qing Dynasty Emperor Daoguang. Gradually, more and more people from neighboring districts of China went to Hong Kong to improve their livelihood, and the influx increased after the onset of the Taiping Rebellion in 1850. Deeply conservative in mentality and outlook and ignorant of the outside world altogether, those Chinese were facing foreigners for the first time and were suspicious of their motives and bewildered by what they perceived to be highly strange ways and customs. This was the society the HK Government had to deal with at the beginning, and it wisely adopted a policy of laissez-faire noninterference (see pp. 109- 113).

The practice of traditional medicine was regarded by all Chinese as a valid, social custom. In any case, the Government had no intention to impose Western medicine on the people. Here, a parallel must be drawn between what Westerners did in China and in Hong Kong. In China, the Protestant medical missionaries made a deliberate, concerted effort to introduce Western medicine and eventually changed the medical outlook. HK's first hospital, that Dr. Benjamin Hobson established as mentioned earlier, made relatively little impact and soon closed down. The HK Government was slow in organizing a medical service to include the Chinese, so there was no alternative for the people but traditional medicine for a long time. This suited the Chinese very well, for faith in their brand of medicine was not to be easily shaken. Even after Government Civil Hospital was opened, in the words of Dr. Ayres, "the Chinese rarely enter a hospital unless they are so ill as to be unable to support themselves, or are in the last extremity of disease, having a great dislike for any restraint upon their freedom of action."

A distinctive aspect of Chinese civilization, the oldest in the world, traditional medicine is different in both theory and practice from the West. The scene of a practitioner sitting in a herbalist shop, diagnosing patients by feeling the pulse, has never changed and can still be seen today in Chinese communities around in the world. Skill lies in the sensitive and knowledgeable interpretation of the pulse in making diagnoses and prescribing the right herbs for treatment. The Chinese pharmacopoeia includes thousands of herbs which have stood the test of time in effectiveness. Some in fact had been used long before they were known in the West, the best known example is *ma hwang* which contains the alkaloid, ephedrine, for treating asthma. Given a choice between Western or Chinese medicine, most Chinese would prefer the latter. They would not believe that a teaspoon or two of some foul-tasting liquid could be more effective than their copious draughts of herbal concoctions. Such practices as bloodletting and enema were regarded by them as doing more harm than good to a body already weakened by disease. Essentially, they felt that Western medicine did not suit the

Chinese constitition which they believed was very different from that of the Westerners. It could also be that, being smaller in build, they could not tolerate the medicinal dosages usually prescribed for bigger and heavier Europeans.

In any case, in the early 19th Century, Western medicine could offer little that was better except surgery, which the Chinese abhored and traditional practitioners could not perform.

The medical missionaries took advantage of their strong point, and so it was said of Dr. Peter Parker that his lancet "opened the gates of China when European cannons could not heave a bar." The young American missionary succeeded in winning the respect of the Chinese in Canton by removing cataracts, extracting bladder stones and excising disfiguring tumors. Operating without anesthesia, Dr. Parker took pride in learning to perform amputations of severely broken limbs in a few minutes. Nevertheless, the HK Chinese became convinced of the efficacy of Western medicine through the Bubonic Plague Epidemic of 1894 to 1923, the worst disaster to strike Hong Kong other than WW II and the most significant event in its medical history.

The Great Bubonic Plague Epidemic

The epidemic originated from Yunan Province where it had been endemic for some years. In 1893, it started to spread across to Guangxi Province to reach Guangdong Province a year later. Cases began to appear in Canton, the capital city of Guangdong, in March and because the two cities are neighbors, the plague reached HK in May 1894. On May 8th, Dr. J. A. Lowson, a Government medical officer, saw and diagnosed the first case -- a ward boy in the Government Civil Hospital, who died shortly after he lapsed into coma. No effective treatment was then available. Long known as the "Black Death" in Europe, its devastation of London in 1665 was reduced through quarantines. In plague-stricken Rome in the 3rd century, 5,000 succumbed each day. From 1334-1354, bubonic plague killed three-fourths of Europe's and Asia's populations.

In the first few months, Lowson was in charge of the service in the absence of the Colonial Surgeon, Dr. Ayres, who was on leave. A strong-willed, uncompromising and rather self-conceited man as seen from his diaries, Lowson was the unsung hero of the Epidemic (Choa, 1993). Having quarreled with higher officials, he was probably never forgiven for his rash behavior and did not receive any recognition or award for his contributions in the early phase of the epidemic. After the initial discovery, many cases appeared in the notorious district of Tai Ping Shan where the poorer Chinese lived together with pigs and other animals in appallingly overcrowded, insanitary conditions, without proper ventilation, water supply and drainage -- a perfect breeding ground for rats, which were found to be a host of the bacteria two years later in India.

To eradicate this focus, about 300 structures were eventually demolished, dislodging some 7,000 inhabitants. They were replaced by new houses built according to standards laid down in newly enacted legislation with the provision of windows, privies and space in front and back. Action was taken immediately to give the entire environment a thorough cleanup. To enforce notification of cases and deaths, British soldiers from the Shropshire Regiment were deployed to conduct house-to-house searches for unsanitary conditions. Plague patients were isolated in a hospital ship anchored in the middle of the harbor and also in converted hospitals. As their houses were sprayed and fumigated, inhabitants were forced to present their clothes, beddings and other belongings for disinfection. The Chinese community objected violently to these measures, which they argued as unwarranted intrusion into their privacy and causing unnecessary inconvenience and hardship. They even went to the extreme of hiding their sick and dead to avoid having their houses quarantined for nine days.

The epidemic lasted three decades from 1894 to 1923. During the entire period, 21,867 cases were reported with 20,489 deaths, a mortality rate of 93.7%. The incidence fluctuated from year to year with typical lapses between bad outbreaks. Eventually, the epidemic ended abruptly. The majority of the cases occurred among the Chinese but it should be remembered that the population was 95% Chinese.

There were deaths among Europeans, in spite of their better living standards and hygiene. Some British soldiers and two British nurses fell victim through patient contact. One 1895 graduate of the HK College of Medicine, Dr. U. I. Kai, died of the disease while serving as house surgeon at the Alice Memorial Hospital. The high mortality reflected the uselessness of the then available treatments, whether by anti-plague serum or Chinese herbs. Many, both expatriates and Chinese, panicked and fled the territory in large numbers. Consequently, the economy suffered badly and life nearly came to a standstill. "As far as trade and commerce were concerned, the plague epidemic assumed unexampled calamnity," reported Gov. Robinson to the Home Government (Sayers, 1975).

Vigilance continued long after the epidemic ended. Older residents recall two measures which were retained until shortly after World War II. The first was the tin boxes attached to lamp posts for people to deposit rats that they caught. The other was the periodic cleaning exercise regularly carried out in certain districts when streets, lanes and backyards were swept with water containing quicklime and Jeye's fluid deposited in tanks at convenient locations for people to wash their beddings, furniture and household utensils. People were therefore constantly reminded that sanitation was essential to protect community health and prevent disease.

The Kitasato-Yersin controversy. During HK's battle with the plague epidemic, the causative organism was identified, a scientific breakthrough that put Hong Kong forever into the history of medicine. Controversy over which scientist was the first to identify the bacillus still illuminates the discovery. Drs. Shibasahuro Kitasato and Alexandre Yersin, a Swiss of French ancestry, announced their respective plague bacillus within days of each other.

Director of the Institute of Infectious Diseases in Japan, Kitasato was trained by the famed Robert Koch, the German bacteriologist who first established the bacterial cause of infectious diseases, such as anthrax and tuberculosis. Working with Dr. Emil Behring at Koch's laboratory, Kitasato helped to develop immunization antitoxins for tetanus and diphtheria for which Behring was awarded the Nobel prize in medicine in 1901. Dr. Kitasato's credentials seemed impeccable. Inspector General of the Pasteur Institutes at Saigon, Hanoi, and at Da Lat in Indochina (Vietnam today), Dr. Yersin had helped P. P. E. Roux to develop a diphtheria antitoxin at the Pasteur Institute in Paris.

Kitasato arrived in Hong Kong on June 12, 1894 and discovered his bacillus two days later. He immediately wired the medical journal, the *Lancet*, and issued a public announcement and addressed a public gathering. The *Hong Kong Weekly Press* reported his presentation on July 15th: "In the first day he was able to discover the bacillus in the bubo, lungs, liver and spleen of dead patients and he immediately made a culture in agar agar, on the same day he took with all precautions some blood from the finger tips of patients suffering from the disease in a severe form and again found the bacillus. He then inoculated mice, guinea pigs and rabbits with the virus, and in every instance the animals so inoculated displayed the symptoms of the disease and died."

Much younger than his Japanese rival, Yersin arrived in Hong Kong on June 15, 1894 and made his discovery on the 20th according to his diary. Declining to share Kitasato's laboratory matshed, Yersin set up his own and soon accused Kitasato of obstructing his work. Unable to perform autopsies, he obtained buboes by bribing those removing dead bodies. Typically, the lymph glands of plague victims swell in the armpits and groins after the onset of high fever; those glands are called buboes, hence the name, bubonic. After his own discovery, Dr. Yersin sent a report and some specimen material to Paris without fanfare.

Much debate followed the release of Kitasato's and Yersin's findings. Who was first? Which of the two bacilli was the actual source of plague, since they appeared to have different characteristics? A summary of Kitasato's findings was published by Dr. E. Larange (1926), who had been Yersin's assistant in Indochina. The *Lancet* issue of August 11, 1894 quoted Kitasato as reporting: "The organism, which is a bacterium resembling the bacilli found in the haemorrhagic seticaemias, except that the ends are somewhat rounded, when stained lightly appears more like an encapsulated diplococci, but when more deeply stained, it has the appearance of an ovoid bacillus. When, however, it is focussed more accurately, it is still possible to see the diplococci form."

This was how Kitasato first described his bacillus. In *Lancet*'s August 25, 1894 issue, he wrote: "The bacillus is found in the blood, the bubos, the spleen and the viscera. It is a rod with rounded ends with bipolar staining. I am at present unable to say whether or not Gram's double staining method can be employed. The bacilli show very little movement." This description prompted Larange to comment: "On this Kitasato's claim rests, it is the only basis of his priority. But the fact that he could not decide upon the reaction to the Gram stain and that he observed mobility of the bacterium, shows that he was in doubt between several bacilli which were present in his slides and cultures and that he could not separate or distinguish them apart." Larange concluded that Kitasato was careless in his rush to publish first.

Others have also expressed their doubts, notably Dr. Aoyama (1895), a member of Kitasato's team in Hong Kong and who actually conducted the autopsies. In fact, after nicking his finger during an autopsy, he caught the disease and was fortunate to survive. Aoyama wrote: "As the bacilli present in the blood differ in size and staining properties by the Gram method, I think that they are not the same as those present in the glands. When the streptococci are broken from their chains and are liberated, they may produce the appearance of the blood bacilli. As the streptococci are mostly present in the blood vessels of the lymphatic glands, I think Kitasato's bacilli need to be considered as streptococci circulating in the blood." With his experience and expertise, it was extraordinary that Kitasato could have committed such a blunder.

Yersin described the characteristics of his bacillus in his diary. The following is quoted from Larange (1926): "June 20th: . . . a film is prepared and put under the microscope; at the first glance, I see a real mass of bacilli, all identical. They are very small rods and lightly coloured (Loeffler Blue)." Excerpts of Yersin's original paper, translated from French into English, has been reproduced in Butler (1983), who said that Yersin wrote:

> It seemed logical to start first by looking for a microbe in the blood of patients and in the pulp of the buboes (which) . . . . always contains masses of short, stubby bacilli which are rather easy to stain with aniline dyes and are not stained by the method of Gram. The ends of the bacillia are colored more strongly than the center. Sometimes the bacilli seem to be surrounded by a capsule. One can find them in large numbers in the buboes and lymph nodes of the disease persons. They are seen in the blood from time to time, but less abundantly than in the buboes and the lymph nodes, and only in very serious and rapidly fatal cases. . . . the bacillus has a very characteristic appearance resembling that of the erysipelas culture: clear liquid with lumps deposition on the walls and bottom of the tube. Microscopic examination of the cultures reveals true chains of short bacilli interspersed with larger spherical bodies.

Comparing Yersin's and Kitasato's original descriptions of their bacilli, Butler (1983) has explained how the controversy was settled in Yersin's favor, after whom the bacillus is now named *Yersinia pestis* in honor of the Swiss as the true discoverer.

Although Kitasato abandoned work on his bacillus, Yersin returned to Roux's laboratory in Paris where he succeeded in immunizing small laboratory animals and horses with a plague vaccine. In 1896, Yersin returned to Asia to test his antiserum on humans and cured his first case in Canton in one day. In Xiamen, he healed 21 out of 23 cases. Known as *Bacillium pestis* initially, the bacillus was renamed *Bacillus pestis* in 1900. After 1923, it became known as *Pasteurella pestis* and in 1944, the name, *Yersinia pestis*, was finally adopted. Confusion continues today because encyclopedias continue to credit both researchers for discovering the plague bacillus (e.g., Chernow & Vallasi, 1993, p. 2163).

Breakthrough for Western medicine. The epidemic changed Hong Kong's history by opening the opportunity for Western medicine to be introduced into that stronghold of Chinese medicine, the Tung Wah Hospital, with far-reaching consequences. Although it was called a hospital, patients were treated with herbal medicine by traditional practitioners and did not receive any nursing care. Tung Wah was severely criticized by the health authorities, for during the epidemic the management failed to give effective assistance. Not only was patient care assessed to be unsatisfactory but from the public health point of view, routine measures as segregation of patients and contacts, disposal of the dead, and accurate reporting of cases were not properly carried out. Tung Wah's management even resisted health officers' inspections. Protesting the Government's interference at one point, relatives of Tung Wah patients wanted to take them to Canton. When this was not allowed, a mob stoned the Chairman of the Tung Wah Board of Directors, Lau Wai Chuen, also a member of the Sanitary Board, and overturned his sedan chair.

However, health officers protested so strongly that the Governor appointed a commission of inquiry into the workings of the hospital. It was chaired by the Colonial Secretary, J. H. (later Sir James) Stewart-Lockhart. Members included Ho Kai, and C. P. (later Sir Paul) Chater, the well-known merchant and philanthropist, in their capacities as members of Legco.

Meeting in June and July 1896, already two years after the first outbreak, the Commission called many witnesses, both European and Chinese. Its report agreed that Tung Wah Hospital should remain in the hands of the Chinese and that Chinese treatment be maintained. However, another body was appointed to be its Permanent Board of Directors with members consisting of Chinese of high standing, experience with the hospital, and whose advice would be accepted by the public. Appointed to supervise the management of Tung Wah Hospital, the new Board's leading recommendation was that a registered doctor be appointed Medical Superintendent whose salary was to be paid by the Government. To defer to the wishes of the Chinese, it was agreed that the doctor would have to be a Chinese. Instead of treating patients, the Superintendent's primary charge was to investigate the cause of all patients' deaths and supply accurate reports to the Government, a task that no herbalist could perform.

The door was thus opened for a Western-trained doctor to join the staff, and Dr. Chung Boon Chor was first appointed. Although he was given the duties of a health officer, he gradually introduced Western medicine to Tung Wah patients and in 1889 amputated a leg, the first major operation ever performed at the hospital. After new premises were completed in 1902, more Western-trained doctors were appointed to the staff. In a survey of 3,200 inpatients completed about the year 1907, 1,815 chose Western treatment and 1,385 opted for Chinese medicine, thus confirming the increased acceptance of Western medicine.

Ho Kai, Chinese member of the Commission and a Western-trained doctor, was instrumental in initiating the process of converting the Tung Wah Hospital into a proper hospital. For all of Ho Kai's many accomplishments (undoubtedly one of the most illustrious personalities in HK's early years), he is remembered today only by a piece of land that he bought with a friend, Au Tak, which they named Kai Tak Bund. In congested use until the new Chek Lap Lok Airport opened in mid-1998, Kai Tak International Airport lies on their former Bund as it has since before World War II. This is all that commemorates Sir Kai Ho Kai, who died at the early age of 55 in 1914 and did so much to modernize and benefit Hong Kong and bring East and West together into one (Choa, 1981).

Earlier it was mentioned that Ho Kai found more demand for his legal than medical expertise. As more doctors graduated from the College of Medicine, Government posts and private practice steadily expanded. Attitudes towards Western medicine began to turn positive. Chinese practitioners opened clinics in the prestigious Central District.

Dr. Kwan Sum Yin, the first graduate of the College of Medicine to practice in Hong Kong, set up at No. 18A Stanley Street. Graduating in 1893, he was house surgeon at the Alice Memorial Hospital for three years and then was an army surgeon in the Chinese Government for another four years before returning to Hong Kong to enter private practice. Besides Dr. Kwan, Chinese doctors who gained entry in the Oriental Social and Professionals Biographies Section of Wright's (1908) blue book included: Drs. Wan Tun Mo, Ho Ko Tsun, Coxion To, and Ho Nai Hop. All of them, except Dr. Wan, were graduates of the College of Medicine; and all except Dr. Ho Nai Hop, had been house officers at the Alice Memorial Hospital.

The first to practice in Kowloon, still developing at the turn of the century, was Dr. Wong Cheong Lam, followed by Dr. Ip Kam Wah. Once there was only one doctor in the whole of the New Territories, Dr. Ho Nai Hop, who graduated in 1899 and was posted as officer-in-charge at the Government Offices Headquarters in Tai Po.

Doctors in those days were general practitioners, handling everything including minor surgery and obstetrics. Though few in number, they formed close relationships with patients as family doctors. By virtue of their humanity and dedication, they helped immensely to popularize Western medicine. Another milestone was reached in 1927 when the first female medical student graduated from HKU. Dr. Eva Ho Tung was a daughter of Sir Robert Ho Tung, often called the "Grand Old Man of Hong Kong," whose life story will always be a part of the Hong Kong's history. Specializing in obstetrics and gynaecology, Dr. Ho Tung set a trend for other lady doctors to follow, much welcomed by female patients.

Expatriate practitioners were not uncommon in Hong Kong. Since all Government medical officers were allowed private practices, Europeans provided both public and private medical services. The aforementioned Drs. Manson and Cantlie were the most prominent, but one other deserves attention. He was Dr. G. P. Jordan, a nephew of Sir Paul Chater, who arrived in 1885. Jordan was appointed Port Health Officer and joined the teaching staff of the HK College of Medicine after it was founded. Playing an active role in HKU's founding, Dr. Jordan was appointed its first Pro-Vice-Chancellor (Vice-President). Working with several partners, he finally teamed up with Dr. G. E. Aubrey. Their firm, located in the first Alexandra Building on Des Voeux Road, was the precursor of the present-day Anderson and Partners (Mattock, 1984).

Beyond 1997

As British administration of Hong Kong came to an end on June 30, 1997, it left a record of achievement in the medical and health field of which the British can be proud. In the course of some 150 years, despite many vicissitudes, Hong Kong had been transformed from poor healthiness to one of the fittest places to live in the world as described in the foregoing sections (Department of Health Report, 1996; Howlett, 1996, Chapter 11). What changes if any come after the turnover? Some answers may be found in the following concluding comments.

1. Medical and health services. There is no reason to expect that any significant changes will have to be made in this area. The people of Hong Kong have long been provided modern and low-cost medical and health services, cheap enough for them to boast that they pay small health charges without having to contribute to a central provident fund or national insurance scheme. As at the end of 1995, there were 68 general outpatients clinics in the first of the HK Government's three-tier medical system as well as clinics operated by private doctors in the housing estates who are given subsidized rentals in exchange for lower charges. Altogether, there are 29,000 hospital beds available, of which 25,000 are in Government and subverted hospitals, or 4.6 beds/1000 population.

It has often been criticized that in planning the health and medical services that more attention is paid to cure and not enough to prevention. That criticism is false for the results of prevention are slow to appear, while immediate demands for care services continue to expand. Geriatric care is one future problem, which will become more acute and deserve top priority in planning as Hong Kong enters the next century. People over 65 years account for 10% of the 6.3 million population, a statistic that will steadily increase as true worldwide.

The financial burden of medical and health services falls on the Government, which subsidizes the services heavily. For example, 81% for an attendance at a General Outpatients Clinic and 91% for a bed in an acute General Hospital. In estimates for 1995-96, expenditures on health was over $23 billion or 13% of the total government budget. The Department of Health was allocated 10% and the Hospital Authority received the rest. Out of the Department of Health's budget, certain services are provided free of charge, e.g., maternal and child health, tuberculosis, social hygiene and others (Towards Better Health, 1993). Under the Hospital Authority, each hospital has its own special budget with freedom as to its expenditure. The cost of hospital care is becoming more expensive as new and

and sophisticated methods of diagnosis and treatment are introduced. As long as HK's prosperity continues, there should be no problem in maintaining the present modus operandi of the medical and health service. If there is a recession, the HK Government would have no alternative but to reduce its spending on the services as well as in other areas. This will present difficulties for both the Administration and the general public. Deciding which areas to reduce or worse still closure of some services would be an extremely invidious exercise, since the services have expanded so much to meet the demands of an ever growing population. The public now takes the wide range and distribution of health and medical facilities for granted.

In any case, free health services must be maintained so as not to jeopardize the present excellent state of health as shown by health statistics that are among the world's best. Similarly, if the Hospital Authority tries to cover costs by increasing charges, it would not be fair to the patients, who expect Government and subverted hospitals to charge less than the private hospitals. Whether to make changes in this legacy of benevolent colonial government or not is therefore an essentially economic and not a political consideration (see p. 18 of the Overview on proposed user-pays changes).

2. Medical education. Hong Kong's two faculties of medicine are not expected to change their standard five-year course of study followed by one year of internship. Also, English will still be used as the medium of instruction, as it is desirable to continue educating young people to be bilingual in both Chinese and English. In recruiting staff, the policy should remain the same, that posts go to the best candidates irrespective of nationality. Hong Kong has gained a respectable name in the medical world that should be preserved; thus, academic medicine must be open to all.

In order to maintain and even to improve the standard of medical practice, the profession has made good preparations for the future in recent years. Hitherto, Hong Kong and the various Royal Colleges have maintained close ties and graduates seek British professional memberships or fellowship examinations to qualify as specialists. Those ties should not be severed altogether, but the time has come for Hong Kong to organize its own examinations and accreditation. To this end, a number of colleges have been established, one for each major specialty, e.g., internal medicine, surgery, etc., including general practice. Each college has formulated its requirements for qualifying as a specialist, including the number of years in training before and after an examination, and a rotation program for training posts. Every practicing doctor in HK will eventually be either a member or a fellow of a college. Overseeing the colleges is the HK Academy of Medicine set up in 1993. It is a statutory body with the authority to approve, assess and accredit all post-internship training. Continued medical education has also been introduced. To remain on the register, specialists must achieve a certain number of points within a given period of time, so everyone must keep up-to-date. Therefore, the standard of practice in HK will not only be safeguarded but also enhanced.

The Medical Registration Ordinance has been amended to require all doctors qualified abroad to take an examination before they are allowed to practice in Hong Kong. This step should not be interpreted as imposing a restriction on doctors from any particular country or countries. It is another way to maintain the standard of practice and prevent an oversupply of doctors; the number of graduates from HK's two faculties of medicine is now over 300 a year. As of December 1995, there were 8,476 doctors on the register, thus the doctor/ population (at 6.3+ million) ratio was 1:743, a very reasonable figure in Asia.

For similar reasons, most Commonwealth countries have withdrawn reciprocal recognition of degrees registrable with the General Medical Council of the United Kingdom. However, exemption or provisional registration is granted to academics who come to teach or conduct research at HKU or CU. After passing the examination, the doctors are still required to serve an internship but there may be difficulties to find posts for them as local graduates have priority in assigning internships. It is hoped that exemption will be freely given, as there is no point to insist that those who have been trained in well-recognized institutions abroad should have to waste time and services in having them repeat requirements.

3. Chinese traditional medicine. Since the inauguration of the People's Republic of China, there has been a resurgence of Chinese traditional medicine, which actually started during the war years when medical supply was extremely short in Mao Zedong's stronghold in Yenan. World interest in Chinese medicine has grown especially after reports on the use of acupuncture in inducing anaesthesia and treatment of painful conditions were published and confirmed by Westerners after President Richard Nixon's historic visit to China in 1972. It cannot be denied that traditional medicine must have its usefulness, since it has sustained a nation for thousands of years.

Practitioners in China now have their own hospitals and training schools. Very often both Chinese herbs and Western drugs are used together. The status of traditional practitioners has been raised to an equal level with Western-trained doctors. Now is the time for Hong Kong to reappraise its situation and the HK Government's nonintervention policy. Traditional practitioners in Hong Kong are not allowed by law to use Western methods of treatment, such as giving injections, treating eye diseases, or prescribe and store dangerous drugs, poisons and antibiotics. Other than that, there is no other control. Thus, the public is not sufficiently safeguarded against the danger of malpractice by ignorant practitioners. Some steps are now being taken at last to regulate the practice of traditional medicine. In 1994, after the Working Party on Chinese Medicine published its report, a Preparatory Committee was appointed in 1995 to advise on the criteria and procedure for the eventual registration of practitioners of traditional medicine. The Committee should lay down such guidelines as the length of the course of instructions, the contents of the curriculum, the facilities for preclinical and clinical practical classes, and the qualification of teachers that all institutions must meet before they can start new schools. The standards should also be used by a statutory body such as the Medical Council to admit and register practitioners whose training can fulfill the requirements. Such steps will help to clear up the chaotic state of affairs in which almost anyone with or without professional knowledge and training can go into practice.

Attention should also be paid to the training and qualification of so-called dispensers. Recently, Hong Kong has experienced cases when the wrong herbs were dispensed and patients suffered severe side effects. Hong Kong offers ideal opportunities for research on Chinese medicine as the community provides much interest and expertise. All that is needed are adequate financial support and rearch facilities. So far, work has been mainly on the pharmacological properties of herbs known to be effective in certain diseases. Less attention has been paid to the theories concerning the origin of disease and the rationale of certain treatment methods. For instance, while the reactions of the two forces, *Yin* and *Yang*, and the interaction of the five elements, gold, wood, water, fire and earth, have philosophical explanations, they do not accord with Western science. Empirical explanations of how they actually work have not been found. In acupuncture and acupressure, the body points have yet to be fully studied in order to establish their anatomical origins and physiological functions. Then there is the latest introduction of *qigong* as a remedy for a wide range of conditions; so far its rationale has not been fully explored.

The objective of research should be to remove the myths and mysteries surrounding traditional medicine and put it on a scientific basis. Once achieved, traditional medicine will have its rightful place along with Western medicine as a true and legitimate alternative.

References

Aoyama, T. (1895). Uber die Pestepidemie in Hong Kong in Jahre, 1894-1895 (On the plague epidemic in Hong Kong in the years 1894 to 1895). *Mitteilungen an der Med. Fac. der Kais Japan Universitat, Tokio. 3*, 115-238.

Butler, Thomas C. (1983). *Plague and other Yersinia infections.* New York: Plennum.

Chernow, Barbara A. & Vallasi, George A. (1993). *The Columbia encyclopedia* (5th ed.). New York: Columbia University Press.

Choa, G. H. (1970). *A history of medicine of Hong Kong. Hong Kong medical directory* (1st ed.). Hong Kong: Federation of Medical Societies of Hong Kong.

Choa, G. H. (1976). *Some obervations on the phenomenon of drug addiction. Journal of the Society of Community Medicine* (Hong Kong), *7*(2), 6-17.

Choa, G. H. (1981). *The life and times of Sir Kai Ho Kai.* Hong Kong: The Chinese University Press, 1981.

Choa, G. H. (1990). *"Heal the sick" was their motto: Protestant medical missionaries in China.* Hong Kong: The Chinese University Press.

Choa, G. H. (1992). Hong Kong, medicine and Sun Yat Sen. *Journal of the Hong Kong College of Practitioners, 14*(5), 2067-2074.

Choa, G. H. (1993). The Lowson diaries: A record of the early months of the Bubonic Plague Epidemic. *Journal of the Hong Kong Branch of the Royal Asiatic Society, 33*, 129-146.

Choa, G. H. (1994). *A history of medical education in Hong Kong: Synapse.* Hong Kong College of Physicians, Supplement 2, 3-6.

Department of Health Report, 1995-199 (1997). Hong Kong: Government Information Service Department.

Eitel, E. J. (1895). *Europe in China.* Hong Kong: Oxford University Press, reprinted 1983.

Endacott, G. B. (1973). *History of Hong Kong* (2nd ed., rev.). Hong Kong: Oxford University Press.

Evans, D. E. (1987). *Constancy of purpose.* Hong Kong: Hong Kong University Press.

Howlett, Bob (Ed.) (1996). *Hong Kong 1996.* Hong Kong: Government Information Service Department.

Humphries, M. (1996). *Ruttonjee Sanatorium, life and times.* Hong Kong: Ruttonjee Estate Continuation Ltd.

Lagrange, E. (1926). Concerning the discovery of the plague bacillus. *Journal of Tropical Medicine and Hygiene, 29*(17), 299-302.

Li Shu Fan (1964). *A Hong Kong surgeon.* Hong Kong: Li Shu Fan Foundation Ltd.

Lo Xianglin (1967). *Dr. Sun Yat Sun and the Hong Kong College of Medicine* (in Chinese). Taipei: Commercial Press Taiwan.

Manson, P. & Alcock, A. (1927). *The life and work of Sir Patrick Manson.* London.

Mattock, K. (1984). *Hong Kong practice, Drs. Anderson and Partners, the first hundred years*. Hong Kong: Linkprint & Co.

Patterson, E. H. (1987). *A hospital for Hong Kong*. Published privately.

Ride, L. T. (1962). *The faculty of medicine in The University of Hong Kong: The first fifty years*. Hong Kong: Hong Kong University Press.

Rydings, H. A. (1973). Transactions of the China Medico-Chirugical Society 1845-1846. *Journal of the Hong Kong Branch of the Royal Society of Hong Kong, 13*, 13-27.

Sayers, G. R. (1975). *Hong Kong 1841-1862*. Hong Kong: Hong Kong University Press.

Selwyn-Clarke, P. S. (1962). *Footprints*. Hong Kong: SinoAmerican Publishing Co.

Sinn, E. (1989). *Power and charity, the early history of the Tung Wah Hospital*. Hong Kong: Oxford University Press.

Stewart, J. (1983). *The quality of mercy*. Hong Kong: George Allen and Unwin.

Towards better health: A consultation document (1993). Hong Kong: Government Information Services Department.

Walker, R. T. (1984). The noble story. *British Dental Journal*, October 20, pp. 291-294.

Wright, A. (1908). *Twentieth century impressions of Hong Kong and other treaty ports*. London: Lloyd's Great Britain Publishing Co.

CHAPTER FOUR

The Media and Communications Networks of Hong Kong

George Shen

The people may be made to follow a path of action, but they may not be made to understand it. Confucius, *Analects* (8:9)

Few dispute the fact that the world's freest economy resides in Hong Kong. Among the many factors that contribute to this unique characteristic and arguably the most important are the free rights of press and speech.

Years before Hong Kong reverted to China's sovereignty on July 1, 1997, members of both the local and international media were already concerned about whether or not Hong Kong would continue to enjoy the same degree of freedom in press and speech that it has taken for granted.

As the historic day approached, the public sensed that the media were exercising self-censorship, but no member of the media would openly admit such self-degrading practices. However, after some journalists privately admitted their fears to visiting U.S. legislators, Congressman John Porter introduced a bill to grant up to 2,000 U.S. passports to HK journalists. A Chinese University survey in the spring of 1997 found that one in five reporters admitted that they practiced self-censorship. Activist and former *Far Eastern Economic Review* journalist, Emily Lau Wai-hing said on TV: "The growing phenomenon of self-censorship prompted by the fear of upsetting the Chinese government has directly undermined the credibility of many news organizations" (Cheung, 1997).

Then, following the appointment of Tung Chee-hwa as the Chief Executive designate of the Hong Kong Special Administrative Region (HKSAR), the situation became clearer when Tung announced his decision to repeal or amend certain existing legislation which Beijing considered to be contradictory to the Basic Law. Granting that the Basic Law contains provisions on press freedom, media members seemed to agree that their work would not be the same after July 1, 1997

1997; their views ranged from encouragingly optimistic to distressingly pessimistic.

It would be premature to predict what effect the handover will have on Hong Kong's media and press rights. It would be inappropriate to speculate on the darkest outcomes. As this chapter attempts to present a fair and objective assessment of the prospects for HK's media, let us first review some history before examining the freedom issue from a number of parameters, including the Government and media, the Mainland China factor, conflicting interests within the media, and the media and public. As this chapter cannot cover the very recent cinema of Hong Kong, which includes Ann Hui, Stanley Kwan, Wong Kar-wai, etc., see Abbas (1997).

Learning from the Past

As those in power learned long ago how important it was to control information, rulers and governments have established their own news organs and more often than not, exerted tight control over information sources. The Roman Empire was known to have distributed or publicly posted government gazettes to inform the people of government policies. Ancient regimes of China pasted posters at city gates to spread information to its subjects. Such posters ranged from seeking the people's advice on state affairs to offering rewards for criminals. The Nazis and Communists bombarded their people with nonstop propaganda broadcasting. In all such instances, the dissemination of information was under the control of the rulers; the people seldom if ever had the right to express themselves. Although the Magna Carta curbed the power of the King of England by protecting baronial privileges, it did not give the people freedom of speech. Perhaps it was not until the First Amendment to the U.S. Constitution and its legal enforcement that a nation truly protected its people's free press and speech rights.

While freedom of the press has long been a pillar of democratic societies, authoritatian nations use propaganda as an important tool of regimentation and all media are expected to serve that purpose. Lenin openly professed the dictatorship of the proletariat and subjected the media to the Communist Party's Propaganda Department. Stalin put Lenin's words into practice by stifling press and speech freedom in the Soviet Union and its Eastern European satellite states and set the pattern for other communist regimes. This is not leading to any implication that the media will be subject to severe curtailments under the SAR. As we review HK's media from a historical perspective, the reader may agree that no radical changes will take place.

Depending on how origins are viewed, HK's first or second newspaper was *The Hong Kong Register*. James Matheson, who along with his partner William Jardine had derived vast fortunes in opium, started *The Canton Register* in Canton on November 8, 1827. After Matheson moved the paper to the new colony in 1843, he changed the name to the *Hong Kong Register* and the paper continued until 1859 when it was sold. Another paper, the *Friend of China*, was first publish-ed in Hong Kong on March 24, 1842 by American Baptist missionaries. The *Friend* locked horns with the *Register* over opium and boldly predicted that HK would "become the base of naval and military operations, which sooner or later, must revolutionize, or subvert, the existing state of things in China" (Welsh, 1993, p. 140). One chief concern of the People's Republic of China (PRC) during the drafting of the Basic Law of Hong Kong, in the later 1980s to early 1990s, was that HK might become a base of subversion. Therefore, it appears that the edi-tors of the *Friend of China* had excellent foresight, for Hong Kong was Lord Elgin's operational base during the decisive Second Opium War, 1858-60. Its prophecy remains valid today, since while Beijing did not see any danger of armed operations emanating from HK, it was concerned with possible subversive actions that the SAR could raise on basic human rights, including freedom of speech and the press.

In the early days of HK's colonization, whatever media there were served British interests. Wanting to trade as freely as possible, Jardine and Matheson made great use of *The Canton Register* and pamphlets in their all-out campaign to secure a Chinese port under British laws and administration. Of all the opium barons at Canton lobbying the British Government, particularly Foreign Secre-tary Lord Palmerston, to pursue hostilities against China to gain trade conces-sions, Jardine and Matheson should be remembered as the most responsible in-dividuals for instigating the First Opium War (1840-42) and Britain's 156 years' rule of HK (See Overview, pp. 1-10). That their success was achieved in part through the *Register* and other publications illustrates the long and important role that the foreign media have played in Hong Kong's and China's history. As James Matheson published in 1836 (Yee, 1992, p. 20):

> If the lion's paw is to be put down on any of the south side of China, let it be Hong Kong: let the lion declare it to be under his guarantee a free port, and in 10 years it will be the most considerable mart east of the Cape. The Portuguese made a mistake; they adopted shallow water and exculsive rules (Macau). Hong Kong, deep water and a free port forever!

Although the Chinese press in early HK was no doubt meager due to the lack of educated Chinese and a sizable population that did not reach 30,000 until the 1850s, they differed in allegiance to the Qing Dynasty. Founded by Wang Tao in 1874, the first known newspaper, *Tsun Wan Jih Pao* (Circular Daily), paid hom-age to Qing China and called for the court to make reforms (Lau, 1997, p. 153). It is interesting to note that this paper was revived several times after World War II and finally shut down in the 1960s. The second well-known Chinese language paper, which appeared towards the end of the last century, was published by Hsin Chung Hui, (Association for the Revival of China), the revolutionary body founded by Dr. Sun Yat-sen. Its paper was called *Chung Kuo Jih Pao* (China Daily) and called for the overthrow of the Qing Dynasty.

Since the British continued to recognize the Qing Government because of their Opium War treaty agreements, it tried to appease China by passing the Chinese Publications (Prevention) Ordinance in 1907 to prevent HK from becoming a base of sedition. Four years thereafter, the Qing Dynasty was overthrown by the Revolution of 1911, but China remained divided. Thus, the colony had many Chinese-language papers representing contrasting viewpoints that were not subservient to the Peking Government and Canton by tradition or mandate. Old HK residents recall how in the 1920s local Chinese newspapers supported Dr. Sun's breakaway government in Canton rather than the Peking warlords. Through this period, the media either paid little heed to the Chinese Publications (Prevention) Ordinance or the colonial authorities decided not to make an issue of the situation and allow unhampered freedom of the press.

The longest and perhaps only period in HK's history when the Government thoroughly controlled the media was during the 44 months of Japanese occupation in World War II. Understandably, HK's media had no alternative but to heed their Japanese masters' policies -- the English-language media serving as the mouthpiece of the military and the Chinese media showing allegiance to Wang Jing-wei's puppet government in Nanjing. Whether history will repeat itself under the SAR Government remains to be seen.

Shanghai progressives go to Hong Kong. Before Japan began its war of aggression against China in 1937, the local Chinese press was generally supportive of Chiang Kai-shek's Nationalist Government. However, some dared to express sympathy for "progressive elements" (meaning those supporting the Chinese Communist Party or CCP). After 1937 and prior to Pearl Harbor, leftist influences started to emerge more openly in Hong Kong. More importantly, HK's film industry came under the direct influence of progressive elements as many famous film directors and playwrights fled from Shanghai to Hong Kong (Cheng, 1963, pp. 75-94).

Up to that time, all motion pictures produced in China were in the Mandarin dialect and were considered superior to the Cantonese dialect films produced in HK. Realizing full well that Cantonese was the dialect of the Overseas Chinese, the film workers from Shanghai saw the impracticality of producing Mandarin films in HK and switched to Cantonese, thus invigorating the local film industry and elevating the quality of its productions.

Because many of the newcomers were also well-known writers, they soon began to contribute articles for local Chinese language newspapers. As many of them had progressive leanings, they propagated the merits of a patriotic united front against the Japanese to save China. This suited the editorial policy of the Chinese language newspapers in Hong Kong and their articles became very popular. While the British authorities tolerated such views in the press, at the same time they discretely sought to avoid any confrontation with Japan, with whom Britain and its Allies were not yet at war. While Japan's conquest and occupation of Hong Kong forced the Shanghai film workers to flee once again, the pre-1941 years had sowed the seeds of leftist influence over HK's media in general and the film industry in particular. During the occupation, the press and Radio Hong Kong were of course controlled by the Japanese military and forced to toe their official line.

Civil War alliances. After World War II ended, China was torn by civil war; and HK's media divided into two contending camps -- those supporting either the Kuomintang Nationalist Party (KMT) of Chiang Kai-shek or the Chinese Communist Party (CCP) of Mao Zedong. Media favoring the latter were muted because they were only branches set up in Hong Kong by their respective main offices operating in KMT China. By 1949 when Chiang and his KMT forces fled to Taiwan, however, the editorial policy of the left in HK became obvious as *Ta Kung Pao* and *Wen Wei Pao* openly supported Mao and the CCP regime in China. For years, *Ta Kung Pao*'s English-language weekly had a limited readership overseas, including the United States.

Following President Richard Nixon's visit to China in early 1972, a surge of interest in Chinese affairs developed and the weekly became well-known within certain sectors of the U.S. In 1950, the *New Evening Post*, which was run by almost the same editorial and managerial staff of *Ta Kung Pao* (No Bias), became one of HK's most popular newspapers. Even so, perhaps because of the HK's capitalist nature, most Chinese papers remained loyal to the KMT. Instead of using the Gregorian calendar reckoning of the year as adopted in the People's Republic of China (PRC), the KMT-oriented newspapers and magazines continued to use the year of the Republic of China in their banner headings.

For several decades, the situation remained more or less the same. New Chinese-language publications of both the right and left came and went, but use of the Republic of China banner gradually faded away as Taiwan's influence waned. By the 1980s, with the exception of a few staunch KMT supporters and KMT-run publications, the Gregorian calendar year appeared on almost all printed media. Then, after the pro-Taiwan *Industrial and Commercial Daily* and the *Hong Kong Times* closed in the early 1990s, the printed media became either pro-CCP or neutral.

The same can be said of radio and television. In the early days, the Government's Radio Hong Kong was the only broadcasting station in the territory, providing English and Chinese language broadcasts on separate frequencies. Commercial radio stations are a relatively late phenomenon in Hong Kong. The first to break the Government's monopoly was Rediffusion, a British company, which started wired broadcasting services in HK in the late 1940s. Commercial Radio and Metro Radio came much later. Radio Hong Kong, of course, followed the overall policy of Britain -- officially recognizing the PRC as the only legitimate government of the whole of China but wary of communist influence. Rediffusion followed the same policy. When it introduced television service to HK in 1957 in the form of "Wired-Vision," most staff members responsible for news editing and telecasting were neutral with a slant towards Taiwan and carefully kept the PRC at arm's length. Sensitivities were especially keen. For instance, when music by a long-dead Chinese composer who had received his music training in Moscow was broadcast during a listener's request program, it caused some anxiety among the staff and management merely because no one had done it before. This stir occurred despite the fact that the commercially available gramophone records had been purchased with the approval of the management. Similar sensitivities were felt at television stations years later.

Becoming independent and pragmatic. It was only in the 1970s that radio and television stations in Hong Kong matured into independent pragmatism. Touchy inhibitions started to decline in the early 1980s after China opened its doors and started an ambitious economic reform program. The 1984 signing of the Sino-British Joint Declaration and promising business opportunities in China encouraged media bosses to adjust their attitude towards Beijing. Nobody wanted to be seen as unfriendly to HK's future master or "unpatriotic to the motherland." This resulted in almost everyone in the media jumping on the Mainland China band-wagon. Although the media still criticized Beijing's policies towards Hong Kong, such criticisms were no longer expressed solely from KMT or British viewpoints. Rather, they were oriented towards what was best for HK's self-interest or voiced out of the concern that the territory's status as the world's most competitive economy after Singapore might be eroded (World Economic Forum, 1997).

Hong Kong came of age when economists, such as Nobel laureate Milton Friedman (1981, p. 26), extolled HK as "the modern exemplar of free markets and limited government."

Film Industry's Second Spring

As mentioned, the brief boom in HK's film industry before December 1941 ended with Japan's occupation. Following the war, from 1945 to 1949, a new wave of film workers came to Hong Kong from Shanghai. Some of them were the same left-wing intellectuals who had fled the Japanese in 1937, but this time they were escaping repression by the KMT Nationalists then in power in China. The same wave also included many right-wing film workers and their wealthy capitalist friends who were afraid of the imminent collapse of the KMT and Mao Zedong's subsequent victory in the civil war. Thus, the British colony was suddenly flooded with first-rate talent with diverse views.

However, as they began production, unlike the first wave of Shanghai film people, the new companies this time produced Mandarin instead of Cantonese dialect films, albeit for political versus financial reasons. To pursue their mission, which was to expose the sins and rottenness of the old regime and to propagate the birth of a new China, the leftists deemed Mandarin as the most appropriate medium. However, the rightists who came to Hong Kong wanted first and all to rebuild their business. As they had access to capital transferred to HK from China, they started to produce lavish epic dramas and star-studded romances in Mandarin, which became so successful that they nearly destroyed the local Cantonese film market. Films from both Shanghai groups enjoyed success not only in HK but also in Southeast Asia where there are large ethnic Chinese populations, which were then still allowed to learn Mandarin in Chinese-language schools. HK's film industry thus experienced a second spring.

The first major film company established by refugee capital was Yung Hua, which recruited almost all of the best Shanghai talent, whether from the left or right camps. One of its first productions, "The Sorrows of the Forbidden City," was produced in 1948. It is translated as the "Secret History of the Ch'ing Court" in Jay Leyda's (1972) book. The "Sorrows" film was a box-office hit and won wide acclaim at the 1950 Locarno International Film Festival in Switzerland. Written by Yao Ke and directed by Chu Shih-ling, this historical spectacle depicted the last days of Emperor Guangxu who reigned from 1875 to 1908 but has been considered a puppet manipulated by the Empress Dowager.

The young Emperor had tried to introduce some political reforms, but his efforts were in vain as the Empress Dowger put him under house arrest and executed officials who proposed the reforms. The film reached its climax when the Boxer Rebellion broke out and the rulers had to flee the Forbidden City. During the turmoil, Guangxu's favorite concubine was thrown into a well and died tragically by order of the Empress Dowager. According to the film, the Emperor never overcame his grief. During the Cultural Revolution of 1966-76, Jiang Qing, Mao's wife who led the radical Gang of Four, denounced then PRC President Liu Shao-chi on many spurious accounts, one being failure to criticize "The Sorrows of the Forbidden City" when it was first shown in China in 1950.

Another major film company that took root in HK was the Great Wall. After producing some very popular melodramas, Great Wall came under leftish influence and later became the bulwark of the progressives. During the 1950s, Great Wall was the most respected film company in Hong Kong and enjoyed the ardent support of Overseas Chinese. Boasting some of the best veteran film directors from Shanghai and the most popular new film stars, such as Hsia Moon, Shek Hui, and Fu Chi, its films had showings at international film festivals. However, filmmakers with "patriotic" bents worked at Feng Huang (Phoenix), led by the famed veteran director Chu Shih-ling of "The Sorrows of Forbidden City" fame. A wide spectum of people found its productions appealing, as they reflected the plight and sentiments of many Chinese -- struggling intellectuals as well as the common people.

While these companies and their films gained popularity, two Singapore-based companies, Shaw's and Cathay theater networks, controlled film distribution in the Southeast Asian markets where good profits were to be made. Long-time distributors of Hollywood-produced films, the two companies managed to control the distribution of almost all of the Mandarin films produced in Hong Kong. Later, they began film production through their respective arms, Shaw Brothers and Motion Picture and General Investment (known as MP & GI), each building modern film studios in HK and holding exclusive contracts with famous directors, such as Tao Ching and Li Han-hsiang and popular movie stars, such as Li Li-hua and Lin Dai.

By the 1960s, Shaw's and MP & GI gained the upper-hand in the film industry because they controlled distribution, whereas Great Wall and Feng Huang had to depend upon their very film competitors to distribute their productions. Since then, many independent producers have entered the market, but Shaw's remained one of the major active players, especially after the untimely death of MP & GI's head, Datu Lok Wan-tho, in an air accident in 1964 that led to the decline of the company. Today, Shaw's media empire relies mainly on revenues from television and the distribution of films, video tapes and discs. The company has been under the leadership of Sir Run Run Shaw for almost five decades and is still prospering. Sir Run Run, reputed to be HK's best known film entrepreneur and perhaps philantrophist as well, was married at the age of 90 to his long-time companion, Mona Fong, who was once a night-club singer but became a very capable manager and administrator of the Shaw empire.

In the 1970s, a new company by the name of Golden Harvest emerged and soon built a successful reputation locally and internationally through kung-fu films, starring the legendary Bruce Lee. Its founder, Raymond Chow, had worked with Shaw's, from which he learned everything he needed to know about the film business. Also, he saw the trend in the 1970s that Cantonese films had a wider audience in Hong Kong than Mandarin movies, and started to produce large-budget productions in Cantonese, dubbing them into other dialects or languages for markets outside Hong Kong. Chow had been educated at the former elite St. John's University in Shanghai, and his excellent command of English and understanding of both Chinese and Western cultures enabled him to become a truly international film producer. Among other innovations, he entered into joint ventures with foreign companies and set up a network of distribution outlets in many parts of the world.

The 1970s revival of Cantonese films was a reflection of the HK people's search for a new identity. Unlike their parents who had come from the mainland, the new generation had been born and raised in a Cantonese-speaking environment. Thus, even when Mandarin films were dominating the scene in the 1950s and 1960s, Cantonese films somehow managed to survive, mainly by producing low-budget and Cantonese opera films. However, as the situation reversed in the 1970s, Mandarin films were seldom produced in Hong Kong.

When the Cantonese film industry was languishing, one company, Chung Luen, which had the support of veteran Cantonese directors, actors and actresses, produced films at quality levels comparable to their Mandarin competitors. Many of these veterans had been the first wave of Shanghai film people who made "patriotic" movies during the Sino-Japanese war from 1937-1941 before HK was occupied by the Japanese. That is how Chung Luen came under leftist influence and views that HK disfavored. Ironically, therefore, as Cantonese films came to the forefront, Chung Luen became dormant and is seldom heard of nowadays.

Since the film industry is about the most influential sector of Hong Kong's media, it is only natural that politics should play an active role. It is a well-known fact that after World War II HK's film industry was clearly divided into leftist and rightist camps, with workers from the former joining the South China Film Workers Union and those from the latter belonging to the Free Film Workers Union. Films with leftist union members were permitted to be shown in Mainland China but not in Taiwan, and vice versa. In private life, however, many of the film workers were old friends and continued to socialize despite their political differences.

Although the HK Government kept a watchful eye over both camps, Great Wall and Feng Huang activities were generally under strict scrutiny and their left-leaning productions were more carefully censored before release. Whenever someone defected from one camp to the other, an event which created a stir in the industry depending on the prominence of the turncoats, government authorities would sometimes provide discrete protection lest harm should befall the defectors, which was why nothing serious ever happened. The only exception was in the early 1960s when a young Great Wall film director by the name of Su Cheng-sou defected to the rightist camp. He publicly displayed his defection by making a speech at HK's KMT "Double Tenth" National Day celebration. However, Su did not go to Taiwan because soon afterwards he was "persuaded" to leave Hong Kong and live in China. He eventually returned to Hong Kong in the 1980s and later died with little notice.

Many suspected that the HK Government deliberately tried to antagonize the two camps so that conflicts between them would weaken their respective influence, but no evidence ever emerged to support such suspicions. Yet it was quite clear that the authorities maintained surveillance over key figures who were closely tied with either Beijing or Taipei. Despite the precautions, two political riots erupted -- one in 1956 which was instigated by pro-Taiwan forces and one in 1967 masterminded by CCP agents in HK and blindly followed by adherents of Mao Zedong's Cultural Revolution in China. As the 1956 riot had very little to do with the pro-Taiwan film workers, the Free Film Workers Union was little affected. Nevertheless, the Government exercised strict vigilance over all rightist forces, including the pro-Taiwan workers.

However, the explosive 1967 riot was quite a different matter. Prominent film stars were mobilized to take part in anti-British demonstrations and, as a result, the police arrested some left-wing film workers, including the most famous husband and wife stars, Fu Chi and Shek Hui. When the HK Government later tried to deport them to the Mainland, the PRC refused to accept them, leaving Fu and Shek to make headlines by camping on the Lowu Bridge at the border to protest the explusion. In the end, the HK Government allowed them to remain in the territory. Such incidents made it clear the the authorities would not hesitate to enforce control over the film industry and its contending political factions.

The Game of Check and Balance

Having touched upon the Hong Kong Government's watchfulness over the film industry, we should survey the whole of HK's media with an interesting question in mind. That is, throughout British rule and the last half century after World War II in particular, what posture did the Government take towards the media? True, the colonial government possessed almost absolute power in governing the territory and ordinances were at its disposal to regulate, control or even suppress the media. But such powers were seldom used. In British tradition, the HK Government used a very careful if somewhat cunning strategy to check and balance relations between the various political forces and their influence. Before the mid-1950s, there was a distinct bias against leftist forces loyal to Maoism as well as a notable tolerance of, if not acquiescence to, pro-Taiwan activities. While labor unions were weakened by their division into two contending camps, they were always under constant surveillance, with leftists receiving more stringent treatment than the rightist unions.

On January 10, 1952, for example, the Government deported eight film workers, including scenarists and actors, on suspicion of their spreading pro-communist ideology among fellow film workers. Deportation of a second group of filmmakers took place later the same month (Leyda, 1972, p. 274). On the other hand, when Eric Chow, a senior editorial staff member of *Ta Kung Pao*, a leading communist paper, defected a few years later, he did not join the pro-Taiwan faction but sought and received police protection and was granted asylum in Britain where he late died. It was believed that Chow did not go to Taiwan because he had written many articles critical of Chiang Kai-shek in the *New Evening Post*.

The British were very good at their game. Chief points of their strategy might be described as two-pronged: (1) seeing that neither camp gained the upper hand at the expense of the other, and (2) ensuring that no camp became so strong that it would be difficult to control. In other words, by favoring neither camp the HK Government could maintain British interests.

Since Beijing controlled leftist media of all kinds after 1949, the British and HK Governments were often targets of harsh criticism, especially by the Chinese-language, leftist press. However, since colonial rule upheld the freedom of the press and of speech, anti-Western news reports and commentaries were tolerated, as long as they were within the generous limits of law and order, such as never slurring the Queen. However, this did not mean that harassment never occurred. For example, all films, no matter whether made in HK or elsewhere, had to be submitted to the Film Censorship Authority for approval prior to their release. Armed with provisions of the Film Censorship Ordinance, the Film Authority would often order pro-China film companies to cut certain scenes from their productions with suspicion that they might contain hidden messages. As the

Authority had almost absolute say, there was nothing producers could do except comply if they wanted their films to be shown in the colony, even though there was supposed to be freedom of speech.

For instance, shots in a Great Wall Motion Picture Co.'s film were asked to be cut because of a phrase in the dialogue, "He is my colleague." The reason was that the word, "colleague," pronounced *tong-shi* in Mandarin, sounded like "comrade" or *tong-chi* and was therefore deemed unacceptable. Ironically, four decades later, the same Film Censorship Ordinance was used in favor of the PRC. Applying Section 10 of the Ordinance, the Government banned films that would "seriously damage good relations with other territories."

Taking on Ta Kung Pao. The most outstanding case of the HK Government pressuring the local media was the prosecution and conviction of *Ta Kung Pao*. On March 5, 1952 during the Korean War when Hong Kong suffered terribly from the United Nations' and America's embargoes against China trade, *Ta Kung Pao* reprinted a short commentary published by the *People's Daily* of Beijing on the previous day. The commentary protested "the oppression of Chinese residents" and "the illegal arrest and deportation of representatives of Chinese film workers and Kowloon fire victims by HK British authorities" and "the dispatch of army and police to massacre Chinese residents on May 1."

The "massacre" referred to took place on May 1st when one demonstrator was killed. The HK Government prosecuted Fei Yi-ming, publisher of *Ta Kung Pao*, Pao Li-chu, manager of the printing company which printed the paper, and Lee Tsun-ying, editor, on the basis of Section 4, paragraph 1(c) of the Instigation Ordinances.

During the trial which started on April 16, one of the defense attorneys, Barrister Percy Chen, and the First Defendant, Fei Yi-ming, focused their defense on the translation of the Chinese counterpart to the English word, "massacre." They argued that while massacre in English implied more than one death, Chinese usage did not have singular or plural forms. Claiming that the reprinted commentary in Chinese had merely reported the fact of one death, the defendants said that it was not inflammatory. Nevertheless, the jury found *Ta Kung Pao* guilty and the judge handed down a verdict to suspend the paper from publishing for six months. *Ta Kung Pao* appealed, and the paper was allowed to resume publishing 12 days later after Beijing intervened.

While the case ended with *Ta Kung Pao* winning the appeal and no further action was taken against the defendants, Percy Chen's victory helped to solidify his name in Hong Kong and abroad as an educated PRC activist and local left-wing advocate and dignitary, often in the news before his death in 1989. His Marco Polo Club dinners hosted speakers and guests of all stripes. The case also enhanced the reputation of Fei Yi-ming as a journalist. The Chinese Communists exploited his fame to their fullest advantage, using him to socialize with foreign media dignitaries because he spoke fluent French and English. At their insistence, he led protests against the British authorities during the 1967 riots. In return,

Fei was given prominent political limelight in Beijing and often visited Deng Xiaoping until the paramount leader's death in May 1988. Li Tsun-ying became editor of the English monthly, *Eastern Horizon*, a post he held until the late 1980s when he retired to live in Canada.

Although subtle bias against pro-PRC media was not uncommon in the 1950s, few punitive incidents took place after the *Ta Kung Pao* case. However, the case has been resurrected in recent years. The pro-Mainland media have highlighted the *Ta Kung Pao* case to demonstrate the unreliability of press freedom under British rule and to counter allegations that press freedom would be curtailed under the SAR Government. However, now that the British are gone, it remains to be seen whether the media will be allowed to rebroadcast or reprint any views originating outside of Hong Kong that criticize the SAR and Beijing Governments in language similar to *Ta Kung Pao*'s in 1952. The answer is probably no, not so much because the HKSAR Government will prosecute any offenders, but because of self-censorship. More about this later, but let's continue our discussion on the role of the HK Government vis-à-vis the media.

As already said, the HK Government practiced a policy of check and balance between the various political factions in the local media. Prior to the mid-1960s, it was inclined to favor the pro-Nationalist and pro-Western forces. This was only natural in view of Britain's alignment with other Western powers against communist Russia and China. However, the policy was adjusted after the 1956 riots in Kowloon led by pro-Taiwan trade unions, when civilians were intimidated and pro-PRC workers were attacked and some killed. To quell the volatile riots, the HK Police had to call for support from the army garrison. Following the riots, pro-PRC trade unions grew rapidly and became very influential, while the HK Government carefully scrutinized the activities of the pro-Taiwan unions.

In Search of A New Identity

Then came the PRC's Great Proletarian Cultural Revolution (1966-76) and the leftist riots of 1966-67 in Hong Kong that became so serious that the British army had to support the police again. Because of their ferocity and duration, the riots drew worldwide attention and had far-reaching consequences in HK. Although actions of the extreme left were unpopular, they aroused the suppressed dissent of the HK people, especially the less privileged.

As a result of the riots, the British sensed the danger of social unrest. This led to an awakening of the HK Government during Sir David Trench's tenure as Governor (1964-71) to the many staggering problems faced by the ordinary people, problems common in rapidly developing societies (see pp. 144-147). The reality was that Hong Kong had started to prosper as a manufacturing center and a major exporter of light industry products. As per capita income rose, a middle class emerged. Protesting their substandard wages and living conditions, especially the plight of the many thousands living in decrepit squatter shacks, the common people demanded equitable treatment and a corrupt-free society that would address their needs. They also sought a voice in public affairs through representation at various levels.

The HK Government began to realize that its past policies had only managed to maintain a superficial equilibrium with little regard to social justice and the plight and opinions of the common people, especially those who had fled China as refugees. Government corruption was one serious area of concern. Thus, the administration of Governor Murray Maclehose (1971-82) succeeding Trench's sought to alleviate the situation by establishing an Independent Commission Against Corruption (ICAC), initiating housing developments and reforms in education, and expanding and creating advisory bodies for more private-sector leaders to participate in Government affairs (See pp. 146-147 on the ICAC and housing programs and pp. 238-239 on educational development). In hindsight, it can be said that the seeds of democracy were sowed at that time. Those policy changes did not arise voluntarily from the HK Government, but by public demand, which ironically gained impetus from the tumultuous 1966-67 riots ignited in HK by Mao Zedong's Cultural Revolution.

Although the changes diminished leftist fervor, it did not mean that pro-Taiwan elements regained favor among the masses. The HK people had come of age and, instead of seeking direction from traditional sources, i.e., either from the PRC or from KMT-controlled Taiwan, they started to seek their own identity. More importantly, the new generation of Hong Kongers born after the Chinese civil war of the late 1940s differed greatly from their parents' generation. Born and raised in HK, their primary attachment was not to any external political entity, but to Hong Kong itself. Their main concern was the improvement of their own livelihood and the lives of their children. In other words, they wanted to see HK become a better place to live, to work and to raise their families, and hence there was growing sentiment that the HK people should have some say in the territory's affairs.

Reliable opinion polls continue to verify HK's growing sense of identity and community awareness. The 1970s economic miracle and HK's status as one of Asia's "Four Little Dragons" (the newly industrializing economies (NIEs) of Hong Kong, Singapore, South Korea, Taiwan), further strengthened the people's self-consciousness as well as self-confidence.

While Mao's Cultural Revolution diminished the image of the Chinese in the West, coincidentally as the territory's economy took off, the HK people saw more reason to develop their own new identity. World as well as local media played a significant role in shaping and propagating the new image, for one reason the world, especially developing economies, were eager to learn how and why HK and Asian NIEs in general flourished as they did before the recent downturn beginning in late 1997. It was through such world interest and local self-reflection that the HK people began to grasp the true meaning of having a free economy and the factors that contributed to prosperity. By the early 1980s, almost everyone believed that the pillars of HK's success were free enterprise, freedom of the press and of speech, rule of law, and its sophisticated infrastructure which included modern financial facilities, transportation and shipping, telecommunications and a relatively efficient, corruption-free government.

All of this triggered a quantum leap in the people's longing for a more democratic political system, which is to be expected as education, professional skills and prosperity as well as greater awareness of the world expanded. The British started to take notice of the situation but were extremely slow to respond. Much to the disappointment of the HK people, without hesitation China issued stern warnings to nip any democratization in the bud. Thus, the hands of the British were tied when they finally decided to heed public opinion. Yet it was already too late to do much as the 1997 issue would soon appear on the agenda.

Mao Zedong's death in 1976 brought an end to the Cultural Revolution, and everyone but Mao's small clique declared the decade to have been an unmitigated disaster for the Mainland. Taking charge in 1978, Deng Xiaoping initiated his economic reforms by putting a halt to Mao's agricultural communes and allowing farmers to sell their produce on the open market. Deng began to remove barriers to foreign investment and enterprise by establishing Special Economic Zones (SECs) with favorable investment incentives. Just across HK's northern border in Guangdong Province, Shenzhen (see Map 2) became the most prominent SEC as many local industrialists moved their manufacturing operations to the Mainland and began to integrate the economies of Hong Kong and the PRC.

As business opportunities in the PRC yielded excellent profits and growth prospects seemed boundless, HK looked more and more towards the Mainland as the 1980s passed. As China fever grew, many wanted to know more about the PRC and its economic reform program, and all elements of the pro-Beijing and neutral media eagerly filled the demand for up-to-date information on the PRC. The traditional pro-Taiwan media lost their remaining audience and quietly modified their stance. It even tried to capitalize on China fever by starting daily newspapers and periodicals in HK, but such ventures proved to be short-lived.

At the same time, the English-language media also gave more prominence to economic and political news from China and became very popular because they were the few daily venues by which the greater foreign community could learn about events and developments in China. Newspapers, *The South China Morning Post, Asian Wall Street Journal*, and *Hong Kong Standard*, and magazines, *Far Eastern Economic Review* and *Asiaweek,* are leading examples. The *SCMP* and *HKS* are accessible by Internet. Americans are very much involved, as *AWSJ* and *FEER* are owned by the Dow Jones Corp. However, English-language newspapers and magazines do not have the scope of coverage as Chinese counterparts. Since the Chinese media is unrivaled for in-depth analysis of political and economic developments in the Mainland and Hong Kong, it is imperative that those who are seriously interested in China learn the language and have access to the Chinese press, much of which is on the Internet.

However, excessive enthusiasm often led to inflated media reports of the investment environment in the PRC. To sort out facts, readers had to grope through a maze of glossy reports. Fortunately, some journalists upheld the principles of reporting without fear or favor and expressed unbiased, independent viewpoints that commanded respect among businessmen, intellectuals and government circles alike. For awhile, HK's media seemed to bury their age-long, political differences. It was at this very moment that the PRC and Britain reached agreement in 1984 on HK's reversion to China on July 1, 1997, followed by the drafting of the Basic Law. It was clear that Beijing wanted to maintain the status quo in Hong Kong, not only economically but also constitutionally, under the slogan "fifty years without change." However, the prospect of HK returning to the motherland was viewed with mixed feelings, and it was at this historical moment that the HK people and media became divided again.

The China Factor

After the Sino-British Joint Declaration was signed, disparities between media factions were no longer determined by old animosities, chiefly the PRC versus Taiwan issue. Most of HK's people were committed to the territory and felt it was theirs. Reflecting public opinion over the 1997 changeover, the media divided between those who were pro-PCR and "patriotic" versus those who were HK-centered and pro-democracy. While the first group was unqualifiedly pleased with Mainland China's takeover, the second group reflected many uncertainties and wariness of Beijing's totalitarian rule.

Differences escalated when constitutional changes proposed by Governor Christopher Patten (1992-1997) responded to popular demand for more democracy. HK's majority, which had deep concerns with the PRC, wanted steps taken to ensure the realization of the "one country, two systems" policy after reversion. Business types were uniformly pro-PRC and confident that HK would continue to prosper after being reunited with the Mainland. However, skeptics demanded that vestiges of colonialism be abolished before the changeover, such as the draconian security ordinances that the British rarely used but did apply during the 1966-67 riots (see pp. 96-97 & 144-145). Thus, public opinion was heated and divided and so were the media.

Tragically, turning day into night in a flash, the Tiananmen Square massacre of June 4, 1989 shocked Hong Kong and the world. Surprisingly, the leading PRC-controlled daily papers, *Ta Kung Pao* and *Wen Wei Pao*, expressed sympathy for the young victims. The day after the massacre, *Wen Wei Pao* printed in place of its editorial four large Chinese characters, *tong xin ji shou*, which convey a meaning that is far more severe than the literal translation of "sick at heart and resent deeply," to denounce the act. While an amazed public praised the papers' editorial stand, PRC authorities took immediate action. After officials from the New China News Agency's HK Branch visited the paper, the publisher and many senior editorial staff resigned immediately. The next day, editorials and news reporting of pro-Beijing papers on Tiananmen turned 180 degrees, adhering to Beijing's official line to the letter.   Other pro-PRC newspapers also relented and immediately changed their stand to denounce the students and their demonstrations as a "counter-revolutionary riot." Astounding the hardened HK public, which thought it had seen everything already, the swift, overnight conversion of the newspapers threw new light on the meaning of press freedom and reliability and possible post-1997 dangers.

Subsequently, many elements of the HK media diluted their pro-student stand. As time passed, a new division among the media gradually took place. Being pro-PRC was no longer the monopoly of the leftists. Many media leaders, among them Louis Cha, founder of *Ming Pao*, were invited to visit Beijing and were received by senior officials; following which, their editorial policy "mellowed." In the eyes of the people, their publications could no longer claim to be neutral. Only a few members of the printed media remained truly independent amidst Beijing's arm-twisting and maneuvers. By 1993, even the traditionally pro-Taiwan English language daily, *Hong Kong Standard*, showed traces of tilting towards Beijing, which caused it to be viewed as an "English-language voice of Xinhua," the PRC's New China News Agency in HK (Moriarty, 1994). By September 1994, the *Standard* became the first private, foreign-language paper to receive permission to print in the PRC, but the contract was terminated four months later. Such dramatic shifts in editorial policy were used to trumpet the freedom of HK's media to formulate their editorial policy, although the reverse seemed arguable too as shown in the case of the two PRC-friendly papers.

Political developments and the ensuing Sino-British brawl over democratization in Hong Kong further affected the media. When Governor Patten took office in 1992, he received almost universal praise. However, after he unveiled his plans in October of that year to allow more members of the Legislative Council to be elected, directly or indirectly through functional bodies, Beijing became suspicious of Britain's intentions and thundered against Governor Patten's democratic reforms and motives (see pp. 309-313). As China thrust itself into HK's affairs, the media divided sharply again on two main issues -- democratization which was political and expenditures on the Chek Lap Kok airport and container terminal projects which were financial. Then a new factor, not ideological, arose to create more schisms within the media.

Internal Contradictions

In earlier times, Hong Kong newspapers and periodicals were started and operated by missionaries and others who wanted to disseminate their viewpoints and profit from the great demand for news vital to business, trade, and local affairs. Recall that opium free trader, James Matheson, owned HK's early paper, *The Hong Kong Register*. However, with changing times and modern formats, publishing a newspaper or operating a television station developed into business enterprises with profits solely in mind rather than just somebody's cause or hobby. Moreover, when media enterprises became public companies listed on the Hong Kong Stock Exchange, the interest of shareholders had to be taken into account. Single-minded focus on profits thus raised contradictions that shook the reputable traditions of media institutions. For ease of discussion to illustrate what is meant, we shall call these different players the boss, the management and the reporters.

The boss is usually the major shareholder and may be more than one person, but there is always someone representing the boss at the helm of a newspaper or a broadcasting station who has the final say and may not even be a HK resident. The management consists of the editor and sub-editors who are professional, seasoned journalists, but they are salaried workers and receive orders from the boss. The reporters are usually youngsters eager to serve their profession; they have ideals, are liberal-minded, and have a strong sense of identity as Hong Kongers. The boss has his own and his group's interests and those of the shareholders to think about, all of whom are committed to profits. The management is entrusted with the efficient production of news, commentaries and advertisements in printed and electronic form to suit the tastes of the market and to win as large a readership as possible. The journalists are the ones who procure news for the management who in turn edit the finished products. Now here is a hypothetical example where disagreements among the players can occur.

A reporter finds a story which he or she thinks is very good. He writes it up and submits it to the editorial staff. The duty editor finds that the story may offend Beijing and thus may have adverse effects on the boss' business investments. Hence he makes changes if it is to be printed. The reporter feels that the editing has twisted his story and protests, and his next story meets with the same treatment. He goes to the chief editor or even to the boss, but to no avail. He either learns to conform to his superiors' wishes, or continues to write unwelcome stories and eventually resigns, if not actually fired. This is what is happening and it is called self-censorship.

Now here is an actual case. In 1994, Asia Television Limited, known as ATV, declined to show a film shot by a Spanish crew in Tiananmen Square on the night of June 4, 1989. Six journalists at the station resigned in protest. Eventually the film was telecast, but its contents appeared to serve China's contention that there had been no violence in the square itself. The six stood by their resignation on the grounds that ATV had exercised self-censorship (Moriarty, 1994, pp. 390).

Here is another hypothetical example. A reporter filed a news story in favor of Governor Patten which the editorial staff not only printed with prominence, but the editor or the lead writer even wrote an editorial to analyze the situation and to say that Patten was doing the right thing in rebuffing China. The next day the boss received an invitation to lunch from Xinhua. Returning to his office, the boss beckoned the editorial's author to give him a stern warning. The author remained on the payroll, but he knew that he had better not repeat the same.

The personal experience of a group of HK editors in Shenzhen in May 1994 may serve to demonstrate interference and indoctrination. A group of editors received invitations to Shenzhen to attend the opening of a new theme park and the short trip seemed to be only a public relations exercise. However, they were briefed in a closed-door, off-the-record session one evening till midnight by officials of the State Council News Office. The essential message of the meeting was simply that journalists are not free to criticize or comment unfavorably upon events in China under the "one country, two systems" principle (Moriarty, 1994, pp. 393). While the message had a chilling effect in 1994, it is reality today.

The above variations on a self-censorship theme were taken as a fact of life by media bosses, many of whom either had or were planning to pursue other business interests in China. One well-known example was the dropping of BBC programs from the Rupert Murdock owned Asia-wide satellite STAR-TV service in April 1994, because the media magnate had a big stake in the PRC, where officials were displeased with BBC (see p. 56). This kind of top-to-bottom self-censorship caused deep rifts within the media, because most reporters looked upon it as violation of their journalistic code of conduct and an affront upon their integrity. However, editorial staffs were obliged to exercise self-discipline in order to toe management's policy line, if not to keep their jobs.

All of HK's media experienced high rates of turnover in recent years, which is typically explained by greater competition and salary enticements. But reporters and editors seeking more compatible working environments was an important factor behind job-hopping. In the old days, the media enjoyed the respect and support of the public because owners, editors, and the reporters shared common professional goals. Nowadays, internal conflicts of interest invariably affect the integrity of news reporting and in the end newspapers and TVstation lose their credibility. Conflict between profits and self-censorship versus editorial integrity are common throughout the media world, but HK's situation has been most intense and unsettling.

In a survey conducted by the Department of Journalism and Communication at the Chinese University of Hong Kong in early 1996 on the credibility of HK's media, it was found that of the six electronic media, 21 newspapers, nine magazines and two others, the HK Government Information Services and the New China News Agency or Xinhua, all of which the survey covered, the Chinese-language daily, the *Hong Kong Economic Journal* was ranked first in credibility trailed by the *South China Morning Post*. Researchers who conducted the survey noted that *SCMP*'s drop to second place in 1996 from first in 1990 was statistically significant. While the HK Government Information Services ranked fifth at 6.81, Xinhua was rated third from the bottom at only 4.68 as were *Wen Wei Po* and *Ta Kung Pao*, but better than the *Next Magazine's* 3.97, the threesome being PRC publications (Chan, Ma, & So, 1997, pp. 462-463). Chairman Mao frequently quoted the famous Chinese saying: "The people's eyes are as bright as snow," which means that no one can deceive the people. Results of the CUHK survey can be interpreted as the people's verdict on HK's media.

The China Youth Daily newspaper in Beijing conducted a survey of China's media credibility (China in transition, 1997) and found that only 36%, 29% and 50% of college students, college teachers, and Chinese in general, respectively, beieved that Mainland media is credible. The paper warned that "growing cynicism and demand for higher reporting standards threaten the media's role as purveyor of party policy."

In 1995-96, this writer was often invited to speak at seminars and meetings of business communities in Hong Kong and elsewhere on the prospects of HK's press freedom after 1997. The view expressed then was that it would be unlikely for China to curtail press freedom openly, because such action would adversely affect HKSAR's status as a financial center. Although the Basic Law protects press freedom, the media will have to abide by a different set of rules than in the past. After all, journalists everywhere must abide by the laws of the country in which they operate, and HK will not be an exception. However, any danger of the media losing press freedom would be due less to imposition of harsh measures from the outside, such as government control, and more to self-restraint and self-censorship from within. Choosing to give up something without anybody taking it away, the media will be spelling their own doom and have no one else to blame. I stand by the same views today.

Opportunism, Profit and Integrity

Some reference should be given to the relationship between the media and the public. It is not the intention of this writer to undertake an exhaustive review, since more information can be obtained from official reports issued by the HK Government, which has an Internet website and offices in New York, London, San Francisco, and in Washington, DC.

Foreign journalists are typically astonished by the number of newspapers and magazines in HK. Granted that some registered publications do not appear regularly, the latest count reveals that HK boasts over 60 newspapers and almost 600 magazines. For a territory with 6.3+ million, the number of news publications and modern printing presses in HK far exceeds any other metropolis of similar size. Some of the news publishing companies are listed on the HK Stock Exchange, and their annual reports show that they have been generally profitable.

In terms of per share earnings, the English-language daily, the *South China Morning Post*, is reputed to have been one of the most profitable newspapers in the world. In September 1998, Kuok Khoon Ean, Chairman of the Board of Directors for the *SCMP* (Holdings) Ltd. (inc. in Bermuda) reported that its shareholders' profits for the year ending June 30, 1998 was HK$412.1 million or about US$53.2 m. 1997 profits were higher: HK$805.3 m.) from a turnover of HK$2,236 million or about US$289 m. (in 1997: HK$2,352 m.). Although turnover decreased about 5% from the banner year of the handover, the dividend payout remained at HK$519.3 million or US$67 m. (1.731 billion shares) (*SCMP*'s website, December 12, 1998). On April 30, 1998, *SCMP* reported (and confirmed by the HK Audit Bureau of Circulation) that the paper had a record average daily level of 119,921 in the second half of 1997.

SCMP's classified ads are the most popular, lengthy, and expensive in HK. It is a well-known fact that newspapers depend on income from advertisements to make profits; net income from sales cannot pay for the cost of newsprint alone. Though their ads are not nearly as lucrative as *SCMP*'s, the best-selling Chinese-language newspapers and magazines also manage to make handsome profits year after year. Of course, as higher circulation justifies higher advertisement rates, many mass circulation newspapers and magazines have resorted to sex and sensationalism to achieve their goal. According to the records of the Obscene Articles Tribunal over the years, several popular Chinese publications have often been found guilty of printing indecent material, proving that the ethical code of conduct of some proprietors is dubious in their drive to compete.

Opportunist or idealist? On the very day their publication began a few years ago, the Chinese language weeklies, *Next Magazine* and the *Apple Daily*, became the talk of the town. Through what it calls investigative reporting, *Next Magazine* digs up sensational stories about well-known personalities, whereas *Apple Daily* pursues sensationalism and news through questionable means, one being reporters forming so-called "doggie regiments" or *kau-tsai-dui* in Cantonese to follow their news targets around constantly, like hound dogs sniffing at everything, i.e., paparazzi. Moreover, their proprietor, Jimmy Lai, takes up the pen himself from time to time to blast the PRC and its leaders in ferocious language. Thus, he has often been portrayed by the Western media as a democracy fighter because of his outspokenness.

When the *Next Magazine* could not find a merchant banker in Hong Kong to sponsor its initial public offering attempt in 1997, it was widely rumored that that was due to pressure from China. Yet, Lai has not been very popular with his major competitors, because it was alleged that *Apple Daily* started an unprecedented price war among Chinese-language newspapers in 1995. It all began when *Apple Daily* reduced its price from HK$5.00 to $4.00 per copy, causing its major competitors to suffer declines in circulation. *Oriental Daily* lowered its price per copy to $2.00 (~US26¢), and several other papers followed suit, one of which even lowered to $1.00 per copy. With the exception of a few specialized papers, such as the *Hong Kong Economic Journal*, most newspapers were affected. The price war ended with readers as the winners. The papers also fought over fat discounts to advertisers in an effort to undercut their competitors. When another price war broke out in 1997, it failed because readers ignored it.

When someone such as Jimmy Lai invaded the printed media through unorthodox sales gimmicks, stories naturally circulate about him, such as those commenting on his management style and his treatment of the staff. Doubts arose that he might be more of an opportunist than a supporter of democracy. No doubt, *Next Magazine* and *Apple Daily* found a niche. However, time will tell whether China-bashing was merely exploited as one of Jimmy Lai's sales tactics. Beijing has seemed quite annoyed by *Apple Daily's* reporting style, and its reporters were sometimes banned from the PRC. Were he to be closed down, Jimmy Lai has obtained more than a handsome return from his investment and he would gain the enviable reputation of being a victim of communist persecution.

While Lai profited from China-bashing in almost blasphemous language, *Ming Pao* built its reputation on quality China-reporting. It started as a mass circulation daily for intellectuals and prospered thanks to its well-written editorials and news stories on the exodus from the Mainland to Hong Kong in 1962, the Cultural Revolution of 1966-76, and then the opening up of China from 1978. After the paper went public in the late 1980s, its founder, Louis Cha, sold his stake reportedly for over a billion HK dollars (~US$135 million). This made him the first and foremost Chinese journalist to have amassed a fortune through newspaper publishing, and perhaps also the last. He is even more famous as a popular kung-fu novel writer under the pen name of Jing Yong. Since leaving *Ming Pao*, Cha has turned his attention to other pursuits, including politics, but his political views have drawn diverse reactions.

Among Chinese daily newspapers, the editiorials of the *Hong Kong Economic Journal* have been rated the most respected and widely read. Almost all of its editorials from *HKEJ*'s founding on July 3, 1973 have been authored by Lam Shan-muk, its founder, who writes under the pen-name of Lin Xing-zhi. An economist who studied in the United Kingdom, Mr. Lam is a firm believer in free market economy but refuses to be swayed by the opinions of academic authorities, including Nobel laureates. He has never hestitated to criticize the HK and the PRC Governments when they deserved it. Because of his outspokenness, a real-estate tycoon once withdrew advertising from the paper because he alleged that the *Journal* had disparaged China (Chan & Lee, 1991, p. 54).

As mentioned, *HKEJ* has enjoyed top credibility ratings, much of the honor due to Lam's editorials. He has ceased writing daily editorials since April 1997, but continues to write a special column almost every day. Vista Publishing Co. of Taiwan has published Lam's editorials which he wrote over a span of 24 years in 41 volumes, unpredecedented for any editor worldwide. Many doubted that *HKEJ* could maintain its independent editorial policy after July 1, 1997, but there has been no change yet. There is no better test case on the integrity of the SAR's media in the years to come than to see what happens to the *Hong Kong Economic Journal*.

The master's voice. Among its many reverberations, the 1997 handover thrust politics into the sale of a major newspaper. When the popular and respected *South China Morning Post* was sold in 1993 by Rupert Murdock to Robert Kuok, a Malaysian investor, Kuok's close ties with Beijing raised eyebrows; but no immediate changes in the paper's editorial contents ensued. Changes came in 1996 when a cartoon strip was dropped and the artist discharged and many of the senior non-Chinese editorial staff members of the *Sunday Post* were terminated. In 1997, Feng Xiliang, the chief editor emeritus of Beijing's English paper, *China News*, became the paper's advisor. Yet personnel changes in journalism are not uncommon, especially in HK. What's important is that readers cannot be fooled in the long run; they will know in time whether a paper has bowed to political or not.

Speaking of integrity, some media workers have not hesitated to file lawsuits to seek damages when their dubious backgrounds have been unmasked. For instance, the *Oriential Daily* initiated legal action in recent years against a number of their peers or competitors on the grounds that they had published articles alleging that the *OD* proprietor's family members had engaged in illegal business. Claiming to be a worthy member of the media, the *OD* family said that they did not do anything improper to impair the integrity of their rivals.

On the other hand, when the HK Government takes action against media members implying that some crime might have been committed, the seriousness cannot be ignored. On June 4, 1997, for instance, 30 ICAC investigators suddenly pounced on the executive offices and residences of the Sing Tao publishing group. They arrested six serving and former senior executives of the *Hong Kong Standard* for an alleged corrupt scheme to inflate the newspaper's circulation figures up to 23,000 extra copies daily to order to deceive advertisement clients and a British circulation audit company. The HK News Executives'Association said that it was very unusual to have officers entering a publishing organization to arrest people, especially "on the eve of the handover" (Fraser, 1997). Three having been found guilty and imprisoned for up to six months in January 1999, it is a serious blow to the integrity of the HK media as a whole.

As for radio and television, the HK Government-run Radio and Television Hong Kong (RTHK) finally ended plans to go private as mooted in 1985. The reason was plain and simple: Beijing's objection. There are similarities between RTHK and Britain's BBC, the most prominent feature being their independent editorial and programming policy. For instance, RTHK's panel discussion and commentary programs have often invited people from different walks of life to present their views, many critical of the Government. Operating television and radio stations differently, China's media serves as the mouthpiece of the CCP; so the last thing Beijing wants in Hong Kong is an incorporated and more independent RTHK. HK's international business community would be alarmed if RTHK's programming is significantly changed, because commerce and finances rely heavily on open and reliable news and commentary.

Language and Its Impact

Hong Kong broadcasting services experienced one noticeable change in recent years, as all radio and television stations reduced their air time for English-language programs to order to expand Cantonese and Mandarin programs. Before television, the dialect used by mainstream motion pictures and popular songs was Mandarin. When television was introduced in 1957, the overwhelming proportion of Chinese programs was in Cantonese; English was negligible and movies and pop songs started to switch from Mandarin to Cantonese. By the late 1960s and early 1970s, the Cantonese dialect not only dominated radio and TV programs but also HK-produced motion pictures. All local pop songs were sung in Cantonese. Second-generation Hong Kongers all spoke Cantonese as their mother tongue. While the rest of China used Mandarin as the medium of instruction in primary and secondary schools, Cantonese remained HK's educational language, although English was supposed to receive more emphasis in most secondary schools. As the Cantonese dialect often differs from written Chinese, the children's lack of exposure to Mandarin has been used to explain the deterioration of Chinese-language proficiency in Hong Kong.

Interestingly, South China experienced the same phenomenon. After the PRC started its economic reform and relaxed its rigid control over the installation of antennas, people living across HK's border received television from the territory. As a result, despite many years of using Mandarin, they began to switch back to their native tongue of Cantonese. But the switch was not total, because PRC schools continued to use Mandarin as the medium of instruction. In Hong Kong, there had been calls for "mother tongue education" to replace the use of English as the medium of instruction in primary and secondary levels. Since Cantonese has always been spoken in Hong Kong, it becomes tautological to use the expression, "mother tongue," for Mandarin. It would be more accurate to regard it as the PRC's national tongue. The fact that Hong Kong had few qualified teachers who could teach in Mandarin made the issue hard to tackle, but the number is increasing (see p. 264). Also, now that British restrictions are passé, it is expected that competent teachers from the PRC can be recognized and accepted officially in HK, making it possible to expand the use of Mandarin in schools.

However, the continued domination of TV and radio programs by the Cantonese dialect might remain a deterring factor to Mandarin until drastic changes are mandated, such as nations that converted to the metric system. Although most people agree that a major effort should be devoted to improving their overall quality, HK's radio and televised programs are often quite good.

For instance, some programs produced by RTHK, which commercial stations were obliged by law to air, have been of high quality and welcomed by the public. Also, Cable TV, a relatively recent player in the arena, provides educational, science, art and documentary programs, which unfortunately usually have poor audience ratings. As elsewhere, HK's radio and TV programs, especially the latter, cater to the taste of the common people. When newspapers resort to sensationalism and scandals to sustain their circulation, it is only natural that radio and television stations do the same. As long as advertisement income constitutes the rice bowl of commercial stations, the quality of most radio and TV programs seems destined to remain at their present level.

The film industry experienced the same. As mentioned earlier, major studios of the local film industry used to produce only Mandarin films. But, from the 1970s on, almost all produced Cantonese dialect movies. This was parity because the once active and popular Great Wall and Feng Huang film companies, considered to be pro-PRC, became dormant after the 1967 riots. Even the other major studios virtually stopped producing Mandarin films. Whether or not Mandarin films will be revived in Hong Kong will be interesting to see.

Telecommunications or Incommunicado

In the area of telecommunications, satellite uplinking and even digital mobile phones, the HK Government betrayed its poor grasp of rapid technological advances. International broadcasters criticized HK's regulatory procedures and its snail-paced review of satellite uplinking and license granting policies. The Government seemed frustratingly inept in fulfilling the public's demand to obtain the latest technology in personal communications services. For instance, in such fields as Personal Communications Services (PCS), Video on Demand (VOD), and Internet Service Provider (ISP), overly cautious authorities wasted valuable time deciding what to do and who to license. As local and international groups vied for the lucrative HK market, some speculated that telecommunication decisions were delayed in order to consult China and that there were conflicting views among PRC officials.

In any case, the telecommunications monopoly enjoyed by the British firm, Cable and Wireless, was at an end and replaced by local and PRC-backed entities. But because of historical reasons, it is likely that Hong Kong Telecom, the local arm of Cable and Wireless, will maintain its influence in the SAR, albeit at a diminished scale. Among the powerful bidders locally were the Hutchison-Whampoa Group headed by tycoon Li Ka-shing, and the Wharf Group, headed by the family of the late Sir Y. K. Pao and now run by Pao's son-in-law, Peter Woo. H-W controls such vital sectors of HK's economy as telecommunications, broadcasting, container terminals, retail chains, and electricity, not to mention real estate and huge investments in Mainland China. Wharf's sway in Hong Kong is comparable. Besides, both enjoy excellent relations with PRC cadre and leaders.

Apart from local companies, China's state-run enterprises and their off-shoots are also major players in Hong Kong telecommunications. For instance, on June 6, 1997, China's state-run telephone company, China Telecom, was reported to be buying a 5.5 % stake in Hongkong Telecommunications Ltd. for US$1.8 billion from Cable and Wireless, thus gaining a strong niche in HK's telephone market. Also, the launching of several telecommunication satellites all involved Chinese partners. At the end of May 1997, there were four HK-related telecommunications satellites functioning and collecting revenues. They were AsiaSat I and AsiaSat II in which the Hutchison Group holds a big stake; and the two satelletes, APStar 1 and APStar 1A, of the China-Thailand-Taiwan consortium's APT Satellite Company, which is closely related to the Wharf Group. The APT company put its most powerful satellite to date for digital television and telephone communications into orbit in 1997 with the PRC's new Long March rocket launcher, the 3B. Although Long March launchers have been erratic and have incurred costly mishaps, China's position in HK's telecommunications market brooks no other choice.

Although Hong Kong wants to match the pace of other societies' telecommunications advances and be at the forefront of the information age, HKSAR's media is still mired in primitive one-way communications. Newspapers, radio and television all follow the conventional role of providing information and treating readers and viewers as recipients of information. Worse, they have been complacent with the status quo even after their production operations were computerized in the mid-1980s. Some are even opposed to the introduction of new technology for fear of competition, as in the case of Wharf Group's objection to its competitor's application for VOD licensing because of the potential threat to its cable TV monopoly. In a nutshell, HK's media seems content to remain in the conventional provider/recipient communications mode, mainly because it is familiar ground. However, the world has already entered the information age full force by introducing high-speed, high-capacity, interactive communications systems without delay. HK should overcome its inhibitions and foster two-way communications systems, but old habits die hard.

Access to HK newspapers on the Internet provide their editorials, news reports and commentaries to readers throughout the world (see p. 30). With many eager personal computer users who are on-line, the HK people have been a step ahead of most local media, and their efforts to access world news have enhanced the free flow of information and its dissemination in the territory.

Thus far, HK's slow pace in telecommunications can be attributed to existing monopolies and Government policy. Hopefully, future developments in this field will not evolve into one monopoly replacing another. The HK Government has indicated that it favored a more flexible and diversified policy that would put the territory more prominently on the world telecommunications map. The local and international business communities as well as the general public would certainly welcome policies that would enhance access to state-of-the-art technology at an early date and at reasonable costs. All seems ready except for the Government's will to proceed.

Vox Populi

With freedom of the press and speech fully protected by the Bill of Rights and the Basic Law, it seems reasonable to expect that Government policy should not hamper future developments in HK's media and communications networks. The media should be of service to the public, whether collectively or individually, and the public, as users and generators but not merely recipients of information, should have the freedom to choose and access information by whatever means possible through advancing technology. Of course, this would not mean the total lack of regulatory measures. But such measures should be viewed as a necessary evil rather than the prerogative of the Government. In fact, with rapid advances in technology, it would be very difficult or even impossible for the SAR Government to control the flow of communications. Sooner or later, two-way, interactive communications will become an inseparable part of daily life. By then, it will be the public, rather than the HK Government, who will have control over the free flow of information. But what about the PRC and its keen control of the media and communications within the mainland?

Unfortunately, China's several millennia history has a tradition quite different from the realities of modern media and communications and their respective roles in society. The great sage, Confucius (551-479 BC), whose teachings became established as the official Chinese state philosophy about two thousand years ago, was a relatively conservative thinker even by the standards of his times. Confucius stressed the obligations of individuals rather than their rights (Hart, 1982). One of his famous teachings is in Chapter 9, the 8th Book of his famous analects, "Lunyu," the English translation of which by the renowned Sinologist James Legge in the 1830s is quoted at the beginning of this chapter. What Confucius professed was that the government might inform the people and tell them what to do, but the people need not know why.

People in today's information age, including the HK Chinese, are eager to know why as well as what, etc. Faulting any government that attempts to decide what the public should or should not read, hear or see, Hong Kongers would surely disagree with Confucius in this particular respect.

Recognizing HK's role as an international financial center and a regional center of management, the media and all of those engaged in communications should reflect upon themselves and reexamine their role. Free trade and enterprise require that there be free press and speech.

It is high time that responsible government officials (public servants) seriously rethink the role of the government vis-à-vis the media and information flow. Should the media be the voice of the people or a mouthpiece of the government? Should one-way communications tell the people what to know and do without explaining and discussing opinions? People have the right to tell the government what they think. With advanced technology and media participation, such a right is no longer just empty talk; it can be put into practice.

As already mentioned, ever since HK's economy took off in the 1970s, Hong Kongers have been searching for a new identity and have longed to have a say in their own affairs. And today's affairs and conditions are already vastly different from those of almost a quarter of century ago. For HK to continue to prosper with stability, there is a vital role for the media to play, especially in promoting two-way communications between the government and the public, in fostering interactive communications among the people, and in encouraging and accelerating the process of democratization. It is most ironic that as Hong Kong moves apace into the information age with modern advances in communications technology at its fingertips, it has been returned to the fold of authoritarianism.

Post-Handover Blues

Midnight, June 30, 1997 marked the end of 156 years of British rule in Hong Kong (meaning Fragrant Harbor), during which a "barren rock" was transformed into one of the world's most successful market economies. As China regained sovereignty at zero hour, July 1, 1997, the former British colony formally became the Hong Kong Special Administrative Region (HKSAR) or *Xianggang Tebie Xingzheng Qu* -- "*Xiang*" and "*Gang*" are the *pinyin* forms of the Chinese characters "fragrant" and "harbor" respectively. The handover was one of the year's hottest news stories and attracted unprecedented worldwide media coverage. The mood of Hong Kong was jubilant -- the stock market was as vibrant as ever, property prices soared, and the Democrats staged their protest at the Legislative Council chambers without police interference. Rainy weather added a touch of melancholy to the scene at the pier when the Prince of Wales and Governor Patten bid farewell to the ex-colony. Everything went smoothly, a good sign that Hong Kong would enjoy prosperity and stability when it entered a new chapter in history.

Unfortunately, the euphoria was short-lived. First came torrent rains, then the bird virus and the Government's draconian decision to slaughter 1.2 million chickens. Western media wasted no time in transmitting photos of helpless hens and cocks having their throats slit and being thrown into plastic bags with their wings still flapping. In the meantime, subtle changes were taking place. Reporters started to feel that the attitude of the police had become sterner and even harsher, especially in measures taken to protect Beijing VIPs.

Unexpectedly, from nowhere an devastating economic and financial crisis befell SE Asian countries in late 1997. Spectulators cracked the region's currency bubbles and governments and banks beset by mismanagement were helpless to defend their currencies. Suddenly, Hong Kong discovered how vulnerable their economy really was, especially its strong dollar-pegged currency.

The Hang Seng Index plunged and continued to fall. Property prices dropped an average of 20% or more, and many rumors of devaluation plagued the HK Monetary Authority, causing it to raise interest rates over 10%. Precipitated by Thailand, Indonesia, and Malaysia, the crisis caught Singapore, SE Asia's financial bulwark, in its wake and spread to South Korea. Although the external storm was beyond HK's control, crisis management by the SAR Government was anemic at first. As HK's economic competitiveness (World Economic Forum, 1997 & 1998) dropped in 1997 to eight from first and second rankings in previous years, the SAR Government was slow to develop meaningful strategy. Although the people remained confident but wary entering 1999, the liquidation and downsizing of well-known businesses and rise in unemployment set the stage for demoralization should the financial turmoil continued for long.

When Chief Editor of the *Hong Kong Economic Journal*, I stated on numerous occasions that the threat to press freedom would not be from outside but from within. In March 1998, my public warning was manifested by an attack on the Government-funded Radio Television Hong Kong network by Tsui Sze-man (Xu Simin), publisher of the Hong Kong-based *Mirror* and a long-time member of the Chinese People's Political Consultative Conference. Mr. Xu was in Beijing attending the Conference when he lashed out at RTHK by alleging that it was often used to criticize Beijing and the SAR Government. Asking "Who gave them the power?," Xu charged that RTHK "teases the country and leadership." Also, "When you want to influence political opinion, the first thing you have to do is to grab control of the radio. Whoever can grab control can create and control public opinion."

Causing a furor in Hong Kong, Mr. Xu's comments were tantamount to inviting Beijing to interfere in RTHK's editorial policy and programs. Every branch of the media refuted Xu's accusations, and public opinion was overwhelmingly against him. Eventually, he fell into silence. With credit to them, senior CCP officials, including President Jiang and then Vice-Premiers Zhu and Qian, reemphasized the "one country, two systems" policy. The Conference, therefore, never followed up Xu's attack. Nonetheless, HK had a serious scare and people began to realize where the real threat to autonomy came from. Martin Lee, leader of the Democrat Party, commented: "What Mr. Xu wants to do is transplant the communist system into HK. It will be HK people who kill Hong Kong, not Beijing."

While Xu Simin's attempt to incur China's intervention failed, the HK media began to shoot itself in the foot. The *Oriental Daily*, which antagonized its peers with sensational law suits before the handover, raised its hooks in January 1998. This time it decided to assign teams of reporters to harass a Court of Appeals judge night and day whom it accused of making an unfavorable verdict. Promptly condemning the action, the HK Human Rights Monitor stated on January 15th: ". . . the explicit threats printed in the newspaper and the newspaper's express intention of influencing the judge's future decisions, go far outside the legitimate role of the press and are a deliberate challenge to the rule of law." While the *Oriental Daily* might have had reasons to bear a grudge against the judge, its poor judgment provided an opportunity for the SAR Government to curtail press freedom if it wanted to do so on the grounds of protecting privacy. In other words, by exercising its "right" to stalk a judge, OD might have sowed the seeds for stricter control by the authorities over the media. Fortunately, the *OD* was fined for its harrassment without the imposition of new measures of media control.

HK's media also made headlines in March 1998 when the pre-handover ICAC raid on the *Hong Kong Standard*, mentioned earlier, took a new twist. The Government prosecuted two staff members and one former employee of the newspaper for conspiring with Sally Aw Sian, Chairman of the Sing Tao parent of *HKS*, for defrauding advertisers by inflating its circulation figures. In January 1999, the three were jailed. However, the Secretary for Justice, Elsie Leung Oisie, decided not to charge Miss Aw. Although it is the prerogative of the Secretary for Justice (formerly the Attorney General under the British) to decide whether to prosecute or not, Leung's decision immediately aroused public controversy and skepticism. Wild and varied speculation thrashed about why Miss Aw was "exempted" from prosecution along with her executives. Was it because Aw was a member of the Chinese People's Political Consultative Conference (along with Xu or could it be because the SAR Chief Executive, Tung Chee-hwa, had served as a Sing Tao director? Critics said that what was at stake was the rule of law, one of the main pillars for HK's stability and prosperity.

Widespread agitation fomented a motion by Legco's legal representative, Margaret Ng Ngoi-yee, of no confidence in Secretary Leung in March 1999, which failed when pro-Beijing and business members supported the Government. After Sing Tao reported a half-year (to Sept. '98) loss of US$1.8 million compared to the same period profit of $15.7 m. in 1997, Ms. Aw sold her Sing Tao holdings to a HK investment bank to pay debts of US$35 million on March 23, 1999.

Months after the handover, these incidents taught the HK people that the integrity of some media elements was questionable. The media's image was tarnished, not only in its intramural bickering but also by *Oriental Daily*'s vindictive methods in the name of press freedom. It became increasingly obvious that HK's media had more to fear from factors from within rather than outside.

Sine Qua Non

This chapter on HK's media and communications systems would be remiss if it did not stress an important fact and recommendation, that is, anyone who wishes to have a true working understanding of HK's media should possess a good knowledge of the Chinese language. Unfortunately, most Westerners have access only to news stories, commentaries and analyses published by the English-language media. Thus, a Westerner may attribute more importance to such news organs as the *SCMP*, *Far Eastern Economic Review*, or *Asian Wall Street Journal* than Chinese publications; but HK's readers, 99% of whom are Chinese, consider the HK Chinese-language media as more accurate and faithful in reflecting their points of view.

Also, Westerners may look upon personalities or publications often mentioned by the Western media as more influential than their Chinese peers. With due respect to the English-language publications and personalities, the fact remains that unless one is in regular contact with the Chinese-language media, it would be very difficult to grasp a true and complete picture of the HK scene. The sheer number and volume of Chinese-language papers and magazines versus those in English justifies this claim.

This is why this chapter has emphasized Chinese media personalities and downplayed Western counterparts. For instance, Derek Davies, for many years the editor of the *Far Eastern Economic Review*, played an important role in helping English-language readers understand Hong Kong and the Asian region. But we must also remember that his predecessor, Kayser Sung, a much-revered figure, is still active as publisher and editor of a monthly periodical on the textile industry. Also, Louis Cha, founder of the Chinese daily, *Ming Pao*, is certainly one of the best known newspaper publishers and writers over a period of almost three decades from the 1950s.

Yet, Lam Shan-muk, founder of the *Hong Kong Economic Journal*, is no less influential and respected through his editorials since 1973. In fact, HK Government officials, executives, and professionals as well as all key PRC Government officials, members of research and academic institutes are known to be *HKEJ* readers. Despite the fact that *HKEJ* is often highly critical of China, it is nevertheless the most frequently quoted newspaper in China's *Can-kao-xiao-xi* (Reference News), a news bulletin circulated among PRC cadre.

Also, to gauge the views of the HK populace, it is important to listen to the Cantonese radio and TV programs, especially the phone-in programs and talk shows. Further, street hawkers and fishmongers are the ones who often make remarks that reflect the man in the street. After all, it is through Cantonese that the HK people air their views.

British officials used to keep in touch with the Chinese media through translated copy. HK translation services have become a lively business and are profitable at just under US$.40 per word. Western journalists should emulate diplomats, missionaries, and others who want to work and communicate uninhibited in HK, the PRC, Singapore, and Taiwan -- study Chinese and become competent in speaking, reading, and writing Chinese. Although linguistic aptitude varies among people, almost anybody can learn Chinese through commitment and immersion in reliable language programs.

The prospects for freedom of the press and freedom of speech in Hong Kong do not hinge on whether or not the English-language media will carry on as before. This is because Chinese authorities always consider non-Chinese media as less influential and would probably not bother to control them. Westerners may therefore get a false impression that everything is normal in Hong Kong as long as papers, such as the *SCMP*, continue to publish without harassment.

On the other hand, some pro-China, "patriotic" Hong Kongers did observe years before the handover that the *HKEJ* might not survive after July 1, 1997. In 1999, the *HKEJ* continues as it has in the past. Therefore, such freedoms depend very much on whether or not key members of the Chinese media will be able to continue their present editorial policy and style. The free flow of information being one of the pillars of HK's economy, the world should therefore keep a careful watch over the future of HK's Chinese media for accurate, post-1997 assessments of the question, Whither Hong Kong?

Let's illustrate my urgent recommendation that Western observers of Hong Kong and China learn and master the Chinese language. They will not only fail to assess public opinion, they will also be unaware of the nuance and humor of articles and cartoons that fill the local media. For instance, Governor Chris Patten was affectionately nicknamed "Fei Pang" by the locals, "Fei" meaning "fat" or "fatty" and "Pang" being Patten's surname in his official Chinese (Cantonese) name of Pang Ting Hong. When Patten first arrived in Hong Kong, he was overweight. Mr. Patten's predecessor, Sir David Wilson (now Lord Wilson), was learned in Chinese and had an original Chinese name. However, because his surname was pronounced "ngai" in Cantonese, meaning "danger," and included the

Chinese radical for "kwai" or "ghost," it was deemed unsuitable for a governor. Thus, the HK Government changed his Chinese name to Wai Yik-shun (Wei Yixin) and Wilson had to go along with it.

Borrowed from a popular Japanese television series, which included a young female protagonist named Ah Shun (Ah Xin), Governor Wilson was nicknamed Ah Shun by Hong Kongers. The *HKEJ* ran a daily cartoon strip entitled, "The Story of Ah Shun," during Wilson's tenure and another series called "Fei Pang Theater" during Patten's Governorship. Both cartoon runs were tremendously popular and it is known that both governors enjoyed the humor along with the public. Since the handover, *HKEJ* has been running a cartoon strip on Chief Executive Tung Chee Wah, who has not expressed displeasure.

Without good knowledge of the Chinese language, it would be next to impossible for foreign journalists to understand Hong Kong and China, especially to monitor subtle changes in press freedom. Let us conclude this chapter by quoting another saying by Confucius: "The mechanic, who wishes to do his work well, must first sharpen his tools."

References

Abbas, Ackbar (1997). *Hong Kong: Culture and the politics of disappearance.* Minneapolis, MN: University of Minnesota Press.

Chan, Joseph Man & Lee, Chin-Chuan (1991). *Mass media and political transition: The Hong Kong press in China's orbit.* New York: Guilford.

Chan, Joseph Man, Ma, Eric K. W., & So, Clement Y. K. (1997). Back to the future: A retrospect and prospects for the Hong Kong mass media. In Joseph Y. S. Cheng (Ed.), *The other Hong Kong report 1997* (pp. 455-481). Hong Kong: The Chinese University Press.

China in transition (1997, August 28). *Far Eastern Economic Review*, p. 26.

Cheng, Jihua (1963). *Zhongguo dianying fazhan shi.* Beijing: Zhongguo Dianying Chubanshe.

Cheung, Jimmy (1997, May 12). Self-censorship hits press credibility: Lau. *Hong Kong Standard*, Internet edition.

Fraser, Niall (1997, June 5). Six executives held after ICAC raid on newspaper. *South China Morning Post*, Internet edition.

Friedman, Milton, & Friedman, Rose (1981). *Free to choose.* New York: Avon.

Hart, Michael H. (1982). *The 100 -- A ranking of the most influential persons in history.* New York: Galahad.

Lau, Chi Kuen (1997). *Hong Kong's colonial legacy.* Hong Kong: The Chinese University Press.

Leyda, Jay (1972). *Dianying -- An account of films and the film audience in China.* Cambridge, MA: MIT Press.

Moriarty, Francis (1994). The media. In Donald H. McMillen and Man Si-wai (Eds.), *The other Hong Kong report 1994.* Hong Kong: The Chinese University Press.

Welsh, Frank (1993). *A history of Hong Kong.* London: HarperCollins.

World Economic Forum (1997 & 1998). *World competitiveness report, 1997 and 1998.* Geneva: World Economic Forum.

Yee, Albert H. (1992). *A people misruled: The Chinese stepping-stone syndrome* (2nd ed., rev.). Singapore: Heinemann Asia.

CHAPTER FIVE

Hong Kong's Educational System: The Universities

Albert H. Yee

To bring comfort to the old, to be trusted by my friends, and to cherish the young.
Confucius (*Analects*, 5:26), when asked his aims in life

Education in Hong Kong combines the worst of British and Chinese education.
Often heard in Hong Kong

A Blank Canvas

Almost desolate when Great Britain acquired it in 1841, Hong Kong by 1999 was a world center with a population of 6.3+ million and 2,200+ educational institutions. This chapter relates the development of education in Hong Kong with emphasis on its Sino-British characteristics and higher education. Endacott (1973, p. 132) wrote that: "Neither British nor Chinese had any tradition of state education, and in the early days of the colony neither demanded it." Whether there was any demand for schools or not, there was great need. Educationally, Hong Kong was a blank canvas, a void that the Morrison Education Society led by the American missionary, Elijah C. Bridgman, first penetrated by opening a one-room school on land donated by Governor Sir Henry Pottinger. Thus, Morrison Hill (by Happy Valley & Wan Chai), Hong Kong's first school, and the Society itself were all named in honor of Dr. Robert Morrison, the first Protestant (Presbyterian) missionary in China (Ride, 1957).

Before the cession of Hong Kong. Sailing from Britain to New York and from there to China in a Yankee clipper ship, Morrison reached the foreign compound in Canton after a long, trying journey in 1807. Dominating the only trade center open to foreigners in China, merchants of the British East India Company shunned missionaries, fearing that they might upset the authorities. Thus, seeking time to find a way to make himself useful and acceptable, Morrison pretended to be an American at first.

A facile linguist, he became so fluent in Chinese that the Company made him its official translator in 1809. By 1813, aided by his colleague, William Milne, Morrison translated the New Testament into Chinese. After the two completed a *Grammar of the Chinese Language* (1815) and embarked on their ambitious *Dictionary of the Chinese Language, in Three Parts* (1815-23), they printed their translation of the whole Bible in 1821. Converting only ten during his 27 years in China, Morrison made his mark through arduous scholarship and his inspirational influence on other missionaries.

Restrictions against the foreigners' movements and contact with the people severely hampered the work of the missionaries until extraterritoriality was won in the Second Opium War ending 1860, which allowed Westerners to do about whatever they wished in China (see pp. 76-81). Prevented from opening a school in Canton, Morrison and Milne established the Anglo-Chinese College far south at the trading center of Malacca (SE Malaysia today) in 1818, for "the cultivation of English and Chinese literature in order to encourage the spread of the Gospel of Jesus Christ" (Harrison, 1979). Self-supporting apostles of the London Missionary Society, by the late 1820s Morrison and his colleagues suffered from overwork, disappointments, and ill health.

Morrison spoke to his American friend, David W. C. Olyphant, of his desperate need for help. Olyphant, one of few merchants who refused to trade in opium, offered the American Board of Commissioners for Foreign Missions free passage to and room and board at the Canton trading center for any missionary that the Board sponsored. With the U.S. ablaze in religious revival, the timing could not have been better.

That's how Elijah Coleman Bridgman, a Massachusetts Congregationalist and graduate of Andover Theological Seminary got to China. Bridgman was hastily ordained at age 28 along with David Abeel, and the two young missionaries shipped aboard an Olyphant & Co. merchantman in 1830 to become the first American missionaries to enter China. Sailing with them was Charles King, David Olyphant's representative in Canton and a strong opponent of opium, as was his employer.

At the foreign compound in Canton, each nationality had what was called their "factory" where they lived and worked. Rented by Olyphant & Co., the American factory was nicknamed "Zion's corner" because its residents were regarded as very pious. Bridgman and Morrison soon formed a close friendship until the passing of the senior missionary from Northumberland in 1834.

That same year, another American began work at Zion's Corner. Missionary and surgeon, the incomparable Peter Parker opened the Opthalmic Hospital at Zion's Corner and performed surgery unknown to the Chinese (see pp. 161 & 175). Dr. Parker's successes brought wide acclaim for Western medicine and attracted many Chinese to medical training. Convinced that ignorance was the chief barrier to their efforts for "The Word of Life," Bridgman often said that Dr.

Parker did more for their cause in his first two years than all of Morrison's 27 years. Because of him, the Chinese began to accept Western learning.

Unlike Morrison, Bridgman's fluency in Chinese never passed the makeshift *pidgin* level. Unable to support himself as a translator, Bridgman launched a monthly periodical in 1832, the *Chinese Repository*, which he would later move from Canton to Macao, the Portuguese getaway where Westerners were relatively free of Chinese officialdom, and then to Hong Kong. With the help of S. Wells Williams, an American missionary skilled in printing, Bridgman continued the *Repository* for 19 years. It is an information tove of those times. Illustrating the versatility of the missionaries, Williams accompanied Commodore Matthew Perry's mission to "open" Japan in 1853. After 40 years in East Asia and writing *The Middle Kingdom*, the most comprehensive book on China of that era, Williams joined Yale University as America's leading sinologist.

Fay's (1975, p. 84) description of the *Repository* gives insight into the missionaries: It ". . . was a remarkable work . . . . contained . . . a seriousness, an impenetrability even, that would have done credit to any reputable European or American review. Most of the English and American missionaries wrote for it. So did a number of merchants, ... But Bridgman wrote more than any of the others . . . . (He) made sure that the journal lived up to its name." It had 200 subscribers in the Pearl River delta, 150 in America, and others from London to Calcutta. As Bridgman intended, the periodical helped Westerners to understand China and the Chinese. It was this scholar-missionary and his colleagues who opened Hong Kong's first school.

In contrast to the avarice of the foreign traders, the humanitarianism and intellect that Anglo-American missionaries devoted to their work in China and Hong Kong extended far beyond the Pearl River Delta. They campaigned against opium with activist groups, such as the Society for the Suppression of the Opium Trade and the U.S. Philippine Commission on Opium, which kept the issue alive in Britain and America (Lodwick, 1996).

Early Decades

Dr. Parker's success in training Chinese medics re-energized the American missionaries and caused them to focus more on education. Their first school opened in Macao in 1838. Three years later, they moved it to Hong Kong, the colony's first school. From Yale, Rev. Samuel Brown, was the first headmaster (Welsh, 1993, p. 153). Returning home in 1847, Brown took a pupil named Yung Wing (Rong Wong) with him. The first Chinese graduate of an U.S. university (Yale in 1854), Yung developed China's arsenals and became prominent, married an American lady, and educated his children at Yale. A naturalized citizen, his attempt to join the Union Army during the Civil War was politely declined. Yung's (1909) fine academic record and ability to relate with Westerners and modern machinery greatly encouraged the missionaries and their supporters. American visions of changing China through education had no bounds.

Similar to England, public education in Hong Kong developed through voluntarism, mostly by religious societies supported by funds raised locally and at home. After Governor Pottinger left the territory in 1844, the Morrison Education Society gradually lost ground to the London Missionary Society which the new Governor, Sir John Davis, favored. When the great opium empire of Dent & Co. collapsed in 1867, the Morrison Education Society lost its chief patron and faded away. Elijah Bridgman, its shining light, went to Shanghai where he died and was buried in 1860.

While HK's educational development became British, American missionaries used the colony as a stepping-stone after extraterritoriality offset China's barriers to foreigners. Although Anglican Bishop George Smith declared in 1846 that the colony was unsuitable for missionaries because of its shocking crime and squalor (Endacott, 1973, p. 71), HK became a base for Anglo-American mission efforts in China. As the Overview discussed, Americans had a special affinity for China and its people; the commitment of their mission groups in China was immense.

The Middle Kingdom had academies for classical studies, but nothing resembling Western institutions of higher learning. During Japan's Meiji Restoration (1868-1912) when European institutions were adopted *en bloc*, universities mushroomed. Illustrating the sociopolitical chasm between the two nations, China's first universities were founded by Americans. U.S. Protestant groups established 12 colleges and universities and many schools and clinics, mostly maintained until Mao's victory in 1949. A British-Canadian Protestant group organized West China Union University in Chengtu; and Catholics founded three universities, the largest being Aurora in Shanghai. Started in 1879 by the American Episcopal Mission, St. John's College (University in 1905) in Shanghai was the first missionary institution of higher learning in China.

Highly sought after, graduates of St. John's, Nanking, Yenching, etc. became officials and professionals -- eventually providing enthusiasm and knowhow to the Nationalists and Communists on opposite sides of the Formosa Strait. Funded by the Rockefeller Foundation from 1915-1950, Peking Union Medical College became a model institution although it graduated relatively few MD's (Yee, 1994, pp. 5-13).

After prodigious efforts and expense from 1860-1950, many missionaries, especially the most evangelical, felt disillusioned with their results in China. Lutz (1971, p. 529) wrote: "Their contribution to China was of lasting importance; . . . Sinifying Christianity was marginal. The colleges aided the Chinese in defining themselves and in defining the West," especially in nationalistic terms. Calling the Americans, "sentimental imperialists," Thomson et al. (1981, pp. 59-60) wrote: "China was not won for Christ . . . had mysterious qualities of success. China was, in fact, transformed through their help. But the transformation was not of their design." Although the evangelists found little success in converts, their educational results were far-reaching. In China, Hong Kong, and the USA, the many prominent Chinese with degrees from the missionary universities whom I have encountered reflects the power of education and its impact on China.

The Government Assumes Responsibility

Education funding by the Hong Kong Government remained minor for sometime; by 1851, five one-room schools each received grants of $10 monthly. The first Governor to take much interest in education, Sir John Bowring initiated liberal changes in 1854 to overcome the "monstrous" fact that the "instruction of the people" received only 120 pounds annually versus the police which got 8,620 pounds. That same year five subsidized schools enrolled only 150 students against the census count of 8,800 children. The Education Committee proposed an increase from five to 19 schools with an enrollment of 873 boys and 64 girls at an annual cost of 1,200 pounds by 1859.

Bowring's successor, Sir Hercules Robinson, accelerated educational reform. Working with Dr. James Legge of the London Missionary Society, who was a prominent community leader and scholar, Robinson's administration decided to centralize, expand, and take responsibility for education, a highly significant policy decision for its time. A large school would be established to consolidate many of the one-room schools, and an European would be hired as headmaster to establish and promote school standards and English-language instruction.

On January 1, 1862, two decades after the ceding of Hong Kong, Central School (later renamed Queen's College) opened for boys in rented facilities with Dr. Frederick Stewart as headmaster and the territory's school inspector. Despite those big steps, school curriculum was evenly divided between scriptures and Chinese classics with little English-language instruction. The missionaries had devised the narrow curriculum and it suited them, since they regarded the schools as feeders to St. Paul's College which they opened in 1853 to prepare Anglican clergy. With his failed Anglo-Chinese College in mind, Dr. Legge was a notable exception among the missionaries and convinced Governor Robinson that the Government schools should be secular as in England.

In full accord since he did not believe that it was the Government's duty to convert the Chinese, Stewart opposed cleric-oriented education and bided the right moment to act. Between one bishop's return home and his successor's arrival, Stewart made the bold move of abolishing the Board of Education which the Bishop chaired and other clerics filled as members. The *coup de main* in 1865 made it possible to separate public education from the church, impose secular education, and centralize curriculum and administration in one fell swoop. Except for the new bishop, the Protestants generally acquiesced out of respect to Legge. However, Catholic Bishop T. Raimondi from Portugal sternly opposed school secularism (Eitel, 1895, pp. 392-393).

Before Central School, Government schools were viewed as pauper schools, and families preferred the private Chinese schools. For those willing to accept Christian influence, the mission schools were considered better than the public schools. For girls, the religious schools provided the best educational opportunities, such as the Diocesan Native Female School opened by Jane Baxter, whom

Endacott identified as "a great pioneer of education for girls" (p. 143). However, Baxter's experiment to instruct girls in English was dropped after many of her students became mistresses for Europeans. Among the private schools were various Catholic groups, including the Portuguese seminaries and schools, the Italian Daughters of Charity and French Sisters of Charity. The London Missionary Society and Church Missionary Society maintained the Protestant cause. HK's educational canvas began to take on diverse, colorful shades.

Development of Public Education

Special access to the archives at the HK Government Secretariat Library in 1989 provided invaluable material for this section. School Inspector Stewart released Hong Kong's first report on education in 1866 with over 6,000 words, the colony's longest in the 19th century, and with candor that's refreshing when compared to today's educationese. He wrote that Central School, the best then, provided only "instruction . . . of an elementary character" similiar to "English education as taught in the National Schools at home," and that textbooks adopted from the Commissioners for National Education in Ireland were ill-suited for Chinese students.

However, "As to the progress of the boys I have every reason to be satisfied. Up to a certain period it is, in fact, remarkable." After the third year, however, only five or six students remained out of a class of 30. Stewart blamed the high drop-out rate and lack of further proficiency on the students' inabilities to deal with "those subjects which depend more on the independent exercise of their own intellectual faculties . . ." Boys also dropped-out to capitalize on their new English proficiency with companies in Hong Kong, the treaty ports, California, and Japan. He found that the students did well with translations they had been taught directly, but "more minute enquiry would show . . . that memory had been cultivated at the expense of judgment; . . . for, when the correct translation has once been given them they rarely forget it; but, if teacher or scholars were to rely on this as an evidence of progress nothing could be more facillacious. Much of the blame . . . is due to their previous training. The Chinese have no *education* in the real sense of the word. No attempt is made at a simultaneous development of the mental powers. These are all sacrificed to the cultivation of the memory."

Stewart continued: "If a boy is able to remain at School for six or eight years he may then be able to explain what he has read or committed to memory, but those who cannot afford to do so must be content to read without understanding. To the majority the language is an *end*, and a *means*. It is an accomplishment which may be very showy in the eyes of the Chinese themselves, but which contains within it none of the elements of the *useful* or of the *improving*." Stewart was forced to conclude that "no great or immediate reformation in education can be hoped for in Hong Kong." But it was vital to "take advantage of opportunities as they occur" and seek improvements. His report is still pertinent, as Stewart saw prospects as follows: "Before any real good can be effected the Chinese must have learnt to appreciate the value of education, and of their *own* education, such as it is. Nothing seems to find favour with them which does not bear a market value . . . . the comparative success of the Central School, English being convertible into *dollars*; hence, also, the neglect of the Vernacular Schools, Chinese being *unsaleable.*"

Stewart found that many students came from China for Western learning. Investigating where and how the students lived, he blasted the impoverished, crowded conditions in which the common people lived (see Chapter Three's pp. 175-179 on the great plague). In 1865, the population was 125,504 of which 97% were Chinese as today. Stewart wrote of his frustrations with the colony's slow educational development and squalid conditions. Although improvements were made, Colonial Surgeon Ayres reported in 1874 that up to 10 families would share a house "not considered fit to put pigs" and that three to eight families would live in one room. "Pigs were universally kept," a favorite place for them being under the beds (Endacott, 1973, pp. 183-197).

Thus, Stewart, who repeatedly used the word "evil" to characterize conditions, expressed concern for his 1,870 "scholars" but could do little. He reported that over 12,000 children did not attend school and were "growing up uneducated and neglected;" because "engrossed in the pursuit of gain, the Chinese who have flocked to Hongkong have left behind them their traditional regard for education, and allowed themselves to settle into an apathy characteristic only of barbarism." The Schools Inspector urged the Government to realize how important it was for education to take hold and to fund it more adequately. Obviously, this Scot was enthusiastic and possessed the same determination and humanitarianism as his contemporary, Florence Nightingale.

Twelve years later in 1878, Stewart could boast of an increased public enrollment of over 2,000 and an examination system by which he ranked the territory's 41 schools. The top five that year were: St. Stephen's School, Sai Ying-p'un; Baxter School, Sai Ying-p'un; London Mission School; T'ai-ping Shan; Basel Mission School, Shau-kei Wan; and Victoria School, Girls. Later, the examination system that Stewart initiated would be greatly expanded.

From those early times to the present, HK's education system has been a diverse mix of schools and sponsors. Brimer (1988, p. 333) said that this was the result of British policy to avoid "provision and administration of education for the masses" and up to World War II the "colonial custodianship" left "the responsibility for education largely in the hands of the voluntary bodies." This diversity also reflected the contrasting secular and sectarian goals of the Westerners and the transient, illiterate nature of the HK Chinese of those times, who approached schooling and Western culture generally in terms of limited, short-term gain. The gap was evident in the Inspector's attempts to develop schooling in the outlying villages where most of the teachers did not hold classes and the one at Tai Tam Tuk turned out to be a highway robber. If they taught at all, their instruction dealt more with "busy work" than real learning. Children were paid to come to school and sit all day when an inspection was expected.

The first school grant-in-aid: Personalities and feuds. The progressive administration of Governor Arthur Kennedy made a crucial decision in 1873 when it reversed a policy of benign neglect towards private education and instituted a grant-in-aid scheme that continues today. The innovative scheme provided mission and non-profit schools financial support ostensibly so that they could maintain themselves. Yet, to receive funds, the schools had to meet the Government's standards. Five types of elementary schools with a minimum enrollment of 200 qualified for grants; those that provided: (1) Chinese education; (2) Chinese education with some English; (3) an European education in Chinese; (4) an European education in any European language; and (5) an European education in any European language with some Chinese.

Some subjects were mandated with a detailed syllabus for six standards (academic levels) and five classes (grades). Funding went from $2 per child in the lowest Standard in first grade, $8 in the highest Standard in grades I & II, and $10 each in the highest Standard of grades III, IV, and V. An extra 50¢ per child was provided grades II and V in schools that taught a second language (Endacott, 1973, pp. 232-233).

Frederick Stewart, of course, opposed grants-in-aid to private schools, but he could take satisfaction that the scheme did establish the principle of funding by results and maintained the secular basis of aid. When Sir John Pope Hennessy became Governor in 1879, Stewart was crestfallen (see pp. 128-130). Most sympathetic to the church schools, Hennessy expanded the grant-in-aid scheme to include financial support to grades higher than elementary, dashed secular restrictions, and provided grants for new classrooms.

Engrossed in the development of education in early Hong Kong for 17 years, Stewart took home leave in 1879 perhaps in part to escape the volatile Governor. As he was about to depart, Stewart was jolted by Hennessy's allegation that the English standard of Central School students was poor and that Stewart was at fault. Sir John's evidence was his misconstruction of Stewart's report. The Government's *Gazette* covered this explosive confrontation between Hennessy and Stewart with statements from both, in which it can be seen that Hennessy went so far as to try to cause Stewart to miss his sailing. Stewart proved that Hennessy had misconstrued his report and that Central's standards were not poor. On his return to Hong Kong, Stewart presented his appointment by the Colonial Office as acting Colonial Secretary, second to the Governor.

A German vicar who had gone to China as a Lutheran missionary and then joined the London Missionary Society, the versatile Ernst Johann Eitel became Hennessy's Private Secretary, a post in which he faithfully assisted the Governor. Long before the Colonial Office replaced Hennessy in 1882, however, Eitel had himself safely appointed School Inspector in 1878, a post he would hold until 1897. Although Eitel (1895) omitted confrontations involving himself, his book is the earliest history of Hong Kong which discusses education.

In his next post as Registrar-General, Stewart found ways to challenge his adversaries and continue his interests in education. In 1883, he conducted a school survey confirming suspicions that many teachers and schools continued to abuse the grants support scheme through misleading attendance records. His report charged that only one-third of the reported students actually attended classes with any regularity and that the schools were overcrowded and in scandalous condition. The report no doubt increased Eitel's work load. After prolonged hearings over the scandal, the grant-in-aid scheme was revised to reduce the required attendance roll from 200 to 100 for aided schools in order to encourage more attention to quality.

Despite Stewart's blistering report, Inspector Eitel's *Annual Report on Education* of 1883 only complained that poor English competence hindered learning and recommended greater use of the native tongue, a hot issue that continues today. He boasted that the best school was Central, "owing to the unrivalled range of subjects it comprises," although Eitel also quarreled with headmaster Bateson Wright. Noting the care with which the boys were tested, 331 out of 363 boys passing or 91.18% (Eitel reported the two decimal places), he praised the results to be "highly creditable to the new Head-Master of the Central School and to his staff."

One great difference between Stewart and Eitel arose from Stewart's prejudice towards Chinese education. Criticizing China's lack of public education and reliance on an ancient examination system to promote learning, Stewart firmly believed that Anglo-Chinese education that stressed the English language had to be developed. His insistence on quality teaching and pupil results were his greatest contributions. A former vicar, Eitel naturally supported the mission schools. The *HK Education Annual Report* of 1951-52 said that when Eitel became the Inspector of Schools in 1878, the "missionary grant-in-aid schools had rendered many government institutions redundant, and (Central School) was saved from dissolution only by (removing it from the control of) the Education Department" (p. 4). By 1896, mission schools had risen from 37 to 101and Government schools had dropped from 35 to 16. Clearly, HK's early educational leaders acted out of conviction and pursued accountablity, which is grossly negligent today.

Maintaining sectarian goals while receiving public funds, the mission schools enjoyed the best of all worlds; but that privilege would change. By 1900, education in the colony was progressive when compared to China but not to Japan.

Twentieth-Century Developments

Unlike colonies that the British used more as military and power bases, such as India and Singapore, Hong Kong's history shows an unique compromise between East and West. Much can be said about the tenacious character of the Cantonese people in HK, who still retain their native tongue and customs and make the most of the stepping-stone away from and to China (see pp. 14-17).

When everything was new and the population limited, change and growth came like bold brush strokes on a blank canvas. Promoting education decades before and after the ceding of Hong Kong, Anglo-American missionaries should be ever honored as well as diligent civil servants who helped to shape its early education.

The University of Hong Kong

Early in the 20th century, public-minded Chinese, Parsees, British and Americans of diverse backgrounds, a modern generation of Hong Kongers, came to the belief that HK should represent something more than greed and materialism. Since Hong Kong has never abided pessimists, optimists interpreted the debacle Boxer Upheaval (1899-90) as the end of the Qing Dynasty and the beginning of China's awakening. After the 1911 Revolution, euphoric impetus sped the idea that a secure, independent Hong Kong could serve China by becoming its visionary gleam, especially through education of its future leaders.

The HK stepping-stone could also be the bridge between East and West, an exemplar of what China could become if it received helpful support, know-how, and encouragement. Beyond altruism, helping to modernize China would also benefit HK's prosperity. There is no better symbol of that spirit than the formation of the University of Hong Kong.

Filled with revolutionary fervor, Chinese students flocked to Japan in search of modern knowledge; 15,000 in 1908 alone. However, Japan became less attractive after Tokyo began to clamp down on the students' political activities after the Qing Court protested. Thoughtful Europeans, such as W. H. Donald of the *China Mail*, argued that HK should become the educational center for China's new leaders. They pointed to the fact that China was so short of teachers of modern learning that many Japanese teachers taught in China. "The duel was between Materialism as represented by the Japanese, and the Christian Gospel as represented by the missions, and Education was to be the weapon" (Mellor, 1980, p. 16). Also, the gentry wanted an alternative to sending their offspring abroad.

The territory's system of higher education originated with the Hong Kong College of Medicine for the Chinese, a private institution founded in 1887 by Dr. Patrick Manson to provide Western-trained doctors for China (see pp. 167-170 in Chapter Three). As Dr. Peter Parker had shown, medical science could assuage Chinese attitudes towards the West. Overcoming ethnic biases, many joined hand to establish the college and in so doing, forged a healthy pattern for HK's future development. Their impact on the Chinese Revolution and China's future through one student alone would have far-reaching effects.

The medical college opened in 1887 with Dr. Manson as Dean and two students, one being the young Sun Yat-sen destined to become China's revolutionary father. Among his teachers were Drs. James Cantlie and Ho Kai, who encouraged Sun's modern thinking during his five years in training (Lo, 1963). Speaking to a cheering crowd of students at the University of Hong Kong in 1923, Dr. Sun said his revolutionary ideas originated while studying at the Hong

Kong College of Medicine (see p. 45). After his graduation, he went to Peking to offer his services but left after finding corruption there far worse than in Canton (Jen & Ride, 1970, pp. 21-22; Park, 1997).

Supporters for the university pointed to the founding of Calcutta University in 1857 as a colonial precedent and the HK College of Medicine and the HK Technical Institute started by Governor Matthew Nathan in 1907 as ready harbingers. Also, a local gentry with wealth and education stood ready to promote humanitarianism and HK's progress. When Sir Frederick Lugard, a respected colonial administrator, became Governor in 1907 (see pp. 133-135), he quickly embraced the idea of an university. In 1908, presenting prizes at St. Stephen's College, Lugard said: "I think that Hong Kong should be the Oxford and Cambridge of the Far East . . . . I believe myself in the awakening of China and in the opportunities for reciprocal benefits which that awakening will give to us and I believe that we must either now take those opportunities or leave them to others to take" (Mellor, 1980, p. 17).

First to contribute was Hormusjee Nowrojee Mody, a Parsee merchant who had resided in Hong Kong for 50 years, with $150,000 for the building and $30,000 for an endowment. Then Ng Li-hing offered to fund a new medical college and an anatomy building and Cheung Pat Sze contributed to the arts faculty. Lukewarm to the idea and calling it Lugard's "pet lamb," the Foreign Office insisted that contributions come from China as well, which Lady Lugard obtained through Viceroy Chang Jen-chun and other Canton leaders. J. H. Scott of John Swire & Sons collected business contributions. Others rose to the challenge, such as an endowment for a chair of surgery in 1916 and building grants by Robert Ho Tung (Cheng, 1976).

On March 16, 1910, the foundation stone of the new university's Main Building (still in use) was laid by Governor Lugard with Mody, then aged 70 and frail, standing by. Reflecting on his colonial experience in Nigeria, Lugard said that Britain's empire was "no longer an age of acquisition in which we live, but an age of development . . . . the graduates of this University, its doctors of medicine, its scientific engineers, and its trained administrators, will exert an influence which will be immeasurable in the future, among the 400 millions of China's population." As the ceremony closed, he surprised everyone especially the recipient by declaring that King Edward VII had appointed Mody to a Knighthood and asked that the announcement be made after the foundation stone had been laid. Few universities have enjoyed such an auspicious beginning.

The University of Hong Kong (HKU) did not take the Oxbridge model for its constitution but instead it followed the pattern of the new civic universities in Birmingham, Liverpool, and Leeds. English was the language of instruction from the start, and HKU would be secular with moral education handled as an extracurricular activity. In London when the Association of Commonwealth Universities was established in 1912 with HKU as one of the founders, Gov. Lugard spoke of HKU's high academic and moral standards without sectarian coercion inhibiting personal religious preference. Sir Charles Eliot was appointed HKU's first vice-chancellor, the governor being the titular chancellor by British custom. In his book, *Hinduism and Buddhism*, Eliot wrote: "I cannot share the confidence in the superiority of Europeans and their ways which is prevalent in the West." With an open mind unprejudiced towards the Chinese, he toured China on vacation, studied the Chinese language daily, and gave HKU a proper start. According to the former HKU historian, Mellor (1980, pp 49-59), "Before he left HK in 1918, it was said that there was at least one student at the University from each of China's eighteen provinces . . . ."

However, Welsh (1993, p. 358) portrayed Eliot negatively. He noted that while in Africa with the Diplomatic and Foreign Service, Eliot degraded Africans and was a poor manager of funds, leaving HKU with a debt of $1.7 million, which the Government covered with opium revenues. Before proceeding further, some attention to Singapore and Macao can provide some interesting perspective.

Singapore

In contrast to Hong Kong, education in the British colony of Singapore progressed at a grudgingly slow pace. Founded in 1921 to provide general education and train teachers, Raffles College's enrollment was only 29 students 13 years later. Unlike the community spirit that stimulated HKU's founding in 1910, Singapore's authorities set up Raffles College to foil a well-financed proposal by Americans to establish an Anglo-American college.

The authorities responded reluctantly to Chinese initiatives for a Western medical school similar to the HK College of Medicine. After Tan Jiak Kim raised $87,000, a medical school was allowed in 1905 which became so successful that it was named the King Edward VII College of Medicine 16 years later in 1921. After much time, dentistry (1929) and pharmacy (1935) were added. It was only after World War II that a university was formed bringing the medical school and Raffles under the administration of the new University of Malaya in Singapore (UMS) in 1949. Engineering (1955), law (1957), and agriculture (1961) were gradually added.

Since Malaya and Singapore were both parts of the Straits Settlement colony and then neighboring British colonies (1946) until the Federation of Malaysia became an independent state in 1957, higher education was a joint operation. In 1961, the UM-S branch was renamed the University of Singapore (US) and became autonomous in 1962. Similar to its parent University of Malaya, the US was organized as a British institution and staffed by Commonwealth faculty; both colonial universities operated as at home with little regard to East-West relations. Also in contrast to HKU, Singapore's community was less involved with the US. After Britain turned Singapore over to Malaysia in 1963, Singapore separated into an independent state under Lee Kwan Yew two years later.

The history of Nanyang University (NU) exemplifies the difference between educational development in Singapore and Hong Kong. In contrast to HK's missionary presence and absence of organized native animosity towards the British, many Chinese who had settled along the Strait of Malacca were divided between a majority that resented the British versus a minority group tied to the authorities. The former were generally the have-nots who labored for pittance in the tin mines and rubber plantations and the latter were those who rose from poverty to wealth and status aiding the British as intermediaries in opium and sundry trade. When the British naturalized their collaborators to protect them while they worked in China, the Chinese regarded them as "traitors" and officials eventually forced them to uncover themselves by requiring all who carried foreign passports to wear Western clothing (Trocki, 1990, p. 237-238; Fairbank, 1969, 215-216). Therefore, relationships in Singapore and the Straits were far more polarized than in Hong Kong (see pp. 37 & 44-45).

Appalled by the easy victory of the Japanese over the British in World War II, Asians viewed their colonial masters as paper tigers. When Britain reclaimed its colonies after the war, the people demanded independence. An armed insurrection of Straits leftists beginning in 1948 took the British 12 years to crush. Resentment remains clear in the following excerpt from the Republic of Singapore's web site:

> The advent of World War Two and the failure of the British Army protecting the people of her colonies from the atrocities of the invading Imperial Japanese Army served to whip up the torrents of nationalism in her occupied territories. The Japanese capitulation saw the return of British rule, but the independence movement in Singapore, . . . was too strong for the British to suppress.

Complicating the postwar situation, Mao Zedong's 1949 conquest of mainland China threw Straits Chinese into confusion once again. China ties were put in jeopardy; everything was upside down. Amoy University in Xiamen which the wealthy Singaporean, Tan Kah Kee, had founded in 1924 could no longer educate Straits Chinese. With this troubled backdrop, Chinese leaders established a private, Chinese-language university in Singapore, named Nanyang, to educate graduates of Chinese schools and preserve Chinese culture. Although Lin Yutang, internationally known for his popular, philosophical writings, served as Nanyang Chancellor for a period, other administrators were Maoists and the university was known as a hotbed for pro-PRC politics. As proficiency in English held precedence in employment and Nanyang's academic and political problems could not be ignored, the Singapore Government finally closed Nanyang University by merging it with the University of Singapore in 1980. See Lim's (1994) comparison of higher education in Singapore and Malaysia.

Today, Singapore's educational system is extensively developed from 191 primary schools to the National University of Singapore, Nanyang Technological University, four polytechnics, and 14 junior colleges. Of the 191 primary schools, 41 are government-aided and the rest are government schools. The Republic has 143 secondary schools of which 107 are government, 28 are aided, and eight are independent, including Raffles Institution for boys and Raffles Girls' School (Sec.). There are also five, primary through secondary, "full schools."

Visiting Maris Stella High School in Singapore, a "full school" for boys run by the Marist Brothers, I was very impressed with the excellent, modern school. Eager and enthusiastic, the boys made one feel that it would be wonderful to teach such students. Asked to speak to a large student group, I made a joke that went over well by using Singapore's favorite *pidgin* expression to translate Hamlet's "To be or not to be" line as "Can do or cannot do." The Lion City's school facilities and the training and dedication of faculty and professional staff are probably the best in Asia. English is the language of instruction and study of a "mother tongue" is also required, Mandarin for most.

Primary Four (4th Grade) pupils are given a life-determining test that channels them into "formal streaming," i.e., classify pupils by IQ. Those identified as bright and deserving of enrichment are treated as elite. Rigid streaming is questionable in light of psychological and educational sciences, but the faith of Singapore's leaders in outdated theories of testing and inherited intelligence continues strong. Through word and tax incentives, Lee Kwan Yew and the People's Action Party have urged educated, intelligent women to marry and have children to raise the population's IQ level. Administered towards the end of primary schooling, the Primary School Leaving Examination (PSLE) determines which secondary schools a student may attend. Since academic achievement to the Chinese is viewed with almost life-and-death concern, parents and pupils become anxious as the Primary 4 exam and PSLE approach. Also similar to HK, Singapore supports both sectarian and private schools with a few self-support institutions. Schools are ranked by PSLE levels and the number of graduates gaining university admission.

Although Singapore and Hong Kong are both world-class, rival entrepots with British and opium roots and majority Chinese populations (76% in Singapore, mainly Fujianese; 97% in Hong Kong, mainly Cantonese), their differences overwhelm the similarities. The greatest distinctions are that Singapore is an independent state and instead of China (about 750 miles north), its neighbors are the Muslin nations of Malaysia and Indonesia, which presents different concerns.

A *Far Eastern Economic Review* survey once advised that while the Lion City's modernity and cleanliness would serve Westerners as an introductory primer to Asia, Hong Kong with its Chineseness, bustle, and brashness could be the advanced course of study. Yet, those who know both places cannot help but see that the same family and cultural values are still irrepressibly commonplace.

Macau

After almost 450 years as a Portuguese settlement, Macau (Macao) will revert to the People's Republic of China (PRC) on December 20, 1999. The mere, six-mile-square enclave lies at the western edge of the Pearl River estuary with Hong Kong an hour's jetfoil ride to the east (see Map One). While HK outdistanced its neighbor in all respects long ago, Macau with lingering touches of its picturesque, old-world past will have the distinction of being the last European enclave in Asia,

30 months after British rule ended in Hong Kong. So the first to come will be the last to go. Established one year before Elizabeth I was crowned and 287 years before the ccssion of Hong Kong, the tiny place witnessed much history through that great span of time, including the rise and fall of Portugal as a power, e.g., ruled by Spain (1580-1640) and England's defeat of the Spanish Armada in 1588.

Catholic missionaries have been prominent in Macao's history. In keeping with their fame as educators, the Jesuits built schools and an institution of higher learning. In 1762, Portugal's dictator, the Marquis of Pombal, ended two centuries of Jesuit service in Asia by forcing them home in chains. Pombal's harsh expulsion was part of his world vendetta against the Jesuits as dramatized in the 1987 movie, *The Mission* (Yee, 1987).

Jesuits claim that the Madre de Deus School of St. Paul's University College, founded in Macao in 1594, was "the first European style university in the Far East, 25 years before the creation of the University of S Tomas in Manila" (Pires, 1987, p. 16). Boasting East Asia's largest Western library, a printing press, etc., St. Paul's was where 700 Jesuit missionaries prepared to work in China across the better part of two centuries, the first being Father Matteo Ricci towards the close of the 16th century. Despite disputes over which university should be considered the first in East Asia, the Dominican University of Santo Tomas has been in existence nearly 390 years since its founding in 1611(but closed during WW II).

Erupting in Spain's 17th-century Manila, the disputes over which order and institution were the first to confer academic degrees in Asia rose over contradictory papal decisions. Was the Jesuit College of Manila the first with Holy See authorizations in 1643, 1552, 1578, and 1621 or did Pope Innocent X's authorization to raise Santo Tomas to an academy in 1647 definitive? The controversy persisted for long, until Pope Clement XIV dissolved the Society of Jesus (also Pompal-instigated) in 1773, thus closing the issue. Pope Pius VII reestablished the order in 1814.

In light of Macau's disaster in losing the Jesuits, the issue of the universities is moot. Not only did Macau lose its educational and spiritual leaders; but it also lost its most enterprising merchants as the Jesuits supported their programs through trade, especially with Japan. In the span of 219 years, from 1762's closure of St. Paul's University College to 1981, when an enlightened group of Hong Kong businessmen (Ricci Island West Co.) founded the University of East Asia (UEA), Macau lacked higher education altogether. Acquiring UEA in 1988 and relieving the Ricci Island West Co. of its debts, the Macau Government renamed it the University of Macau in 1991 (Yee, 1988).

Schools in Macau are classified as *oficial* or public, *oficializado* or semi-official, and *privado* or private, which translates into Portuguese, Portuguese/ Chinese (Macanese), and Chinese categories. There was a total of 58,686 students enrolled in all Macao schools and grades in the academic year of 1985-86. Six percent or 3,478 students attended the "public" schools and one percent or 719 in the semi-official sector. The bulk of the school-age population, 54,489 or

93 percent, attended Chinese private schools. Schooling breaks down uniformly for the three types of schools, as follows: pre-school -- 3 years; primary -- 4 years; pre-secondary -- 2 years; and secondary -- 3 years. Macao does not have system-wide examinations as in Hong Kong and Singapore, but schools have their own examinations, especially the Catholic schools, which lower enrollments by about 30% at the end of Year 7, the first secondary year. While compulsory attendance ends at the same time, the exams decide who continues.

With Macau's total of 2,114 teachers in 1988, student-teacher ratios reveal a systematic bias operating in Macau. For the so-called "public" schools catering to Portuguese students, the student-teacher ratio was *14*, i.e., one teacher for every 14 students. The student-teacher ratio for the "semi-official" schools for Eurasians was *19*, while the ratio for the "private" or Chinese schools was *30*, more than double the ratio for the public schools.

Education in Macau received about 5-7 % of the annual Government budget before the advent of the University of Macau in 1991. With US$8.6 million provided for education in 1986, the 1987 budget was US$11.7 million. Although the increase of $3.1 million represented a gain of 27 percent in one year, the per student rate remained far below that of its HK neighbor. At $8.6 million, Macau Government's support per student was $146 in 1986. Assuming enrollments held even in 1987, we have almost $200 spent per student by Macau.

In 1987 Hong Kong, US$501 million or over 43 times more than Macau's 1987 budget for education provided for 825,207 primary/secondary students in Government and aided schools. That translated into $607 spent per student using only those gross figures alone. Thus, compared to HK's school budget for 1987, Macau authorities provided only 32 percent of HK's gross per student.

Educational funding by school type clearly reveals the bias in Macau's educational system. Although budget details of the Macau Government are not publicly available as they are in Hong Kong, it is common knowledge (which Macanese officials verified to me personally) that 70% of the educational funds go to the Portuguese public schools or US$8.18 million in 1987. Support per public school student and teacher, the respective figures were $2,353 and $33,268! If such expenditures were widely known, Macau's public school facilities and support would be envied in HK and elsewhere in East Asia.

The 69 other schools (semi-official and private) obtain the remaining 30% of the educational funds or $3.5 million in 1987. Rounding off, that breaks down to only $64 of Government support per student and a gross amount of $1,878 per teacher. The disparity between $2,353 for Portuguese learners and $64 for the Chinese has been highly criticized by non-public school educators, despite the fact that they reported the funding bias has always been a colonial phenomenon. With Macau's return to China approaching, educators I spoke to said they had expected more equitable treatment of the Chinese schools.

Assuming far less responsibility for public education than the HK Government, Macau has exercised laissez-faire administration over the Chinese schools and left them to manage as best they can. Macao's bias towards the Portuguese schools is explained as providing for the expatriate children of officials and others from Portugual who are temporarily in Macau. Thus, the "non-public" or Chinese schools have had to fend mainly for themselves. Catholic schools make up the largest and most prestigious group of non-public institutions, and the PRC supports schools it favors. Dependent on the non-publics, the people would be left with little or no education without the non-government support given to their schools.

Very little has been known about the public school teachers other than their being Portuguese and that most are spouses of civil servants. Except for teaching sisters, non-public schoolteachers have been poorly trained. While few primary teachers have university degrees, most secondary teachers in the non-public schools have academic degrees from the Philippines, Mainland China, and Taiwan, none of which still qualify for teaching posts in HK. When Chapter Two's author was UEA's Secretary in the 1980s, Mr. Topley and I began Macau's first teacher-training program with nearly US$2 million from the Macau Government. Teachers completing the two-year UEA program receive a salary raise from the Macau Government (Yee, 1988, 1990).

In contrast to Hong Kong where officials typically complete life careers, whether local or expatriate, their Macau counterparts come and go according to the patronage of the governor. Typically serving a term of three years through appointment by Portugal's President, Macau governors bring their own hand-picked officers who leave in mass when governors complete their terms of office and return home. Administrative continuity would be hampered if it were not for the Macanese who have filled middle-management posts. Since Portugal's economy has been slack for long, the high salaries paid Portuguese teachers and officials must be strong enticements to accept Macau appointments.

World War II hardships. Obviously, Hong, Kong, Singapore, and Macao differ greatly. Their histories in political and educational development reveal totally different circumstances. Each predominantly Chinese, the three diverge and put the lie to blanket stereotypes of the Chinese. Since Portugal was neutral during World War II, the Japanese did not occupy Macau but still suffered tremendous deprivation because of China's degradation. Its humane Governor, Colonel Gabriel Mauricio Teixeira, permitted Chinese, British, French, German, etc. refugees to overflow the six-square-mile settlement. Chinese refugees alone numbered a million or more.

With farsightedness, Teixeira stockpiled goods, such as cloth, machinery, and fuel, that he expected the Japanese to need during the long war and bartered them for refugee basics, such as rice and firewood. Yet, with insufficient resources for such a huge refugee population over four years, Macao suffered greatly and cannibalism has been charged (personal communication, Monsignor Manuel Teixeira of Macao, October 15, 1996).

The Chinese and POWs suffered harsh deprivation in HK and Singapore (see pp. 92-94). All public schools were closed until a few Japanese-language primary schools were opened in May 1945. Chinese and neutral (Irish & Italian) voluntary groups (Sweeting, 1993, p. 9) offered limited education. HKU's library holdings were burned for fuel. While Tsurumi (1977) characterized education under Japan's long rule in Taiwan as "outstanding," though not as progressive as in the Philippines under America, Japanese administrators in Korea were often inhumane. If the Japanese had serious educational plans for HK, which is doubtful at best, they were hampered by their imminent defeat.

After WW II, damages to the University of Hong Kong were partially compensated for when one million pounds sterling of reparations were given to HKU. Chapter Three (pp. 156 & 171-172) covers the heroism of HKU professors during WW II, a number of whom had been British missionaries in China. Some escaped to Free China and worked with the British Army Aid Group led by Lindsay T. Ride, who became HKU's Vice-Chancellor after the war. HK's educational history has many heroes.

Colonialism in Hong Kong's Schools

For much of HK's history, British children attended an elaborate expatriate school system for them alone. The English Schools served British government and military dependents and children of parents in private life. In the 1980s, the army schools were closed as British troops declined in number and most Gurka dependents remainly in Nepal. The HK Government turned over the English Schools to the English Schools Foundation, which instituted tuitions. ESF's oldest school, King George V, celebrated its Golden Jubilee anniversary in 1987.

When first opened in 1902 in a Kowloon building donated by Sir Robert Ho Tung for English instruction, supposedly open to all, it was called the British School. When the HK Government persuaded Sir Robert to agree to the exclusive use of the building for British children, he "regretted the change . . . 'so much opposed to the spirit which prompted my offer of the school to the colony' " (Endacott, 1973, p. 281).

After Kenneth Topley (Chapter Two's contributor) became Director of Education in 1974 (promoted Secretary of Education and Manpower in 1981), educational funding was equalized for British and Chinese schools. Topley was also the first to encourage international schools and an American school was the first. French, German-Swiss, Japanese, and Singaporean schools also operate as they would at home. While Chinese pupils could attend British schools if they passed an English fluency test, which few could do at first, in time more Chinese passed the test and attended ESF schools. Macau-like bias persisted in HK into the 1970s whereby British youth were better treated; but unlike Macau, HK changed.

Governor Murray Maclehose (1971-1982) propelled HK's growth into a world metropolis and entrepot; for whether cause or effect, colonialism gradually tapered off as educational and social services for the Chinese were equalized and expanded. Since the 1984 Joint Declaration, "localisation" hiring has been the standard operating policy.

From One-Room Schools to Bureaucracy

Hong Kong's educational system took root as governors, civil servants, and missionaries worked to fulfill their sense of moral obligation to promote education. As Chapter Three makes clear, to the credit of the British this was also true in health and medical services. Through grant-in-aid support as discussed earlier, the HK Government steadily expanded its involvement in education. Financial support naturally opened the way to criticize and control the schools. Taking financial support with one hand and regulations with the other, the schools gradually found themselves increasingly dependent on Government support as well as curricula and oversight. In the end, officialdom defined results according to its own judgment and criteria and became intolerant of other views. After all, the HK Government was not accountable to the ballot.

In earlier times when there were only a handful of civil servants in education, they were in direct contact with the schools and knew the teachers, all of which is passé in today's multicultural metroplis. HK's educational bureaucracy includes about 6,000 civil servants in the Education Department (ED) alone. The system is an odd mix of Anglo-Chinese ("Chinglish") colonialism, which as often said in Hong Kong combines the worst of English and Chinese education.

Similar to bureaucracies elsewhere, the system has layers of staff, bureaus, regulations, and mandates that are often contradictory and self-serving. The worst bureaucracies are perhaps in education. For as populations expand and authorities prescribe, the authorities typically impose agendas onto schools and teachers that are already hard-pressed to relate basic curricula. The ED grew in power in the late 1940s when the Government grew fearful of the possible use of the schools for propaganda, whether by the Kuomingtang (KMT) or pro-Mao Communists. A Special Bureau was formed for frequent school inspections to foil any political proselytizing. After findings surfaced that resembled spy thrillers, in February 1949 the HK Government closed the popular Tat Tak Institute, a pro-Maoist school, two and a half years after it was opened by former KMT General Tsai Ting-kai and reputable China academics (Sweeting, 1993, pp. 202-204).

ED's problem is that once an educational goal, even if it's clearly stated and defined by boards, etc., its path through the large school system to implementation is typically convoluted and bureaucratic, which at times can be beneficial when a bad idea is broached. As in most large enterprises, ED specialists are like clogs who know their part but miss the whole. The incubation period during which it is decided how, when, and where to put the goal into practice system-wide can manifest results that scarcely resemble the original intent, such as sex education. This is one reason why the schools have failed so miserably in fulfilling English competence. Big and complex does not necessarily mean better and efficient. Dealing with what is regulated and specific, the Chinglish system negates sensibility and scientific principles of learning. For example, after observing a Primary Three lesson on the Renaissance, I asked the teacher how long the massive topic would continue, whether it wasn't all beyond the third graders, and about the children's restlessness. Her answer was, "They only get this one lesson in P3. Never mind, they will return to the Renaissance in middle school."

Hong Kong's Educational System

Hong Kong's modern educational system reflects the territory's growth and the Government's dominant role. In 1995-96, Hong Kong afforded US$4.36 billion (using HK$7.74 to US$1.00) to formal education. Compared with similar U.S. funding and populations, such as Massachusetts ($6.7 billion), population of 6.07 million and Virginia ($6.1 billion) with 6.6 million citizens, HK's educational budget is not outstanding. Class sizes are huge, often 50; teachers' salaries are lower than in the U.S.; and HK provides only nine years of "free" education. The allocation of $4.36 billion for education represented 22% of the Government's 1995-96 total recurrent expenditure and 6% of capital expenditure, a net increase of one percent from 1994-95. The increase reflected continued willingness to support education, for its total budget of $25.2 billion in 1995-96 kept pace with a perennially high inflation rate, 8+% recently (deemed acceptable).

HK's complex educational system in 1995-96 is outlined in Display 5.1. It highlights particulars of school levels and types, key exams, and various institutions of higher education. Note the much larger secondary enrollment in aided versus Government schools. With 419 grammar schools, 21 technical schools, 26 prevocational schools, and two practical and skills opportunity schools, the vast majority of HK's secondary students attend grammar schools that provide preparation for the crucial HK Certificate of Education Examination (HKCEE).

Complementing Display 5.1, Table 5.1 flowcharts the various stages and demanding exam hurdles to tertiary (higher) education. As shown, a staged, winnowing process begins after primary education.

As seen in Display 5.1 and Table 5.1, the numbers and complexity involved in HK's educational system today are astounding compared to the past; for only recent times did the British advance comprehensive social services. As Welsh (1993, p. 481) has pointed out, "as late as 1971, that critical year, did the Government succeed in providing even comprehensive primary education." Before Sir Murray Maclehose became Governor in 1971, Hong Kong was still known as a "cruel society" where people fended for themselves; but it was far better than China. Shedding colonial pomp and arrogance, Sir Murray attacked the dismal refugee shantytowns by mounting housing developments and expanded health and medical services and the educational system (see pp. 145-147).

When Governor Edward Youde replaced Maclehose in 1982, education and social programs were accelerated. The progessive moves of the Government paralleled the desire of business leaders to mount ambitious changes in education by having the schools address the demand for professional skills and services versus the declining manpower needs of manufacturing. Yet, progressivism did not mean unfettered indulgence. Display 5.1 neglects to mention that the Secondary School Places Allocation System, conducted at the end of primary school, was deliberately devised to cut enrollments.

Computerized analyses of teachers' assessments and aptitude test scores result in life-determining decisions. Determining junior secondary placements (similar to U.S. middle school), the SSPAS usually gives low-achieving students only one choice, a deadend school enrolling similar students. High-achievers are allowed to select from a number of elite schools. The same competitive process works with the Junior Secondary Education Assessment (JSEA) at the end of Secondary 3 to decide which senior secondary school(s) a student may attend. Up to 1987, the JSEA was used to decide whether one could continue studies at all, i.e., move on to Secondary 4 (high school). In 1985, the Government decided to end that policy in 1991, but the outcry from parents and educators was so great the Education Commission initiated the current policy four years earlier. As school placements and HKCEE results are critical to jobs and university admission, SSPAS student placements are clearly life-setting thesholds.

Many low achievers drop out after Secondary 3 when free and compulsory education for nine years ends. As Display 5.1 indicates, full-time enrollment drops from 97% in junior to 85% in senior secondary. Based on achievement and exams, the winnowing process allows little flexibility for "late bloomers" and second chances. Although HK's system differs greatly from America's (see Table 5.2), what's done in HK is more typical worldwide. Valuing educational attainment by China's knowledge-based, examination traditions, the public believes that HK's educational system is fair and equalitarian. For regardless of family income level, many students who commit themselves to arduous, disciplined cramming and memorization do succeed in passing exams and gaining university admission. Few children work during the school year, as poor parents work extra hard so their children can study.

To escape the exam drudgery, many students of families with means attend schools in Britain and North America [9,665 in the U.S. higher education, 1997-98 (Desruisseaux, 1998)]. Strong marketing efforts by Australian schools have drawn many HK and SE Asian students, who have boosted the Aussie economy by US$800 million yearly and benefited budget-strapped institutions. However, enrollments have slowed after bigotry resurfaced in recent times. Everything seems aimed towards diploma status versus lifelong learning.

East Asian Universities: Significant Differences

Universities in East Asia are quite different from those elsewhere (Yee, 1989, 1994). Having taught in Hong Kong, Japan, and Singapore as well as the United States and having lectured in China and conducted research through most of East Asia, I can say that the differences seem more in kind than degree. As education

Education

About 22 per cent of Hong Kong's population is at school or kindergarten and in 1995/96 the approved public spending on education amounted to $33.780 million, representing 21.5 per cent of government's total recurrent expenditure and six per cent of capital expenditure.

There is nine years' free and compulsory education up to the age of 15. In 1996, the government expects to be able to provide subsidised Secondary 4 places for about 81 per cent of the 15-year-olds in a continuing programme.

With both Chinese and English in common use, bilingualism is being adopted in schools.

There are 15 schools operated by the English Schools Foundation offering education to English-speaking children. There are also some international schools which are open to children of all races.

There are three main types of schools—government schools which are wholly operated by the government; aided schools which are fully aided by the government but run by voluntary bodies; and private schools, some of which receive financial assistance from the government.

Kindergartens : Voluntary organisations and private bodies provide education for children in the 3–5 age group. These kindergartens are registered with and supervised by the Education Department.

The government gives assistance in the forms of reimbursement of rates and rent to non-profit-making kindergartens; government subsidy under the Kindergarten Subsidy Scheme; allocation of kindergarten premises in public housing estates; fee remission to needy parents; and providing in-service teacher training facilities.

	No. of Kindergartens	Enrolment
Non-profit-making	425	112 133
Profit-making	306	68 184
Total	731	180 317

Primary Education : Primary schooling starts at the age of six. Most primary schools operate in two sessions. In 1971, free and compulsory primary education was introduced in all government primary schools and in the majority of aided primary schools. The aim of the 6-year primary course is to provide a good general education appropriate to the age range and particular environment of the children. Chinese is the language of instruction in most schools with English taught as a second language. A new Primary 1 Admission System was introduced in 1983 to monitor admission to Primary 1 in government and aided primary schools.

	No. of Day Schools	Enrolment
Government and government-aided	773	419 402
Private	87	48 316
Total	860	467 718

School enrolment for the 6–11 age group approaches 99 per cent

Secondary Education : On completion of the primary course, pupils are allocated free junior secondary places in government, government-aided and private secondary schools with bought places. The allocation system, known as the Secondary School Places Allocation System, is based on internal school assessment, scaled by a centrally administered Academic Aptitude Test, parental choices and the division of the territory into 18 school nets.

Junior secondary education (Secondary 1–3), which became compulsory in September 1979, has been free since September 1978.

A centralised system of selection and allocation for subsidised school places for senior secondary education (Secondary 4–5), known as the Junior Secondary Education Assessment (JSEA) System, was first introduced in 1981. Effective from 1994, an allocation method known as the Secondary Four Places Allocation Method has been adopted. The performance of students in the school internal assessments and parental choices form the basis for selection and allocation of Secondary 3 students to subsidised Secondary 4 places. Students may also choose to continue their studies in post-Secondary 3 craft courses offered by technical institutes and industrial training centres.

Based on school curriculum there are three main types of secondary schools in Hong Kong - grammar, technical and prevocational. They offer a 5-year course leading to the Hong Kong Certificate of Education Examination (HKCEE). Prevocational schools, which are fully subsidised by the government, provide students with a solid foundation of general knowledge and an introduction to a broadbased technical and practical education upon which future vocational training may be based. They do not set out to provide all the skills and knowledge of a specific trade or occupation. Rather, they provide the link between general education and education for employment through a knowledge of broadbased basic skills and a wide range of applications of modern techniques in at least two major fields of local employment.

HKCEE candidates may enter a 2-year sixth form course leading to the Hong Kong Advanced Level Examination for admission to local tertiary institutions like universities. Uniform tuition fees are charged for Secondary 4–7 in government and aided secondary schools and private secondary schools with bought places.

	Day School Enrolment	
Type of School	Secondary 1–5	Secondary 6 & 7
Government	34 078	4 827
Aided	325 958	40 419
Private	47 017	7 546
Total	407 053	52 792

The percentage of children aged 12 to 14 receiving full-time education is 97, and the corresponding figure for the 15 to 16 age group is 85.

Special Education : There are 63 special schools (including one hospital school operating classes at 16 hospitals) providing places for the blind, the deaf, the physically handicapped, the maladjusted and, the mentally handicapped. Non-governmental organisations involved in this work receive financial assistance from the government.

The Services Division of the Education Department administers an integrated programme for mildly disabled

Display 5.1, continued:

children in kindergartens, and runs special education classes in government and aided schools for children with learning difficulties, partially sighted and partially hearing children. The division runs three centres providing assessment, diagnostic, remedial and placement services for children with special educational needs. Other services include free issue of hearing aids, ear-mould production and special education teaching resources. The division also operates intensive remedial teaching programmes and adjustment programmes for children with learning difficulties and for children with behavioural and emotional problems integrated in ordinary schools respectively.

A Combined Screening Programme is conducted for all Primary I pupils. It consists of screening tests for hearing and eyesight and provides checklists for teachers to detect children with speech and learning difficulties so that early identification, follow-up assessment and remedial services can be given.

Post Secondary Education : Shue Yan College is the approved post secondary college registered under the Post Secondary Colleges Ordinance. It is financially independent and has 2 573 students. Government financial assistance in the forms of maintenance grant and loans are available for eligible students at the College.

Teacher Training : The Hong Kong Institute of Education (HKIEd), a Government-funded and autonomous tertiary institution, was established on April 25, 1994 in accordance with the recommendations of the Education Commission's Report No. 5. The Institute comprises the three Colleges of Education (Grantham College of Education, Northcote College of Education and Sir Robert Black College of Education), Hong Kong Technical Teachers' College and the Institute of Language in Education previously under the management of the Education Department, the objective of establishing the HKIEd is to upgrade teacher education and enhance the professional development of teachers in Hong Kong. It admitted its first intake of students in September 1994.

The Institute will initially concentrate on upgrading courses at the pre-degree level while preparing to offer degree programmes as soon as practicable. It has a range of full-time pre-service Certificate in Education programmes for primary and secondary school teachers to prepare them for specialised levels of education. The Institute also offers a range of full-time and part-time in-service programmes for the professional development of teachers in the early childhood, primary, secondary, technical and special education sectors. A Postgraduate Diploma in Education (Primary) has been launched in 1995–96. The Institute also plans to introduce B.Ed. (Honours) degree programmes as soon as possible.

A new purpose-built campus for the Institute, located in a 12.5-hectare site at Tai Po, is scheduled for completion in 1997. The new HKIEd campus will provide academic, sports and amenities facilities for 5 000 full-time equivalent students.

	Enrolment (1995–96)
Full-time courses	2 993
Part-time courses (including in-service courses)	5 580

The University of Hong Kong and the Chinese University of Hong Kong also offer full-time and part-time post-graduate teacher education courses.

The Open Learning Institute of Hong Kong, in association with the City University of Hong Kong, the Hong Kong Polytechnic University and the Hong Kong Institute of Education, offers an in-service Bachelor of Education (Honours) degree programme for primary school teachers. Another consortium which comprises the School of Continuing Education of the Hong Kong Baptist University, the School of Professional and Continuing Education of the University of Hong Kong and the Hong Kong Institute of Education also provides an in-service degree programme in education for primary school teachers.

Higher Education : There are at present seven government-financed institutions of higher education, namely, City University of Hong Kong (CityU), Hong Kong Baptist University (HKBU), Lingnan College (LC), The Chinese University of Hong Kong (CUHK), The Hong Kong Polytechnic University (PolyU), The Hong Kong University of Science and Technology (HKUST) and The University of Hong Kong (HKU).

In 1995–96 CityU has 10 124 full-time and 6 556 part-time students participating in degree and non-degree programmes offered by its five faculties and college. HKBU has 4 220 full-time and 483 part-time students pursuing degree courses in five faculties and schools while LC has 2 059 full-time and two part-time students participating in degree and non-degree courses in three faculties. CUHK comprises four constituent Colleges. It has seven faculties, offering undergraduate and postgraduate courses in both the full-time and part-time modes. In 1995-96, CUHK has an enrolment of 10 330 full-time and 2 545 part-time students. PolyU has six faculties offering degree and non-degree programmes with an enrolment of 10 809 full-time and 9 279 part-time students. HKUST, which was opened in October 1991, comprises four schools with 5 669 full-time and 484 part-time students participating in undergraduate and postgraduate programmes in 1995–96. HKU has nine faculties with an enrolment of 10 341 full-time and 2 620 part-time students, studying at the undergraduate and postgraduate level in 1995–96.

The Open Learning Institute of Hong Kong (OLI), established in 1989, offers degree, non-degree and postgraduate programmes principally through open access and distance education to working adults aged 17 and above. It comprises four schools and has about 20 000 students at present.

Adult Education : The Education Department provides formal and non-formal adult education courses through an evening institute, 10 adult education and recreation centres and 78 subvented agencies. Formal education courses range from literacy classes to secondary and post-secondary studies whilst the adult education and recreation centres organise a wide variety of cultural, social and recreational activities. The Education Department also provides subvention to non-profit-making organisations for the running of an induction programme to help new immigrant children from China to adapt to the local environment and extension programme to raise their standard of English. Thirty-three organisations joined the scheme to serve a target of 10 000 children.

Adult education courses are also provided by the evening sections of technical institutes, the various universities, the Open Learning Institute of Hong Kong and private institutes.

	Enrolment
Evening Institute (Government)	10 445
Adult Education and Recreation Centres (Government)	1 199
Voluntary agencies offering adult education courses under a government subvented scheme	20 300
Private Institutes offering post secondary and adult education courses	84 677

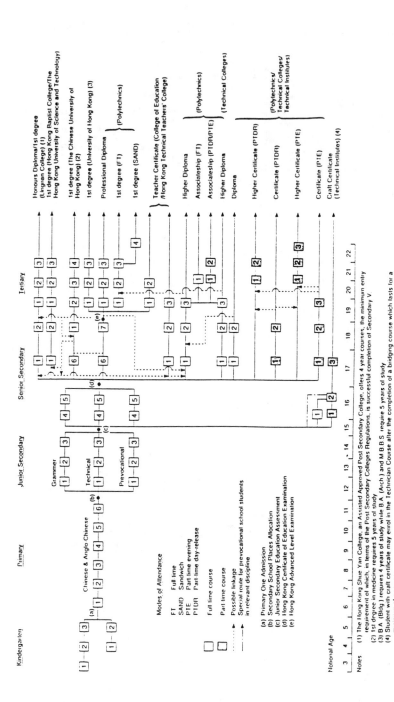

Table 5.1 The Hong Kong Education System (1992/93)

Table 5.2   243

Comparing the Educational Systems of USA and HK

	USA	Hong Kong
Main Purpose	Focus on the individual. Develop individual to fullest potential. Transmitter of a cultural heritage that's still forming.	Focus on effective, lawful citizenry. Develop literacy and skills ready to serve society's needs & self-reliant/productive people. Helps select future corps of leaders.
Instructional Mode	Learner-centered; stress on understanding, application & ability to integrate learnings. Use of educational psychology & varied teaching aids & methods. Learner is motivated through self-interest & is active. Routine promotions. More present-future oriented.	Teacher-centered; stress on knowing factual details & logic of disciplines. Use of lectures, homework & rote learning. Extrinsic motivating force of exams determining advancement & sch/ class placements. Learner is group-oriented and passive. More past-present oriented.
Curricular Orientation	Concern for developing whole person -- cognitive, social-emotional, & physical. Social interaction & human relations seen as tool to promote whole person. Various tracks -- university prep & vocational, for choice by secondary students	Mastery of academic knowledge & skills in preparation for traumatic, subject-matter exams. Linear progression in concepts & skills taught. Curricular status/ prestige hierarchy delimits choice; most secondary students take university prep.
Ideal Secondary School Graduate	Well-rounded, achieving student/ person superior in academics as evidenced by grades. Has extracurricular activities, perhaps as student leader and/or athlete. Perfoms well in aptitude tests.	Outstanding achiever in school, estimation mostly by teachers. Performs outstandingly in major exams, especially for admission to best universities. Good-natured, relates well with superiors & peers
Administrative Control	Administered by local communities through elected boards of education and board-appointed administrators. Each of the 50 states constitutionally responsible; not the federal government. Strong democratic traditions	Policies and procedures centrally controlled by the government with little discretionary power given to local authorities and schools. HK Gov.'s Ed. Dept. directs schools; higher education self-assessing. Far fewer tertiary places than U.S.

Modified from Yee (1989) and Yee & Cheng (1997)

is taken very seriously in East Asia, especially higher education which greatly affects entire school systems, admission into the best university possible is the absorbing and painstaking goal of Asian students and their families (Lin, 1984).

Westerners make the mistake of assuming that Asian universities are much like their own. Since many have studied in the West, however, Asian academicians know better. My research has found that professors and administrators across East Asia assess their universities quite differently from Western universities. When asked what universities were the best in the world, they selected Harvard, Cambridge/Oxford (Oxbridge), and Stanford as the very best. Asians explained their choices by saying that the best had world-class faculty, leading research productivity and support, and superb scholarly environments.

Asked to pick the most respected universities in their own nations and explain their choices, the East Asian academicians said that they were first-tier nationally because their graduates obtained the best jobs, a very surprising difference between their world versus domestic ratings. That finding alone speaks volumes.

The fact that Westerners do not know much about Asian education and universities became clear in 1990-91 when I was a consultant to the directors of U.S. accrediting associations and working as an evaluator of U.S. university branches in Japan. The American accrediting chiefs, whose mission is to certify the standards of universities and colleges, indicated right off that they perceived Asian higher education as similar to that of North America. They were thunderstruck when I began to set them straight. Let's examine three characteristics of East Asian higher education to illustrate what is meant.

University Faculty

Unlike the inbreeding taboo of reputable U.S. universities, faculty appointees in East Asia are often graduates of the university employing them and handpicked by their senior professors. It is unlikely that they have completed doctorates or have had much teaching or independent research experience. Their role as junior faculty is to follow the lead of superiors, usually one senior professor, rather than to initiate and pursue scholarship of their own and develop an independent coterie. The hardest task, therefore, is to land a starting post, i.e., to be handpicked. Junior faculty typically gain permanent employment (tenure) at or within a few years after initial hiring and stay on through their careers. While mobility is very restricted, job security comes early without the years of toil and worry of most Western counterparts.

While HKU formerly hired with a British bias for long, more Chinese academics have been employed in recent decades. In 1972, Dr. Rayson Huang, a HKU graduate in chemistry, became the first Chinese to be appointed Vice-Chancellor of the University of Hong Kong and remained until 1989. Although notices of HK job openings state the required academic qualifications for more than a decade, they also state preference for those who are familiar with the Chinese language and HK. That is merely the tip of the iceberg, for no matter how well qualified, even outstanding applicants should have *quanxi* (see Huang & Jeffrey, 1995, pp. 26-28) i.e., supporting connections and/or HK roots. If not, they are at a great disadvantage. Far more vital than reference letters, which are mostly ignored, *quanxi* represents meaningful person-to-person ties. It is doubtful that my HK teaching post would have come about without the support of a respected *taipan*. Many see little or no difference from their use of *quanxi* and the way the British overwhelmingly selected faculty and administrators from home.

In the past, young lecturers in East Asia worked for several years before they took leave to complete a doctorate overseas. In Japan, the routine has been to complete their terminal degree with the senior professor that supported their hiring. Often their first extended trip abroad, other Asian lecturers returned ready for promotion with doctoral degrees in hand. Their attitudes and English literacy, especially written, often showed that they never really left and that memorization, hard work, and sympathetic institutions and mentors abroad stood them in good stead. As a graduate and research dean and professor in the U.S., I marvelled at the ability of Asian students to work hard, conform, and achieve satisfactorily. Their Ph.D.'s carry immense, lasting value at home, even if they never conduct any scholarship their whole lives. Many use their degrees as stepping-stones to obtain employment and residency in the U.S.

American professors often excuse limited student competence in language and scholarship by saying that such students are returning home. Such rationalizations belittle themselves and their universities as well as the students who might have fulfilled or exceeded standards if only pressed to do so. Since education is supposedly more than course credits hours and academic hurdles, this is not necessarily a criticism of the students so much as institutional indulgence.

Foreign bachelor's and master's degrees are blindly accepted by U.S. and British universities as if they were equivalent to their own. Even if they were of high quality, which is not true for many HK master's, the curricula are hardly the same except perhaps in the hard sciences. Foreign graduate students should be required to fulfill a minimum, one-year requirement in general education before embarking on regular graduate studies. Besides gaining basic concepts, their language competence would profit as well.

One reason for the mollycoddling is that U.S. faculty, especially at lower-tier universities, often lack students for their doctoral programs and accept applicants sight unseen if they claim self-support. In this way, such professors protect their lighter teaching loads and gain research assistants. Once arrived, foreign students with shortcomings are hard to send away, because professors can use them and are indulgent. I have seen cases where professors kept foreign students, who couldn't pass the scrutiny of their peers, under their wings for many years because they felt responsible for them, almost as dependents. Those students usually got their degrees after many years, as did aged examination-takers in old China who failed many times but finally won their degrees for having tried over and over again. Starting in the 1980s, U.S. universities reinforced the likelihood for

for indulgence, etc. when they decentralized graduate studies administration to the school and departmental levels.

Gathering alumni of Harvard and Stanford (latter my alma mater) for a faculty luncheon in 1987, I was surprised that there were only 20 throughout HK's tertiary institutions (6,475 academic and research FTE staff in 1996-97; perhaps 2,500 more than 1987). The same low ratio prevailed from other prestigious universities. A survey of doctoral degrees held by HK university faculties, the highest salaried in the world, could uncover a surprising number from relatively low-tier institutions. Some lecturers have enrolled in scandalous graduate programs, such as one in Britain that granted Ph.D. degrees for merely attending three summers; exemplifying CSS opportunism at its worst. Holding permanent employment, junior faculty members need the doctorate to be promoted. In some departments, it did not matter much where one's final degree came from as long as the institution had some accreditation, an asinine policy that may not exist today.

About the greatest sin in academia, plagiarism has been common in HK and Asia for long, a bad habit that has been generally accepted in the demand for Chinese-language texts and translations of foreign classics. Notwithstanding excellent salaries and benefits, HK professors obtain royalties for such work without notice and remuneration to the unwitting original publisher and author. When a respected HK newspaper accused an academic of plagiarism, no problem befell the translator as his peers elected him to the deanship. Since bicultural, bilingual winks and tricks had been condoned in British HK, what can be expected now? As discussed later, HK's tertiary system lacks quality control.

HK's best academic departments and many professors are at a par with most peers elsewhere; their standing in terms of scholarship and top-level students arise from the commitment of one or more founding or senior professors to represent quality and forsake pettiness and slothfulness. Such dedication and the discipline to demand high standards over the years are hard to maintain against campus politics. When salaries are set by rank and seniority scales as in HK, professors must be self-motivating; otherwise, many see little incentive to exert themselves after reaching their rank ceiling and count their time to retirement.

As behavior is role-related, institutional leaders should accentuate the best in their personnel by enhancing role expectations and rewarding professionalism. For example, HKU's and CU's medical faculties have built-in incentives, as they uphold quality because of professional oversight and their awesome duty to save lives. Historic breakthroughs do the same for those in technology and the natural sciences, such as one CU professor, Charles Kao, who made his mark with fiber-optics and later became vice-chancellor. Faculty caliber has improved in the 1990s, mainly because HK academic salaries have been among the world's highest for years. Younger faculty members have completed terminal degrees at good universities before they were hired. Hopefully, they will help to boost standards.

An educator for 40 years before retiring in 1995, I have observed countless academicians in America and Asia. What never ceased to amaze was that so few were humanists versus specialists. In that respect, HK was not worst nor better.

Top-down Administration

Asian universities are run by career administrators who relate very little with their faculty members. While teaching units initiate petty routines at HK universities, such as office hours, central administrations scrutinize and rubber-stamp everything in Chinglish manner. For instance, to leave the territory, even during holidays, professors must obtain permission through the entire chain of command. The power of department heads and faculties comes in hiring, firing, and promoting staff, which of course is circular in terms of quality and maintaining the status quo. Unlike the U.S. but similar to Britain, Asian academic deans and units have little budgetary control and campus heads lack flexibility of fiscal accounts.

Asian governments control everything possible through an authority hierarchy which works from the education ministries down to the university heads and administrative staff and to the faculty (Yee, 1994). On leave from the University of Wisconsin-Madison, where student riots were the worst during the Vietnam era, to Japan as a Fulbright professor in 1972, I was sought after by heads of public universities. They wanted advice on how to handle the student strikes that were devastating their campuses. My advice, however, was politely declared unrealistic for them. The administrators explained that their campuses had little budgetary and policy authority and had to follow the lead of Japan's Education Ministry or *Monbusho* (see Mori, 1994 & Yamamoto, 1994). Unlike the U.S., other nations' educational systems are directed and funded by national governments (see Table 1.1). Funds strictly enrollment driven -- thus the alarm in 1972 Japan.

HK's University Grants Committee. The UGC is responsible for HK's tertiary institutions. Before the two polytechnics became universities, the UGC was UPGC. With ten overseas academics, four local academics, and four local professionals and businessmen acting as a board, the UGC looks good on paper but is actually run by a tiny group of only 40 civil servants, two-thirds of whom are clerical. None of the UGC executives have had academic career experience. Although they oversee billions of dollars and a huge tertiary system, they are simply sincere civil servants who might have run the transportation or welfare departments during colonialism. Unlike higher education, HK officials directing health and medical services have always been relevant professionals, i.e., MDs.

One board member, an internationally-known scholar, confided that the requirements of his job was merely to agree to everything on the long, tedious agendas several times a year. His spouse interjected that he had better do so: "I don't want to miss our visits to Hong Kong." In its Chinglish, bureaucratized system of education, HK has many ceremonials posturing as decision-making bodies -- "ridiculous fig leafs" according to one critic.

Residents of HK and refusing to be rubber-stamps, a few business and professional members of UGC, such as the scholar and industrialist Ann Tse-Kai, have worked to upgrade HK's tertiary system. One of many who migrated from Shanghai in the 1950s and expanded HK's industry, Dr. Ann served as UPGC Deputy Chairman from 1965-76 and was conferred with a Honorary Degree of Dr. of Law by CU in 1976. Local UPGC members, such as Dr. Ann, were crucial in developing the two polytechnics, both deemed vital to the economy's expansion. UPGC and UGC Chairmen have exerted direction and influence, but few have equalled Dr. Ann's wisdom and scholarly insight.

Typical of the CSS model as discussed in pp. 19-26, the top-down system is bound to foster autocracy and counter-allegiance. It was disappointing when my letters to the UPGC in the late 1980s requesting copies of its annual reports brought chastisement from my campus authorities for daring to contact the UPGC. Deferential replies saying their reports were in the library, librarians never found any. Lacking the reports was no great loss, but the episode portrayed the haughtiness of HK's top-down administration. When HK's Deputy Chief Secretary invited me to dine and heard my story, his coy reaction was, "You were just too polite." Yet in May 1998, the UGC Secretariat welcomed me into its offices and provided useful data that is used in this chapter.

Comprised wholly of civil servants, the UGC Secretariat says that its main mission is to channel Government funds to the universities with little interference (University Grants Committee, 1996a & b; personal communication, UGC visit, May 12, 1998). Given autonomy, the universities are allowed to use funds as they see fit and oversee their own quality control. Since 70-80% of funds go for salaries, the institutions have leeway in managing their budgets as they recruit, hire, fire, and promote faculty. Student enrollments are set by the HK Government in UGC's funding formulas, i.e., so much per fully enrolled student (FTE).

Thus, HK's higher education lacks adequate external quality and policy control, a problem that its system center does not seem to recognize. It's reminiscent of Harold Alexander's generalship in the Mediterranean during World War II. Although Aexander had overall command, his reluctance to use his authority and give direction allowed his two bold and outspoken generals, Bernard Montgomery and George Patton, to do about whatever they wanted (E'Este, 1995). The problems in HK's tertiary system can be traced to negligent oversight and administration by UGC and the Secretariat of Education and Manpower.

Mandarin manners. Those who learn and teach in Hong Kong have little opportunity to initiate. As Chinese officials have always faulted the people to justify autocracy, campus administrators are quick to point out faculty and student flaws. A former vice-chancellor complained bitterly to me that his HK faculty took much of his time seeking advice and permission on everything, even personal matters. One quickly sensed his professors' child-like dependence and offhand counter-allegiance. Although the retired V-C had taught many years at an elite U.S. university where faculty professionalism and governance were maximal, he reverted to mandarin attitudes and ways in HK. Yet, inured to authoritarian paternalism (see pp. 19-34), his faculty no doubt sought such a leader.

The base limits of chauvinism and ignominy at Asian universities can astound those who abhor the unethical and corruption of standards. Assigned to a master's thesis committee chaired by the school head, I eventually learned that the student's English was so deficient that it was impossible to decipher the thinking. Although his conversational English seemed adequate, every written sentence was flawed, a common malady in the educational system. After he presented his thesis at the last minute, I worked with the student for hours. The second faculty member on the committee played it coy and the committee chair was in the U.S. where he was also a tenured university professor.

Showing how opportunism can override integrity, "double-dipping" (receiving two paychecks same time period) has not been uncommon in Hong Kong. One head librarian is alleged to have maintained his job in America as he commuted periodically between the U.S. and the territory. In May 1998, the UGC informed me that it was not involved in such deals and that it had no policy against them. Since HK universities carefully scrutinize consulting work by academicians, in part to share in the fees, I assume that what was meant is that double-dipping is tolerated as long as a non-HK person is involved and receives only one HK salary. The UGC Deputy Director said that campus authorities had autonomy in handling their appointments and finances and had to have made the arrangements themselves. Thus, questions arise regarding possible tax ploys.

Are U.S. institutions aware of the double-dipping? If they are, how do they justify their employees holding two jobs, one with them and another afar in HK? While American professors who accept federal political appointments go on unpaid leave, it appears that games are being played with HK universities that go beyond normal consulting privileges.

A rising administrator at a sister campus, the master's candidate complained that I was holding up his graduation, never mind repeated attempts over more than half a year or more to assist him. Because the director, who had worked full-time in HK for years, was at his U.S. job, the graduate dean stepped in and demanded my grade for the thesis, whereupon I failed him. The other faculty member assigned a "B." Soon I was called before the graduate dean, who angrily ordered that I pass the thesis with a "respectable grade." Arrogantly refusing to listen to my views, he insisted that I obey his instructions on the spot. In shocked frustration, I assigned a "C," still inferior in the inflated grade climate, and added a note on the grade form that I changed the grade after being ordered to do so.

Since the student graduated, the director must have assigned an "A," which would have rounded the thesis grade to "B." After that experience, I declined thesis assignments when HK students exhibited the same profile. It's the diploma that counts, not the learning.

Several students failing my courses had their grades raised through appeal. Without discussing it prior to the changes, the same director explained his administrative action by saying that a "C" was bad enough and the students would remain enrolled. And funds based on enrollment would not be lost, which helps to explain why students in Hong Kong (and Asia) rarely fail to graduate.

I had very good HK students who not only worked diligently but were also cheerful, bright people to instruct. However, they numbered only about 25% in the best classes; the majority disdained learning but did enough to pass. One of the better students was an unforgettable graduate student who decried boss tyranny in his Tuen Mun district. Hospitalized after assailants nearly killed him, he said that he would die for democracy. Before succumbing to leukemia in 1991, my former student was elected to the Legislative Council as a Democrat and attacked HKUST's cost overruns to the end.

Academic autocracy. Endemic to East Asian institutions as discussed on pp. 19-26, autocracy permeates university life. Position and rank direct interpersonal relations in ways that would be regarded as wholly unethical in the West. Authorities resent any embarrassment and feel that they have suffered loss of face if found in errror. Thus, the thing to do is to maintain decorum and avoid any possible confrontation with the mandarins. Some university administrators were reputed to be so rigid that colleagues warned, usually after the fact, never to ask them a question on policy or procedure. For asking them anything implies that they have not instructed well or raises the possibility that they do not know the answer. Many professors seemed of the same genre; but thank goodness for those, Westerners and Chinese, who had some integrity and were more of themselves than pompous pose.

As professors and administrators donned academic garments in a waiting room prior to graduation ceremonies, I saw one man with a cardinal-colored, Stanford gown identical to mine. I went to greet the fellow alumnus whom I had never met. Replying in a cold, officious manner, "I am the Registrar," he set me back; but I still tried to be cordial. Ignoring my natural sociability, he repeated himself, which friends told me later meant that he was a senior administrator and I was out of line.

Whenever I asked office staff about unclear or meaningless edicts or procedures, their pat answers were invariably: "This is Hong Kong." and "That's how it has always been done." When promised travel funds went unpaid, the answer was that others had exhausted the account. Westerners never see such manners. People assumed that my Chinese face meant that my reactions would be Chinese.

If something serious happened, students band together to protest and administrators seek accommodation. However, student activists seeking conflict are clever in pursuing wedge issues that bar easy solution. For example, students commemorating Tiananmen with freedom statues the first week of June 1997 insisted that they be permitted to mount one on the HKU campus. The turmoil ended when Chen Yiu-chung, HKU's Vice-Chancellor, finally gave in to a two-week campus stay of the "Pillar of Shame" statue. V-C Chen went so far as to say that he would protect and maintain academic freedom after the handover.

While tough on professors, who never forget who controls promotions and favors, a former vice-chancellor was famous for fearing activist students and went to great lengths to avoid them. His fear was not losing his job but confrontation itself, which has been typical of Chinese officials. When professors receive unfavorable student evaluations and complaints over grades and course requirements, administrators typically side with the students as water seeks the easiest path. Caught between the students and mandarin administrators, professors with quality standards toe a tightrope. Since the normal retirement age in HK is 60, professors hope that they can teach an extra year through their V-C's grace.

While selection of a new vice-chancellor is handled mysteriously, two qualifications seem absolute -- ability to speak Chinese, preferably both Cantonese and Putonghua and a doctorate from a respectable institution. Learning that the new V-C would reside temporarily in their campus tower before his family and goods arrived, my friend and his wife attended his welcoming session and cordially invited him to dine with them when he wanted, saying they knew what it was like to move, etc. His disappointing reaction was that of a flustered mandarin who couldn't handle his embarrassment by simply giving regrets and thanks. However, a year or so later, the same V-C did himself credit by hampering an unscrupulous ploy by a department clique to dismiss a professor.

Another new V-C, who many expected to be stuffy, entertained faculty and others at his residence with warmth; he and his outgoing wife seemed genuinely eager to be friendly and helpful. Thrice, I accepted his kind invitation to meet, first to see if he was sincere and twice to get advice on projects.

What it must have meant to be a scholar-official in old China and then to be the epitome of all of that as an university V-C or in another administrative role in HK must be petrifying to many and liberalizing to too few. HK needs more role models of the latter type whose style and manner are more akin to the quotation beginning the Overview than hierarchical authority. Chinese administrative styles include a broad range of behavior from the polar extreme of rigid officialism to personal and *quanxi* indulgence. The better leaders follow a middle road. Disdaining the golden mean, autocracy should be considered archaic and dangerous to professionalism and the common good.

Helping others to find a "foothold" and "to attain" should mean more than family and cronies, surely in education. A perennial problem is that universities, like religious institutions, are often consumed by petty politics and self-interest. Some say they are because they must fight over meager resources. My own feeling is that too many professors are actually unsuited to conduct quality scholarship and teach, academic goals that career paths do not reward directly.

The academic senates at HK's universities are mostly sounding boards. As Government employees, faculty cannot organize unions. An example of the melding of East and West, HKU's senate has carried weight and been jealous of its governance role, which developed when the faculty was mostly British. The status quo is the desideratum, since university heads in HK and Asia are relatively free of the persistent fund-raising, alumni activities, athletics (hardly exists), parking chaos (few HK students have cars), and campus high jinks prevalent at U.S. campuses (Matthews, 1997). As more professors go to HK from the PRC, where universities have been oppressed, faculties may become even more conforming.

Quantity versus quality. Philanthropy towards HK universities is expressed in buildings versus out-and-out grants. Sir Run Run Shaw's gifts to CU for a theater and fourth college, each named after him and HKU's Swire Building are examples. Many schools bear the names of tycoons who donated their construction funds. Sharing its horse-racing profits, the HK Jockey Club has been quite generous to HK universities, such as HKUST's initial capital funds of about US$202 million. However, university endowments in HK are minuscule compared to what they are in the U.S. The £1,000 received for WW-II damages put HKU's endowment far ahead of others. HK's tax system gives no allowance for charity.

Since undergraduate education is the chief function of HK's universities, research is underfunded (only US$50 million funded in 1994-95) and graduate studies are less than what would even be found at low-tier institutions in the West. Research funded by the HK Government has had to be applicable to the territory; nothing too abstract. All of which is amazing since HK senior faculty are so well-paid. In the U.S., the average 1997-98 faculty salary at public institutions was $53,296 and $51,448 at private schools (Reynolds, 1998).

Graduate enrollments remain as low as the endowments. Beginning in 1999, postgraduate places will be cut because UGC complained that master's students took longer than two years to complete degrees and doctorates more than the allowed four years (Kwok, 1998a). Indicating that graduate education is not high priority, Dr. Edgar Cheng Wai-kin, the UGC Chairman, declared in June 1998 that the universities would have to afford the extra 1,000 graduate places proposed by the Government's unemployment task force (Kwok, 1998b).

HK's universities have been allocated an increase of 24% in funds beginning in 1999, which comes in part from an increase from seven to eight institutions. Student subsidies were cut 10% but 11,000 student hostel places will be built over five years. The UGC will funnel US$4.57 billion to the universities in recurrent funding for three years (Lai, 1998). For all the money that has been poured into HK's higher education system for years, the results are more quantitative than qualitative -- more faculty and students, more institutions and buildings, etc.

Receiving US$24,493 per student in 1997-98 (total enrollment of 69,723 FTE; total public costs of $1.71 billion), HK's universities are among the best-funded in the world. The expenditure level seems unwarranted for nondegree and undergraduate programs (14,890 subdegree students; 45,823 UGs), the mainstay of HK's universities, especially given the typical standards of the students. In 1997-98, the UGC funded 9,010 postgraduates out of nearly 70,000 FTE (University Grants Committee, 1998, p. 28). Perhaps the universities will begin to justify their costs by increasing enrollments, especially graduate students, developing innovative community services and producing noticeably more world-class research with the participation of quality scientists from the PRC and abroad, but much more is required to justify the high costs. As with obesity, cutting consumption is best.

As UGC Secretary-General Nigel French (UGC's website, June 1, 1998) declared for the future, what is crucial are promoting excellence, determination to become a regional center for diverse, advanced areas of specialization, and increasing foreign students from two to four percent. Also, cost-effectiveness will be raised, which means reducing budgets 10% over three years, which raised protests from academicians inured to steady increases. In response to French, HK Polytechnic University (HKPC) has decided its "excellence areas" will be "accounting with computing, construction and land use, textiles and clothing, and rehabilitation science and bio-engineering" with the PRC. Each area will receive about US$1.35 million for three years before they become self-supporting. Foreign student gains, no doubt from the PRC, have been targeted from the current 20% to one-third.

Exam-Conforming Curriculum

Elitism, supposed status of the best, is built into Asian education. Critical, subject-centered examinations throughout the educational systems of Confucian societies narrow the numbers seeking university entry. In contrast, the egalitarian U.S. system (see Table 5.2) emphasizes successful achievement within institutions, and nearly all American students (65% of college age enrolled) can find some institution of higher learning that will accept them. However, elite U.S. universities, such as Harvard, Stanford, Yale, and UC, Berkeley, are both hard to enter and stay enrolled.

The U.S. accrediting executives, mentioned earlier as misperceiving Asian universities as similar to those in the U.S., were shocked to learn that Asian universities rarely fail any students once admitted. This was indeed shocking, for they suddenly realized that Japanese students enrolled in U.S. university branches in Japan and their families took graduation for granted. The Japanese, of course, wondered why admission was so easy at first but later realized that enrollment depended on hefty tuitions and fees being paid.

Gaining admission after passing grueling examinations for which many memorize entire encyclopedias, students at Japan's elite universities seldom attend lectures or even step foot on campus. This phenomenon was baffling when I was a Senior Fulbright professor at Tokyo University, Japan's premier institution. When I mentioned the students' absenteeism to a Japanese professor, he asked how many attended my lectures and I answered two or three. He replied, "Then why should you complain? Often, not even one student comes to my classes!"

Assured graduation after four years in "fantasyland," Japanese students spend most of their time with extracurricular activities developing networks useful for their future careers in corporations and the government. Thus, it was with relief that I learned that HK students are required to attend classes and fulfill minimum work requirements in order to graduate.

Students in Confucian societies have perfected memorization and study skills so that few fail multiple-choice tests. The world's best test-takers, Chinese, Koreans, and Japanese compete well internationally, especially in math (Geary, 1996). Facing essay exams, however, they are at a loss and resent open-ended work.

Somehow the process works to a degree despite its defects. While only a few have achieved world-class fame (some say only one or two), HK graduates have become successful professionals, managers, teachers, and students abroad.

Tertiary students in Hong Kong are generally the first of their working-class families to attend an university. Their years of drudging memorizing and cramming produce anti-intellectuals who boast of their degrees as status symbols. As admission is license to graduation, some students, much to the disgust of many peers, reveal wild egoticism, such that they believe that they are superior to their professors and act out their arrogance in discourtesies.

Such attitudes can be appreciated when one realizes that the youth of uneducated parents can cram arduously many years to reach the university, i.e., to rise in one generation from cart pushers to supposed gentry can raise the specter of narcissism (Yee, 1992b, pp. 286-304). Unheard of in the West, serious-minded students write letters to HK newspapers to complain of their peers' laziness and disrespect to teachers (Yee, 1992b, pp. 288-290).

In the U.S., where student incompetence, grade inflation, and faculty indulgence are at crisis levels (e.g., Britt, 1998; Trout, 1998), it gratifies one that he is not beginning an academic career today. Given the forced choice of teaching either in Hong Kong or America today, I would choose the former, for at least most students know something and work hard.

Tests are so important in HK that there is a special bureaucracy to produce and administer the Hong Kong Certificate of Education Examination (see Table 5.1; taken at age 15 near completion of Secondary 5) and the Hong Kong Advanced Level Examination (taken at age 17 after finishing Secondary 7) as well as administer the tests of overseas examining bodies, such as the GRE. The HK Examination Authority was set up in 1965 as an independent, self-support statutory agency.

Taken by all students, whether they plan to attend university or not, the HKCEE has been liberalized in the '90s so that the list of subjects has been increased to 42 from which to choose the minimum of five and maximum of nine subjects, two of which must be languages. Assessed by proficiency level, exam results typically show that most students barely pass at the grade of "E." In 1995-96, 117,400 took the HKCEE (60.5% with "E" or higher) and 28,200 sat for the HKALE (70.9% "E" or higher) (Daryanani, 1995, p. 155). Such results are typical.

The steady decline in English proficiency is alarming. Examinations Authority Secretary, Choi Chee-cheong, reported that out of almost 29,000 taking the 1997 HKALE exam for university entry, "Only 40.9 per cent, or 12,000 candidates, achieved Grade D or above in English but there are 14,500 university places . . . Our system is not producing enough quality students" (Kwok, 1997). As straight "A's" are rare, newspapers feature the handful every year. The top achievers all seemed to cherish knowledge and learning and had patient, supportive parents.

Although Confucius' first principles were humanistic learning, self-reflection, and conscientious duty, his influence on disciplined, rote learning has been more prominently pursued. To pass the highest examinations in old China deserved great credit indeed, yet they were based on the classics and memorization.

In late 1997, the HK Curriculum Development Council released results of its two-year study of failed students. Its report confirmed what many have felt for long -- excellent students were failing because of a "demanding but downright boring curriculum." One school principal said: "For students, the core curriculum in schools is too demanding, too competitive and it's so exam-oriented that they don't learn -- they just cram it all in like Beijing barbecue duck." The Council urged teachers to be more sensitive with students' emotional intelligence (EQ) than IQ and to "improve their relationships with children by being more open and making learning more enjoyable" (Smith, 1997). In early 1999, the Education Commission sought comment on a plan to promote "student-centred education" (Lai, 1999), an excellent move. Teaching should "cherish the young," and learning should be viewed as a humanizing and lifelong goal (Yee & Cheng, 1997).

With the university at its pinnacle, HK's educational pyramid follows China's ancient traditions. It is more structured than in Britain, where graduation from a sound secondary school is sufficient for most careers. In Asia, a degree is mandatory for professional-level careers. Thus, compromising East and West, British HK leaned heavily on Chinese traditions for assessment purposes.

HK's universities are not as stultifying inert as in other Asian societies, mainly because they have been on the uptake. However, key characteristics (faculty, administration, and exam conformity) as just reviewed make them tailor-made for any authoritarian moves by the PRC, where corruption and suppression of its universities do not augur well for the SAR's higher education system.

Higher Education in Hong Kong

Besides the HK Open Learning Institute, Display 5.1 mentions seven institutions of higher education. The 1997-98 enrollment of nearly 70,000 FTE represents 18.6% of the 17-20 relevant age group versus 5% in 1985 and 13% in 1991-92. Unlike American usage, "colleges" in Europe are typically secondary schools. In the British mode, colleges extend into the first year or so of American higher education, and studies for the first degree at the university last three years. Since all but one of HK's newer universities were lesser institutions of higher learning in 1985, the increase in students is due to name changes as well as increased admissions overall. Usually more cosmetics than substance, renaming colleges into universities is aimed at resource boosts (Lively, 1997). In HK, status changes have enhanced "university" access and choice for which the Government has been willing to afford. The enrollment rise to 18.6% compares with China's 6%, Singapore's 7%, Britain's 25%, and America's 65%.

Modelled after Britain's outstanding counterpart, the HK Open Learning Institute was founded in 1989. When it was given university status on May 30, 1997, it gave 20,000 students access to degree and nondegree studies through part-time, distance learning. Chartered as self-supporting, the OLI is not funded under the aegis of the University Grants Committee. OLI's head, Dr. Tam Sheungwai, said more programs will be offered in Chinese to benefit students locally and "on the mainland and in other overseas Chinese communities" (*South China Morning Post*, Internet Edition, May 23, 1997). Thus, OLI's outreach could be worldwide if Dr. Tam's ambitious goal comes true.

The Academic Pyramid

Reliable HK professionals inform me that HKU, CU, and HKUST are rated equally as first-tier in prestige and the students' first choice, City University and HKPU as second-tier, and Baptist University and Lingnan as third-tier. As well as granting some degrees, City and HK Poly also offer vocational training in a variety of fields that provide certificate holders good jobs; the same is true at Singapore's polytechnics.

While Asian societies have overemphasized academic degrees, more youth and families are realizing that non-degree skills can be rewarding and take less time and costs to obtain. Asia should heed Germany's exemplary nondegree technical and vocational programs. With traditions honoring craftsmanship and technical skills, however, Germany's sociocultural background contrasts with Confucian values towards education. Making a travesty of academic virtures, degree obses-sion in Indonesia, the Philippines, and Malaysia is compounded by weak stan-dards and funding (Ranuwithardjo, 1994; Yee & Lim, 1994). The outdated stress on diplomas and status versus (lifelong) learnededness and skills has produced many unemployed graduates in India and SE Asia.

A fourth academic tier in HK includes: the teacher-training agency, the Insti-tute of Education, which is headed by China scholar and former Canadian diplo-mat, Dr. Ruth Hayhoe; the privately endowed Hang Sang School of Commerce and Shue Yan College; seven technical institutes and two technical colleges operated by the Government's Vocational Training Council; and the Academy for the Performing Arts (APA) financed by the Recreation and Culture Depart-ment and built in 1985 with a HK$300 million grant from the HK Jockey Club.

The Academy is one of HK's most creative educational programs (Yee, 1994, pp. 45-47). While its degree programs began in 1996 and Governor Patten award-ed diplomas to the first cohort of Bachelor's of Fine Arts (29) the same year, Dis-play 5.1 and Figure 5.1 do not list the Academy. Omitting the APA in their Edu-cation Chapters, the HK Government's annual reports cover it in chapters on Recreation, Sports and the Arts (e.g., Howlett, 1996, pp. 341-342), a distinction that seems to reflect the gap between status and skills.

Tertiary programs are also offered in Hong Kong by foreign universities, pri-marily from Britain, Australia, and America. Profit-making, the distance learning programs attract those who believe that high tuitions are worth the value of for-eign degrees and the ease of studying at their own pace. Associated with the University of Macau, the Asia Pacific Institute has operated in HK on a large variety of degree programs.

In mid-1997, the HK Council for Academic Accreditation began to evaluate courses offered locally by foreign institutions. It was formed in 1990 to review degree programs of non-university institutions such as Lingnan, OLI, and the AFA. However, universities are permitted to manage their own quality control, a weird presumption that is perhaps the most egregious error in HK's higher education system. Both Britain and the U.S. incorporate accreditation systems.

Few places can match the myriad of higher education programs in Hong Kong. Booming from 1984 to 1997, HK's economy absorbed the educated as energy. Besides higher education, worthy of mention are the British Council, Hong Kong Arts Centre, the symphonies, Education Department adult education programs, etc., which enrich the community and help to satisfy lifelong learning and aesthetic interests of the people beyond the craving for certified status.

Founded in 1911, the Univeristy of Hong Kong was discussed earlier as the territory's first tertiary institution. The venerable institution remains at its Pokfulam Road site on HK Island where Main Hall is still in use and HKU's dedication plaque can be found. During the Japanese occupation when HKU was closed, scavengers removed Main Hall's roofing for fuel and material. As more and larger buildings are added to its cramped 40 acres, such as the attractive library completed in 1991, the campus surrenders greenery to steel and concrete. Beyond the campus boundary below Pokfulam Road, the unremitting construction of high rises has sadly obliterated the stunning view of Victoria Harbor, once plied by working junks, West Point, and Stonecutters' Island.

Lingnan College. Headed by economist, Edward K. Y. Chen, former Director of HKU's Centre of Asian Studies, Lingnan College is slated to be HK's next university. Opened as a private college in 1967 by alumni of the original university in Canton on a narrow strip on Stubbs Road, Lingnan developed slowly until it restructured itself to win UGC acceptance in 1991 for public funds. It offers honors degrees for 2,814 residential students. Typical of its expeditious development of campuses, the HK Government finished building a new campus at Fu Tei, Tuen Mun before the 1995-96 academic year. Winning an architectural prize in early 1997, its handsome buildings are modelled after Lingnan University in Canton (renamed Zhongshan in 1952), that was founded by American Presbyterians in 1888 as the Christian College of Canton, renamed Lingnan in 1903 and university in 1927.

A student at the original Lingnan University in 1947-48, I visited the Tuen Mun campus in May 1998 while lecturing at the HK Institute of Education (HKIEd). The new HKIEd campus at Tai Po is located at a picturesque setting, but the plain design and inferior construction give the impression of a PRC industrial plant. In contrast, Lingnan's buildings and grounds are more beautiful and perfect than expected. So thrilled was I by the harmony and spirit of the new Lingnan campus, despite the steady rain, I roamed about and paused reflectively at aesthetic spots for three hours. It is obvious that architects, construction crews, Dr. Chen, staff, and no doubt Lingnan alumni dedicated themselves to bring about a harmonious unity with rare attention to detail, as seen in the classical Chinese garden and fine design and construction of the buildings.

Housed in attractive, well-built, campus dormitories, Lingnan College's 2,121 students mostly pursue first degrees in arts, business, and the social sciences. Despite the ambiance of their beautiful campus and its many benefits, most LC's students as well as those at HK Baptist University would rather be enrolled at higher-tier institutions, which did not accept them. The gross student cost at Lingnan in 1997-98 was a bargain US$16,490 versus $32,286 at HKUST.

The Chinese University of Hong Kong (CU). HK's second university was formed in 1963 by joining together three small private colleges with instruction in Chinese -- New Asia, Chung Chi, and United. In 1986, CU gained a fourth college named after its benefactor, Sir Run Run Shaw, the film mogul (see pp. 193-194). In the late 1950s and early 1960s, many called for a Chinese counterpart to HKU and Western-oriented curricula.

CU was built on a panoramic expanse overlooking Tolo Harbour near Shatin, mostly with public contributions. With its distinctive architecture and hilly, rural location, visitors laud the University's beauty; some say that it is the world's most beautiful campus. Unlike HKU's hodgepodge nature on limited space in the city, CU was built according to an overall architectural plan as were later campuses. No matter the view and passing praise of visitors, the hilly terrain makes biking prohibitive and the distances between buildings necessitate everyone driving or riding buses to keep on schedule. During hot, humid months that make 100 meters an ordeal to avoid, walking is left to "mad dogs and Englishmen."

HKU's campus is also trying since it is sited on a steep slope, but buildings are accessible by foot and vehicles are restricted by limited roads and parking spaces. While teaching in Hong Kong and a Visiting Scholar at the HKU Centre for Asian Studies summers of 1991 and 1992, I made good use of the excellent holdings and services of HKU's Library. Because of the walk up from the Pokfulam Road bus stop to the Library, maybe only 200 meters but rather steep, I seldom checked out books. Coming down was as easy, but trekking up with a load of books was something else. Those afoot in Asia's hot, muggy seasons soon learn to seek the best air-conditioned, even circuitous, routes. In May of 1998, I found summer-like heat and friends said that HK's weather seemed warm throughout the year now.

HK's faculty are provided attractive, furnished living quarters for a fee (7.5% of salary) and subsidized utilities. This practice stems from colonialism when Europeans were provided housing and other perks no matter their pay scale. The rationale for long now is that HK's property market has been a disincentive in attracting and holding desired civil servants. Many take advantage of a housing stipend in lieu of quarters to rent or buy their own residences in the costly property market. Faculty flats include heavy furniture but tenants must obtain their own air conditioners for the hot season of June through October. Those who know such climate also know what it is to brace a strong A/C breeze on coming home. During HK's cooler months, the lack of centralized heating is felt when the temperature nears and falls below 10 Celsius (50 F.). As space heaters are not as efficient as A/Cs; one finds comfort in wearing more clothing. While classrooms have A/C, they lack heating so as in China windows are often open in the winter for fresh air.

CU's name actually means "Chinese Language University of Hong Kong," which visitors from the PRC and Taiwan find peculiar, since universities do not identify themselves by their medium of instruction. CU is not just a language institute, it is a comprehensive university with degree programs and faculties from engineering to the natural and social sciences to medicine. Its name can be understood in light of 1960s politics that made much of East-West, Sino-British differences; language was used to epitomize the differences in culture and political sentiment. Since Putonghua has been China's national tongue for long and will supplant Cantonese in the SAR someday, it shows how circumstances change, i.e., same name but contrasting tongues.

Although its faculty has always had many more Chinese than HKU, CU has classes taught in English and duplicates about everything in both languages. Since the students are Cantonese, Mandarin-speaking faculty have lectured in English, an accommodation that will end in time. CU mixes U.S. and British academic traditions. Until recent times, academic ranks were as in Britain, i.e., each unit usually had one professor, who was generally the head, with ranks of reader, senior lecturer, and lecturer. Today, American titles are utilized, i.e., professor, associate professor, and assistant professor, which match usage in China. However, the UGC continues to use the British nomenclature.

CU fought bitterly but futilely in the early 1990s over Government policy that cut its four-year degree curriculum to resemble Britain's three years. Some CU administrators charged that the change was nothing but a "British plot" to force conformity with England. Wanting to copy CU, HKU and UST argued that student standards were such that four years was needed. Many believe that the SAR will shift from three-year programs to conform with China's four-year courses.

In 1988, HKU's V-C Wang Gungwu said that incoming students were: " deficient in linguistic ability, lack independent judgment, analytical power as well as basic knowledge on world affairs" (also see Huang & Jeffrey, 1995, p. 168). Baptist President, Daniel Tse, said local students did not possess an "attitude of self-learning" and extended secondary-school habits of conformity and memorization to higher education (Yee, 1992b, p. 287).

A decade ago, CU took a jump on HKU's first-choice status by giving high HKCEE scorers provisional admission after satisfactory completion of Secondary 6. Its coup in tapping the best students raised loud protests from HKU and schools offering Secondary 7; yet CU's admission policy continues at a lesser rate. CU's Vice-Chancellor, Arthur K. C. Li, rose from the CU Faculty of Medicine where he enjoyed an excellent reputation as a teacher and medic. His pragmatic approach should help to improve CU in coming years.

Hong Kong University of Science and Technology (UST). Vice-Chancellor
Woo Chai-wei boasted years before UST opened in 1991 that his university
would be the "MIT of Asia," a goal he has tried to meet by handpicking seasoned Chinese professors from U.S. universities and installing state-of-the-art
research facilities. When UST opened, many of its faculty members were senior
professors and researchers who had made their name in the U.S. and were also
graduates of the elite National Taiwan University. Students complained bitterly
of their faculty's high scholastic expectations until the professors relented somewhat.

HK has never had a V-C who has sought the limelight as much as Dr. Woo.
Although he still holds to his goals, the media pays less attention since the public
is skeptical and regards him as flashy and UST as a high-priced "Rolls-Royce."
In 1997, V-C Woo created a campus war of words by insisting that his UST staff
use the expression, "Chinese mainland," instead of "mainland China." Professional Teachers' Union President, Cheung Man-kwong, expressed the general
sentiment: "It's ridiculous that a university head would intervene in freedom of
expression" (*South China Morning Post*, Internet edition, September 16, 1997).

On April 1, 1998, the *South China Morning Post* editorialized that "The
(HKUST) is behaving like a private club." The dispute was between the university and the HK Government over V-C Woo Chai-wei's salary. HKUST's "university council believes that government policy for tertiary institutions is not
applicable to it." The flap over Woo's annual salary of US$328,682 rose from its
being nearly $65,116 more than authorized by the Government; the extra amount
was obtained through private donations and granted by UST's Council. The
SCMP said that donations to universities "are normally designated for scholar-
ships for students or funding the setting up of laboratories or other new facilities. Using donations to subsidise the pay of a university head is unheard of"
('Private club' must answer, 1998). Woo's salary makes him one of the highest paid
university presidents in the world. Many said that the public dispute revealed
once again that advisory councils and boards in HK tend to be rubber stamps.

In the late 1980s, UST's capital development was budgeted for US$257 mil-
lion of which $200 m. was donated by the Jockey Club. Exceeding the already
rich budget and forcing the Government to cover the cost overrun, V-C Woo's
single-minded drive to obtain world-class research facilities drew public scorn.
British HK was keen on top-down administration, but not breaking budgets as is
common among the PRC's state enterprises. Beginning in 1999, UST's superbly
equipped campus and its well-paid faculty will be cut graduate student places because of poor degree completions.

Visiting HKUST in May 1998, I was impressed by the modernistic buildings
and facilities. It is doubtful if any new university in the world can surpass its
technological thrust and advantages. However, what makes UST unparalleled is
the fact that it enrolls only 1,151 postgraduate students and 5,649 undergraduates
in such an elaborate plant. With a 1997-98 budget of US$219.5 million (Univer-
sity Grants Committee, 1998), that is a gross student cost of about $US32,286. With

531 academic staff members, the ratio of faculty to students is about 13. Many question UST's practice of hiring large numbers of visiting faculty and researchers for a year or so.

Hong Kong's Academic Budgets and Salaries

In comparison to UST, HKU has 12,021 students, 1,105 academic staff members. With a 1997-98 total budget of US$343.7 million, HKU's gross cost per student was $28,593 with a staff/student ratio of about 11. Since HKU has costly professional degree programs in medicine, law, and dentistry, which UST lacks, the difference of $3,693/student between the two universities highlights UST's expenditure level (US$32,286/student). Also with a medical school, CU's gross cost per student of $28,309 is also less than UST's. Since the three top-tier universities enroll so few postgraduate students, however, CU looks expensive in comparison to major universities in America and Britain. Since their postgraduate students are chiefly master's-level, HK's universities should be compared with master's-level institutions elsewhere, which if the data were at hand would show how generous tertiary budgets are in the SAR.

Leading American universities include a multitude of programs and activities that HK universities do not pursue or much at all, such as competitive athletics for females and males, extensive alumni affairs, rigorous student recruitment and placement services, multi-million dollar fund-raising drives, highly competitive research, etc. Externally funded research at the best U.S. institutions can exceed instructional costs, such as at Stanford where organized research in 1996 totaled $477 million as compared to instructional costs of $408 m. (data for U.S. universities were obtained from their web sites and e-mail).

In HK, academic research funds are mainly obtained from the Government through UGC, only US$43 million in all for 1996, not even one-tenth of Stanford's research grants. However, the $43 m. is greatly improved over the $12.9 m. allocated in 1990 (University Grants Committee, 1996c).

For further comparisons, Stanford's total operating expenses in 1996-97 were US$1.351 billion. Deleting "organized research," which still leaves many non-instructional activities, the gross cost per student was about $63,266. Harvard's total expenses in 1996 were $1.521 billion. Dropping $319.3 m. in research, the per student cost was $68,073. Quite different from HK's universities, both Stanford and Harvard have extensive postgraduate programs and enrollments. In 1996, Stanford enrolled 6,550 undergraduates and 7,261 postgraduate students and Harvard had 6,635 and 11,018, respectively. Both institutions have renowned programs in about every professional and specialist field.

Professorial salaries in Hong Kong are among the world's highest, if not the highest. The average salary for senior, non-medical professors (N=288) as of April 1997 was US$185,279 per annum. The range for academic levels below professor, from senior lecturer (N=596) up to reader (N=254), goes from $104,938 to $145,442 (about twice as much as 1989), and the lowest entry lecturer's salary is $49,193 (University Grants Committee, 1998, pp. 33-34). Despite HK's recession, academic salaries were increased about six percent in 1998 when the HK Government decided to raise civil-service salaries, thus putting the average senior professorial pay at about US$196,396.

Paid about the best in the U.S., non-medical, full professors at Harvard and Stanford average about $115,000 for ten months ($138,000 for 12 months). Averaging US$77,000 per annum, Japan's senior professors supplement their regular salaries by teaching part-time at several universities.

Also unlike most elite U.S. schools, salaries at HK universities are set by rank and seniority on fixed salary charts. As I advised the UGC, with salaries at such levels, Hong Kong should rather consider what elite systems do elsewhere -- negotiate individual professorial contracts with base salaries and increases based on meeting agreed-upon goals, such as generating research grants.

Since Stanford and Harvard are private universities, let's consider two public doctoral-degree institutions in the U.S. for contrast. Below the national average in academic funding and salaries, bargain education is provided by the University of Montana at the cost of $7,000 per student, only 59% of which comes from the State of Montana with the rest gained from tuition and fees.

At the other end of the scale, the University of California, Berkeley (UCB), one of the world's premier insitutions, rivals Stanford and Harvard in prestige. UCB's 1996-97 operating expenses totaled $889 million. With 30,290 students, 21,738 undergraduates and 8,552 postgraduates, the gross student cost is US$29,350, which is highly competitive with HK's universities, especially when UCB's extensive and prestigious postgraduate programs are considered.

Although HK professors earn nearly twice as much as UCB's, they lack the full challenges of postgraduate teaching and research and sponsored research of competitive caliber and magnitude equivalent to grants and contracts from the National Science Foundation, National Institutes of Health, etc. This seems like comparing apples with oranges, for HK's higher education system is different unto itself.

Besides the differences in HK's university funding as compared to Europe and North America, the greatest and most significant disparity is between the SAR and Mainland China. PRC academicians earn less than the likes of taxi drivers and benefits are pathetic. PRC universities are shabby reflections of what they should represent in autonomy, resources, and free inquiry.

The Future

Welsh (1993, p. 481) wrote: "However impressive Hong Kong's health care system, the most surprising advance has been in education." I cannot agree. While education and health care both developed through the humanitarianism of enlightened missionaries and civil servants (see Dr. Choa's Chapter Three) and have been well-supported by the Government, HK's educational system does not merit higher praise than the health and medical system. Comparing the two essential services, however, is rather unfair since health and medical results can be measured unequivocally and related to other places. Results of the health care system have been impressive. Assessing education, Welsh and others, especially those who have not taught in Hong Kong, assess progress in quantitative terms. With its many modern clinics, hospitals, etc., HK's health and medical system is a huge bureaucracy as is education, but it has the advantage (and accountability) of validating itself beyond faith and numbers in terms of the community's quality of life and individual health (see p. 160).

Somehow, the individual and concern for humanizing qualities were lost in HK's educational system, as anti-intellectualism, rote learning, conformity, and costly expenditures became prevalent. For all of the resources that have been poured into higher education -- from two universities to seven since 1985 and increasing tertiary admissions from 5% to 18.6% of the age group, Chinese and Western values in what education should represent, cherishing the young and the learned, inquiring person, have been neglected. Far from a model of Sino-Western education, Hong Kong's tertiary system is a fiscal bubble ripe for popping.

The best time to affect Chinese institutions is when new leadership and conditions arise, similar to the start of a new dynasty when significant change is possible and the advice of creative scholar-officials are heeded. Even if it had intended to do so before 1984, the 1997 handover obfuscated British HK's options in higher education. Instead of moving towards increased quality, the HK Government used a booming economy to throw more and more money at education and boast of the numbers produced, never mind the waste and consequences. Sad to contemplate since the UGC and universities should be masters of their reforms, the prolonged recession may force the SAR Government to retrench higher education with a poleaxe. If it does, blame may be cast at the British.

Written over 130 years ago, Frederick Stewart's concerns about education in Hong Kong are surprisingly relevant today. Most provocative are what he said about rote learning, fiscal scrutiny, and criticizing those who took to education for its cash versus humanizing value. The desideratum of lifelong learning and becoming a whole person is neglected by HK's schools (Yee & Cheng, 1997).

Instruction in Chinese or English. Stewart's views on English competence remain pertinent, since HK students continue to do poorly with English as business leaders have complained often and bitterly of the declining standard of English that they find in graduates. While the poor quality of English in HK has been criticized since Eitel and Stewart, few have come up with explanations and solutions. Those that have been spelled out are ignored (e.g., Yee, 1992b, pp. 304-306). In short, foreign languages will not be learned effectively if students are unmotivated, rote-strained to exams and learning, and do not have home environments that can reinforce language lessons. On the surface, it seems amazing that HK's rich English-language environment has not promoted competency but it may be understandable from the CSS model (see Overview pp. 19-34 & 31-32).

The Education Department (ED) has swung back and forth on what language should be used in the schools. ED's policy shifted once again in 1997 to mandate the use of Chinese ("mother tongue") versus the Chinese-English mix. Believing that their children will do better in university exams and life if they knew English, parents insist on English instruction. With the latest shift, families are pursuing overseas secondary-school education for their youth. Bemoaning the poor English competence of their students, HK universities have been granted UGC language enhancement grants for years, e.g., from US$3.23 million in 1991-1992 to $5.17 million in 1994-95 (University Grants Committee, 1996c, p. 18).

The language issue has enlarged now that Putonghua (Mandarin), China's spoken tongue, is being introduced; but it should be less of a problem than English. While China and Singapore simplified many characters long ago, Hong Kong and Taiwan retained the traditional character forms. About 3,000 teachers have been qualified to teach Putonghua, a core subject in both primary and secondary schools; and the HKCEE will include the "language" as a subject in 2000. Since Cantonese and Putonghua are kin, what will happen to English in this triad is easy to guess. As Governor Christopher Patten said in his handover speech, "Hong Kong is a very Chinese city."

Teaching HK's history. A brief word on history. World War II stands as the abyss; the oppression and chaos of 1942-45 should be related fully and objectively in HK's schools. Although HK experienced inhumanity that few would have believed possible, history should not be taught in one-sided, demonizing or sycophantic tones. The way some speak of inculcating "patriotism" raises concern. As British rule was surely more than the Opium Wars, the history of WW II is far more than the culpability of Japan and its military. Facing danger and death when the thought of education was a luxury, many men and women, British, Chinese, Portuguese, and yes, Japanese too, set examples of heroism and humaneness that have been sadly neglected. There would be more enlightenment if history dealt more with intent, character, and humanity and less with hatred, blame, and nationality. That said, the PRC's handling of Hong Kong should not be measured against the grievous war years. Now that British HK is history, the era of 1841-97 can be assessed fully and fairly.

Education in the PRC. The first American social scientist to visit the PRC, I visited many schools from primaries to universities in 1972 amidst China's devastating Cultural Revolution (Yee, 1973) and after. Although life conditions had improved since 1947-48, I witnessed the tyrannic extremism of the CR and the hard-fisted control over the people and institutions. Universities were closed; most professors were working as farmers and laborers and those on campuses did not hold classes and uttered nonsense (e.g., "Soldiers and workers are more knowledgeable and worthy mentors than scholars"). Though captivated by them at first, I later realized that young school children looked and behaved as marionettes. In the early 1980s, while everybody in the PRC condemned the CR, one could see how the CSS model worked -- China's fluctuating authoritarianism and the pliant conformity of the people.

According to Pepper (1996), educational radicalism tapered down after Mao Zedong's death in 1976 and Deng Xiaoping's pragmatic approaches took hold in the 1980s. However, the universities and student movements have suffered strictures since the Tiananmen massacre. China provides children nine years of compulsory education as in HK, six in primary and three in middle school. Those selected by exams and "potential" for senior high school receive three more years of education and prepare to take the higher education examination.

Beginning in September 1997, a mandatory, annual tuition of about 1,500 yuan (US$180) is required of all university students, which is costly to most Chinese. Annual urban incomes average 4,380 yuan per person and half that for most rural people. HK's per capita was comparable to the U.S. While free education ended, PRC university graduates can now seek jobs on their own instead of working where the Government sent them, typically in the back-country. Optional since 1994, the tuition-work policy is intended to accelerate market forces at the cost of welfare programs. Business and foreign languages are the most popular studies (Herting, 1997; Pay as you learn, 1997).

In 1997-98, PRC students enrolled in U.S. colleges and universities numbered 46,958, an increase of 10.5% from the previous year and second only to 47,073 students from Japan; Taiwan was fifth with 30,855 and HK tenth with 9,665 (Desruisseaux, 1998). Because many in the past have not returned, the PRC has been issuing short-term permits to students, which lets them gain knowledge and skills in America but not degrees.

Compared to Oxbridge (12th century) and Harvard (1636), higher education in East Asia is infantile (see p. 233). Few Chinese universities existed a century ago. On May 5, 1998, Beijing (Peking) University, famed for its intellectual and revolutionary leadership (as in the May 4th Movement, 1919, Scalapino & Yu, 1985, pp. 460-463) celebrated its 100th anniversary. Although the number of PRC institutions of higher learning have greatly increased, 1,080 in 1994 with 2.8 million students enrolled (World Bank, 1997, p. 9; Annexes 5 & 6) and more are added each year, the logistics of providing advanced learning for a population of over 1.2 billion is staggering. Compared to HK's 11% and N. America's 20%, only 2% of the PRC's population aged 25 and over have completed tertiary degrees.

For its population of 225 million, the U.S. has about 3,150 institutions of higher learning, more than twice that of the PRC. Of the 1,080 institutions reported in 1994, 70 were designated as "comprehensive universities" to distinguish them from specialized and lower-tier institutions. PRC data for higher education have been questioned, such as by Hamrin (1990, pp. 171-174), who charged that the PRC's higher education figures are highly distorted, such as reporting more tertiary students than secondary graduates in the 1950s. Also, many local universities are mere names, and many have liquid assets of less than US$15,000 and few or no buildings. Earning less than US$100 per month, professors work part-time for extra cash, providing private teaching and industrial skills.

According to the World Bank (1997), which has granted US$910.4 million to eight PRC academic projects from 1981 to 1997, the PRC Government continues to hold tight reins on its higher education system. Although the Government is said to be assessing the universities' readiness to assume "new responsibilities" by gradually shifting from a 'state-control' to 'state-supervising model,' that appears to be no change at all. One detects from the Bank's many recommendations for university reform in the Mainland that the leading problems are state authoritarianism and lack of an " 'enabling environment' in which institutions can have greater financial and managerial autonomy" (pp. viv-xvi). The contrast with HK's tertiary system is like night and day.

On the positive side, however, Hayhoe & Zhong (1994) indicated that university scientists in Mainland China are increasingly productive researchers and their publications are gaining visibility in international database systems, hopeful signs of progress. The PRC honors scientific research in the hard sciences but is wary of social-science publications. Ranking universities by the number of journal articles published internationally and total citations in international journals in 1996, China's State Science and Technology Commission ranked the top five universities as follows: Nanjing University, Beijing University, Qinhua University, the University of Science and Technology, and Fudan University. The report said that China ranked 11th in the world with the total of 27,569 papers published in international journals and presented at international meetings in 1996 (*HK Standard*, Internet edition, Dec. 21, 1997).

However, as Zhu Lilan (1999), PRC Minister of Science and Technology wrote: The PRC lags far behind the U.S. by only publishing 5% as much research -- "Basic research in China faces problems because of the lack of innovations and major breakthroughs with an international impact, the lack of an effective mechanism for optimal personnel flow, and the lack of young people involved in basic research."

Now that HK is Chinese soil, let us see how universities relate across the PRC/SAR border. Originating from the same remarkable Anglo-American sources reviewed earlier and building on Asian ingenuity and industry as well as the knowledge and practices of leading world universities, Hong Kong's higher education system could represent the best of East and West if its decision-makers would only define their institutions as such and worked at it qualitatively. Also, the UGC must institute and enforce central accountability. What HK's universities are today is neither East nor West; they can only be accepted in local terms.

This chapter began by likening Hong Kong's educational void in 1841 to a blank canvas, i.e., a clean slate. When Britain returned what had been its foster child for 156 years to the PRC, rich and clashing colors and forms swarmed over the educational canvas. How would pioneers, humanitarians all and mostly Westerners, such as Morrison, Bridgman, Parker, Legge, Baxter, Stewart, Eitel, Manson, Cantlie, Ho Kai, King, Ride, etc., assess the outcome today?

Churning and fat, Hong Kong's educational system has grown by leaps and bounds in recent times, particularly in higher education. Recession or not, Hong

Kong's universities are high-priced enterprises that do not compare well with world-class institutions elsewhere and what they produce. Looming in the background is the fact that one of the most glaring contrasts between the PRC and its SAR lies in their higher education systems -- world's richest and poorest.

It is one thing to view institutions philosophically as having a free press and another thing when they are government facilities, personnel, and budgets. The latter being material, they can be grasped and turned around more easily, no matter what they were intended to represent. Therefore, despite the "one country, two systems" policy, will SAR and PRC authorities as well as Mainland universities, their being among the most regimented and underfunded in the world, begin to question the gaping differences between the PRC's higher education system and that of their compatriots? If they do, let it be that higher education in the PRC gains, not through HK's loss so much as to bring greater quality to both. Whatever happens in the coming decades of the new century, Hong Kong's higher education system presents an intriguing case study for scholars in economics, management, public administration, and higher education.

References

A national identity crisis (1996, December 14). *Economist*, pp. 39-41.

Beeching, Jack (1975). *The Chinese opium wars*. NY: Harcourt Brace Jovanovich.

Brimer, M. A. (1988). Hong Kong. In T. N. Postlethwaite (Ed.), *The encyclopedia of comparative education and national systems of education*. Oxford: Pergamon.

Britt, Suzanne (1998, December). Generation A+. *Sky*, pp. 30-33.

Cheng, Irene (1976). *Clara Ho Tung: A Hong Kong lady, her family and her times*. Hong Kong: The Chinese University of Hong Kong.

Daryanani, Renu (Ed.) (1995). *Hong Kong 1995*. Hong Kong: HK Government Printing Department.

Desruisseaux, Paul (1998, December 11). 2-year colleges at crest of wave in U.S. enrollment by foreign students. *Chronicle of Higher Education*, pp. A66- A71.

D'Este, Carlo (1995). *Patton: A genius for war*. New York: HarperCollins.

Eitel, E. J. (1895). *Europe in China*. Hong Kong: Kelly & Walsh (Reprinted Oxford University Press, Hong Kong, 1983).

Endacott, G. B. (1973). *A history of Hong Kong* (2nd ed., rev.). Hong Kong: Oxford Univesity Press.

Fairbank, John King (1969). *Trade and diplomacy on the China coast*. Stanford: Stanford University Press.

Fay, Peter Ward (1975). *The opium war 1840-1842*. New York: Norton.

Geary, David C. (1996). International differences in mathematical achievement: Their nature, causes, and consequences. *Psychological Science, 5*(5), 133-137.

Hamrin, Carol Lee (1990). *China and the challenge of the future: Changing political patterns*. Boulder, CO: Westview.

Harrison, Brian (1979). *Waiting for China*. Hong Kong: HK University Press.

Hayhoe, Ruth & Zhong, Wenhui (1994). Universities and science in China: New visibility in the world community. In A. H. Yee (Ed.), *East Asian higher education: Traditions and transformations* (pp. 122-134). Oxford: Pergamon.

Herting, James (1997, May 16). China will charge tuition at all of its universities. *Chronicle of Higher Education*, p. A39.

Howlett, Bob (Ed.) (1996). *Hong Kong 1996*. HK: HK Government Printing Dept.

Huang, Evelyn & Jeffrey, Lawrence (1995). *Hong Kong: Portraits of power*. London: Weidenfelf & Nicolson.

Jen, Y. W. & Ride, Lindsay (1970). *Sun Yat-sen: Two commemorative essays*. Hong Kong: Centre of Asian Studies: University of Hong Kong.

Kwok, Shirley (1997, July 11). Worsening English 'to cut college standards.' *South China Morning Post*, Internet Edition.

Kwok, Shirley (1998, March 26). Students told to get act together. *South China Morning Post*, Internet Edition

Lai, Chloe (1998, March 29). Universities to receive more funding. *HK Standard*, Internet Edition.

Lai, Chloe (1999, January 24). Views sought on students of the future. *HK Standard*, Internet Edition.

Lim, Teck Ghee (1994). Malaysian and Singaporean higher education: Common roots but differing directions. In A. H. Yee (Ed.), *East Asian higher education: Traditions and transformations* (pp. 69-83). Oxford: Pergamon/Elsevier.

Lin, T. Y. (1984). Mental health and family values. Public lecture at Chung Chi College, Chinese University of Hong Kong, March 1.

Lively, Kit (1997, June 13). What's in a name? Just ask colleges that want to be called universities. *Chronicle of Higher Education*, pp. A33-A34.

Lo, H. L. (1963). *The role of Hong Kong in the cultural interchange between East and West*. Tokyo: Centre for East Asian Cultural Studies, Tokyo University.

Lodwick, Kathleen D. (1996). *Against opium: Protestant missionaries in China, 1874-1912*. Lexington, KT: University Press of Kentucky.

Lutz, J. G. (1971). *China and the Christian colleges 1850-1950*. Ithaca, NY: Cornell University Press.

Matthew, Anne (1997). *Bright college years: Inside the American campus today*. New York: Simon & Schuster.

Mellor, G. (1980). *The University of Hong Kong* (Vol. 1). HK: HK University Press.

Mori, Watari (1994). The University of Tokyo: The graduate school reformation project. In A. H. Yee (Ed.), *East Asian higher education: Traditions and transformations* (pp. 22-24). Oxford: Pergamon.

Park, Nancy E. (1997). Corruption in eighteenth-century China. *Journal of Asia Studies, 56*(4), 967-1005.

Pay as you learn (1997, May 10). *Economist*, pp. 32-33.

Pepper, Suzanne (1996). *Radicalism and education reform in 20th century China*. Cambridge: Cambridge University Press.

Pires, B. V. (1987). Originis and early history of Macau. In R. C. Cremer (Ed.), *Macau: City of commerce and culture* (pp. 7-21). Hong Kong: UEA Press.

'Private club' must answer to public (1998, April 1). *South China Morning Post*, Internet Edition.

Ranuwihardjo, Sukadji (1994). Higher education in Indonesia: Its development, problems, and prospects. In A. H. Yee (Ed.), *East Asian higher education: Traditions and transformations* (pp. 84-91). Oxford: Pergamon/Elsevier.

Reischauer, E. O. (1971). *The Japanese*. Cambridge, MA: Belknap Press.

Reynolds, Jason M. (1998, May 22). Faculty salaries rose 3.2% this year at public and private colleges, survey says. *Chronicle of Higher Education*, p. A14.

Ride, Lindsay (1957). *Robert Morrison: The scholar and the man*. Hong Kong: University of Hong Kong Press.

Scalapino, Robert A. & Yu, George T. (1985). *Modern China and its revolutionary Process*. Berkeley, CA: University of California Press.

Smith, Alison (1997, December 13). Bright students fall victim to boring, stressful curriculum. *South China Morning Post*, Internet Edition.

Sweeting, Anthony (1993). *A phoenix transformed: The reconstruction of education in post-war Hong Kong*. Hong Kong: Oxford University Press.

Thomson, J. C., Stanley, P. W., & Perry, J. C. (1981). *Sentimental imperialists: The American experience in East Asia*. New York: Harper & Row.

Trocki, Carl A. (1990). *Opium and empire: Chinese society in colonial Singapore, 1800-1910*. Ithaca, NY: Cornell University Press.

Trout, Paul A. (1998, July 24). Incivility in the classroom breeds "education lite.' *Chronicle of Higher Education*, p. A40.

Tsurumi, E. Patricia (1977). *Japanese colonial education in Taiwan, 1895-1945*. Cambridge, MA: Harvard University Press.

University Grants Committee (1996a). *Report for July 1991 to June 1995*. Hong Kong: UGC Secretariat.

University Grants Committee (1996b). *Higher education in Hong Kong*. Hong Kong: UGC Secretariat.

University Grants Committee (1996c). *Research grants council of Hong Kong: Annual report*. Hong Kong: UGC Secretariat.

University Grants Committee (1998). *Facts and figures 1997*. Hong Kong: UGC Secretariat.

Welsh, Frank (1993). *A history of Hong Kong*. London: HarperCollins.

World Bank (1997). *China: Higher education reform*. Washington, DC: World Bank.

Yamamoto, Shinichi (1994). Traditionalism versus research and development at Japanese universities. In Albert H. Yee (Ed.), *East Asian higher education: Traditions and transformations* (pp. 25-35). Oxford: Pergamon.

Yee, Albert H. (1973a). Psychology in China bows to the Cultural Revolution. *APA Monitor, 4*(3), 1 & 4.

Yee, Albert H. (1987). Missionary education in Macau and Brazil: Tragic conflict between the Jesuits and dictatorship. *New Horizons, 28*, 109-116.

Yee, Albert H. (1988). Universities in Hong Kong and Macau: A tale of two colonies. *Higher Education Policy, 1*(4), 16-22.

Yee, Albert H. (1989). Cross-cultural perspectives on higher education in East Asia: Psychological effects upon Asian students. *Journal of Multilingual and Multicultural Development, 10*(3), 213-232.

Yee, Albert H. (1990). A comparative study of Macau's education system: Changing colonial patronage and native self-reliance. *Comparative Education, 26*(1), 61-71.

Yee, Albert H. (1992a) Asians as stereotypes and students: Misperceptions that persist. *Educational Psychology Review, 4*(1), 95-132.

Yee, Albert H. (1992b). *A people misruled: The Chinese stepping-stone syndrome* (2nd ed., rev.). Singapore: Heinemann Asia.

Yee, Albert H. (Ed.) (1994). *East Asian higher education: Traditions and transformations*. Oxford: Pergamon/Elsevier.

Yee, Albert H. & Cheng, Joseph Y.S. (1997). Lifelong learning in the United States and Hong Kong: Before 1997 and after. In Michael J. Hatton (Ed.), *Lifelong learning: Policies, practices, and programs*. Toronto: Humber College.

Yee, Albert H. & Lim, Teck Ghee (1994). Educational supply and demand in East Asia: Private higher education. In A. H. Yee (Ed.), *East Asian higher education: Traditions and transformations* (pp. 179-192). Oxford: Pergamon/ Elsevier.

Yung Wing (1909). *My life in China and America*. New York: Henry Holt.

Zhu, Lilan (1999). Basic research in China. *Science, 283*, 637.

CHAPTER SIX

Barren Rock to World Entrepot:
Economic Developments and Issues

Ian K. Perkin

To get rich is glorious. Deng Xiaoping, 1988

Hong Kong has always been an economic city, never a political city. Lu Ping, Former Director, China's Hong Kong and Macau Affairs Office, in Hong Kong, 1994.

Millions of people around the world identify with Hong Kong through its mid-1997 return to Chinese sovereignty, the globally televised ceremonies of the "handover" on June 30, 1997, and the continuing media coverage of the post-transition process. Few know much about Hong Kong's history, especially its economic history, and what they may know probably only extends from the arrival of the British in 1841. Most Westerners' knowledge of this place on the southern edge of the vast Chinese mainland may involve memories of a tourist stop on the way to China or elsewhere, or perhaps its manufactured products and films.

Yet Hong Kong, in its former guise as a British colony, or its new one as a Special Administrative Region (SAR) of the People's Republic of China (PRC), is one of the economic powerhouses of East Asia. This chapter will provide a brief background to Hong Kong's economic development from a "barren rock" (as the then British Foreign Secretary, Lord Palmerston, dismissively described it in 1841) to a world trade and financial entrepot, its current economic progress, and prospects as the HKSAR of the People's Republic of China.

Hong Kong's Place in the World

Hong Kong remains an economic and political oddity on the global stage. Ceded to Imperial Great Britain in war in 1841, it was returned to Chinese sovereignty in 1997 in peace. A relatively small economic entity [6.3+ million people in 1,000 square kilometres with a Gross Domestic Product (GDP) of some US$160 billion, or a high US$25,000+ per capita], Hong Kong nevertheless plays a far larger role on the global business and financial stage than its size suggests. One of the freest and most-open marketplaces anywhere on the globe, it has found its way in the modern world through the ingenuity and drive of its people, its low taxes, rule of law, respect for business and property rights, tremendous physical infrastructure and unbridled capitalism. A free and open society in most ways, its political development has been restricted, first by its colonial status under British rule and subsequently under the sovereignty of the PRC and its Chinese Communist Party (CCP) rule.

Hong Kong is unique, too, in the manner in which it was returned to its former and present "motherland" of China. It is not just that it was returned, rich and in peace, to China, but the manner of its return is important to its economic and political future and its prospective place in the world. Britain agreed to HK's return to the PRC under an elaborate set of arrangements known as the Sino-British Joint Declaration. It effectively set down the timetable and the conditions under which Hong Kong would be returned on July 1, 1997 and how it would operate, economically and politically in the post-return environment.

Containing many complex details that cover all aspects of Hong Kong's economic, political and social life, the Declaration is essentially summed up in three phrases used popularly to describe HK's status. The first, "one country, two systems" recognizes China as a single country but with two systems of operation, one capitalist, the other socialist. The second, a "high degree of autonomy," meaning HK would run itself and have its own place in world economic affairs. And the third, "Hong Kong people ruling Hong Kong," meaning rule would be by local people, not by Beijing and CCP officials. Key exceptions to HK's governance are, however, are in the fields of foreign affairs and defense, where the sovereign state has authority. Finally, and importantly, the arrangements are to remain in place for a period of 50 years to the year 2047.

Subsequently, the major provisions of the Declaration between Britain and China, as well as some other matters, were formalized further in the Basic Law of the SAR. This document was the product of a Basic Law Drafting Committee comprised of HK and PRC representatives. Like the Declaration, the Basic Law not only deals with HK's political development but also its future economic status as well. Described as the "mini-constitution" of the HKSAR, it sets the political, social and, importantly, economic ground rules under which the new entity should operate. Therefore, with HK's return to China, all developments in the SAR must be measured against provisions of the Basic Law.

Hong Kong and China: Historic Economic Links

Throughout its entire economic history, HK's development has been determined through its relations -- or absence of relations -- with its natural parent. This point was made most eloquently in 1997 by Professor Richard Wong Yue-chim, Director, the Hong Kong Center for Economic Research at the University of Hong Kong, in an instructive speech "Hong Kong Growing As Part of China: A Historical Perspective, 1997." In that address, he said: "Hong Kong's relationship with the Chinese Mainland is fundamental in defining the shape and scope of economic and social affairs in the territory. It sets in motion forces which their totality determine the environment for public policy choices which the HK Government faces not only in political affairs, but also in economic and social matters."

While knowledge and discussion of Hong Kong in the West tends to date from 1841when the British took possession of the territory during the First Opium War (See the Overview and Chapter One), the place did have a prior history and, of course, an economic role. As Professor Wong pointed out, HK and its immediate environs were active commercially long before the British arrived on the scene. Hong Kong and the immediate region of southern China were, as he says, a natural crossroads and entry point to China well before the Europeans arrived. The Pearl River Delta (see Map One), where HK is situated was well-known for its salt pans, producing an important trading commodity. As Wong said, from the limited available records of HK's early history, two points stand out: "First, the territory was a natural crossroads for trade and cultural intercourse . . . by virtue of its geographic location and natural endowments. Second, the territory thrived in the Tang and Song dynasties when governments of China pursued an open door policy, and declined in the Yuan, Ming and early Qing dynasties when policies turned inward and became insular. The forcible opening of China in the Qing Dynasty . . . and the loss of Hong Kong to Britain heralded a new chapter in the development of Hong Kong." It brought about the beginnings of HK's thriving role as a trading post, or entrepot, between China and the rest of the world. It established a key link between East and West, which the Overview describes as the vital stepping-stone.

During the 50 years since the PRC was created in 1949, the economic entity that is HK has recreated itself several times. First, it emerged from its pre-World War II entrepot role to become a dynamic light manufacturing center for consumer goods. Then, in the 1980s, it moved from being a light manufacturing center in its own right to become a major trade, business and financial services center for the PRC, the East Asian region and the world. The most important factor in each of HK's transformations was its relationship with China. The first changeover in the early 1950s resembles what happened during the Yuan, Ming and early Qing dynasties, in that it involved an effective closing of the Mainland to foreigners, causing Hong Kong to rely on its own resources. The second transformation approximates what happened during the Tang and Song dynasties as the PRC economy opened to the outside world. In this second transformation, HK moved its manufacturing to cheaper production areas in Southern China itself and resumed its role as a city of commerce, finance and shipping for its region and beyond.

With its return to Chinese sovereignty, HK effectively converted itself yet again. As the new political entity of SAR of the PRC came to being at midnight, June 30, 1997, HK became China's most advanced business and financial center with no disruptions because of the elaborate preparations.

Coping with Change

Dramatic change is definitely something that Hong Kong can handle well. As mentioned, throughout 156 years of British rule, Hong Kong reinvented itself several times -- from a sleepy fishing village on China's south coast to a thriving entreport for China trade; then to light manufacturing center in the 1950s; and from light manufacturing to services center in the 1980s. Embargoes during the Korean War (1950-53) by the United Nations and United States effectively cut off HK's commerce with China. In the 1950s, therefore, HK became a substantial manufacturing base in order to survive economically, while it was separated from its natural parent and lacked the sustenance of bilateral trade and investment with its natural hinterland. After the late paramount leader, Deng Xiaoping, implemented the PRC's "open door policy" in 1978-79, Hong Kong initially returned gradually and then rapidly to its entrepot role of international shipping and commerce. It also shifted manufacturing into China and established itself as a services base for China and the region.

However, despite the business-as-usual atmosphere, HK's return to China has raised questions about the SAR's future economic direction. For example, what role will HK assume in its SAR relation to Mainland China and outwardly, in relation to the Asian region and the rest of the world? Will HK maintain its role as a major international city for free trade and finance or will it become increasingly China orientated? Since HK's manufacturing base has been operating across the border in the PRC for many years, will its trade and financial services sectors also follow when major PRC cities have appropriate, reliable infrastructures in place? As HK is already an expensive place to do business in regional and global terms, will it be able to maintain its lead roles as a major trading and financial services center for the region and the world? Faced with fierce competition throughout East Asia (from Singapore and Sydney) and from within China (Shanghai, Guangzhou, Beijing), how will Hong Kong retain its competitive advantage? Will ultimate control over HK's future by the SAR Government and China alter the views of international business towards HK and its future as a regional and global international center? These are questions that the SAR Administration is addressing.

For their part, Beijing authorities have made it clear that as long as Hong Kong remains an "economic city" and does not become a "political city," it will retain a high degree of autonomy in its determining its own future. This has been the long-standing policy of Beijing and is reflected in the quotation at the beginning of this chapter from Lu Ping, formerly head of Beijing's department overseeing HK's return to China. It can be seen that the high degree of autonomy guaranteed Hong Kong enables the SAR to change its economic role if it is deemed necessary. Indeed, the Basic Law, the SAR's mini-constitution, guarantees the freedom to act as an independent business center for 50 years to 2047. This clearly opens the way for a change of direction from within. On the other hand, Beijing has also clearly signaled that it want to use HK for what was in the past and what it remains today, a free port and international financial center.

Radical Economic Restructuring

There is no denying that HK's economy has radically changed since Deng's policies began in 1978. As Table 6.1 dramatically shows, as services began to dominate the economy, the manufacturing sector shrank as a proportion of overall GDP, the total output of goods and services. For some, this dramatic change has brought with it a potential economic fragility which may well have been exposed by the onset of East Asia's financial crisis mid-way through the handover year of 1997.

Alert to these developments, the HK Government and business community moved to protect its economy vis-a-vis other centers in the region. To ensure that Hong Kong retain its competitive position, the previous British adminis- tration established steps that the new SAR Government continues to follow. Those steps attempt to enhance HK's vital trading and services industry base. The SAR Administration under Chief Executive, Tung Chee-hwa, has announced new initiatives in information technology, industry and innovation policies aimed at ensuring HK's regional leadership. With each major policy initiative, the Chief Executive has appeared to take this new approach one step further, leaning towards a more interventionist stance by the Government in determining the SAR's economic future, through industrial policies and apparently encouraging the re-development of a higher valued-added manufacturing industry.

While the SAR obviously holds a strategic and infrastructural advantage in serving the PRC and East Asia, particularly in trading, finance and other services, it realizes that it does not have a permanent monopoly. This was brought home all the more solidly to the new SAR administration with the onset of East Asia's financial turmoil from the middle of 1997. The crisis and HK's reaction had direct effects on HK's relative competitiveness, its over-all financial status in East Asia, and its standing as a world financial center. Across the border, Beijing has its own ambitions and, while still favoring Hong Kong, has extended its links further afield in seeking the services it requires.

Table 6.1

ECONOMIC CHANGE IN HONG KONG 1979-1997[4]			
	1997[3]	1984[2]	1979[1]
GDP (US$ billion)	170.1	32.9	14.3
GDP per capita (US$)	26,166	6,092	2,906
GDP by sector (%) (1995)			
- Industry	16.0	32.2	32.0
- Manufacturing	8.8	24.3	23.7
- Agriculture	0.1	0.5	0.8
- Services	83.8	67.3	67.2
Trade – China Share (%)			
- Total Exports	34.9	17.8	8.3
- Total Imports	37.7	25.0	17.6
- Outward Processing"	82.0	N.A.	N.A.
Employment by Sector (%)			
- Industry	14.0	34.2	44.0
- Other (inc. Services)	86.0	65.8	56.0
Enterprises by Sector (%)			
- Industry	9.0	27.4	32.0
- Other (inc. Services)	91.0	72.6	68.0
Investment (US$ billion)			
- Hong Kong in China	72.0	0.7	0.3
- China in Hong Kong	42.5	N.A.	N.A.
Travel (million)			
- Visitors from China	2.29	0.3	0.1
- Visitors to China	33.68	8.0	3.0

Notes: (1) China "Open door" policy adopted
(2) Joint Declaration signed (19 December 1984)
(3) Current figures
(4) Updated: March 1998 (All conversions at HK$7.80 = US$1.00)

The PCR's ability to provide domestic services skills in all areas, including finance, will also improve as it builds its infrastructure and skills base. HK realizes that its own cost base increased substantially in recent years, chiefly through rapid rises in wages and rents, although these declined rapidly in late 1997 and 1998 as the East Asian contagion hit Hong Kong hard.

Concerned with this threat to its competitive edge, the HK Government, as mentioned earlier, had launched a program to promote HK's role as a services center, an activity that is continuing. This program's framework for action has targeted key segments of the services sector, especially trade in services (HK's services skills overseas), telecommunications and information technology, tourism development and the expansion of the financial services sector. Within financial services, particular attention has been directed at the development of the HK debt market establishment of a Mortgage Corporation and a planned Mandatory Provident Fund (MPF) for compulsory, fully-funded retirement schemes in the private sector. Directed against the aggressive marketing of services regionally and globally by Singapore and other centers, the HK initiative was sure to bring counteraction. In fact, as HK's campaign became even more aggressive towards the close of 1998, Singapore countered by cost-cutting and taking deregulatory and direct competitive moves. The SAR Government, however, believes it has one chief card that no other center can play -- its intimate, political and geographic ties with China and its possible future role as a major service center for the potentially huge Mainland market.

At the same time, the SAR government has gone into an entirely new direction which the British were unwilling to explore. Under pressure from some sectors of the business and wider community that believe the SAR's economic structure has become unbalanced by being tipped too far in the direction of services, the SAR Government has begun to examine the prospect of introducing some sort of industry policy. This would be aimed at directly encouraging higher value-added and higher technology industries in all areas. Still others in the community are opposed to any more overt Government intervention to encourage the redevelopment of the SAR's domestic economic base. They argue that Hong Kong now has to be viewed as part of a bigger whole, having its manufacturing base in southern China and the services center for that cross-border base situated in HK itself. They also argue that public and private sector attention directed to manufacturing renewal might see HK's services strengths side-lined and ignored.

Unlike Singapore, where government direction is the norm in promoting broad-based economic development, it has been anathema in Hong Kong, one big difference that helps to explain the nature of both entrepots.

On the Way to Transition

Fortunately, during the nearly 13 years leading up to the handover in mid-1997 after the Sino-British Joint Declaration was signed in 1984, HK's economic performance was devoid of trauma and characterized by steady, if unspectacular, growth by modern East Asian standards. This had less to do with the political, economic and social aspects of the transition process than it did with changes initiated in conjunction with China, in particular, the dramatic alteration in the structure of HK's economy during the almost two decades of China's "open door policy" (1978 to 1997 and beyond). As HK moved rapidly towards a greater service-based economy (less than 7% of its GDP now comes from manufacturing), so too did its medium-term growth rate moderate to an expected range of 2-6% annually.

Only events of catastrophic impact, such as a global recession, a slump in major markets (the USA, China, Europe and Japan) and a major regional financial crisis shattering domestic confidence, were believed to have the potential to throw HK's economy from its projected growth. This was dramatically illustrated by the onset of East Asia's financial crisis when the SAR's economic expansion suddenly came to a halt. After growth in excess of 5.3% in the handover year of 1997, with the fastest pace being in the first six months, the SAR economy contracted dramatically in 1998 by some five percent.

Hong Kong's great advantages, economically and politically, in its momentous transition were three-fold: (1) the generous length of time given to adjust to the circumstances of the transition, i.e., ample preparation during the 12 years, 6 months and 12 days from the December 19, 1984 signing of the Declaration to the handover date of July 1, 1997; (2) the great economic changes that have occurred in China since 1978-79, which provided a very conducive environment in China for the reunion; and (3) HK's domestic prosperity. For the most part, HK had enjoyed the third circumstance since 1984.

Historically, transitions from colonial rule, whether in Asia, Africa or elsewhere, were characterized by economic dislocation for the country or territory undergoing the transformation, usually to some sort of self-rule. HK's case was different, of course, with the territory being returned to China under the unique "one country, two systems" prescription. Instead of taking total responsibility for HK's destiny, China promised a "high degree of autonomy" under its sovereignty. The expansion of Mainland business interests and direct investment in HK in recent years by state-and provincially-owned corporations also added a special dimension to Beijing's direct and growing financial interest in the territory's economy as well.

Establishing the groundwork: The 1996 Recovery. While frequent political crises and economic uncertainties affected Hong Kong in 1996, there was gradual recovery in economic growth, better consumer price inflation and employment outcomes and, importantly, a resumption of the upward spiral in both the residential property and equity markets. The year was essentially an economic drama performed in two acts. The first half of 1996 saw the economy hitting its low point before a hesitant recovery began in the face of external political crises (the cross-straits tensions between China and Taiwan and later the Daioyu Island dispute) and trade uncertainties (USA-PRC disputes over intellectual property, textiles, and arms sales).

Other concerns were also on the fore-front front -- controversy in the U.S. over China's Most Favored Nation status and fears that the U.S. Federal Reserve Board would raise short term interest rates to slow the U.S. economy and head-off any developing inflationary pressures.

With these external political and trade uncertainties removed and a U.S. economy with low inflation taking pressure off the interest rate front, HK's pace of economic growth picked up during the second half of 1996. Both the residential property and equity markets surged ahead to near- and record levels, respectively. These developments were accompanied by slightly better domestic consumption in the latter half of 1996. There was also a continued strong investment performance in both the public and private sectors as the year progressed. While external trade in goods continued to be weak throughout the year, services trade performed well (although not up to original expectations because of the easing in demand for the trade-related services as merchandise trade growth fell away as the year progressed).

Calendar 1996, therefore, was a mirror image of 1995 when a good start to the year was followed by a gradual decline in economic activity and expectations. Fortunately for the 1997 handover, the better economic times were to continue into the transition year -- at least until the Asian crisis hit home later in the year.

The economy during the transition year. As HK entered its last year under British rule, it became apparent that economic recovery was going to smooth the transfer process. The territory's financial markets, in typical fashion, led the way with the HK share market's Hang Seng Index soaring to record levels in the second half of the 1996 calendar year and continuing through the handover into August 1997 when the market peaked at 16,600 points on August 8th. The local property market responded well to the better economic and interest rate outlook and prices rose in all sectors, although most notably in the upper end of the residential market. More moderate consumer price inflation and stable interest rates were positive for increased levels of activity in most sectors and the growth rate in GDP picked up throughout the year. HK's finances were extremely healthy with strong fiscal and foreign reserves. Budget surpluses in 1996 were expected to continue in subsequent years before the fiscal crisis hit.

The HK dollar remained on the strong side of the HK$7.80 linked rate (dollar "peg" controlled by HK's Currency Board System) to the U.S. dollar as capital inflows and confidence remained firm. Employment growth was extremely positive throughout 1997 and unemployment, after a brief increase in late 1995 and early 1996, again declined to historically acceptable levels.

Surveys of public opinion showed economic and political confidence improving substantially throughout the year. While there were still some weaknesses in the real economy, principally in modest external merchandise trade growth and domestic consumption, there were some very real strengths as well, especially in investment and external services trade and property market activity.

As the all-important year of 1997 approached, the immediate outlook for global growth with low inflation was also positive for the SAR and a smooth handover, providing HK and Beijing with a comfortable economic environment for the return of sovereignty. Also, Britain could depart with more grace than what might have been in 1998-1999. Although Asian regional expansion slowed somewhat during 1996 and into 1997, overall economic growth was still relatively strong. Beijing authorities were confident that their country's economy, which had become so important to HK's economic health, had reached the fabled "soft landing" with growth moderating to around the 8% target rate and national inflation well below expectations at less than 5%.

The forercast for the transition year in Hong Kong itself was for steady growth in excess of the then HK Government's medium range forecast growth rate for GDP of 5%, relatively low consumer price inflation and continuing low unemployment. The HK dollar was forecasted to remain on the firm side of the HK $7.80 "pegged rate" to the US dollar, interest rates were expected to remain low, all sectors of the property market strong, and the Government's own finances in an extremely healthy state. Government spending on capital works, especially the new US$21+ billion Chek Lap Kok airport complex and related projects was expected to slow somewhat during the transition year, but private sector investment was forecasted to improve along with overall consumption spending as a result of transitional factors.

Swelled by the flow-on effects of the handover celebrations and the accompanying influx of tourists and others during at least the first half of the transition year, domestic consumption was expected to improve. But the one-time positive impact on growth was expected to be offset by continued weakness on the external merchandise trade account.

Assessing the Transition Year

The historic importance of Hong Kong's 1997 transition made economic forecasting less difficult in some respects and more difficult in others. It became apparent, for example, that HK's return would bring a substantial injection of vigor into the economy, with expenditures on a whole range of events associated with it, as well as a huge influx of visitors in the first half of the year at least. There was greater uncertainty, however, as to how the almost exclusive focus on sovereignty issues might detract attention from other aspects of the economy. In addition, there were concerns about the actual outcome in the second half of the year. Although many expected that the post-handover period would lift domestic demand above the more restrained levels of the previous two years, onset of the East Asian crisis more than confirmed the skeptics.

Continued spending on the expansive Chek Lap Kok Airport complex (opened on July 6, 1998) and other infrastructure projects helped to boost HK's growth in 1997. Private sector investments also continued. Beyond HK's control, however, a question mark still existed over the likely direction of the merchandise trade account -- concerns over flat demand from major foreign markets (the USA,

EU and Japan), intra-regional trade growth slowing, and probable modest growth in China trade. Trade squabbles, especially regarding textiles and intelleclectual property as well as the annual ordeal of MFN trade status renewal by the U.S. for China, would bring momentary uncertainties. As for the Mainland's economy itself, growth was expected to be fairly steady around 8-10% as Beijing made it clear that they did not want to see the economy balloon the way it did in 1993 and 1994 with consequent inflationary risks. External trade-in-services were expected to continue to show good growth but not provide a substantial boost to the overall economy.

The property market was expected to remain firm. As the HK stock market in moved into totally uncharted territory in 1996, a question mark was hanging over its future performance. Much would also depend on the future direction of the U.S. economy, both in terms of the likely economic growth rate in that premier market and in the future direction of interest rates. On balance, however, expectations were for a modest upturn in real economic growth to something above 5.8 per cent, with relatively low inflation (5-6% annual average) and continued strong employment performance, with low unemployment rate (around 2.5%).

It was the unexpected which was the major concern for economic stability in 1997, with crisis in the financial or equity markets seemingly the most likely potential culprit. With hindsight, this proved all too accurate as East Asia's crisis fell. Yet there had been warnings. In a special handover preview article in *The South China Morning Post*, virtually on the eve of the return of sovereignty (June 29, 1997), I wrote that economic difficulties could be more important than changeover problems for the new SAR Administration: "There is a very real case to be made that decisions in the economic area in the first 12 months (of the handover) could be as important as the political process that must necessarily be gone through . . . . The danger is that economic conditions may move against the SAR globally and, more specifically, in the region and China, in the coming twelve months and the very open HK economy will feel the effects very substantially."

As Hong Kong prepared itself for its all-important transition, however, it was apparent that the economy would have a positive run-up to the July 1st handover. The economy continued to be buoyed by capital investment, initially in public projects (including the massive airport core program) and then from greater private sector investment. There was some recovery in domestic consumption and services trade (including tourism) stayed positive. Activity in the property and share markets also improved substantially.

A negative for growth continued to be external merchandise trade growth, with significant decline in domestic exports and much slower growth in re-export activity and transshipment. However, imports also slowed, reducing the trade deficit and the burden on overall GDP growth. The weakness in domestic exports was also reflected in domestic production, with orders on hand in manufacturing declining throughout the year. Far more satisfactory from an overall economic perspective was the continued easing of inflationary pressures during the year.

All four measures of consumer price inflation eased throughout the 1996 year and were running, on average, a good two or three percent below the past year's levels and this improved positive continued into 1997.

The Transition Year:
Recent Economic Performance

In economics, it is the unexpected that always causes the greatest trauma. And so it was with Hong Kong as it made its historic transition from British colony to China's SAR in mid-1997. Barely had the Royal Yacht Britannia left on its own last official voyage with the Prince of Wales and last Governor of Hong Kong, Chris Patten, on board, the economic clouds began to gather in East Asia. Soon after the senior Chinese leadership of President Jiang Zemin, then Prime Minister Li Peng, and Prime Minister-to-be Zhu Rongji proudly witnessed the return of Hong Kong, the East Asian economic miracle began to collapse.

HK's return to China was an immerse success, despite the inclement weather of that historic day. Historically, politically, socially and emotionally, it was unlike anything had ever seen before, as more than six million Hong Kongers, hundreds of thousands of visitors and several thousands dignitaries shared in the historic event. Waiting in the wings, however, on July 2nd, the day after HK's return to China, Thailand devalued its currency, the Baht, and set off a string of financial collapse around the region, the impact of which will last for years.

At first, it seemed that HK, with its strong "peg" to the US dollar, its healthy economy and robust financial markets would be immune to the crisis. There was a brief shudder during July, as interest rates rose to protect the HK-US dollar link in the wake of the devaluation of the Thai Baht. But it was to be short-lived and the local share and property markets, so central to HK's economic health, held. In early August 1997, the HK stock market reached its historic high point of more than 16,600 points, and the property market remain firm and extremely active.

But HKSAR was not going to be able to hold out for long. When the crisis hit, it was going to hit hard. As liquidity tightened around the region, it became apparent that HK could not remain above the financial turmoil that had engulfed almost every country in the region, with the notable exception of China. For the SAR, the crisis unleashed its full force In the third week of October 1997. Liquidity dried up, interest rates sharply, and the share and property markets, always sensitive to liquidity and interest rates, collapsed.

For the SAR, which had expected political debate to dominate its early months of existence, economics instead became the key focus of attention. As the HK Government battled to maintain the peg, the domestic economy became a casualty. Before the year was out the share market had dropped by more than one-third and the property market had seen two-fifths of its value wiped out. The local

local economy which had experienced 6.3% real growth in the opening nine months of the year, slumped to 2.8% growth in the final quarter of the year.

Tourism dried up as the number of East Asian visitors slumped by some 25% overall, up to half fewer Japanese. Domestic consumption and investment dried up as consumers looked instead to their bank balances and investors decided to postpone major projects not already into the construction phase. The external trade account, which had been weak, now merely compounded the weaknesses in the domestic economy. It was clear that the downturn would not end quickly.

Major weaknesses in the economy were initially external, with both merchandise and services trade performing poorly and a big increase in the SAR's physical trade and current account deficits being a drag on growth. There was also a substantial withdrawal of international liquidity from the HK financial system, particularly by Japanese banks hard-pressed by their own capital problems at home and difficulties with their loan portfolios in the region. A steady appreciation of the HK dollar throughout the year (in line with its peg to the US dollar), also may have affected external trade and the SAR's growth.

It also became clear that the PRC's burgeoning export trade (up 26% in the first six months of 1997) started to bypass Hong Kong (with SAR's exports up only 4% in the same period). This was highlighted by HK traders as a possible major concern for the future if the trend continued, as it not only affected the physical goods shipped through HK, but also the services supporting China trade in such service sectors as insurance, transport and trade facilitation. Although both HK and the PRC at first were largely unaffected by the currency uncertainties which affected SE Asia mid-year, the SAR Government did move to ward off any attempt by speculators to attack the HK dollar and break its peg to the US currency.

By the close of 1997, however, the SAR Government and business community felt relatively comfortable that Hong Kong would be able to ward off the worst effects of the Asian financial crisis. It was a false hope, with the early months of 1998 showing a further economic weakening.

Beyond the Handover: The 1998 Year

As each month of 1998 passed with the release of new figures documenting the dramatic economic slowdown, it became apparent that recession was inevitable. It would be the first for Hong Kong in 13 years. Although the new SAR Government continued to put a brave face on problems right up to the May 24th election of the First SAR Legislative Council, it was apparent that the economy was turning sour. As the region's economic crisis continued, political disarray increased (most especially in Indonesia and Malaysia). Moreover, Hong Kong was also hit by a series of non-economic crises on the domestic front (Avian flu in the poultry industry, a red tide of pollution in the fishing industry and problems in the hospital system). Together with the collapse in the share and property markets, these non-economic crises of varying dimensions rapidly sapped domestic confidence in the economic outlook and in the Government's performance. On February 18, 1998, the HK Government produced a fiscal 1998-1999 (April to March) Budget aimed at stimulating growth through increased spending (especially infrastructure projects), tax cuts, freezes in fees and charges and higher welfare benefits. But even then, it was clear that it was not going to be enough.

After the election for the Legislative Council was completed on May 24, 1998, the HK Government admitted that the SAR was suffering and that recession was likely. Two days after the election, the SAR Chief Executive, Tung Chee-hwa, in an otherwise unremarkable speech, announced that Hong Kong had been suffering from an economic and asset price "bubble." He said that the bubble had now burst as a result of the liquidity crisis in East Asia. Tung said as a consequence the new SAR was likely to experience several quarters of negative economic growth, which proved to be all too accurate. Three days later, the SAR Financial Secretary, Sir Donald Tsang Yarn-kuen, announced that his 3.5% growth target for the economy was "unattainable" in 1998.

Government action not words needed. Calling for greater action, the public viewed the Government's admission of recession as tardy and weak-kneed. In a few days, the Financial Secretary announced the first of a series of measures aimed at supporting the ailing property market, improving liquidity, and addressing the worsening unemployment situation.

As the economic crisis deepened; however, it became apparent that the Government's "seven bold measures" as they were called were inadequate to combat the impact of the economic downturn. Several actions aimed at alleviating the problems in the property, financial and labour markets followed. On June 22th, the Financial Secretary announced another eight measures aimed at alleviating the impact of the recession and boosting the all-important property sector. Most importantly, these included the suspension of all Government land sales for the remaining nine months of the 1998-99 financial year through to the end of March 1999. As the only supplier of new land for development, this action ensured the supply of land would remain what it was (thereby, hopefully, underpinning prices of existing property). But it also savaged the Government's revenue from land sales (which accounted for something like one-third of its revenue in the previous fiscal year).

Despite these measures, the property and share markets continued to fall and the local economy continued to contract. Inevitably, the Government was urged by politicians and business to do more, but no one was prepared for the bombshell the Financial Secretary was about to drop on the local financial markets.

On August 14, 1998, when the HK stock market languished around the 6,600 point level (down from its August peak a year earlier of 16,600 points), the SAR Administration dropped a bomb. Using its fiscal reserves in the Exchange Fund, which is managed by the HK Monetary Authority (de facto central bank), the HK Government moved into the securities markets to buy shares on the stock market and trade stock index futures on the local futures market. Speculation was the catalyst for this draconian event. Regarded as a market free of Government interference, except for the legal regulation of activities, HK's shares market was under pressure by speculators who were alleged to be manipulating the HK currency and securities. They were in fact doing a "double play" -- trading in the foreign exchange market to bring about interest rate rises and weaknesses in the stock and futures markets where they had previously short-sold stock. The Financial Secretary's plan of action was to "squeeze" the speculators by forcing the shares market higher. There followed tremendous activity in the securities markets as the HK Government bought massive quantities (US$15.2 billion) of the 33 shares which make up HK's chief stock index, the Hang Seng Index.

By the end of August 1998, the HK Government had acquired large holdings in all the constituent stocks of the Hang Seng Index, including three property groups in which it now has a greater than 10% interest. It also bought up shares in the international banking group, HSBC Holdings, in which it has an 8.8% stake. At first, financial and market leaders viewed the massive action with horror, because it marked a substantial break with HK's "free market" past.

That initial response toned down, but the intervention introduced another risk factor to trading in the stock market. Will the Government intervene again and how it will ultimately dispose of its large share-holdings, which when sold could precipitate a market plunge? Subsequently, perceptions of the intervention has been helped by the subsequent share market rise (largely in response to interest rate cuts in the U.S. and HK) and the handsome profits it has made as a result. The debate remains open, however, about whether the intervention marks a change in the Government's previous laissez-faire approach to the markets. Among those who have claimed the action has damaged HK's reputation as an open and free market are: U.S. Federal Reserve Chairman, Alan Greenspan, Nobel Laureate Merton Miller, and the conservative Heritage Foundation in the U.S., which issued a report with the title, "Hong Kong no Longer Has Worlds Freest Economy." According to Heritage, by HK's action Singapore became the freest.

What is certain, however, is that while the interventions helped lift the share market dramatically (at least in the short term) and may have helped underpin the important local property and banking sectors, it did little or nothing to boost the real economy. When this chapter was completed in early 1999, HK's economy was heading for its first year of negative economic growth -- an overall contraction in the output of goods and services -- ever since GDP records were started in 1961. In the first nine months of the 1998 calendar year, the HK economy actually shrank by five percent and little improvement was expected for the rest of the year. Continuing weakness was also predicted for the economy as it moved into 1999. From the perspective of future historians, it is apparent that the year of 1997 will be remembered for two highlights -- when HK returned to PRC sovereignty and when the financial crisis of East Asia hit home. The year of 1998 will be remembered for the SAR Government's shares-market intervention and concerns over whether the action marked a lasting change in the stance of the HK Government towards market intervention.

Beyond Transition : Into the New Millennium

Central to Hong Kong's economic outlook, irrespective of the transition process, is the territory's historic and present-day dependence on external factors largely beyond its immediate control. With external trade equal to two-and-a-half to three times its GDP last year and exports equivalent to 1.5 times GDP (including services exports), Hong Kong has the highest reliance on external trade in the world. Moreover, continued growth in other countries is vital to the SAR's own economic performance. Its dollar peg also means the territory's economic outlook is determined by the decisions of the U.S. Federal Reserve Board in monetary policy. Any assessment of the local economy's performance must make certain assumptions about these outside factors -- global growth of around 3-4%, world trade growth at least double that, the PRC's growth of about 8-9%, and positive U.S. growth of about 2-4% with no big swings in interest rates.

Given those factors in place, it is reasonably easy to plot relatively steady growth path for the local economy through 2001, especially with HK's relatively new role as a maturing, service-based economy. However, East Asia's financial crisis in late 1997 and 1998 changed all that, at least for the short term. Charting the economy has become for more difficult as a result. Nevertheless, the most likely scenario for the years immediately ahead is outlined in Table 6.2.

In 1997, the local economy grew in excess of the Government's medium range growth forecast of 5%, at 5.3% for the year. Growth in the first half of the year was predicted to be 6.3%, with slightly slower growth of 4.3% in the second half of the year as the East Asian crisis took hold. The worst quarter was the fourth when growth was only 2.8%. Both domestic (weaker tourism levels, easier domestic demand) and external factors (Asian currency uncertainties, appreciation of the HK dollar along with its U.S. counterpart and weaker external trade growth) played a role in this easier outlook.

Medium term growth is now expected to be around 2% to 3%, although 1999 is expected to show a further economic contraction of one percent, before positive growth resumes at 2.5% in 2000. Reasons for some confidence in the medium term includes forecasts of positive world trade and economic growth, steady, if slightly slower growth in the PRC and the U.S. economy, and stable U.S. and HK interest rates in the near term. These are expected to offset the weaknesses elsewhere in Asia as a result of the recent economic uncertainties.

To achieve a more negative economic scenario for HK over the medium term would require some further severely adverse factors to emerge, especially factors external to Hong Kong. These might include events such as a dramatic downturn in the China and/or USA economies, global recession or financial crisis, or unusual trade or diplomatic friction between the U.S. and China. Further deterioration of SE Asian economies following the currency crisis would also have an adverse impact on HK, especially if it were to continue for long. The "likely" scenario for Hong Kong's economic medium term growth, therefore, translates in-

Table 6.2

SAR ECONOMY TO 2001
[Real GDP Growth, Per Cent)

Year	1997	1998	1999	2000	2001
Q1	+5.7	-2.7	-4.0	+3.0	+2.0
Q2	+6.9	-5.2	-2.0	+2.0	+3.0
Q3	+6.1	-7.0	+2.0	+2.0	+3.0
Q4	+2.8	-5.0	+3.0	+3.0	+4.0
Annual	+5.3	-5.0	-1.0	+2.5	+3.0

to steady growth in line with the SAR's role as a "maturing service-based economy," servicing China, East Asia and, to a lesser extent, the wider international community. Key positives for the HKSAR are its continuing sound economic and financial fundamentals, its key links to the Mainland and, as a result, its overall attractiveness to international business.

Positive prospects for Hong Kong. As far as local and international business communities are concerned, HK's role as a place in which to do business in China and East Asia remains extremely positive as outlined in Table 6.3. HK's most vital economic advantages come from its reunion and relations with China. Those positives include:

(1) Relative Autonomy -- In all but defense and foreign affairs (and perhaps some other matters), and especially as an economic entity, with its own currency, customs territory, tax system, etc;

(2) A Fiscally Strong Government -- On June 30, 1997, the HK Government transferred reserves of more than HK$320 billion (US$42 billion) to the new SAR Government, a very sound financial base indeed, and these have now grown to some US$60 billion;

(3) Strong External Reserves -- As of the end of 1998, Hong Kong had underlying foreign exchange assets in the Exchange Fund (the fund used to hold reserves and support the HK dollar) of US$90 billion;

(4) Global Trading Presence -- Including its re-export trade with the PRC, the territory is the world's eighth largest merchandise trading entity (1996) and the 11th largest in services. Considering a "One China" bloc, the Mainland, Hong Kong and Taiwan comprise the world's fourth largest trading entity after the EU, Japan and NAFTA;

(5) International Financial Center -- Hong Kong is one of the world's major currency, futures and equities trading centers and a large banking, insurance and fund management center;

(6) Competent "De-Facto" Central Bank -- The Hong Kong Monetary Authority (HKMA) has taken on a powerful role in the economy and has good relations with monetary authorities in Beijing;

(7) Unrivaled International Links and Goodwill -- Hong Kong is a major business and travel center with connections to the world's major cities, a business bridge to China and the biggest base for regional headquarters in Asia; and

Table 6.3

WHAT MAKES HONG KONG ATTRACTIVE TO BUSINESS?

TODAY	POST-1997	RATING
Geographical Location	China Link	+
"International City"	reduced role, possible	+
		-
Political Stability	stable but different	+
Rule of Law	relatively positive - which laws?	+
		-
Corruption Control	potential problem	-
Infrastructure	still positive	+
- Port	still positive	+
- Airport	still positive	+
- Communications	still positive	+
- Housing supply	negative	+
- Housing costs	negative	-
Population skill	still OK	+
Labour availability	shortage?	-
Immigration/Emigration	still uncertain	-
Regulatory environment and business freedom	some tigher regulations?	+
Financial and Professional Services	supply and skills tight	+
		-
Economic Growth	Slower	+
Operating Costs	High Cost Centre	-
Taxation	No change	+
Currency System ($ Link)	No change	+
Life Style	still OK, but potential for change	+

(8) Backing from China -- Recent statements from the PRC leadership have stressed HK's economic autonomy under the provisions of the Joint Declaration and the Basic Law, and have also pledged Beijing's support for the territory's economic and fiscal policies.

A Key Financial and Commercial Center

Despite the unexpected onset of East Asia's financial crisis in 1997 and its severe impact on the economy of the newly created SAR, Hong Kong remains the key financial and commercial center in East Asia, outside of Japan. Its current challenger is Singapore; in the future, it could be Shanghai.

Singapore's challenge has been long-standing, but the Lion City gained renewed momentum in 1997 and 1998 as it responded quickly to East Asia's turmoil by instituting measures to cut costs (including payrolls, taxes and rents) and increase its competitiveness in financial services. In particular, it instituted further deregulation of its financial markets in order to attract the fund management industry to the city. It also announced the proposed merger of its equity market, the Singapore Stock Exchange, and its SIMEX futures market.

Rather than competition, however, it is more likely that the SAR and Singapore will continue to complement each other, with Singapore developing as the financial center for SE Asia and Hong Kong concentrating on the PRC and NE Asia. Shanghai is already the PRC's dominant domestic financial center and, with Beijing's backing, is intent on developing into a major international center over time. Any challenge to HK, however, will require time and a greater opening of the PRC's financial markets, including full convertibility of the Chinese currency, the yuan, to be successful. In any case, the PRC's financial demands will be so great as to require more than one major international financial center.

Hong Kong's many strengths. In terms of commerce, Hong Kong remains a key regional and global trading center, with its total trade in goods equivalent to 250% of its GDP. The HKSAR is the world's eighth largest trading center (if reexports, mainly to and from China, are included) and the fifth in size if the European Union is included as one. Not surprisingly, it is also the world's biggest container port, handling 14.5 million TEUs a year. Its new airport at Chek Lap Kok, as was its predecessor at Kai Tak, is one of the busiest in terms of both air cargo and passengers. HK is the 12th largest trader in services. It has the fourth largest foreign exchange reserves in the world at more than US$90 billion and it has fiscal (budgetary) reserves of some US$60 billion. It has a per capita GDP in excess of US$25,000, one of the highest in the world. The SAR is also the region's leader in the location of regional headquarters and offices of major international companies, with some 1,800 foreign operations based there, some 700 being headquarters and the remainder offices of one type or another in Mainland China and East Asia.

On the financial side, the SAR has a strong financial and banking system and modern and prudent supervision of its financial markets. It has a low, consistent and simple tax structure, an open and accountable government and a competent and corruption-free civil service, as well as the rule of law. Hong Kong has the second largest stock market in Asia, after Japan's (with a capitalization of some US$250 billion in August 1998). It is the fifth largest foreign exchange center in the world in terms of turnover and it is the sixth largest banking center in terms of the volume of external banking transactions.

The SAR also has one of the most active futures exchanges and gold markets in the region. In mid-1998, there were 345 authorized banking or deposit-taking institutions in HK, 175 of them being fully licensed banks. There were also 212 insurance companies operating in the SAR. In recent years, the SAR Government and the HK Monetary Authority have been actively encouraging the development of the debt market, both for government short-to-medium term paper and for the commercial sector. The SAR also has one of the biggest and most active funds management sectors in the world, with some 1,500 unit trusts and mutual funds registered to operate locally. Surely, HK's commerical, financial, logistical, etc. strengths must be recognized and taken seriously.

Assessing the SAR Administration and Chief Executive

The HKSAR's first Chief Executive, Tung Chee-hwa, has done a creditable job so far. He has had to reassure the HK people about their future in adverse circumstances, arranging the election for the first legislature of the SAR in May 1998, and addressing trying problems facing the local economy (principally housing supply and prices, welfare and education). He has also made several overseas visits to promote the HKSAR, which included trips to the USA, where he met with President Bill Clinton among others, and to Singapore, Malaysia, London and Brussels, Australia and New Zealand. He also delivered two major policy statements in October 1997 and 1998 that attempted to project a new vision of the SAR's future and were quite upbeat about medium terms prospects.

From an economic perspective, it appears that he heeded the advice given him ahead of the handover: "Take your time, settle into the job, show you are intent on having a command of all aspects of Government, gather around you a competent team of advisers and ensure you gain the confidence of the community as a whole and -- importantly -- both the domestic and international business and financial sectors." Unfortunately, Asia's financial crisis has made his job far tougher than it otherwise might have been. It also made for harsher community judgments on his performance and his popularity, which began at extremely high levels immediately after the handover and has fallen precipitously since. Because everyone in Hong Kong knows that Tung's appointment as the SAR's first Chief Executive had been influenced if not downright decided by Beijing, his allegiance to the HK people vis-a-vis CCP authorities will always be an open question. That is why the Democrats led by Martin Lee demand that HK's chief executive should be openly elected.

The first months of any new administration, whether national, provincial or local, is always critical to its future. Often referred to as the "honeymoon" period, when broad-based support and goodwill ensue before hard realities set in, the SAR's first 18 months may very well determine the tone of the new Administration's long-term relationship with the HK people. Will it be a relationship based on mutual trust and respect, founded on common goals and aspirations, and openness and the sharing of information? If so, then it could be constructive and long-lasting. Or will it be an administration founded on distrust and suspicion, lack of communication, and misunderstanding, and therefore lead to destructive and unproductive results? Or could it be a mixed bag of pluses and minuses that frustrates everyone?

Tung appeared to be aware of the importance of the opening months to his administration when he delivered his first Policy Address, titled, "Building Hong Kong for a New Era." Speaking to the Provisional Legislative for two hours and ten minutes on October 8, 1997, Mr Tung said: "Each step we take today will set our course for decades. Hong Kong has finally broken free from the psychological constraints of the colonial era. We should have the courage to set aside past modes of thought and plan Hong Kong's future with vision. We must work to build Hong Kong for ourselves and for future generation: a Hong Kong that is civilized, prosperous, stable democratic, filled with a new vitality."

Viewed in its broadest sense, the future of the SAR will depend on three factors -- (1) the application of the Basic Law and adherence to it; (2) events in China (political and economic); and (3) important world perceptions of how the territory is being governed, by China as well as the SAR Government, and what this means for HK's attractiveness as an international business and financial center. In accordance with the provisions of the Sino-British Joint Declaration and the Basic Law, the international community is expecting Hong Kong to be governed with "a high degree of autonomy" under the principle of "one country, two systems." Decisions of the SAR Government in the economic as well as the political sphere will be measured against this yardstick.

Tung's early months may well have set the tone and the substance of his Administration in economic and political matters. The world, especially the international business community, has been monitoring developments closely. HK's fundamental economic advantages are geographic -- (a) its unique link with China and (b) its pivotal position in East Asia, which has been severely affected by the recent crisis, but is likely to once again grow rapidly once it has been dealt with. The HKSAR Government must build on these basic geographic and economic advantages if Hong Kong is to be the preeminent business and financial center for the immediate region into the 21st Century.

The Synergism of China and Hong Kong

Addressing the opening session of the World Bank - International Monetary Fund Annual Meetings in HK in September 1997, the then PRC Premier Li Peng was clearly intent on impressing on all the importance of the occasion to Hong Kong and its reunion with China. "As a Chinese saying goes, seeing it once is better than hearing about it a hundred times," he told the assembled delegates. "Now you are in Hong Kong, you can see with your own eyes that the Chinese Government's basic policies of 'one country, two system,' 'Hong Kong people administering Hong Kong,' and a 'high degree of autonomy' have been carried out in earnest, and the SAR government headed by Tung Chee-hwa is operating normally and effectively in accordance with the Basic Law."

Premier Li's purpose was to stress to the assembled elite of the global financial community that the new HKSAR was still very much open for business; that the unique transfer of sovereignty had gone smoothly; and that Hong Kong would continue to be a major center for commerce and finance in East Asia. Warming to his theme, Premier Li went on: "Hong Kong, in its continued capacity as a free port and an international financial, trade and shipping center, will play an even more active role in strengthening the economic cooperation between China's mainland and other countries in the world." This anticipated last statement hardly caused a ripple of comment among the assembled delegates; yet more than a truism, it goes to the very heart of the future of the HKSAR in relation to its Mainland sovereign, East Asia and the rest of the world.

What is too often overlooked in most analyses of HK's future is the fact that a fast-growing PRC, rapidly emerging onto the world economic stage, wants Hong Kong to stay as it is. It wants and needs HK to operate in the way it has been operating for the past two decades and longer. It wants Hong Kong to maintain itself as a free port, a major global trading entity, and a free and open financial center with growing equity, debt capital and foreign exchange markets. It wants the SAR to be a two-way trade and investment bridge to the rest of the world. It needs the territory as a major capital raising center for its own development and its emerging corporate elite. And Mainland China wants HK to be a U.S. dollar-based economy with its currency still linked directly to the greenback.

In short, Beijing wants the SAR as a sort of offshore trading and financial center, inextricably linked to the PRC but separate from it. Beijing wants all this -- in effect, no change from the status quo -- because it sees HK playing an important role in facilitating its own future development and modernization.

Without any doubt, it is the Joint Declaration and the Basic Law which provides formalistic, legal protection for HK's economic and political future. Thus, the SAR's usefulness as an economic entity is its greatest protection against Mainland interference and its greatest asset in assuring its own future development as a world business center.

Questions Over the Hong Kong SAR

Despite this positive view of the PRC's role in relation to HK, the protections offered by the Basic Law and the "light touch" so far exercised by Beijing in its dealings with its new acquisition, there remain serious questions about the SAR's economic future. For the most part, these are not questions related to the PRC, but to the SAR's internal economic development and its relations with the rest of the world.

For example, when will East Asia's financial crisis last? It began in 1997 and HK authorities have predicted it will continue for two or more years. Will it have a lasting impact on HK's economy, or will it recover relatively quickly and easily, as it has done so often in the past? Has there been a marked change in the attitude of the SAR Administration to intervene in the economy? Will it take a more active role in the future in determining the SAR's development path, either in industry or trade and finance? Can the Administration maintain the people's confidence in its approach to economic development, as well as the confidence of international investors? Will HK maintain its standing as an "international" center, or will it become dominated by PRC affairs and business exclusively, i.e., become China's shadow? Can the SAR remain competitive regionally in the face of challenges once they recover from the ravages of the financial crisis?

All of these are important questions that will only be answered with the passage of time. What appears to be beyond doubt, at least for the foreseeable future, is that HK will retain an important role in global trade and finance. In other words, Hong Kong should be expected to do better than survive.

Self-realization. On top of everything else, HK lacks new identity spanning the economic, political and social dimensions of the society, which can involve high-level policy-makers to the average person on the street. What develops will determine what sort of society HK becomes in its post-colonial era. Hong Kong has always been a transient community in many respects -- a "borrowed place, borrowed time," as one author described its colonial past. This was surely true for Westerners. Regarded in China as "sojourners" and hostile to imperialism and colonialism, Hong Kongers have clung closely to their cultural roots, if not to China as a state (see pp. 19-20 & 31-32). Even though many HK families have been in the territory for generations, the population welcomed the handover on July 1, 1997 with enthusiasm.

True, the great majority of the SAR's 6.3+ million citizens are permanent residents. Many have used HK as a convenient "stepping-stone" as the Overview describes, perhaps as many as one million. Possessing foreign passports, they could move at any time, for any reason. Many already divide their time, business and personal lives between Hong Kong and other places -- Canada, the USA, Australia and, increasingly, Mainland China itself. Now, as citizens of the PRC's SAR versus former identities as sojourners and residents in a laissez-faire British colony, Hong Kongers have to find a new sense of purpose, place, and self, which may not be an uniform identity as might be mandated in the PRC but self-realization that fits the nature of the SAR (pp. 48-49 & 198-201 also discuss the development of identity in IIK).

Much will depend on the future direction of community development. It used to be said in earlier times that Hong Kong was run by "the Bank" (the Hongkong and Shanghai Banking group), "the Club" (the Hong Kong Jockey Club) and the Governor, in that order. Now that colonial rule is gone, HK's ruling elites remain, particularly Government leaders, the business community and the Civil Service.

HK has a Legislative Council, but only 20 (out of 60) members are directly elected and are populist, grass-roots politicians; power thus remains with the elites. The last British Governor, Christopher Patten, attempted to belatedly alter the balance of power by the introduction of democratic reforms, but those reforms have now been modified. Nevertheless, the way remains open for the society to change significantly in the years just ahead as pressures are brought to bear on the ruling elites to change policies and practices.

Although the basic structure of the society is set down in the SAR's Basic Law, the economic, political and social battle lines have been already drawn on what future direction the society should take. Economically, there are divisions and obfuscations between those who believe Hong Kong should retain its laissez-faire traditions (i.e., Government's hands-off stance towards the private business sector) and those who suggest the SAR Government should take a more active role in determining its future economic direction.

There are divisions between those who want to see HK continue to develop service strengths and those who want to see a new high value-added industrial base created. Those who see the SAR's entire economic future tied to its new sovereign differ with those who want it to maintain its standing as a city with an international outlook and a global financial center. There are many other complex differences: big business versus the small and medium enterprises; property developers versus renters; international versus local business attitudes; and local entrepreneurs versus newly arrived Mainland counterparts.

In socioeconomic areas, there are also divisions between those who believe the whole purpose of the society is to create wealth and those who would like to see greater attention given to its social redistribution. There are also the inevitable divisions between those with capital and those who provide labor. Such divisions have become more pronounced with the onset of the East Asian crisis.

The political arena. It is in the political process, however, where social and economic differences merge and gain their most vocal expression. At the pinnacle of power, Chief Executive Tung maintains the strong backing of Beijing authorities. His major advisory body, the Executive Council, consists largely of senior business people, civil servants (current and retired), some senior pro-PRC figures. Unlike the past, all Exco members are Chinese. Still headed by the capable and popular Chief Secretary for Administration, Mrs. Anson Chan, the HK Civil Service remains one of the most respected bureaucracies in East Asia.

Disagreements have been rumored between Civil Service seniors and members of the Executive Council, even with Tung himself. The most difficult relationship, however, is between the Executive Branch of Government and the First SAR Legislative Council (Legco), elected on May 24, 1998. A complicated electoral system involving geographical constituencies (20), functional constituencies (30) and representatives chosen by an election committee (10) has resulted in a fractious Legislature. Not only are there divisions between the pro-business and populist parties, but also between Legco members directly elected by the people (who regard themselves as more legitimate) and those indirectly elected (through functional constituencies or the election committee). Within the "grass roots" camp, there are also divisions between the pro-democracy and pro-PRC parties. Additionally, there is a complicated voting system in Legco which can turn an overall majority vote into a losing situation. With much room for political friction, all of this makes decision-making all the more difficult, even in the key areas of economics and business.

When Tung Chee-hwa was sworn in as HKSAR Chief Executive in the early hours of July 1, 1997, he spoke confidently of HK's future: "For the first time in our history, we now have the opportunity to chart our own destiny." In the months since, he has continued to emphasize the tremendous long-term potential of Hong Kong, both globally and in its new relationship with a fast-developing Mainland economy. Although not of HK's nor of the PRC's making, the onset of the East Asian financial crisis has, nevertheless, led to doubts in some quarters about the SAR's future and the ability of its leadership (new and old) to cope with the challenges ahead (see pp. 326-327).

As Hong Kong heads towards the new century, new leadership and goals may develop to affect its economy. Successful leadership will not only carry the community with it, it will also show that it has a greater vision of what the SAR's future should be and the political will and drive to carry it through.

CHAPTER SEVEN

Change, Confrontation, and Community Since 1984

Frank Ching

*I don't believe that general elections are definitely beneficial for Hong Kong . . . .
Matters of Hong Kong's future should naturally be handled by Hong Kong people. Can
these people be elected by universal suffrage? We say these administrators of Hong
Kong's affairs should be Hong Kong people who love the motherland and Hong Kong.
Can such people definitely be chosen through general election?* Deng Xiaoping, when
he addressed members of the Hong Kong Special Administrative Region's Basic Law
Drafting Committee on April 16, 1987

A Disputatious Triad

Fundamental disputes over democracy in Hong Kong marked the years since
the signing in 1984 of the Sino-British Joint Declaration on the Question of
Hong Kong. The disputes were often between the People's Republic of China
(PRC) and Britain, sometimes between Britain and Hong Kong, at times between
Hong Kong and the PRC, and often within Hong Kong. Even though the British
have departed, disputes will not end but are likely to continue for years, both
within Hong Kong and between Hong Kong and China with occasional murmurs
from Great Britain.

A second major theme that marked the 13-year transition period was the question of the identity, specifically, the nationality, of the people of Hong Kong.
Even though the broad outlines of the Sino-British agreement had been known
before the Joint Declaration was made public, there was intense interest in Hong
Kong about the details of the accord. Britain had declared that any agreement
had to be acceptable to Parliament and to the people of Hong Kong. Thus, after
they initialled the Declaration on September 26, 1984, the British called on the HK

public to express their views on the agreement, and an Assessment Office was set up to tabulate the results. Then Governor, Sir Edward Youde, made it clear that the only alternative to acceptance of the agreement was to have no agreement. And that, he said, meant that the PRC would take back Hong Kong anyway on July 1, 1997, and the HK people would not have the benefit of the protection offered by a legally binding international agreement signed by the PRC and Britain.

Given that choice, most people who wrote to the Assessment Office to express their views declared that they found the agreement acceptable. They were encouraged by the surprisingly detailed agreement, which provided for the continuation of their lifestyle for 50 years after the 1997 handover. Up to that point, the British would continue to be responsible for the administration of Hong Kong. And, afterwards, Beijing would not send any officials to run Hong Kong but would allow the territory to run itself under the concept of "one country, two systems" with "Hong Kong people running Hong Kong" with a "high degree of autonomy" in all areas other than defense and foreign affairs.

That is not to say everybody found the Joint Declaration acceptable. Many skeptics did not write to the Assessment Office, knowing that the accord could not be changed. Nevertheless, some did write to express their frustration with the British. In particular, those who were British nationals voiced their strong sense of betrayal. "With one stroke of the pen, you have stripped us of our identity and slotted us into racial categories -- an unforgiveable act," one person wrote, alluding to Britain's decision to downgrade holders of HK British passports so that they became citizens of the British dependent territory of Hong Kong with no right of abode in the United Kingdom. Another who was a naturalized Briton said he had made a solemn oath of allegiance to the Queen, and was "disillusioned by what the British government has done." While reporting such negative views, the Assessment Office concluded: "Most of the people of Hong Kong find the draft agreement acceptable."

The Joint Declaration ended a long period of uncertainty in Hong Kong; people at least knew now what the future held. Those with little confidence in the PRC were able to make plans to transfer assets out of Hong Kong and, in many cases, to move themselves and their families out as well. Ironically, perhaps, while Beijing promised that Hong Kong would not change for 50 years after 1997, the Declaration actually led to immediate changes. This was because the Sino-British agreement provided that the HK Special Administrative Region to be established by the PRC on July 1, 1997 would have a legislature constituted by elections. Up until the signing of the Joint Declaration, the colonial HK legislature was completely appointed. The British felt obliged to transform the Legislative Council (Legco) from an appointed body to one that was elected in 13 years.

In fact, the British made it clear even before the Joint Declaration was finalized that they intended to democratize Hong Kong. In July 1984, two months before the Joint Declaration was initialled, the British asked the HK public for reactions to a Green Paper on representative government in which they said their aim was "to develop progressively a system of government the authority for which is firmly rooted in Hong Kong, which is able to represent authoritatively the views of the people of Hong Kong, and which is more directly accountable to the people of Hong Kong." This was followed four months later, after the Joint Declaration had been made public but before its formal signing, by a White Paper that announced the HK Government's decision, after taking into account the views of the people, to introduce indirect elections in 1985. As for direct elections, the White Paper said: "With few exceptions the bulk of public response from all sources suggested a cautious approach with a gradual start by introducing a very small number of directly elected members in 1988 and building up to a significant number of directly elected members by 1997."

The British took those steps to pave the way for acceptance of the Joint Declaration by both the HK people and by Parliament. By pointing the way to a democratic future, it was felt, Parliament might approve the agreement, and the tactics were successful.

Thus, the Declaration was formally signed on December 19, 1984 in Bejing. On September 26, 1985, the British expanded Legco from 46 to 56 members, 24 of whom were to be elected, with the rest appointed. Of the 24 seats to be elected, 12 were filled by electoral colleges comprising all members of the District Boards, the Urban Council and the Regional Council, and "functional constituencies" elected 12 additional members. Functional constituencies were groups that play an important role in the economy, such as people involved in commerce, in industry and in financial services as well as professionals, such as doctors and lawyers. "Such a system enabled, in 1985, twenty-four members of the Legislative Council to be elected by a total of 25,206 voters, or rather more than half of 1 per cent of those who in a normal system might have had the franchise: hardly a great extension of democracy" (Welsh, 1993, p. 516).

Despite its shortcomings, the 1985 election marked a giant step toward representative government. The British indicated that the next step would be the introduction of direct elections in 1988. Before long, however, Beijing's leading representative in Hong Kong, Xu Jiatun, the outspoken director of the Xinhua News Agency, held a press conference at which he accused Britain of having violated the Declaration by making its own plans for political reforms (see pp. 25-26). Beijing also scorned the idea and scolded Britain for its audacity.

Capitulating to Beijing's wrath, Prime Minister (PM) Thatcher's Government reversed its position. The British accepted the guiding concept of "convergence," i.e., whatever Britain did in Hong Kong before 1997 had to accord with China's plans for Hong Kong after 1997 (Roberti, 1996, pp. 161-164). By agreeing to convergence, the British in effect surrendered their right to take the initiative, a policy that led to many disputes.

For its part, Beijing immediately started the process of drafting the Basic Law, which would be HK's constitutional instrument after 1997. Although the Declaration had provided for the drafting of a Basic Law, the British had thought this would come later in the 13-year transition period and that they would have a free hand in the first few years. However, this was not to be as Beijing announced in July 1985 the creation of a 59-member Basic Law Drafting Committee, with 36 members from China and 23 members from Hong Kong, many of whom were prominent businessmen and leading professionals. Beijing said that, since Hong Kong was to remain a capitalist society, it was natural that capitalists should be given a major role, first in drafting the Basic Law and, later, in running the Hong Kong SAR.

The drafting committee set up a Basic Law Consultative Committee, whose members were meant to "engage in consultative activities within Hong Kong" and then inform the drafting committee of the viewpoints of HK people on various issues. The first Consultative Committee meeting was instructive. At that meeting, Sir Y. K. Pao, one of China's trusted advisers in Hong Kong, read out a list of names of people who would serve as the Committee's officers. After the names were read out, all those present applauded and it was announced to the press that the Committee had "elected" its officers.

When it was pointed out that the Committee's constitution provided for an election process with nominations to be made prior to the holding of an election, December 6, 1985 was scheduled for a proper election to be held. On that day, people whose names were not on Pao's list refused to accept nomination. Thus, all the original appointees were duly elected. This process was an early sign that Beijing may have had a different definition of concepts such as "elections" than Britain and Hong Kong.

As the drafting of the Basic Law progressed, much disagreement arose among Committee members on the pace at which Hong Kong should be democratized. Debate focused on the extent to which members of the legislature should be chosen through direct elections in 1997 and the rate at which this number should be increased in subsequent years. And because the drafting was still in progress, China argued, Britain should not try to pre-empt the Basic Law by introducing direct elections in 1988. Also, since the Basic Law was not expected to be promulgated until 1990, direct elections should not be introduced before then. That created a major dilemma for the British. They had promised in 1984, when announcing indirect elections for 1985, that they would consult the HK people again in 1987 as to whether direct elections should be introduced in 1988. Facing a major confrontation with the PRC, which opposed any "drastic changes," the British looked for a way out of their dilemma.

The Questionable Survey

What the British opted for was an opinion-gathering exercise with a predetermined outcome. They set up an elaborate Survey Office in 1987 and appointed two monitors whose job was to determine if that the Survey Office had done its job properly. Then they hired a private survey company, AGB McNair, to conduct two opinion polls. Mark Roberti (1996), an investigative journalist, tells how the HK Government manipulated the issue. About two million copies of the Green Paper, *The 1987 Review of Developments in Representative Government,* were published on May 27, 1987 with September 30th as the deadline for responses. According to Roberti, the Governor, Sir David Wilson, who took office in 1987 after the death of Governor Edward Youde the year before, told the Executive Council before the deadline that "based on the submissions received by the Survey Office so far, it appears that a majority are not in favor of introducing elections to the Legislative Council in 1988." Roberti (1996, p. 203) commented: "No one questioned whether it was ethical to make a decision before seeing the Survey Office's final report on public opinion. After a brief discussion, the Council agreed . . . that democratic elections would be put off at least until 1991."

The Survey Office's findings were surprising. Most privately conducted surveys had found a significant majority who favored direct elections in 1988. However, the Survey Office came to the opposite conclusion. While the nub of the issue was whether direct elections should be introduced in 1988, the survey asked convoluted questions about technical issues such as the timing and mode of elections. At no time were respondents asked the simple question: Do you want direct elections to be introduced in 1988? Instead, all information was marshalled to support the thesis that the Hong Kong people did not want direct elections in 1988.

A group of academics calling themselves the University and Post Secondary College Staff Concerned Group on Developments in the Government System conducted its own survey in which they gave people a choice of eleven years, from 1987 to 1997, as the best time to introduce direct elections. More people picked 1988 than any other year. Yet when this finding was presented to the public by the Survey Office, it was presented as "1988: 35.9%. Other year 64.1%," suggesting that most of the people were opposed to 1988. Moreover, although the Survey Office decided to ignore a signature campaign in support of direct elections signed by more than 230,000 people, it counted 70,000 form letters as individual submissions, 90% of which opposed direct elections.

Martin Lee, the leader of HK's democratic forces, flew to London (accompanied by this writer and Daniel Fung, now the solicitor general) in a last-ditch attempt to persuade Britain to allow direct elections to be held in 1988. Needless to say, his mission was unsuccessful. Subsequently, the *Far Eastern Economic Review* commissioned Norman Webb, secretary general of the famed Gallup International, to appraise the HK Government's political review and the Survey Office report (Lau, 1988). Webb concluded that the government-sponsored surveys were "deeply flawed." He pointed out that the questionnaire was designed in such a way that respondents had to spend 20 or 30 minutes answering difficult questions before any questions on direct elections appeared "By this time respondents are likely to be no longer as fresh and willing to cooperate as they were when they started the interview," Webb said.

The first question in the Government survey relating to direct elections was worded as follows:

Options related to the composition of the Legislative Council:

1. to make no change in the numbers and relative proportions of Official, Appointed and Elected members.
2. to conclude that direct elections to the Legislative Council are not desirable.
3. to conclude that, in principle, some element of direct elections is desirable, but that it should not be introduced in 1988.
4. If changes are desirable in 1988, it will be possible to make one or more of the following changes, e.g., increase slightly the number of official members, reduce the number of appointed members, increase the number of indirectly elected members or have directly elected members.
5. dont know/no opinion.
6. don't understand the options.
7. not clear about the respective concepts and therefore not asked to choose any options.

Of the seven options, only one, No. 4, provides for the possibility of direct elections in 1988. Those who chose this option were then confronted with the following choices:

Options of changing the composition of the Legislative Council:

1. to increase slightly the number of official members.
2. to reduce the number of appointed members.
3. to increase the number of members elected by functional constituencies.
4. to increase the number of members elected by the electoral college.
5. to introduce a directly elected element in addition to the existing system of election, by means of either territory-wide or constituency-based elections.
6. to replace the system of indirect elections from the electoral college geographical constituencies by a system of direct elections.
7. don't know/no opinion.
8. don't understand the options.

Commenting on the questions, Webb said: "In order to find out what the citizens of Hong Kong wish, it would have been far better to have asked them a number of simple direct questions on the subject. This was not done." Webb also criticized the convoluted language used in the questionnaire, as compared with "the ordinary language with which people would normally communicate." He pointed out that, in one survey, 24% of the respondents did not understand the concepts put to them in the question concerning the Legislature's composition, 3% did not understand the options and 18% did not give an opinion. "The fact that nearly half of them were defeated by this question demonstrates how complicated it must have been," Webb said. He said it was impossible to conclude from the responses to such a "complicated and highly abstruse question" what the true wishes of the HK people were. Moreover, the Gallup expert concluded that on the basis of other territory-wide surveys, sponsored by newspapers and other independent organizations and conducted by well-known professional polling firms, those supporting direct elections in 1988 out-numbered those opposed by a majority of two to one or three to one.

The rigging of the findings by the Survey Office was obvious to many in Hong Kong, and contributed to the growing worry that the British were merely appeasing China until 1997, when they could wash their hands of the territory. Conspiracy fears were confirmed by admissions by "a senior executive at AGB and a senior civil servant at the Survey Office . . . that the document itself was biased" and that at least six resigned from the survey firm amidst the furore (Roberti, 1996, p. 206).

During this period, worries over Hong Kong's future were increasing, rather than abating, as reflected in a sustained "brain drain" exodus of the middle class. While the number of people who left HK during the early 1980s was about 15,000 a year, by the late 1980s it had risen to 45,000. Many more would have immigrated if it was not for the quota limits of free societies, such as Australia, Canada, and the United States; waiting lists were filled for many years. Yet the British Foreign Office and HK Administration chose to ignore this obvious manifestation of worry on the part of HK people. Ignoring the increased exodus, Sir David declared that emigration was a HK tradition and said that Chinatowns around the world, filled with former HK residents, proved his point.

The exodus was not reported to the British Parliament in the required annual reports on Hong Kong. It was not until March 1989 that its first mention was made, under the neutral sounding heading of "Emigration and Immigration." In that report, the British Government commented: "Population mobility has long been a feature of Hong Kong. Many of the territory's residents migrated from China and elsewhere; and many have chosen to move overseas for education, training, career development or permanent settlement." It said emigrants totalled 30,000 in 1987 and 45,000 in 1988, figures challenged by the Canadian Commissioner and others as deceptively low. "At current levels, emigration is not having a serious effect on the economy," according to the report. "However, if the present outflow were to continue for some years, there could be a loss of efficiency."

The Tiananmen Massacre, June 4, 1989

Former CCP party leader, Hu Yaobang, died in Beijing on April 15, 1989. The populist-oriented member of the PRC leadership, Hu lost his job as leader of the Chinese Communist Party (CCP) for being too liberal and was disgraced in 1987 by Politburo conservatives. Hu's death led to a massive outpouring of grief and student demonstrations that evolved into the pro-democracy protests in Tiananmen Square (see pp. 32-33). Many people in HK identified with the students and gave them support, material as well as moral. A million people -- close to one-fifth of the population -- marched in HK in support of the students after Beijing pro- claimed martial law on May 20. When the demonstrators were brutally suppressed in a predawn military crackdown on June 4, 1989, Hong Kong mourned the slain students and workers. For more than a week, unprecedented numbers of demonstrators and marchers expressed sorrow for the martyred youth and support for the pro-democracy cause. As p. 201 in Chapter Four relates, even HK editors and journalists of pro-China publications joined the universal outrage (Hicks, 1990).

Tiananmen, more than anything else during the 13-year transition period, left an indelible mark on Hong Kong. Besides anger at CCP leaders and frustration over their dashed hopes for a progressive China, there was panic as fear spread that what transpired in Beijing could happen in Hong Kong after its 1997 takeover by China. Almost everyone wanted to get out. Wild schemes were floated, such as the transplantation of Hong Kong to Australia, or to Scotland. When Singapore announced in 1990 that it would take 5,000 HK emigrants, 100,000 people swamped the Singapore Commission to scramble for application forms.

At the same time, a cry arose for Britain to restore to its HK nationals the right of abode in the United Kingdom, a right abolished by London over the years through changes in British immigration laws. Taunting those in Parliament who urged a change in immigration rights, such as Liberal Democrats leader, Paddy Ashdown, PM Thatcher thundered soon after Tiananmen, "Do you want to see more than three million Chinese come to Britain!?" Labour Party leaders agreed to do nothing. Many who listened to Parliament's post-Tiananmen debates on BBC Hong Kong were appalled by Britain's callousness. PM Thatcher's administration had deliberately changed Britain's nationality law in the early 1980s in preparation for the return of Hong Kong to China. Through the British Nationality Act of 1983, HK British subjects were downgraded to the newly created category of British Dependent Territory Citizens, with the right only to reside in Hong Kong.

British afterthoughts. Foreign Secretary Sir Geoffrey Howe was the target of protestors when he arrived in Hong Kong in the aftermath of Tiananmen Square. Every group he met demanded the restoration of the right of abode in the United Kingdom for all British passport holders. Facing worldwide concern for the people of Hong Kong, the British finally decided in July 1990 that something had to be done to restore confidence in HK. One measure was to give the right of abode in Britain, not to all 3.3 million British nationals in HK but to 50,000 carefully chosen "key" families, with the idea that they would have the confidence to remain in the territory, knowing that they could leave if things went wrong. The British estimate of 225,000 people covered by the heads of households scheme was found to be highly exaggerated by demographer Paul Kwong of the Chinese University of Hong Kong, who said the figure is more like 150,000. Dr. Kwong commented: "It's nothing less than a confidence trick to talk in terms of 225,000" (Yee, 1992, pp. 338-339).

Another step Britain took was to give Hong Kong a Bill of Rights. This move had been consistently rejected by the British in past years, when they said that a Bill of Rights was unnecessary because existing HK laws already fully protected the rights of the people. This had been Britain's position since 1976, when it signed the International Covenant on Civil and Political Rights, the main United Nations human rights convention, and extended it to Hong Kong. The British also informed PRCofficials about this during the negotiations that led to the signing of the Joint Declaration. But, to help restore confidence, Britain decided to give Hong Kong a Bill of Rights by turning the International Covenant into domestic HK law. A third step to promote confidence after Tiananmen was Governor Wilson's announcement in October 1989 that a world-class airport would be built at Lantau Island to replace Kai Tak Airport, which had been operating far past capacity for many years.

For each step taken by Britain, Beijing devised a countermeasure. Thus, it declared that PRC would not recognize the passports Britain would distribute under its nationality scheme. The holders of such passports, China said, would continue to be regarded as Chinese nationals and so would not be able to enjoy British consular protection; and the passports would not be considered valid travel documents. In fact, Beijing even argued that the nationality package violated the Joint Declaration. In an exchange of memoranda attached to the Declaration, Beijing had agreed in 1984 that Hong Kong people could continue to use British travel documents after 1997, and Britain had agreed that British Dependent Territory Citizens would be given an "appropriate status" after 1997 that would "entitle them to continue to use passports issued by the Government of the United Kingdom" but would do so "without conferring the right of abode."

As for the Bill of Rights, the PRC announced that it reserved the right to review this legislation after 1997 with a view to either amending or repealing it. It argued that the Bill of Rights was a violation of the Basic Law. The reasoning was that the Basic Law was meant to be superior to all other laws in Hong Kong but the British, by making the Bill of Rights override all other laws, were usurping the position of the Basic Law. Subsequently, Sir T. L. Yang, the Chief Justice, expressed the view that the Bill of Rights had created three tiers of laws and, while it did not override the Basic Law, it was a separate tier between the Basic Law and all other laws.

Beijing did not respond immediately to the announced decision to build the new Chek Lap Kok airport. Perhaps this was because the move was apolitical and a new airport was much overdue. London took the position that it was a decision that Hong Kong could make on its own. However, the HK Government soon found that bankers were unwilling to extend financing for the new airport unless Beijing approved of the project. After all, the project was meant to be finished in 1997, but repayment would extend well past the handover, when the British would no longer be responsible for Hong Kong. Gradually, Governor Wilson's administration realized that it had to obtain Beijing's support for the new airport. Yet it insisted for awhile that it would merely inform Beijing of what it was doing, rather than seek its approval. When HK officials were asked to fly to Beijing to discuss the Chek Lap Kok project, PRC officials were invited to come to Hong Kong to get a "briefing" on the new airport. Negotiations over the airport were protracted, but the British eventually admitted that China had to be accorded a formal role. Beijing, on its part, used the airport issue to extract a political price. In the wake of the Tiananmen massacre, China faced worldwide condemnation. When China and Britain reached a preliminary agreement on the airport, the most important provision had nothing to do at all with the airport. It stipulated that the memorandum of understanding on the airport had to be signed in Beijing by the leaders of the two countries. That was how PM John Major in September 1991 became the first leader of a major Western nation to go to the PRC after Tiananmen.

Major was clearly uncomfortable. He had to shake hands with Premier Li Peng -- who was widely regarded as one of the principal people responsible for the massacre -- as well as pose for photograhps with the Premier during the signing ceremony. Maintaining an air of sober presence throughout the day, the Prime Minister partially saved his face by telling a press conference that he had discussed human rights problems with his hosts (Roberti, 1996, p. 294). The entire ordeal must have caused him to begin questioning the wisdom of the Foreign Office and its convergence policy.

Major went on to Hong Kong where soon after his arrival, it was rumored that Governor David Wilson, one of the leading architects of Britain's HK policy, would be removed. The PM publicly denied the rumors but, before year's end, it transpired that Sir David would be leaving Hong Kong and be elevated to the House of Lords.

Just as Tiananmen caused Britain to change its policy toward Hong Kong, so it also caused the PRC to re-evaluate its stance toward the territory. PRC leaders had viewed Hong Kong as a city whose people who were only interested in making money. Now it realized that many of its people had political leanings which, if not curbed, could threaten the survival of the communist regime. Beijing reached this conclusion when it saw that, during the Tiananmen disturbance, HK people had not only provided moral support for the demonstrators -- they had donated money that was used to buy tents for the students in Tiananmen Square. In fact, it has been argued that the demonstrators would have dispersed before June 4th if Hong Kong had not weighed in with its support. Moreover, after the Tiananmen crackdown, many HK people helped smuggle dissidents out of the PRC into the West, such as Chai Ling and Wu'er Kaixi.

Outraged by HK's protests, Beijing adopted a harsher stance. A new article was inserted into HK's draft Basic Law stipulating legislation that addressed the crimes of subversion, secession, sedition, treason and the theft of state secrets. This provision, Article 23 of the Basic Law, calls for the legislation to be passed by the post-1997 Legislative Council. Exactly how such legislation would be worded raised great concern, since it would presumably restrict the rights of free speech and assembly.

Hong Kong's First Direct Elections, 1991

September 1991 deserves to be remembered. It was the month the airport agreement was signed in Beijing by Li Peng and John Major and when direct elections were held, the first truly democratic elections since British rule began in 1841. Eighteen of the 60 seats in the legislature were open to direct election, with 21 being filled by elections through functional constituencies. Three government officials served in an ex officio capacity, and an additional 18 were appointed by the Governor. Since Tiananmen remained a hot issue, much of the campaign hinged on the candidates' views towards China's Communist Party rule.

While liberals, led by the newly formed United Democrats of Hong Kong, swept the elections, all pro-PRC candidates were defeated. Following the election, the United Democrats (UD) urged Governor Wilson to use his power of appoint- ment to reflect the public mood and to include more liberals onto the Legislative Council by way of the Governor's allotment of 21 appointees. Their argument was that the people had shown their will by voting for pro-democracy candidates and it followed that the Governor should appoint accordingly. They also asked him to appoint UD members onto the Executive Council, the Governor's cabinet, but Sir David refused. In his 18 appointments to Legco, the Governor chose people who did not have overt political backgrounds and were, therefore, on the whole, more conservative than those who had been directly elected. Wilson's appointees also suited Beijing's preference.

"Our position is very clear," said Ambassador Guo Fengmin, the Chinese head of the Joint Liaison Group. "We are of the view that the admission of those people who are against the Basic Law and openly propagate subversion against the legitimate government of China will not be conducive to the stability of Hong Kong. Therefore we oppose this." While the names of UD leaders, Martin Lee and Szeto Wah, were never mentioned, Hong Kong knew that Ambassador Guo was alluding to them. Yet even without this warning, Wilson never would have appointed any United Democrats onto the Executive Council.

More Subterfuge -- The Court of Final Appeal

Another major development in September 1991 was an agreement by London and Beijing on the establishment of a Court of Final Appeal in Hong Kong. The Joint Declaration had stipulated that appeals to the Privy Council in London would end after June 30, 1997, and in its place a Court of Final Appeal would be set up, in Hong Kong rather than Beijing. Attempting to instill confidence in the independence of the court, the Joint Declaration provided that "the court of final appeal . . . may as required invite judges from other common law jurisdictions to sit on the court of final appeal." The thinking was that distinguished foreign judges would not only lend stature to the HK court but would also make it less vulnerable to political pressure by China.

However, Britain surrendered to China's demand that only one overseas judge at the most should be allowed to sit on the five-judge court at any one time, despite the plural of "judges" in the Declaration of 1984. The 1991 Sino-British deal on the Court's composition was immediately attacked by liberal legislators and the legal profession in Hong Kong. Believing that China would never accept a majority of overseas judges, Britain had proposed that two of the five judges should be from overseas jurisdictions. In the face of Chinese opposition, the British retreated and agreed that only one overseas judge would serve on the Court of Final Appeal at any one time.

The Legislative Council, containing directly elected members for the first time, held a heated debate on the issue, with Martin Lee, Chairman of the United Democrats, denouncing the agreement as "a joint breach of the Joint Declaration." The debate marked the first time that Hong Kong had been given a voice on a decision regarding its future. In a 34-to-11 vote on December 4, 1991, Legco rejected the Sino-British agreement and called on London and Beijing to negotiate a new accord. Britain's hope to see a Court of Final Appeal up and running well before 1997 could not be realized.

Revisiting the Court issue in 1995, Britain and China not only confirmed that there would be only one overseas judge out of the five but agreed that the Court would begin work on July 1, 1997 when China was in control. The deal also agreed that the Court of Final Appeal would not have jurisdiction over cases involving acts of the state, such as defense. The exact implications of this are still unclear but, according to Roberti (1996, p. 300), the latter clearly "meant China would interfere in sensitive cases *before* they went to trial."

A British Change of Policy Evolves

Although it yielded to Bejing's will on many important issues, after the massacre of June 1989 the British Government must have begun an anguishing reassessment of its HK policy. Margaret Thatcher, whose words and actions indicated little warmth for the HK people, was under attack by fellow Conservatives on domestic issues and finally replaced as Prime Minister by John Major in 1990. Major's confidence soared after April 1992 when his Conservatives scored a surprising victory at the polls and retained power, a feat attributed to Party Chairman, Christropher Patten. But, ironically, Patten's tireless efforts for the Party caused him to lose his own seat in Parliament representing the city of Bath. PM Major offered his loyal ally the Governorship of Hong Kong, a strategic job that would give Patten international exposure. In accepting the offer, Patten became the

28th and last British Governor of Hong Kong.

After the Tiananmen bloodbath, Britain adopted a more assertive Hong Kong policy in which fewer decisions were made according to the PRC's wishes. Thus, despite Beijing's opposition, in 1990 Britain went ahead with the Nationality Scheme and introduced the Bill of Rights mentioned earlier. Although the new, bold policy became identified with Christopher Patten, he was simply implementing a more assertive British policy to regain the initiative in Hong Kong, which it had lost years ago when it agreed to convergence. Before his arrival, the new Governor made it clear that he was going to be different. Instead of repeating the standard formula of wanting to preserve HK's "prosperity and stability," he pointedly said that he wanted to "preserve the territory's stability and prosperity and freedom." Yet he came in without a free hand. A decade of Sino-British convergence had resulted in a slew of agreements that could not be easily overturned.

Arriving in Hong Kong on July 9, 1992, Patten was immediately sworn in as Governor. He eschewed the traditional, white colonial uniform, topped off by a pith helmet with ostrich feathers. Patten settled for a business suit for his inauguration and passed up the knighthood which, since the colony's early years, always accompanied the job of HK Governor. Patten's populist approach quickly won him acceptance in Hong Kong. He acted as if he was campaigning for office, walking the streets and picking up children to hug and kiss. A PRC official upbraided the Governor, saying he was not running for office. Governor Patten spent his first three months in office meeting people, getting a good feel for Hong Kong, and avoiding policy statements. His position on key issues, he said, would be disclosed when he made the Governor's annual address to Legco in October 1992.

The Governor's Platform and China's Reactions

In that address, Patten responded to Beijing's pressure not to appoint leaders of the United Democrats Party to the Executive Council -- and pressure to appoint its members to his cabinet -- by announcing a policy of only appointing people who were not involved in politics. Thus, he satisfied China on this issue without at the same time appearing to bow to its pressure. Yet the Governor could not avoid antagonizing Beijing with his reform package. In the past, the British had always negotiated with the PRC first and then informed the HK people what the two governments had decided to do. Reversing the procedure, he unveiled his electoral reform proposals before seeking Beijing's views.

Patten announced electoral proposals that, he said, were consistent with the Basic Law. That document provides for a 60-seat legislature in 1997, with 20 seats filled by direct elections, 30 by functional constituencies and 10 by an election committee. Patten said that he hoped that the Legislative Council elected in 1995 would be able to serve beyond 1997. The 1995 elections would be the first time when all 60 seats in the legislature were filled by election. One of his main proposals related to the creation of nine new functional constituencies and another was the setting up of an Election Committee; both steps were required by the Basic Law.

While technically adhering to the Basic Law, Governor Patten widened the franchise significantly. Previously, functional constituencies were all narrowly based. However, Patten proposed that every working person should have a vote in a functional constituency. He created nine new functional constituencies in which he included everyone in the territory who had a job. The effect was to make these seats scarcely distinguishable from the 20 directly-elected seats. He also proposed the total phasing out of appointments to district boards and municipal councils, and proposed that the Election Committee be made up of directly-elected district board members.

The rest of Patten's package had to do with lowering the voting age from 21 to 18 and a widening of the franchise in some of the existing functional constituencies. But the most controversial proposals were those relating to the nine new functional constituencies and the Election Committee, which were widely seen as thinly disguised attempts to increase the number of democratically elected seats from the 20 laid down in the Basic Law to a total of 39 legislators.

Hong Kong's initial response to Patten's reform proposals was extremely positive. But the atmosphere clouded quickly when Beijing unfurled its implacable opposition. When Patten went to Bejing to explain his proposals, not one senior member of the PRC leadership met him and his talks with Lu Ping, Director of the Hong Kong and Macau Affairs Office under the State Council, did not go well. This became obvious when, within minutes of the Governor's departure from Beijing, Lu Ping held a news conference in which he denounced Patten's proposals and threatened that the PRC would, if necessary, "build a second stove," or create its own governmental structure for Hong Kong, if the British went ahead with Patten's plans. Attacking the proposed reforms with vehemence, PRC leaders hurled insults at Governor Patten, such as the enigmatic epithet, "sinner for 1,000 years!"

One thing that emerged from the visit was a disclosure by Beijing that, in addition to the Joint Declaration and the Basic Law, there were "other relevant understandings and agreements" between London and Beijing. Lu Ping disclosed that there had been an exchange of letters between Foreign Minister Qian Qichen and Foreign Secretary Douglas Hurd in early 1990 that Patten's proposals for the election committee contradicted. Surprisingly, Patten appeared to have been unaware of the Qian-Hurd understandings and initially resisted demands that the letters be made public. Ultimately, seven letters were released, which showed that the British had actually asked for much less democracy than Hong Kong had wanted and, eventually, settled for even less than that. Instead of insisting that 30 seats, or 50 per cent of the legislature, be directly elected in 1997, Hurd asked for only 24 seats to be directly elected. He ultimately settled for 20 seats. This agreement was then incorporated into the Basic Law. The letters showed that Hurd said he agreed "in principle" that the Basic Law's provision for the Election Committee would be put into effect in Hong Kong in 1995. This was quite different from Patten's proposal that the Committee be composed of elected district board members. It therefore appeared to Beijing that the British were reneging on a previous understanding.

The new Governor changed the political alignment within Hong Kong. The United Democrats, who were firmly in the opposition during the Wilson years, became a pro-Government party. And the Cooperative Resources Center, made up of pro-business conservatives, was transformed from a pro-Government party into an opposition group.

The five years of Patten's administration saw a strong surge in the development of political parties. A pro-Beijing party, the Democratic Alliance for the Betterment of Hong Kong (DAB) was inaugurated the day after Patten's arrival in Hong Kong and headed by Tsang Yok-sing, principal of a "patriotic" school and whose family was closely identified with the PRC. His brother, Tsang Tak-sing, was a member of China's National People's Congress and the editor of the pro-communist newspaper, *Ta Kung Pao* (see pp. 191, 197-198, & 204). After discussions with other liberal groups, the United Democrats merged with the Meeting Point group in 1993 to become the Democratic Party. Ultimately, the conservative Cooperative Resources Center changed its name to the Liberal Party.

PRC officials made good their threat to set up a "second stove" in July 1993, when they created a new body, the Preliminary Working Committee of the Preparatory Committee of the Hong Kong SAR. The Basic Law stipulated that the Preparatory Committee would be formed in 1996 to handle issues relating to the transition. Because the British were no longer as cooperative as before, Beijing stepped up the timing for the transitional body. In order to appear consistent with the Basic Law, it created what was called the Preliminary Working Committee. However, because the Basic Law says nothing about a PWC, the British and HK Governments refused to cooperate with a body that they viewed as illegitimate.

After Patten's Beijing visit, Lu Ping, speaking for the Communist Party leadership, called on him to withdraw his proposals, while the British asked for negotiations. In the end, Beijing agreed to hold talks, which continued for seven months. Little progress was made except on relatively minor issues, such as lowering the voting age from 21 to 18 (The voting age is 18 in Britain and PRC).

The British then announced towards the end of 1993 that time was running out, and they had to enact legislation for the 1994 district board and municipal council elections. They made it clear that they would propose legislation in line with Patten's proposals and asked Beijing to remain at the negotiating table to discuss the 1995 Legislative Council elections. However, the Chinese refused to negotiate, pointing out that the British were taking unilateral action. Patten's reform proposals were then presented to Legco. In a marathon session that went on until 2:30 AM, Legco approved the electoral proposals and passed them into law on June 30, 1994, exactly three years before the handover.

By and large, 1994 was marked by quarrels between Britain and the PRC. One of the few agreements that they reached was on the handling of military property in Hong Kong. Britain promised to turn over all land held by its military to the PRC's People's Liberation Army (PLA). Beijing agreed that they would not use the land for commercial purposes and, if any land was no longer required by the PLA garrison, it would be turned over to the HK Government. The principal quarrel remained Patten's reforms. Still hurling insults, especially at Patten, Beijing made it clear that since Britain had acted unilaterally, Beijing, too, would go its own way. On August 31, 1994, the Standing Committee of the National People's Congress passed a resolution declaring that the terms of office for HK's three tiers of elected bodies -- district boards, municipal councils and the legislature -- would terminate on June 30, 1997. Subsequently, the Preliminary Working Committee decided to set up a provisional legislature as of July 1, 1997, a decision that provoked great controversy in Hong Kong, since the Basic Law does not mention a provisional legislature.

Furore also followed the PWC's proposal to excise key sections of the Bill of Rights: one repealed all existing legislation that was inconsistent with the Bill of Rights; another prohibited the introduction of new legislation inconsistent with the Bill of Rights. Critics felt that the removal of these two sections would result in the emasculation of the Bill of Rights. To support their position, the PWC cited previous British statements. Britain had informed the United Nations in 1978, when it presented its first report on Hong Kong, that the rights set out in the International Covenant on Civil and Political Rights were protected by "safeguards of different kinds operating . . . independently of the covenant but in full conformity with it." Moreover, the British said that all existing legislation in Hong Kong was fully consistent with the covenant. They held that there was no need for special legislation, such as a Bill of Rights, to implement the covenant. This was the British position until Tiananmen and the public demand for civil liberties guarantees.

In addition to its desire to water down the Bill of Rights, the Preliminary Working Committee also urged that some of the dozens of laws repealed or amended by the Bill of Rights, such as draconian security measures last used during the chaotic riots of the late 1960s, should be restored to their original form. PRC officials argued that the British had needed those laws to administer Hong Kong and, now that they were leaving, they were handicapping the new SAR by depriving them of the very tools they had used to run the territory.

The Legislative Council Elections of September 1995

Although campaigning was as vigorous as ever, the Democrats did not have high expectations in the 1995 Legco elections, the first time all seats would be filled by democratic elections. In 1991, the United Democrats had benefited from the Tiananmen backlash; but conventional wisdom suggested that this time voters would choose people who were less confrontational toward China. Ballot results, however, showed that support for the Democrats had not eroded. The Party secured 19 seats, making it the largest bloc in Legco. By contrast, three of the four leaders of the pro-Beijing party, DAB, were defeated, although some lesser known candidates did win. The outcome was widely seen as another rebuff for the PRC and a strong affirmation of the people's desire to maintain their way of life and to preserve their rights and freedoms. Part of the reason for the Democrats' success was their ability to field incumbents, all of whom were re-elected. The only incumbents in the election who lost were defeated by other incumbents. Yet, good as it was, the media, especially the international press, exagggerated the magnitude of the Democrats' triumph, for they actually did no better than they did in 1991 when they ran as the United Democrats.

The pro-business Liberal Party was second to the Democrats with 10 seats, representing a loss of five seats. No new Liberal party candidates won, a fact that did not bode well for the Liberals' future. The pro-PRC party did surprisingly well, despite the loss of its stars, as it increased its representation in Legco from one seat to six. In four races that pitted Democrats against DAB candidates, each side won two and lost two. After the handover, pro-China candidates were expected to do better, whereas the Democrats might decline, especially if they maintained a hostile attitude toward China. However, as will be seen shortly, conventional wisdom was proven wrong .

A "Solemn, Grand & Decent" Turnover

The agreement on the Court of Final Appeal improved relations somewhat between the PRC and Britain and led to a long-awaited visit to London by China's Foreign Minister, Qian Qichen, which took place in October 1995. Talks during the visit resulted in agreement on four points. First, the HK Goverment would set up a liaison office to work with the Preparatory Committee to be set up by Beijing in January 1996. Second, a new structure would be established for improving communications between HK civil servants and CCP officials. Third, efforts would be intensified to end the deadlock over the construction of Container Terminal 9 and to ensure progress on other port developments. And, fourth, an expert group would be formed to prepare the handover ceremonies, which were to be "solemn, grand and decent."

However, Sino-British disputes did not end with the accords. A liaison office was set up in January 1996, but relations between the HK Government and the Preparatory Committee were cool. The diplomatic deadlock over Container Terminal 9 was resolved by the two governments saying the parties involved in the project should work things out themselves. Even discussions of the handover ceremonies ran into big problems, with Patten suggesting at one point that, if necessary, there could be separate ceremonies. The only accord that went relatively smoothly was the second and easiest one -- senior HK civil servants and CCP officials held a series of meetings to enhance mutual understanding.

The year 1996 opened with the PRC's creation of the 150-member Preparatory Committee of the HKSAR. Ninety-six members were from Hong Kong, mostly from the business community, with the rest from the PRC. Since Beijing appointed all members, including those from HK, China's influence over the Committee was considerable. Formation of the Preparatory Committee marked the opening of a new chapter, heralding as it did the impending transfer of sovereignty. The PRC's National People's Congress had given the Preparatory Committee the task of "preparing the establishment of the (Special Administrative) Region." In doing so it "shall prescribe the specific method for forming the first government and the first Legislative Council."

Because Beijing had decided that the Legco members elected in 1995 would not serve beyond June 30, 1997, the Preparatory Committee was to decide how to set up a new legislature. In addition, of course, it had to decide how to choose the first Chief Executive who would head the HKSAR. Although the Basic Law provides that the chief executive "shall be selected by election or through consultations held locally and be appointed by the Central People's Government," the general belief in Hong Kong was that Beijing would choose the Chief Executive. PRC officials were frequently asked who they preferred, and who was on their short list, and, through 1996, they did nothing to deny that they would, indeed, be making the choice.

In 1996, however, there were signs of a more moderate stance on various issues, including the choice of the future Chief Executive. First, in early January, Shiu Sin-por, Deputy Secretary-General of the Preparatory Committee, asserted that Beijing was prepared to deal with the Democratic Party. "It is a reality that the Democratic Party represents a certain portion of Hong Kong people," he said. "The Chinese government knows it very well."

Another unexpected sign of enhanced moderation came from Lu Ping, Director of the PRC's Hong Kong and Macau Affairs Office, who said that the Jardines Group was welcome to return to the territory. Having supported Patten's political reforms, Jardines had been disfavored by Beijing and had moved the stock listings of all its associated companies from Hong Kong in 1995 to Singapore. Its primary listing had been moved to London previously. In the new conciliatory mood, Lu Ping declared: "If they (Jardines) find that Singapore is not as good as Hong Kong, we welcome them to return to Hong Kong."

Lu also tried to bolster HK's confidence by declaring that the CCP would not send a party secretary to act as a "power behind the throne." He strongly denied suggestions that there would be an "overlord" who would be more powerful than HK's Chief Executive. Subsequently, similar reassurances were made in HK by Zhang Junsheng, Deputy Director of the Xinhua News Agency. Their statements suggested that Beijing wanted to show moderation and calm HK's nerves in the remaining months of British rule to assure a smooth transition.

Revealing missteps. Efforts to boost confidence were marred by an incident that caused many to question Beijing's integrity once again. Would it really tolerate a high degree of autonomy in Hong Kong? The incident was precipitated by plans of the Geneva-based Lutheran World Federation to hold its 50th anniversary assembly in Hong Kong in July 1997, soon after the establishment of the SAR.

According to HK's traditions of free speech, press, and assembly, the British and the HK Governments never played a role in deciding whether a private group could hold a conference in Hong Kong. Wanting to ensure there would be no trouble, however, the Lutherans sought assurances from PRC officials. Instead of saying that there was no need to ask for permission, PRC officials actually entered into negotiations with the Lutherans. Officials warned the Lutherans not to hold their assembly in Hong Kong and even threatened to withhold visas from delegates. They asked if Lutherans from Taiwan would participate, and if the Taiwan flag would be flown. Beijing finally withdrew its objections after being assured that the meeting was purely religious in nature.

In fact, Beijing should have been delighted at the prospect of a major religious meeting so soon after the birth of the SAR, since it would have provided early proof to the world that basic freedoms, including those of religion and assembly, continued to exist in HK. Instead, the Lutheran incident highlighted a CCP proclivity to want to control and dictate.

Another misstep arose when the Preparatory Committee endorsed the recommendation in March 1996 by the Preliminary Working Committee to establish a Provisional Legislative Council to replace the legislature elected in 1995. The motion was opposed by only one member of the Preparatory Committee, Frederick Fung, chairman of the Association for Democracy and People's Liveliood. Fung's solitary no vote apparently brought down Beijing's wrath and appeared to confirm the CCP's intolerance of any dissent. Director Lu Ping told Fung that he had disqualified himself from serving on either the Selection Committee or the provisional legislature. After a public outcry, Lu Ping withdrew the threat and said he had only expressed a personal opinion. But Fung privately revealed that other PRC officials had also warned him in similar terms not to cast a negative vote or at least to abstain. It was quite clear that Lu had expressed an official position. Governor Patten hailed Fung as a hero and called the development a "black day for democracy."

Beijing's missteps renewed the fears of many HK people about the impending takeover. Once again, their nervousness turned feverish; long lines formed at the Immigration Department as people sought to apply for naturalization to become British Dependent Territory Citizens, even though they knew that such citizenship status would expire on June 30, 1997, when Hong Kong ceased to be a British colony. While BDTC status would not give anyone the right of abode in Britain, it did entitle the person to a British National (Overseas) passport, which could be used to enter many countries without a visa.

The HK Government had announced in 1993 that applications for naturalization would not be accepted after March 31, 1996. By mid-March, the street outside the Immigration Department (ID) was packed solid everyday as thousands of people, young and old, stood in line to submit application forms for second-class British citizenship. Towards the end of the month, the ID kept its doors open 24 hours a day to handle the ever-lengthening queue. March 31st was a Sunday, but the ID put its officers on overtime and accepted applications until one minute to midnight. On that day, more than 54,000 people applied to be naturalized as BDT citizens and risked Beijing's ire, for the applicants would have to swear allegiance to the British monarch before they could be naturalized.

Some standing in line explained why they were seeking British papers by referring to recent incidents, such as the Frederick Fung case. But PRC officials in HK kept silent, pretending that the long lines outside the Immigration Department had nothing do with a lack of confidence in HK's future or in the future HKSAR passport.

(S)electing the Chief Executive

Also in the spring of 1996, Beijing repeatedly emphasized that it would not impose a chief executive on HK who was not acceptable to the territory's populace. For much of 1996, Lo Tak-shing, a pro-Beijing lawyer, was the only declared candidate. With only one percent of the population supporting him, Lo was not popular and the prospect that he might be the Chief Executive worried many. Tung Chee-hwa, the shipping magnate, who many believed to be Beijing's choice, maintained a low profile; and the general belief was that he was reluctant to be a candidate. Beijing tried to end speculation on the identity of the Chief Executive. The PRC's headman in Hong Kong, Zhou Nan, for example, said it was too early to talk about candidates and that discussion should not begin until the 400-member Selection Committee, responsible for choosing the Chief Executive, had been formed.

PRC President Jiang Zemin himself played a reassuring role when he met with the British Deputy Prime Minister, Michael Heseltine. Jiang said the choice of Chief Executive would not be made by Beijing and then imposed on Hong Kong. He said whoever it was had to be someone who was widely acceptable to HK people. "The Chinese side will not arbitrarily make a decision on the post," he said. Those remarks not only reassured the public that they would not be saddled with a decision made in Beijing, they also encouraged potential candidates to step forward and declare their interest in the job. The assertion that Beijing did not have a pre-ordained candidate was subsequently repeated by Vice Premier Qian Qichen, PRC's Foreign Minister, on more than one occasion. Such statements did much to improve the atmosphere.

Beijing made an apparent overture to the Democrats when Lu Ping said in an interview with ABC News that the Democratic Party could continue to exist and participate in elections after 1997. "I think they can continue to exist if they abide by the law," Lu said. "I don't think there will be any difficulty for them."

An even stronger signal was given by Vice Premier Qian in August 1996. In a keynote address to the Preparatory Committee, Qian -- without mentioning the Democrats -- suggested that Beijing was willing to talk to them. "There are some people in Hong Kong who support the return to the motherland but hold different views about the course and pace of democratic development," he said. "As long as they share the common ground of support for the resumption of sovereignty and hope for a smooth transition, we can sit down and discuss Hong Kong questions to make things better." Qian did not indicate what issues he would be willing to discuss with the Democrats, but Beijing's apparent softening stirred much discussion in HK and improved the atmosphere further.

Many people felt that, since Beijing had made a concession, the Democrats led by Martin Lee should also make one. Opinion surveys showed that a majority of the public felt the Democrats should drop their opposition to the provisional legislature, and should in fact, be willing to serve on it. The Democrats conducted their own opinion survey and, to their surprise, discovered that public opinion in felt they should join the Selection Committee and the provisional legislature. However, the Democrats decided to stick to their original position and announced that their members would not join either body. But they said that they welcomed a dialogue with Beijing. Letters were despatched to senior PRC officials but nothing concrete ever developed. The olive branch, it appeared, was primarily an attempt to get the Democrats to end their opposition to the provisional legislature.

In fact, Zhou Nan suggested that the PRC was not offering to conduct a dialogue with the Democrats at all. He said that if the Democrats realized the error of their ways, then of course Beijing would be willing to accept their return to the fold. Perhaps there was more than one school of thought in the CCP hierarchy, which is often the case. In fact, it was difficult to see what there was to discuss, since Beijing had already made all the major decisions relating to HK's transition. Professor Lau Siu-kai, a member of the Preparatory Committee, summed up the situation by describing Qian's words as "only a goodwill gesture to improve relations."

Although the Democrats decided to boycott the Selection Committee, others did not share their compunctions; the 400 slots available were greatly oversubscribed. Even Frederick Fung, who had been chastised for voting against the provisional legislature, decided that members of his Association would seek seats on the Selection Committee, even though one of its tasks would be to choose members of the provisional legislature. Even two members of Governor Patten's Executive Council, businessman Raymond Chien and banker Vincent Cheng, submitted applications. When the HK Government forbade senior civil servants and members of the police force from joining the Selection Committee, the civil servants took their case to court, claiming that their human rights were being violated. The court upheld the Government's stance. In the end, almost 6,000 of HK's most prominent people applied to join the 400-member body.

Even before the campaign for membership on the Selection Committee ended, the campaign for HKSAR Chief Executive heated up. In September, the Chief Justice, Sir Ti-liang Yang, announced his candidacy, joining Tak-shing Lo, who had tossed his hat into the ring in a May interview with *Ming Pao*. Yang resigned as Chief Justice in order to campaign, and to comply with the Basic Law, Yang also gave up his British passport and offered to forego his knighthood. He was supported by pro-PRC publisher, Xu Simin (see pp. 213-214), and appeared to have the support of some PRC officials. Polls showed substantial public support for Yang. Many who did not like the idea of a businessman as Chief Executive thought a judge would be a good choice since a judge, presumably, would have few vested interests and would be more likely to uphold the rule of law.

But support for a businessman as chief executive was strong within the Preparatory Committee. Billionaire tycoon, Li Ka-shing, who wields great power in HK, made no secret of his support for shipping magnate, Tung Chee-hwa, who was widely thought to be Beijing's choice as well. Tung also had the support of Allen Lee, Chairman of the pro-business Liberal Party. But Tung refused to declare his candidacy, giving every indication of being reluctant to abandon business for politics. In late September, he called a press conference, not to announce his candidacy but to say that he was trying to decide whether to run. The following month Tung confirmed that he was, indeed, a candidate.

Another leading businessman, Peter Woo, a son-in-law of the late Sir Yue-kong Pao, was less reticent. On September 30, Woo issued a statement announcing his candidacy, promising the HK people vision and leadership. Launching a U.S. presidential-style campaign, he issued a manifesto stating his position on major issues and held public meetings with many political groupings. In fact, Peter Woo set the tone and style of the campaign. This was because, once he started to discuss issues in public, it became impossible for other candidates to remain silent. As a result, the public felt a sense of involvement in the entire process, even though only the Selection Committee's 400 members had the right to vote. The feeling grew that public opinion would induce something of a election. Thus, an undemocratic process became about as palatable as possible.

Meanwhile, opinion polls continued to show Lo Tak-shing with the lowest popularity and in time he withdrew, which paved the way for the announcement of another major candidate. This was Simon Li, a retired appelate court judge. Li had given his support to Lo and so felt he could not declare his candidacy as long as Lo was still officially in the race. Chief Secretary Anson Chan, who continued to top the popularity polls, officially declared that she would not join the race. That left Yang, Li, Tung, and Woo as the four viable contenders, two retired judges and two businessmen.

Throughout the media hype, Beijing officials refrained from comment and from endorsing any of the candidates. Vice Premier Qian, in an address to the Preparatory Committee, said: "Some people say the selection process is just a formality, or that we are putting up a show. I want to make it very clear to everyone that this is incorrect." Beijing's efforts to improve HK's political atmosphere were successful, as surveys conducted between January and May 1996 found more and more people willing to accept the PRC. Clearly, the HK people were beginning to feel more relaxed about the impending change in sovereignty, that is, until Beijing did it again.

Concerns over the possible erosion of rights and freedoms after July 1, 1997 resurfaced after Vice Premier Qian gave an interview to the *Asian Wall Street Journal*. The Foreign Minister warned HK people not to take part in "political activities which directly interfere in the affairs of the mainland of China," such as rallies to mark the anniversary of the June 4 military crackdown in Tiananmen Square in 1989. His other remarks were interpreted as indications that there would be restrictions on the media after 1997. The media "can put forward criticism, but not rumors or lies. Nor can they put forward personal attacks on Chinese leaders." Qian's tough remarks followed similar statements by Director Lu Ping in the spring when he warned that, after 1997, newspapers would not be allowed to advocate certain key views, such as "two Chinas," "one China, one Taiwan," the independence of Taiwan and the independence of Hong Kong.

How HK's Chief Executive was (s)elected. Members of the Selection Committee were chosen on November 2, 1996 by the 150-member Preparatory Committee. As expected, the Committee was dominated by business people as well as members of pro-Beijing groups. Since mainlanders accounted for a third of the PC's members, Beijing could decisively influence the make-up of the Selection Committee. Now the campaign for HK's Chief Executive entered a final, decisive phase, as self-proclaimed candidates campaigned actively for the support of Committee members and not just to gain public popularity. They lobbied individual members of the Selection Committee furiously in an attempt to secure support. They also kept a wary eye on Beijing, knowing that everything that they said would be scrutinized by PRC officials.

The rules required that each would-be candidate obtain nominations from 50 members of the Selection Committeee before being considered an official candidate. Nomination day was November 15, 1996, the first meeting of the Selection Committee. Newspaper reports suggested that Tung would have little trouble in securing 50 nominations as well as Yang, because of his public popularity. While Peter Woo was doubtful, Simon Li, despite his low standing in the popularity polls, was considered safe since he had strong ties with pro-PRC figures. The results were surprising. Li received only 43 nominations and was disqualified as a candidate. Woo scraped through with 54 votes and Yang received 82. Showing the breadth and depth of his support, Tung received 206 nominations, or more than half the membership of the Selection Committee and was formally elected on December 11, 1996.

In the weeks leading up to the actual vote, Tung's public popularity rose steadily to overtake that of Yang. This made it possible for PRC leaders to claim, with some justification, that the Chief Executive chosen by the Selection Committee was not someone imposed by Beijing but was someone who was acceptable to the HK people, even though not democratically elected by them.

Ten days after Tung's victory, the Selection Committee met again and elected the 60 members of the provisional legislature. Because the Basic Law limits foreign nationals and people with the right of abode in foreign nations to no more than 20 percent of the seats, several candidates announced that they were giving up their foreign passports, which suggested that they were "patriotic" Chinese who were confident about HK's future.

Double jeopardy. Coinciding with those important events, a controversy erupted about the right to consular protection on the part of beneficiaries of the British Nationality Selection Scheme. Francis Cornish, the British Trade Commissioner, who was scheduled to become the first British Consul General in HK after the 1997 handover, said at a press briefing that members of the 50,000 families who received British passports under the scheme would be ineligible for consular protection. The public outcry that ensued caused Governor Patten to call a special session of the Legco to explain the legal details.

Patten asserted that all British passport holders would be treated in the same way, regardless of how their passports were obtained. He added that only Britain can decide who is or is not a British citizen. However, he also explained that, under international law, Britain would be unable to offer consular protection to anyone who had both British and Chinese nationality. While Patten tried to be reassuring, he could not escape the fact that Beijing had said from the beginning that it would not recognize as British nationals those who obtained their passports under the nationality scheme. Since the vast majority of those people are ethnic Chinese, the PRC would consider them to be Chinese nationals. And, just as no one can tell Britain who is or is not a British national, no one can tell the PRC who is or is not a Chinese national. The fact that consular protection was still a major issue at the end of 1996 showed that, despite the improved atmosphere, many HK people remained apprehensive about the future.

Their apprehension was also reflected in another Sino-British dispute at this point -- the decision by the HK Government to introduce legislation, mandated by Article 23 of the Basic Law, covering subversion, secession, sedition and treason. This was part of Britain's attempt to ensure that any post-handover legislation would not be unduly harsh. The British decision to introduce such legislation was made after they failed to get Beijing to accept their ideas in the Joint Liaison Group. Predictably, PRC officials accused the Patten administration of attempting to preempt the HKSAR legislature and the Basic Law.

The first half of 1997 saw the trends of the previous year continuing, as HK enjoyed a strong economy (see pp. 279-280) and opinion polls showed that confidence in the future continued to rise. While out-migration continued, the numbers of emigrants were at the 40,000-a-year range. Even more noteworthy was the fact that more of those who had left in earlier years were returning, no doubt in response to HK's economic boom (see pp. 47-48). Precise figures are not available, but some estimates are that up to a fifth of those who left in earlier years had returned. At the same time, more foreigners were pouring into the city.

It seemed that few believed that July 1, 1997 would bring an abrupt end to Hong Kong's economic vibrancy.

Good times garnish handover. The Hong Kong stock market rose to record levels, setting one record after another, before closing at another historic high on June 27, 1997, the last trading day before the handover. The bullish atmosphere was also reflected in real estate prices. Businessmen, including virtually all of the foreign chambers of commerce, were optimistic about HK's future. A pre-handover survey by the American Chamber of Commerce in HK showed that 95% of its member companies predicted that HK's business environment in the next five years would be "favorable" or "very favorable."

Opinion surveys of the public conducted by the HK Government, the media, and academics differed only in terms of the actual figures; all pointed to the same thing: an increased sense of confidence in the future. In fact, the surveys showed confidence higher than at any time since the Declaration was signed in 1984. Perhaps the public was simply bowing to the inevitable, but the surveys showed more people favoring HK's reunification with the PRC than those who favored independence or remaining a British colony. To be sure, much of the confidence reflected the excellent economy. Thus, many more people were confident of HK's economic future than of its political future.

As the British era ebbed, PRC leaders continued their campaign to raise confidence in Hong Kong. Vice Premier Qian, who had raised anxiety levels last year by what he told the *Asian Wall Street Journal*, gave another interview to the *South China Morning Post* in which he was asked about his previous statements that HK newspapers should not publish rumors and should not make attacks on PRC leaders: Did that mean that freedom of the press would be restricted in HK? Apparently welcoming the opportunity to clarify his previous remarks, Qian declared that what he had said represented only his personal views. He said that quality newspapers anywhere in the world should not engage in rumor-mongering. But he said that Beijing would not regulate HK newspapers; they would only have to abide by SAR laws (See Chapter Four on self-censorship).

After the Handover and Into the Beyond

No doubt, there is still widespread concern about the future. Yet there is recognition that HK's future belongs with China now rather than with Britain. In recognition of that reality, the place has changed greatly since the Joint Declaration was signed in 1984 when few people had foreign passports. By mid-1997, something like 10% of the population had foreign passports, and an additional 25% had close relatives abroad who could sponsor their emigration if necessary. The population had become much more mobile. If things went wrong, very many people are positioned to leave very quickly, a fact that Beijing is surely aware of, for Hong Kong has been the classic geographic and psychological stepping-stone away from and to China for the Chinese people for more than a century and a half (see pp. 14-17).

But this does not mean that people are packed and planning to leave soon. Rather, a new sense of community may be developing now that the territory has been restored to the motherland. In fact, the HK Transition Project, a respected polling concern, found that while in the past a majority of people preferred Hong Kong to remain a British colony or to become independent, by early 1997 a majority of people actually wanted HK to join China, a finding that was reconfirmed in a follow-up survey in June 1997, virtually on the eve of the historic handover.

Another polling firm, Asian Commercial Research, had been compiling a "Happiness Index" by asking people since 1994 if they expected to be happy or sad on the night of June 30, 1997. In October 1994, when the index was first compiled, 37% said they expected to be sad, and 26% said they expected to be happy, while the rest were unsure. By July 1996, however, for the first time, those who expected to be happy outnumbered those who expected to be sad by a ratio of 38% to 28%. By March 1996, the "Happiness Index" was 66% happy and only 11% sad. However, David Bottomley, ACR's head, wrote in the *South China Morning Post* on June 26, 1997 that, while "people will feel happy about the handover event," it "does not mean the majority accept the idea of Chinese sovereignty. They don't." Bottomley said that, in over a decade of polling, 13,000 people had been asked "what status they would prefer for Hong Kong in 1997, if they could control history." He said that the answers have fluctuated, "but in none of the 21 readings has a majority wanted Hong Kong to be part of China."

Be that as it may, the trends were clear. Surveys taken by the HK Government since 1983 showed that a large majority of people had confidence that Hong Kong would remain prosperous and stable. But there was much greater confidence in HK's economic outlook than in its political development. Overall, optimists still outnumbered pessimists by a ratio of at least two to one. Because the leading concern of most people clearly had to do with the retention of their political rights and freedoms, it was perhaps appropriate that, at the handover ceremonies held on the night of June 30, all of the key participants emphasized the importance of democracy in Hong Kong. In his address at the handover ceremonies on July 1, 1997, PRC's President Jiang Zemin virtually repeated all the principal points in the Joint Declaration, underlining the fact that the PRC had not deviated from its promises of 13 years ago, even though a new generation was now in charge of the CCP and the Mainland Government.

In conclusion, it seems fair to say that in the early days of the HKSAR the mood in general was relaxed. A significant portion of the community supported reunification and were generally confident about the general future. No matter the merits of the British, there was always that sense of contradiction among HK Chinese that foreigners ruled them. Now that sovereignty has been returned to China, the people feel that they could shed such ambiguities and will be able to expand their identity with the community. However, it also needs to be pointed out that confidence is still fragile and needs to be nurtured. Any major political reverses or a downturn in the economy, which came in late 1997 and continued into 1999, could result in a setback in the sensitive climate. But the overall trend of 1996-97 was that the HK people had increasing confidence in their future and were anxious to play a part in the shaping of their community's future.

The weeks following the transition were also marked by legal challenges regarding the legality of the provisional legislature. One challenge was defeated in the first month, but other challenges were visible on the horizon. Predictions of doom and gloom failed to materialize, as life continued much as before. True, laws regarding the holding of demonstrations and the formation of societies had been passed, but no one had been forbidden to stage a protest, or to organize a society. Still, the SAR Government now holds the legal power to crack down if it should want to -- power that the British colonial government also held until the early 1990s.

All attention turned to the legislative elections scheduled for May 1998. The SAR Government maintained that the elections would be fair, open, and acceptable to the HK people. Its critics, however, maintained that the elections were being rigged to reduce the number of pro-democracy candidates in the legislature. The visit by Chief Executive Tung to the U.S. in September 1997 were smoothly -- something that certainly could not have been anticipated six months earlier. However, both the White House and the Congress made it clear that much would depend on how the 1998 elections were conducted. President Jiang Zemin's grand visit to America followed Tung's tour.

As *The Economist* (Greeting the dragon, 1997) editorialized a week before President Jiang's state visit to the U.S., "No country inflames American passions quite as much as China." Whether Tiananmen, Taiwan or Tibet, trade disputes, religious oppression, China's arms sales to rogue nations, human rights and pro-democracy dissidents, cheap goods produced by Chinese prisons, abortion policies, "a geostrategic threat comparable to the old Soviet Union," potential demise of Hong Kong's capitalistic society and nature, etc., Americans can work themselves into frenzy over the PRC. *The Economist* concluded its editorial by saying that "The stakes are high: how the natural rivalry between America and China plays out will affect the stability, and thus the prosperity, of the entire East Asian region. And perhaps the world."

Handled with great deliberation and fanfare, President Jiang Zemin's state visit a month after Tung's whirlwind stop represented a potentially important, turning point in US-PRC relations. Working with the White House, Chinese diplomats demanded that Jiang's trip should be treated with the same grandioseness as Deng Xiaoping's historic visit in 1985. In the same mood, the Americans proposed the use of a large tent in the garden for the state dinner so more guests could be included, but the Chinese insisted that the event be held inside the White House, i.e., no change from Deng's visit. As Jiang told Bill Clinton, "We share extensive common interests bearing on the survival of mankind." In reply,

Clinton said, "Twenty-five years ago, China stood apart from, and closed to, the international community. Now, China is a member of more than 1,000 international organizations, from the International Civil Aviation Organization to the International Fund for Agricultural Development" (Mann, 1997). During their extensive discussions, President Clinton insisted that America wanted the PRC to maintain and protect HK's autonomy and permit its democratic development.

A modern China involved internationally could be a great boon to American exports, such as shown by the $3 billion contract for 50 Boeing aircraft that was signed during Jiang's visit. It would also boost the PRC's growing trade with the U.S. and the world, all of which would benefit the HKSAR.

A few weeks after the summit, the PRC released Wei Jingsheng from prison, the PRC's most famous democracy dissident, and sent him to the U.S. for medical care. For all but six months, Wei had been imprisoned for the last 18 years. An electrician at the Beijing zoo, in 1978 he dared to mount a wall poster that said that China could never become a modern, advanced nation without true democracy. That he should have been released after many years of protests by the U.S. and world suggests that Beijing interpreted the Sino-American summit as positive and decided that its goodwill should be expanded. Later in early 1998, student democracy leader, Wang Dan, was released to his family for health reasons and went to the U.S. There can be no mistaking the favorable symbolism intended in the 1997 releases.

President Jiang differs from paramount leader Deng and other old guard leaders. He is not an idealogue hard-liner. During the student demonstrations for democracy in 1987 and 1989, Jiang was the mayor of Shanghai and then the city's Party Secretary, when he defused tensions by visiting the campuses, recited Lincoln's Gettysburg Address, and spread the impression that he understood the students' democratic goals, etc. Unlike mayhem in the capital, Shanghai simmered down. Deng selected Jiang to be his heir apparent and brought him to Beijing for high office and grooming. Few expected him to last long after Deng died, but his pragmatic, behind-the-scenes strengths appear to have succeeded in forming and staying his power. People in Mainland China say that their President is just the right leader for the times -- unconnected with the Long March generation and ideologue radicals, a systems engineer, a builder through strategy and consensus, unpretentious yet worldly, and one who delegates authority instead of grasping all that he can. These positives, however, may not represent the complete man.

The People Vote for Democracy

The massive voter turnout in the Hong Kong Special Administrative Region election on May 24, 1998 took everyone by surprise. HK authorities have taken the turnout as an endorsement of the "one country, two systems" policy, while the Democratic Party regards it as a sign of discontent and, in fact, a mandate to push for a full directly elected legislature.

Before the election, pollsters had predicted a low turnout. Michael deGolyer, head of the HK Transition Project, released a report days before the election that said: "The key measure of the (election's) success will be whether the number of geographic voters exceed one million. If numbers fall below 900,000, the SAR's first elections will have to be deemed an overall rejection of the system . . . One million voters will comprise a provisional, lukewarm endorsement."

If one million meant a lukewarm endorsement, one and a half million should be considered a warm embrace. But this is not how the results were read. Instead, many saw the big turnout as reflecting unhappiness with the SAR Administration and transition process.

Critics of the electoral system had called on voters to cast blank ballots in protest, a ploy that failed. The number of spoiled ballots was smaller than in 1995, even though there more voters.

Several Chinese-language newspapers conducted surveys on what motivated voters to go to the polling station. The *Apple Daily*, often seen as a champion of democracy in Hong Kong, reported that 65% of nearly 300 respondents said they voted out of civic duty. A sizable minority, 13.5%, said they wanted to express dissatisfaction with the provisional legislature (which replaced the Legislative Council elected in 1995), while another 13.5% said they voted because they wanted to improve the economy.

The *Oriental Daily* interviewed over 400 voters. Of those, 62% said that they voted because it was their civic responsibility, 13% because they were unhappy with the provisional legislature. And 10% said they voted to voice dissatisfaction with the SAR government.

And *Ming Pao* polled 747 voters, 54.8% of whom said they voted to implement the principle of "Hong Kong people running Hong Kong." A third said they voted because they disapproved of the provisional legislature. Some also said they wanted the election souvenir cards, but the vast majority, it seems clear, voted to take part in the political process, not to repudiate it.

One explanation for the inaccuracy of some forecasts is that those who intended to vote for the pro-Beijing Democratic Alliance for Betterment of Hong Kong were too embarrassed to admit it. Instead, they simply answered "don't know" when asked whom they would vote for. This seems to reflect a shift in sentiment within HK away from an adamantly anti-PRC stance. Even feelings about the Tiananmen Square crackdown are changing. Asked if Beijing was right to send tanks into Tiananmen, 71.9% said no in 1995, compared to 55.2% three years later. Similarly, those who supported the crackdown rose from 9% in 1995 to 13.3% today.

Since the recent election was for a legislature -- not a full government -- the voters were, in a sense, choosing an opposition. It is not surprising, therefore, that they chose people who have a record of being critical of the establishment.

The absence of a government party is a serious flaw in HK's constitutional make-up. The Basic Law says the ultimate goal is to have the entire legislature chosen through universal suffrage. When that happens, it would clearly be untenable for the Government not also to be elected. Hong Kong will eventually have to evolve into either a parliamentary system or something like the American system.

Even now, with an "executive-led" system, the SAR Administration has already been put on the defensive. On June 3, 1998, seven political parties, who together command a majority of the new legislature, agreed on a package of proposals to stimulate the economy, showing that aside from their attitude towards Beijing, the parties are not far apart on major economic and social issues. On the defensive, the HK Government had to consider some of the proposals; otherwise, it would have great difficulty getting its own proposals adopted.

Patten Returns to Hong Kong SAR

The administration of Chief Executive Tung Chee-hwa is in for a rough two years, especially with the SAR and East Asia in recession (see pp. 283-290). And, chances are, things will not improve and will continue as they are into 2000, when the next round of elections will be held.

In 1999, Hong Kong looks, acts, and feels differently from its handover year of 1997. When there had been euphoria and a strong economy (before the handover), nothing has epitomized the changed atmosphere better than former Governor Christopher Patten's first return to HK in November 1998. Promoting his controversial book, *East and West* (see p. 56), Patten was mobbed by fans and admirers. The tumultuous welcome given him underlines the extent to which he had won the hearts and minds of many HK people during his five years as Governor. One young woman waiting for an autographed copy of his book said that she wished Patten was still Governor.

Patten himself, of course, rejected all suggestions that Hong Kong would not have faced severe economic problems if he was still Governor. Over and over, he said that Chief Executive Tung had had to face difficulties that he did not have. When a journalist asked if his outgoing style, unlike Tung's, was a reflection on the Chief Executive, the HK Governor-turned-author immediately dissociated himself from the observation.

Surely, Patten was the only Governor to take the British Government to task for having failed to prepare HK for democracy. In his book, he condemned Britain for "denying Hong Kong the chance to grow its own self-confident political culture." His close friends, former PM John Major and Foreign Secretary Douglas Hurd, gave him a virtually free hand in running HK and in dealing with Beijing. Left to his own devices, Patten managed to snatch back some semblance of British honor.

He won passports for war widows and ethnic minorities, passports which mean-spirited bureaucrats in London had withheld for decades. And, while he did not get full British passports for HK's British nationals, he was able to secure visa-free entry to Britain for holders of the SAR passport. Patten staked everything on pushing democracy. Without a doubt, he violated the spirit, if not the letter, of prior Sino-British agreements, by shifting from convergence to confrontation. His electoral reforms reversed prior British policies and raised questions about Beijing's intentions. Thus, he derailed the "through train," under which the Legislative Council elected freely and openly in 1995 would have served until 1999. That forced the creation of a provisional legislature by Beijing and enhanced suspicions all around. Thus, some say that Governor Patten's reforms did HK a disservice by provoking Beijing. Yet, a good case can be made that the process raised the political consciousness of the HK people and made them more responsible, reflective individuals.

Patten also made HK's Administration more open and accountable In fact, everyday, the SAR Government and Chief Executive Tung are being measured against standards that Patten set. Tung's biggest achievement -- and it is a huge one -- has been to curtail Beijing's fear and suspicion of HK. Because PRC leaders trust Tung, they have not openly interfered in HK's affairs. Although no one questions Tung's sincerity, the Chief Executive should stop trying to be so politically correct. His second Policy Address on October 7, 1998 disappointed the HK people who were hoping for a bold or imaginative move from a visionary leader. Tung's attempts to transform HK into a Chinese city will nullify China's "one country, two systems" policy. In less than two years, the place has become much less international. To a large extent, that is the result of the Tung Administration's actions, asking the people to emulate China, a formula for disaster, and downgrading HK's status as a unique, international city.

Indeed, by insisting on electoral reforms and showing sincere concern for the common people, Patten gave Hong Kong a taste of democracy, long the forbidden fruit. HK lived through some harrowing years of serious politics with him, but in the long run the price may have been worth paying. Now we can look ahead to the elections of 2000.

References

Greeting the dragon (1997, October 25). *The Economist*, pp. 15-16.

Hicks, George (Ed.) (1990). *The broken mirror: China after Tiananmen.* Essex, UK: Longman.

Lau, Emily (1988, March 10). 'Lies, damn lies and statistics.' *Far Eastern Economic Review*, pp. 32-33.

Mann, Paul (1997, November 3). Clinton, Jiang break the ice. *Aviation Week & Space Technology*, pp. 32-33.

Patten, Christopher (1998). *East and West: China, power, and the future of Asia.* New York: Times/Random House.

Roberti, Mark (1996). *The fall of Hong Kong: China's triumph & Britain's betrayal* (rev.). New York: Wiley.

Welsh, Frank (1993). *A history of Hong Kong.* London: HarperCollins.

Yee, Albert H. (1992). *A people misruled: The Chinese stepping-stone syndrome* (2nd ed., rev.). Singapore: Heinemann Asia.

The Contributors and Editor

Frank Ching has been a Senior Editor of the *Far Eastern Economic Review* for many years and is a regular *Review* columnist. Author of the landmark book, *Ancestors*, and many other works, he became internationally known as the Beijing correspondent for the *Wall Street Journal* and *New York Times* for many years.

Gerald Hugh Choa served with great distinction as Hong Kong's Director of the Medical and Health Services and as Foundation Dean, Faculty of Medicine, The Chinese University of Hong Kong Medical School. Possessing extensive knowledge of Hong Kong's medical history, he has authored many publications. Dr. Choa remains active in clinical practice and is Foundation Chairman of the Hong Kong Museum of Medical Sciences Society.

Oliver Lindsay, CBE, served in Hong Kong in the mid-70's and throughout the world during his distinguished military career of 35 years. His family has served in the British Army from father to son since 1795. Also in the family tradition, he is a member of the Queen's Body Guard for Scotland. A Fellow of the Royal Historical Society, his most recent book is *Once a Grenadier*. Colonel Lindsay has worked with disabled young people through the Treloar Trust and is Editor of the *Guards Magazine*.

Ian K. Perkin has been Chief Economist and Assistant Director of the HK General Chamber of Commerce since 1991 with responsibility for the Chamber's policies on economic, legal, taxation, and social issues. From 1989-1991, he was Business Editor of *The South China Morning Post*. Earlier, Mr. Perkin was a staff adviser to the leader of the Australian Liberal (Conservative) Party, former Foreign Minister Andrew Peacock, now Australia's Ambassador to the U.S. He has also been Associate Editor and Chief Political Correspondent of the leading national daily, *The Australian.*

George Shen served as Chief Editor of the *Hong Kong Economic Journal* for many years and continues to be active in journalism. He pioneered television in Hong Kong in the 1950s and was in broadcasting and films. Before his journalistic career, Dr. Shen was Head of Administration at the Asian Productivity Organization in Tokyo. He has authored *Essays on China's Economy* and *My Views of Japan* (in Chinese).

Kenneth Topley was a distinguished civil servant in Malaysia and Hong Kong from 1950-1983. During his 27 years service in Hong Kong, he rose from cadet to become Hong Kong's Secretary of Education and Manpower. His honors include the Companion of the Order of St. Michael and St. George (CMG) and Commander of the Order of Arts and Letters (France). Prior to his return to England, he was the Secretary of the Asia Pacific Institute (in Hong Kong) as well as the University of East Asia (now University of Macau) from 1984-90.

Albert Hoy Yee was a professor and academic dean at universities in the U.S. and East Asia. He has taught at Tokyo University, the Chinese University of Hong Kong, and the National University of Singapore. He assisted in White House preparations for President Nixon's historic visit to China. In 1972, he became the first U.S. social scientist to tour the PRC -- a mission to establish communications with the Chinese psychologists for the American Psychological Association. Dr. Yee is a Fellow of the APA and other national societies. *Whither Hong Kong?* is his tenth book.

Index